WORK AND IDLENESS:
The Political Economy of Full Employment

RECENT ECONOMIC THOUGHT SERIES

Editors:

Other books in the series:

Klein, Philip A.: THE ROLE OF ECONOMIC THEORY
Semmler, Willi.: BUSINESS CYCLES: THEORY AND EMPIRICS
Little, Daniel: ON THE RELIABILITY OF ECONOMIC MODELS: ESSAYS IN THE PHILOSOPHY OF ECONOMICS
Weimer, David L.: INSTITUTIONAL DESIGN
Davis, John B.: THE STATE OF THE INTERPRETATION OF KEYNES
Wells, Paul: POST-KEYNESIAN ECONOMIC THEORY
Hoover, Kevin D.: MACROECONOMETRICS: DEVELOPMENTS, TENSIONS AND PROSPECTS
Kendrick, John W.: THE NEW SYSTEMS OF NATURAL ACCOUNTS
Groenewegen, John: TRANSACTION COST ECONOMICS AND BEYOND
King, J.E.: AN ALTERNATIVE MACROECONOMIC THEORY
Schofield, Norman: COLLECTIVE DECISION-MAKING: SOCIAL CHOICE AND POLITICAL ECONOMY
Menchik, Paul L.: HOUSEHOLD AND FAMILY ECONOMICS
Gupta, Kanhaya L.: EXPERIENCES WITH FINANCIAL LIBERALIZATION
Cohen, Avi J., Hagemann, Harald, and Smithin, John: MONEY FINANCIAL INSTITUTIONS AND MACROECONOMICS
Mason, P.L. and Williams, R.M.: RACE, MARKETS, AND SOCIAL OUTCOMES
Gupta, Satya Dev: THE POLITICAL ECONOMY OF GLOBALIZATION
Fisher, R.C.: INTERGOVERNMENTAL FISCAL RELATIONS
Mariussen, Å. and Wheelock, J.: HOUSEHOLDS, WORK AND ECONOMIC CHANGE: A COMPARATIVE INSTITUTIONAL PERSPECTIVE
Gupta, Satya Dev: GLOBALIZATION, GROWTH AND SUSTAINABILITY
Gupta, Satya Dev: DYNAMICS OF GLOBALIZATION AND DEVELOPMENT
Medema, Steven G.: COASEAN ECONOMICS: LAW AND ECONOMICS AND THE NEW INSTITUTIONAL ECONOMICS
Peoples, James: REGULATORY REFORM AND LABOR MARKETS
Dennis, Ken: RATIONALITY IN ECONOMICS: ALTERNATIVE PERSPECTIVES
Ahiakpor, James C.W.: KEYNES AND THE CLASSICS RECONSIDERED
Wolfson, Murray: THE POLITICAL ECONOMY OF WAR AND PEACE
Jain, A.K.: ECONOMICS OF CORRUPTION

WORK AND IDLENESS:
The Political Economy of Full Employment

edited by

Jane Wheelock
John Vail

University of Newcastle
Newcastle upon Tyne
United Kingdom

Kluwer Academic Publishers
Boston/Dordrecht/London

Distributors for North, Central and South America:
Kluwer Academic Publishers
101 Philip Drive
Assinippi Park
Norwell, Massachusetts 02061 USA
Telephone (781) 871-6600
Fax (781) 871-6528
E-Mail <kluwer@wkap.com>

Distributors for all other countries:
Kluwer Academic Publishers Group
Distribution Centre
Post Office Box 322
3300 AH Dordrecht, THE NETHERLANDS
Telephone 31 78 6392 392
Fax 31 78 6546 474
E-Mail <orderdept@wkap.nl>

Electronic Services <http://www.wkap.nl>

Library of Congress Cataloging-in-Publication Data

Printed on acid-free paper.

Printed in the United States of America

CONTENTS

List of contributors xiii

Acknowledgments xv

INTRODUCTION

Chapter 1 A feasible capitalist response to a changing political economy 1
Jane Wheelock and John Vail

Introduction: the moment for a redistribution of work? 1
The problem: insecure times in the labour market 3
The sources of the problem: working all the hours that God sends 7
Policy prescriptions for full employment 10
Redistributing the rewards of work 12
  Basic income: the right to idleness?
  Working hours: the right to personal and family time?
  Third sector: the right to work?

PART I THEORIES OF FULL EMPLOYMENT

Chapter 2 A Keynesian view of the redistribution of work 23
John Wells

Introduction 23
Keynesian economics and employment theory 23
Mass unemployment and increased inequality in the UK: a statistical picture 29
Mass unemployment and increased inequality in the UK: a Keynesian account 31
Unemployment and the polarisation between households in access to paid employment 35
  Increasing the size of the economic cake
  The redistribution of working time

Chapter 3 Neo-classical perspectives on unemployment and labour supply: the macro environment and micro responses 51
Tim Barmby and Martin Robson

Introduction 51
A macro-economic perspective on the causes of unemployment 51
  The model
  Unemployment and inflation
  Explaining unemployment differences across countries and over time

Why does unemployment persist?
Policies to reduce unemployment: a macro-economic perspective
Household responses to unemployment 60
A neo-classical view of household labour supply decisions
Inside the black box of the household
Demand side effects and the impact of unemployment on household labour supply decisions

Chapter 4 Whose full employment? A feminist perspective on work redistribution 69
Irene Bruegel, Deborah M. Figart and Ellen Mutari

Introduction 69
Whose full employment? Gender in the post-war order 72
Gendered work time and flexibility strategies 75
The emerging crisis of caring 78
Prospects for a new vision of full employment 81

Chapter 5 A green approach to work and idleness 85
Christer Sanne

Introduction 85
Green views of the productive environment 86
A modest environmentalism? 89
A green analysis of work 91
A green agenda for work 94

PART II WHO NEEDS WORK?

Chapter 6 Crap jobs, 'govy' schemes and trainspotting: reassessing the youth, employment and idleness debate 99
Robert Hollands

Introduction 99
The 'idleness of youth' in political economy 101
Interpretations of 'idle youth' 104
Rethinking work and idleness: symbolic work, altered transitions and generational separation 107
Conclusion: a new deal for youth? 112

Chapter 7 Managing the end of occupational life 119
Geneviève Reday-Mulvey

End of career management: towards a new consensus 120
Gradual retirement: recent trends 122
From early to gradual retirement: the French case 124

Unpaid work for older workers 126
Conclusion 127

Chapter 8 Working opportunities for disabled people 131
Neil Lunt and Patricia Thornton

Introduction 131
Disabled people, poverty and participation 132
Disabled workers and the new labour market 134
Part-time work
Self-employment
Casual and temporary jobs
Flexible benefits and services 137
Barriers to effective participation 139
Third sector employment and disabled people 140
Conclusion 141

Chapter 9 Reducing the burden of work on women? 143
Rachel Woodward

Introduction 143
Women's double burden? 143
Strategies for reducing the double burden 149
The employment of waged domestic labour
Getting men to take responsibility
Flexible working arrangements as a strategy
Concluding comments 153

PART III BLUEPRINTS FOR ACTION

Chapter 10 The US model: the wages of inequality 157
Jared Bernstein, Lawrence Mishel and John Schmitt

Wage inequality 158
Income inequality 159
Causes and consequences of inequality 160
Job creation 163
Job security 164
Some conclusions 165

Chapter 11 'The cult of training'; unemployment and capitalist employment policy 183
Gregory Albo

Neo-liberal policy on training and unemployment 186
Social democratic policy on training and unemployment 192
Capitalism, training and employment policy 200

Chapter 12 Redistributing work: the role of the welfare state 205
David Purdy

The changing worlds of welfare capitalism 206
Work redistribution and well-being 209
Reduced working time 211
Citizen's income 214
Liberal workfare 216

Chapter 13 Working time in Europe: current trends 219
Giuseppe Fajertag

Introduction 219
A diversity of working time arrangements 219
Recent developments in legal, negotiated and actual working hours in Europe 221
Reduction of working hours through collective bargaining: the German and Dutch experience 222
Reductions of working hour through centralised framework negotiations or legislation: the French case 224
The Swedish/Scandinavian approach: individual negotiated flexibility over the life cycle 226
Conclusions 227

Chapter 14 Social labour and democratic capital: the margins or the main-stream? 235
Hilary Wainwright and Paul Gosling

Introduction 235
The third sector in practice and theory 236
The third sector in Britain: some exemplary cases 241
Co-operatives
Voluntary sector
Community enterprises
What future for the social economy? 249

Chapter 15 The feasible utopia of a redistribution of work: radical alternatives for full employment 253
John Vail

Introduction 253
When is radical reform possible under capitalism? 254
Improving material well being
Solving a problem for capitalists (and the state)
Constructing a new general interest

The feasibility of redistribution of work 258
Redistributive conflicts 258
Working time: basic income; third sector;
Macro-economic issues 262
Working time; basic income; third sector;
Political-institutional issues 265
Working time; basic income; third sector
Ideological barriers 270
Working time; basic income; third sector;
Conclusion: can we get there? 274
The synergy solution
Harnessing the role of the state
Building a political coalition for redistribution of work

Bibliography 285

Index 323

ILLUSTRATIONS

Figures

2.1	GB: unemployment as % labour force aged 16-59/65, men and women compared, 1975-96	42
2.2	GB: employment and unemployment as % male population, aged 60-65	42
2.3	GB: male and female employment rates (% population aged 16-59/65) 1975-96	43
2.4	GB: total number of hours actually worked and total number of persons employed, 1979-96	43
2.5	GB: women's % share of total hours actually worked, 1984-96	44
2.6	GB: % distribution of total hours worked in main job between full-time and part-time work, 1979-94	44
2.7	GB: average weekly hours actually worked by different categories of worker, 1984-96	45
3.1	Determination of equilibrium unemployment and the effects of an increase in 'wage pressure'	54
3.2	The labour supply decision	61
3.3	Pareto optimal labour supply	63
3.4	Utility possibility frontier	64
10.1	Growth in real hourly wages, 1973-95	170
10.2	Average annual change in family income	171
10.3	Relative poverty rates for children, mid-1980s to early-1990s	172
13.1	Hours usually worked per week, EU countries, 1995, full-time employees by sector	229
13.1	Part-time work in the EU, 1996, percent of total employment	230

Tables

2.1	GB: persons working 46 hours or more, Spring 1984 and 1996 compared	46
2.2	GB: employment, ILO unemployment, activity and inactivity for working-age population, age 16-59/65, Autumn 1992 and 1996	47
2.3	GB: full-time and part-time work for men and women, Autumn 1992 and 1996 compared	48
2.4	GB: long term ILO unemployment, men and women, Autumn 1992 and 1996 compared	48
2.5	GB: alternative unemployment definitions compared, men and women, Autumn 1992 and 1996	49
2.6	GB: persons wanting a job but not searching, men and women of working age 16-59/65, Autumn 1992 and 1996	50

10.1	Hourly wages for US workers with a four-year college degree, 1979-95	173
10.2	Rate of private-sector, employer-provided benefit coverage, 1979-93	174
10.3	Changes in family hours worked by family type, 1979-94	175
10.4	Percent of persons with low relative income, 1969-95, by race, adjusted for family size	176
10.5	Civilian employment in ten countries, 1959-95	177
10.6	Employment rates for male workers in the US, 1980-93	178
10.7	International job creation and job destruction rates	179
10.8	Rate of job loss, by gender and reason, 1981-95	180
10.9	Employment stability for men, 1970s versus 1980s	181
13.1	Working hours in Europe as determined by law and/or agreement	231
13.2	Average hours usually worked per week, EU countries, employees working full-time, 1994-96	232
13.3	Average hours usually worked per week, EU countries, employees working part-time, 1994-96	233

LIST OF CONTRIBUTORS

Gregory Albo, Department of Political Science, York University, Ontario, Canada
Tim Barmby, Reader in Economics, University of Newcastle, UK
Jared Bernstein, Economic Policy Institute, Washington, US
Irene Bruegel, South Bank University, London, UK
Giuseppe Fajertag, Senior Research Officer, European Trade Union Institute, Brussels, Belgium
Deborah Figart, Social and Behavioural Sciences, Richard Stockton College, New Jersey, USA
Paul Gosling, freelance writer; former co-operative development worker, UK
Robert Hollands, Lecturer, Department of Social Policy, University of Newcastle, UK
Neil Lunt, Department of Social Policy and Social Work, Massey University, New Zealand
Lawrence Mishel, Economic Policy Institute, Washington, US
Ellen Mutari, Monmouth University, New Jersey, USA
Geneviève Reday-Mulvey, International Association for the Study of Insurance Economics, Geneva, Switzerland.
David Purdy, Department of Social Policy, University of Manchester, UK
Martin Robson, Lecturer in Economics, University of Newcastle, UK
Christer Sanne, Department of Infrastructure and Planning, Royal Institute of Technology, Stockholm, Sweden
John Schmitt, Economic Policy Institute, Washington, US
Patricia Thornton, Social Policy Research Unit, University of York, UK
John Vail, Lecturer, Department of Social Policy, University of Newcastle, UK
Hilary Wainwright, Research Fellow, International Centre for Labour Studies, University of Manchester; editor, Red Pepper, UK
John Wells, Lecturer in Economics, Cambridge University, UK
Jane Wheelock, Reader in Social Policy, University of Newcastle, UK
Rachel Woodward, Research Fellow, Centre for Rural Economy, University of Newcastle, UK

ACKNOWLEDGEMENTS

There are many people we would like to acknowledge for their part in the book. Our first thanks go to the authors themselves. We would like to thank our contributors for their thoughtful and incisive chapters and for their patience in putting up with the lengthy gestation of this volume.

Dorothy McLoughlin is owed a special debt of thanks for her extraordinary work and diligence in the preparation of the manuscript. We would also like to thank Frank Popham for putting together the integrated bibliography that follows the text and Brad Robinson and Margaret Tulip for their assistance.

We would like to express our profound gratitude to our partners, Alex Howard and Kate Thompson, for their tolerance of the many hours we spent in completing this project and we hope that they feel our 'time bravado' was well spent.

CHAPTER 1

A FEASIBLE CAPITALIST RESPONSE TO A CHANGING POLITICAL ECONOMY

Jane Wheelock and John Vail

Introduction: the moment for a redistribution of work?

The summit meeting of European leaders in Luxembourg in November, 1997 began with the familiar spectacles that we have grown to expect at these rites of class and gender bonding. There were of course the obligatory photo opportunities of Europe's most powerful leaders, resplendent in their placid smiles and dark suits (these are the real 'men in black'), anxious to provide ongoing evidence of the solidarity and solidity of the continent's leadership class. There were the ritual promises that the onset of the single currency would enshrine a new era of prosperity and growth for the region. What seemed slightly out of place was that for the first time in the forty year history of the European Union, the entire summit was devoted to the issue of unemployment. Over the past decade, unemployment has barely penetrated the collective consciousness of the continent's leaders, passing in and out of the political discourse like a bad dream that faintly lingers throughout the day. Yet with 18 million people officially out of work across Europe, the political establishment finally decided to address the enormity of the problem.

There was animated discussion of the substantial variability of unemployment experience within the continent: Spain faces an unemployment rate of nearly 21 per cent with women and young people particularly disadvantaged; Germany at 13 per cent with racial minorities and former East German workers facing the brunt of the problem; France only slightly behind at 12 per cent with severe pockets of unemployment in its depressed urban areas; the Netherlands at 6 per cent yet with a high disability and sickness toll; and Great Britain at close to 5 per cent yet with the attendant social ills that have flourished as a result of the massive growth of inequality that has plagued the country in the past decades. There were a few tentative suggestions in favour of the 'Social Europe' blueprint espoused by the former head of the European Commission Jacques Delors but European wide solutions were deemed inappropriate by the assembled leaders, not surprising in light of the neo-liberal roots of the European project. (Gill, 1998). The only substantive policy decision made in the three days of deliberations was the rather lukewarm proposal - which, unlike the binding requirements of the financial rules adopted for the single currency, were recommendations only - to have the EU states submit 'national action plans' of how they proposed to cut unemployment.

This anticlimactic finale demonstrated the inability, and transparent lack of desire, on the part of the European political elites to solve this deep crisis. The Kohl government of Germany perfectly illustrated the neo-liberal mentality, which hypocritically embraces fervent calls for an end to mass unemployment with an almost atavistic commitment to policies of fiscal rectitude that only serve to intensify it. The continuing hegemonic sway, if not gravitational pull, of the American 'jobs miracle', was aptly demonstrated by the evangelical zeal with which Tony Blair heralded the American employment record and the remarkable healing powers of flexibility. It was left to his French socialist counterpart, Lionel Jospin, to sound the slightly discordant note. Only a short time before the summit, he had announced plans to implement a nationally imposed reduction to a 35 hour work week by the year 2000.

Lest we give the impression that we believe Jospin's proposals are an augury of a New Jerusalem, let us be clear that we do not believe that he intends to embark on anything like a radical break with capitalism. However, his initiatives demonstrate a willingness to escape from the mental straight-jacket that has plagued employment policy these past decades. His affinity with the more radical alternatives encapsulated in the term 'redistribution of work' links him to wider trends that are shaping Europe and beyond. The French prime minister joins a growing number of government officials, policy experts, trade unions and mass media outlets in a call for reduced working hours.[1] These initiatives are matched by the increasing receptiveness of politicians for a basic income, a policy that has now been endorsed by parliamentary representatives in over a dozen European countries. Finally, when his Minister of Labour, Martine Aubry, announced plans for a £3 billion public spending initiative to create community jobs (where the French state would pay up to 80 per cent of the minimum wage of those who took up employment), she was articulating a willingness to envision the third sector (or social economy as it is also called) as a prime source of job creation.

Full employment has always been an enduring part of the programme of the left. Mass unemployment is an immense social evil on a multitude of levels: it is horribly inefficient and wasteful; it is destructive of human dignity and potential; it is at the root of inequality and social polarisation; it is a prime contributing factor to the crisis of welfare state provision; it is at the heart of social exclusion from not just the world of work but political life as well; it is the genesis of the most destructive political instincts of racism, xenophobia and authoritarianism. Full employment has been at the forefront of transformative projects for social justice, equality and democracy because without it all these objectives become impossible to attain. But conventional measures, either the fetish for deregulation and flexibility of the right or the cult of the supply side of the centre-left, are incapable of creating the millions of jobs needed to restore full employment in Europe. Indeed, we must face up to the fact that the conventional notion of full employment itself is doomed. 'If we understand by 'full employment' continuous full time employment for all - 8 hours a day, 5 days a week, 48 weeks a year, and for 45 years of our lifetime (probably restricted to men as the so-called 'breadwinners of the family', wrote Gunther Schmid, 'then...by this definition full employment is not only a utopian dream but also an old fashioned goal.' (Schmid,

1995a; 429)

'Thinking the unthinkable' is a popular parlour game of the chattering classes and politicians everywhere, one that is usually intended to dress up right wing initiatives - for workfare, privatisation of pensions and social security, pollution futures, for-profit prisons, to name just a few - as inescapable alternatives. Truly radical projects, that have the potential to reconfigure political, economic and social life around principles of democracy, autonomy and solidarity, rarely receive the benefit of such an appellation. This book is an argument for a redistribution of work as the basis for a radical vision of full employment that has the potential to: create sufficient paid jobs for all those who want them; reduce inequalities and serve as the institutional cornerstone of an egalitarian political economy; reformulate gender relations and promote a culture of autonomy and self realisation.

This book develops the view that redistributing employment is a 'feasible capitalist' solution, not just to the unemployment which particular groups suffer from so severely, but also to the over work that others have to contend with, including many women. It argues that for example the policies of the British 'New Labour' government's 'third way' - where paid work is to be the means for the least well off to make a dignified exit from poverty and dependency, and a national childcare strategy relieves the burden of unpaid work on women - need to be placed in the context of a more radical debate. For many men and women - and therefore children and others in need of care in our society - are increasingly threatened with time deprivation, and the stresses that this imposes on lives. Yet others, including the young and the old, are burdened with idleness: with more time than they know what to do with. How do we want to distribute our time between employment, other forms of work, and time to do what we please; and what makes a fair distribution? Putting the redistribution of employment on the policy agenda opens up debate on how to ensure a more equitable and fulfilling relationship between the ways we gain our livelihoods and the lives we lead. We suggest in this introduction that insecurity in labour markets creates a growing divide between those not in work, the 'idle' who have time on their hands, and those who work long hours in paid or unpaid work. By time-sharing between the time-burdened and the time-pressed, we can begin to close the gap between the haves and the have-nots. Fears for the electoral and economic impact of progressive taxation in this neo-liberal era mean that there is little likelihood that the offensive inequalities of income that have become embedded in our economic structure over the last two decades will be decisively reversed in any other way.

The problem: insecure times in the labour market

What people work at, and the ways in which they work have changed substantially over the last quarter of a century. The quantity - and the quality - of work available has altered as market led change has brought about more flexible ways of working, and fragmentation of the institutional context. In Britain and many other parts of western Europe over the post war era, an institutional framework for - largely secure - employment had been broadly settled until the mid-seventies. There was state guaranteed full employment, income security through state-prescribed minima and a redistributive tax system, employment security through regulations on hiring and firing, work security through health and safety regulations and job security through toleration of demarcation practices. As labour markets have been opened up to the operation of market forces, labour has steadily become more commodified. For some, the optimists, the shift in the character of labour markets has provided the opportunity for new, more independent ways of working, with more possibilities for self fulfilment in a context of reflexive post-modernity (Piore and Sabel, 1984; Giddens, 1991). Pessimists observe growing contrasts between work-rich and work-poor individuals and households; between those who work manically hard and those condemned to idleness (Schor, 1992; Baily et al., 1993). There is not full agreement about the scale of the changes that have taken place in labour markets, but there is general consensus for the direction change has taken. In this section we provide a thumb nail sketch of how growing insecurity in labour markets and changing patterns in the commodification of labour have led to a redistribution of paid and unpaid labour time as the structure of power relations, the gender order, discrimination and state regulation have been modified.[2] We take Britain as a paradigmatic example of these changes, for the UK has shifted from a relatively regulated labour market in the continental European mould towards the US model of a deregulated and flexible labour market.

The first main trend affecting insecurity is to *mass unemployment and the growth of workless households*. In Britain 3 million out of a labour force of 24 million were regularly unemployed during the 1980s, a figure that remained at 2 million even in recovery phases of the business-electoral cycle until the late 1990s. In 1975 a fairly disturbing 6.5 per cent of non-pensioner households had no adult member in work, but by 1995 3.3 million, or one in five households were workless, as John Wells points out in his chapter. Since that time, full employment for men has no longer been a reality in many of the advanced capitalist economies, while during the 1980s state policies of full employment have increasingly been modified or even more or less abandoned. In continental Europe, overall rates of unemployment remain high as the millennium approaches. Indeed, changes in the structure of the economy and increasing internationalisation of competition have led to the institutionalisation of mass unemployment, particularly amongst unskilled and blue collar workers in the developed economies (Godfrey, 1986). The only apparent exception to this rule is the US (possibly joined in very recent years by the UK), where rates of unemployment are lower.

Part II of this volume documents the ways in which this shift to mass idleness in the advanced industrial economies has hit some groups particularly hard: the youngest and oldest age cohorts, and other groups who have traditionally suffered discrimination in labour markets including disabled workers. In some countries of the European Union such as the Netherlands and France, less than 40 per cent of the active male population aged 55 to 59 and less than 20 per cent of the 60 to 64 age group are now at work as Geneviève Reday-Mulvey points out in her chapter (Chapter 7). Robert Hollands highlights the plight of youth in Chapter 6. Unemployment rates, even for the 20 to 24 year old grouping of young people are roughly twice the national average for many national economies, and in the European Union, people up to the age of 24 account for more than one third of the total unemployed. Neil Lunt and Patricia Thornton show that in the UK the employment rate of disabled people is only 32 per cent compared with 76 per cent for non-disabled people (Chapter 8)[3]

Until recently, changes in the structure of employment in the developed market economies were largely affecting the levels of security enjoyed by blue collar workers and the unskilled. Increasingly, the only cushion available to workers in these sectors of the economy has been employment in the tertiary, service sector where wages tend to be lower. Now jobs in the primary sector of the labour market - skilled white collar employment - are under siege in a variety of ways. Firms have been using mechanisms which commodify labour and make employees subject to market forces in ways that those in the tertiary sector have long become accustomed to suffering. Indeed this is the route carved out by the US model, and followed with some hesitations by the British. So for example, firms are using pay cuts in addition to layoffs for all sections of their employees. Redundancy is no longer a one-off experience, but is likely to be repeated time and again. Firms now fire experienced employees and then ask them to return as contract workers with less pay. The 1997 UPS strike in the US was caused by the insecurity felt by senior employees as freshly hired employees undertook similar work for lower wages. Experienced and skilled core staff are kept to the bare minimum with widespread use of contingent employees. Manpower Temporary Services is now the largest US employer! The consequences of this commodification is a new, middle class insecurity, particularly in countries like the US and the UK, where idleness, as we noted above, has apparently been held in more check than in continental Europe.

A second notable trend is a *gender based redistribution of hours worked.* In Britain, for example, the number of women in paid employment (11.5 million) has gradually converged on that of men (14.1 million), so that men's share of total hours has fallen from 67.8 per cent in 1984 to 64.5 in 1996 as John Wells indicates in the next chapter. It is because the increase in women's employment has largely been part-time that women's share of total hours has not risen more. Indeed, throughout OECD countries, the growth of part-time employment has gone on alongside rises in women's activity rates. In all OECD countries, less than 12 per cent of men worked part-time (See Chapter 4). Unfortunately, there is declining transparency of working time in Europe thanks to growing discrepancies between agreed hours per week and the number of hours usually worked, as Giuseppe Fajertag points out in his contribution (Chapter 13). It is nevertheless clear that in Britain the proportion of male employees working long hours has increased. Nearly 40 per cent (39.2) of men worked 46 hours or more in 1996, up from 33.9 per cent in 1984. This may take the form of overtime, where in the UK approximately half of full time male workers worked overtime either periodically or regularly. As Irene Bruegel and her colleagues point out in Chapter 4, men also tend to have longer basic working weeks than women, and longer travel time. This limits the possibility of men contributing to domestic work within the household, and in turn restricts women with domestic responsibilities to part-time employment at most.

It is unsurprising that the growing insecurity attributable to mass idleness also results in the intensification of work for those who are employed. There is in fact a trend towards *intensification* of both men's and women's work. For men this takes the form of pressure to undertake more hours in the labour market. There is also some evidence for a very limited increase in the hours of unpaid work that men contribute within the household, but it is not sufficient to offset the increase in the hours that women are working in the labour market (Anderson et al., 1994). For women, work intensification therefore takes the form of an increasing double burden of paid and unpaid work, and the pressures that arise from juggling two major roles, as Rachel Woodward describes it in Chapter 9. Juliet Schor's study of overall hours of work in the United States (Schor, 1992) confirms that work loads of both men and women have intensified since the end of the 1960s. She shows that hours of paid and unpaid work have risen by 163 hours - the equivalent of an extra month a year - even after taking into account those who are idle through unemployment. The struggle for security represented by over one hundred years of campaigning for shorter hours appears to have been decisively reversed!

The third major trend is a *shift from full-time waged work to full-time self-employment* which has occurred throughout the OECD economies (Mason, 1991). Even Britain, which started from a relatively low base at the end of the 1970s, now has one in eight of the labour force in self employment. For the optimists, this trend represents a shift towards more independence and self reliance in obtaining a livelihood. Policy makers in almost all the developed economies have seen the growth of small business as an important element of endogenous growth strategies, though not all have evinced the missionary enthusiasm for stimulating an 'enterprise culture' of the successive British Conservative governments of the 1980s and 90s (Ritchie, 1991; Hutton *et al.*, 1991; Burrows, 1991). Yet historical evidence indicates that growth in self employment and in unemployment go hand in hand (Foreman-Peck, 1985; Steindl, 1945). The pessimistic view is that rising insecurity of employment pushes people in to self employment as a next best way of obtaining a livelihood (Wheelock and Baines, 1998). That pressures remain for those who have taken this route is evident from the hours they work. The full time self employed work longer hours than their waged counterparts: in Britain over half (51 per cent) of self employed men worked over 46 hours a week in 1996, while 22.5 per cent of self employed women (compared with 9.3 per cent of employed women) did the same[4].

Part I of this book presents what the main economic theories say about the forces driving the continuing divide between the intensification of work and employment and the extension of idleness. There is an important difference between theories which see these changes as opening up choice for individuals and their families, and those which see people as constrained or even coerced. For the latter theories, institutional constraints may limit the choices available to individuals and their households. But they may also limit our societal choices in terms of social reproduction. These are choices over the way we care for the future, whether in terms of our children or our environment. Each theoretical approach struggles to define work, and idleness, doing so in ways which place differing emphases on the role of power in social relations.

In Chapter 3, Tim Barmby and Martin Robson utilise a neo-classical model to explain persistent international differences in unemployment rates between the USA and the EU. They posit that self interest is the basis for action in terms of both the demand for and supply of labour. Although the neo-classical model of self equilibrating markets should not give rise to 'involuntary' idleness, real-world imperfect competition and labour market shocks can reduce the effectiveness of market mechanisms in responding to individual choices. The authors model the impact of the resulting mistakes in wage and price setting behaviour, arguing that policies which reduce wage pressure can minimise such institutional problems. Institutional forces at the micro level of the household are also likely to mean that idleness affects not just the individual male, but his wife as well, and that choice in number of hours worked may be similarly constrained.

John Wells (in Chapter 2) takes a more radical approach, and uses an empirical analysis based on Keynesian economic theory to explain mass idleness and the inequalities in the distribution of work and idleness between households. There is no self-equilibrating tendency to full employment for two main reasons: economic shocks such as the oil crisis can lead to a cumulative departure from full employment, while the labour market operates quite differently from, say, the market for apples, thanks to its nature as a social institution. Focusing on the UK economy, John Wells shows that total hours of work have remained more or less constant for the past twenty years. Neo-classically based policies to reduce wage pressure will simply lead to the replacement of unemployment with the kind of underemployment evidenced by street sellers and armies of self employed window cleaners. Political as well as economic means are required to expand the job-creation capacity of the economy; it is likely that this will only be achieved by increasing the size of the economic cake, albeit with attendant problems. In Chapter 5, Christer Sanne highlights the impact on the environment if we fail to address the issue of how to break the cycle of 'work-and-spend' that the dominant work ethic can lock the economy in to. He suggests that the acquisitive ethic posited by the neo-classical model does not provide the full story, and maintains that there is considerable evidence that consumers accept a need for 'voluntary simplicity'. Unfortunately there are many distinctly non-transparent ways in which the market locks us in to an environmentally unfriendly economic structure; for example traffic pollution is not measured as a cost of getting to work.

Irene Bruegel and her collaborators argue the case for a complete rethink of the concept of full employment, with the capacity to provide an institutional framework for a reformulation of gender relations. Chapter 4 picks up on the multiple interconnections between labour markets and households, focusing on the theoretical impact of empirical studies of the gendered division of labour inside the household, of job segmentation and of the valuation of unpaid domestic labour. Not only gender, but also class, race, sexuality and nationhood can all act as 'structures of constraint' which limit choice and opportunity. The authors of this chapter show that the conventional definition of full employment is based on the concept of a white, male breadwinner; that flexibility strategies to reduce wage pressure are gendered; and that there is an emerging crisis of caring.

The sources of the problem: working all the hours that God sends

When one of the editors was interviewing households where men had become unemployed in the north east of England in the mid-1980s (Wheelock, 1990) she found several of the middle aged male respondents commenting that they had 'worked all the hours that God sends' right up to the moment when they lost the job that they had usually held for many years. Idleness for some of these men was modified by making - in some cases a substantial - contribution to the unpaid work of the household; there were even two isolated cases of men doing the ironing or cleaning the windows! Some men also did voluntary work: shopping for elderly relatives or visiting sick neighbours in hospital. Since all respondents had wives who worked full or part-time in the labour market, men saw the varying contributions they made to domestic and caring work as 'only fair'. Yet however much some gained from the additional time they were able to spend with their families, none of the men in the sample experienced unpaid work as a complete substitute for the satisfactions of working in the labour market. Time still lay heavy on their hands for few had developed any non-work interests during their time-pressed years as the family breadwinner. Indeed, a number of husbands commented that they now understood why their wives needed to go out to work as well as looking after the family. What came out of this study was that men and women may each want the opportunity to combine paid, unpaid and non-work time.

As they develop their theoretical approach to the redistribution of work, the contributors to Part I each show varying constraints operating on individual, household and societal choices over the distribution of time between paid work, unpaid work and non-work. In this section the editors hope to provoke the reader with an attempt to schematise the ways in which the growing insecurity in labour markets (brought about by the commodification of labour) fragments and reconstructs patterns of power and powerlessness in ways which may consistently constrain choice in the use of time. We draw here on arguments that are made in a forthcoming book,[5] as well as the context provided by contributors in Part III for their policy blueprints. At the risk of oversimplifying, it is possible to distinguish between what Alain Lipietz calls the high road and the low road to flexibility (Lipietz, 1992), or what Jill Rubery calls positive or long term flexibility in contrast with short term or negative flexibility (Rubery, 1996) and Tony Killick sees as responsive versus innovative flexibility (Killick, 1995). We hope to indicate how each can take the form of a gendered social-political construction, which actually constrains the time options available to individuals and families.

Let us follow the low road to flexibility first of all, and see where it leads. Global competition and the structural shift to services put downward pressure on the wages of the unskilled, wages which are already at the lowest end of the market. The expansion of personal services associated with tourism and leisure, or with cleaning and catering in state education and health services, for example, draws in groups with limited training, such as women, youth or ethnic minorities (Baily et al., 1993). The decline in relatively well paid manufacturing jobs means that there are fewer alternative forms of employment, blocking off possibilities for career progression (as Gregory Albo stresses in Chapter 11).

Responsive flexibility is characterised by particular industrial and occupational characteristics which mean that employers can readily offload any risk and uncertainty in their final goods markets onto employees, by hiring and firing as needed (Thurow, 1992; Jared Bernstein and colleagues in Chapter 10). There are of course, minimal requirements for training for those groups that comprise the source of this workforce whose hallmark is insecurity of employment (again, Gregory Albo develops this argument in his chapter). Strategies of 'numerical flexibility' make solidarity between workers harder to maintain, and their encouragement of individualism undermines the social basis for trade union organisation and activity. *Insecurity on the low road takes the form of a constant threat of unemployment, of idleness, in the face of short term (economic recession) and long term (technological) market forces.*

The high road to flexibility in contrast, relies upon employment based on sophisticated technology and innovation to keep abreast of international competition. Those employed in this sector - in high tech industries such as petrochemicals, computing or biotechnology - must be highly trained. They must be prepared to be 'functionally flexible' in the sense that they undertake a range of tasks and learn how to do new ones. In contrast with trade unions, the professional organisations representing such employees are often able to maintain a relatively powerful presence, by for example, restricting access to practising law, medicine or accountancy. In a deregulated and privatised market situation, relationships between employers and employees are individualised, but in a very different way to the low road. The managerial discretion that fragmentation facilitates is likely to be based on strategies to retain and upgrade expensively trained professionals, and avoid poaching by competitor firms. This means the development of promotion and career paths internal to the firm - what have been called internal (as opposed to external) labour markets.

There are of course also risks for those on the high road. Internal labour markets are particularly likely to encourage longer hours of work as a means of establishing that the individual is worthy of promotion in an orgy of 'time bravado' (Robert Hollands uses this term in his chapter). Nor are those in highly trained labour market positions immune to what is euphemistically called 'corporate downsizing'. If developments in technology do not secure a market position, then redundancies for managerial and professional personnel can reduce costs. Those who remain after such cuts will be expected to take on the work of former colleagues. *Insecurity in the upper echelons of the labour market tends then to take the form of pressure on time.*

Let it be recognised that strategies of short and long term flexibility are not gender neutral, but rely upon strategies of gender differentiation which take advantage of socially constructed gender roles (Wheelock and Mariussen, 1997; and as Irene Bruegel and her collaborators point out). The low road to flexibility is only feasible if society has institutions which can pick up the living costs of individuals who lose their jobs. The family is very important here. Married women are seen as the ideal work force where short term flexibility is concerned. Why, the kind of temporary or part-time work found on the low road is actually family friendly; it allows women to combine employment and caring work! The fact that women may also be forced into employment to supplement family incomes hit by falling wages is not so generally remarked upon. For of course the main argument for the low road to flexibility is that lower wages encourage higher rates of job creation, protecting people from unemployment. Yet lower wages undermine livelihoods, and can only be tolerated if more people work for more hours in more jobs within the family household, as Bernstein and his colleagues argue in Chapter 10. *Insecurity on the low road, then, also takes the form of time pressure, but it is time pressure on the whole household.* This time pressure - or caring deficit - will be somewhat relieved in Britain for example, by the combination of the Labour government's modest minimum wage which will be implemented for adults in a year's time, and by its national childcare strategy.

The high road to flexibility involves a very different experience for women. (See Chapters 4 and 9.) The time bravado demanded of those employed on this route tends to favour women without domestic responsibilities; indeed it is noticeable that the age at which women are having their first child is rising relentlessly (Haskey, 1996). Unlike their male counterparts, fast track mothers retain responsibility for organising child care, as Rachel Woodward points out in Chapter 9. But unlike their sisters on the low road, mothers on high salaries can afford to purchase child care; indeed it is often available at a knock-down price from those very sisters (Folbre, 1994; Gelder, 1998). *Whether it be the high road or the low road, insecurity will thus be off-loaded onto our children, the next generation, in the form of an acute lack of time with their parents.* What Irene Breugel and her collaborators aptly call a 'caring deficit' is a feature of short term and long term flexibility. Can this deficit be made good by such policies as the British national childcare strategy? Will it be possible to avoid the conundrum that (low) paid, commoditised child care - almost always employing women - raises for equal opportunities? (Gelder and Wheelock, 1998) Has the New Labour pendulum swung too far back to old communist arguments first put forward by Engels in *The Family, Private Property and the State* that the only way to ensure the liberation of women is for them to devote their time to labour market activity? Don't we need to look more closely at how men as well as women can be encouraged to take on the burdens – and the rewards – of caring?

Policy prescriptions for full employment

Market forces have most notably failed to break down the institutional barriers between the high and the low road. The difficulty and expense of obtaining the education and training that could allow those on the low road to climb to the high road is actually reinforced by the very trends that are supposed to free up markets. Privatisation has made education more of an individual choice - for those who can afford it. Deregulation has pushed training into the hands of individual firms, who then want to establish internal labour markets to retain those they train, making it more difficult for outsiders from the low road. The problem for market-led policies is that education and training are by their nature public goods to a large extent: it is to the benefit of the economy and society as a whole that there should be a sophisticated workforce, but individual firms who put on training cannot guarantee that they will be the beneficiaries, as Gregory Albo argues in his chapter.

If we are correct, the tendency for the low road to flexibility to be unfenced and to allow all passers to eat whatever grass is left, while the high road to flexibility is carefully hedged off for superior grazing, means that there will be a tendency for inequality in wages to increase. It is particularly in countries that have pursued policies of deregulating labour markets most enthusiastically, notably the United States and Britain, that wage differentials have risen most sharply. (John Wells, Chapter 2; Jared Bernstein and colleagues, Chapter 10; Baily et al., 1993). Baily and his colleagues point out that American men have fared worse in this regard than women. Real earnings for young unskilled men have been especially hard hit: those responsible for supporting most of the nation's children. Women have experienced greater gains in part because they are putting in more hours, but also because advantaged women are doing better than in the past.

When it comes to household, rather than individual incomes, the situation is rather different, though again there is a gender element. In the US in the 50s and 60s, it is probable that the household distribution of income remained relatively egalitarian because women from the least affluent households were most likely to enter the labour force. More recently, as wages for well paid women have increased most rapidly, women's earnings have contributed to a widening of household income differentials (Baily et al,. 1993). In the US, growing inequality between households has gone alongside households in all income groups working longer hours over the period since 1979 (Jared Bernstein and colleagues in Chapter 10). This empirical data confirms the theoretical points made earlier that insecure households must intensify their work efforts to stand still.

In Britain, the structure of state welfare regulation makes for an additional set of inequalities: between work poor households, where no household members are in employment, and work rich ones, where husband and wife are both working. For households whose members can at best only command low wages, unemployment of one household member means that the other is not able to earn a wage which will take the household above state benefit levels (Morris, 1990b; Wheelock and Mariussen). Low wages can therefore structure the whole household into unemployment. *Insecurity under these circumstances takes on the further guise of a contrast between time rich households, who have no money to help wile away the hours in any socially meaningful way; and 'the harried leisure class'* (Linder, 1970)*: time poor households who may have so little time to spend their earnings that they make thoughtless purchases of luxury goods.* (Offee and Heinze, 1993).

Part III provides a set of policy prescriptions for loosening the constraints that operate on choice over the use of time. Here we concentrate on the critical contributions from Chapters 10 and 11; the next section deals with the blueprint emerging from the following three chapters. Between them, Jared Bernstein and his collaborators and Gregory Albo provide a powerful critique of the conventional wisdom of employment policy. The US model of promoting 'free' labour markets - where government and trade union measures underpinning the conditions on which labour is supplied are minimised, and employers' power on the demand side is given free reign - is frequently held up as an exemplar for achieving low rates of unemployment. But in Chapter 10, the authors indicate the high costs at which these low rates are obtained: particularly damning are the provocative levels of inequality, rising insecurity and the stagnant or declining levels of real wages. What about the almost universally accepted policy of training? In Chapter 11, Gregory Albo shows that the commonplace justification for training: 'if individual workers adjust their skills ......they will better match labour demand conditions and thereby raise individual and overall social welfare' is misjudged in both neo-liberal and social democratic policies. Neo-liberals do not take account of the widespread market failures that plague a largely public good like training. Social democrats cannot ensure that even leading countries keep their share of 'good' jobs, and the inflation of training qualifications cannot improve the situation. The solution however, is not a counsel of despair: training and employment must be placed in a wider context which takes proper account of technical advances and preserves our ecological and social environment. We now turn to what Gregory Albo calls for: 'more active employment policies that disengage work and incomes from market determination ......[which] remain fundamental to the achievement of high employment and social equality'.

Redistributing the rewards of work

There is growing evidence that the problems of mass unemployment are not likely to be alleviated in the near future. Economic growth can no longer be assumed to have an automatic predisposition for job creation as productivity gains come at the expense of jobs in the new technological climate. The deflationary effects of fulfilling the Maastricht debt and deficit criteria are likely to drive up unemployment across Europe. (Michie and Grieve Smith, 1994) Standard policy prescriptions heretofore have had only negligible effects (at best preserving jobs but not creating them) or else have paid a prohibitively high price for an increase in employment in terms of damaging social costs. The other alternative of redistributing income to those without work is not feasible in a political climate where even social democrats are unwilling to put the case for higher taxation. More importantly, however, providing benefits to those who are unemployed fails to respect the fact that people would rather be in a position to earn their living (Jahoda, 1982).

The potential of work redistribution therefore to offer a partial solution to the crisis is increasingly attractive. Several studies have begun the task of estimating the job impact of a redistribution of work. Although there may be good reasons why these figures should be viewed critically, there is a growing consensus that a redistribution of work can have positive impact on job creation. Many studies have been conducted at the national level that predict a substantial positive effect of both work sharing and third sector employment (ETUI, 1994). In France for example, a leading economic think tank assessed the relative contributions to job growth of the three competing policy alternatives of the three major party formations: Keynesian economic growth, flexible cuts of labour costs, and work sharing. They concluded that while the first two proposals were unlikely to have an impact above 200,000 jobs gained, a reduction in work hours to a 35 hour week could generate a net gain of two million jobs.

Stuart Holland, in a study for the Socialist group of the European parliament, has calculated the potential gains of a European wide initiative: he concluded that between 9.5 and 11 million jobs could be achieved through work time reductions in both the private and public sectors and another 4.5 million from 'labour intensive employment in the social sphere' (what we are calling third sector employment). When added to another 4.5 million that could be created through the direct investment stimulus of a revitalised European Investment Fund, Holland calculated that 20 million new jobs could be created in Europe, more than enough to end mass unemployment. (Holland, 1997) The real obstacle, he concluded, was not the economic feasibility of work redistribution but the political will needed to enact such a far reaching programme.

The impact of a redistribution of work will also be felt beyond the sphere of employment. As Irene Bruegel and her colleagues insist: 'work redistribution cuts to the heart of contemporary debates about gender inequality in society'. A redistribution of work needs to be conceived as an opportunity to abolish the artificial division between paid work and unpaid work and between market production and social reproduction; as an opportunity to combat inequality in all its aspects; as an opportunity to place gender relations in society at the forefront of our strategies for employment policy. Nor must we forget the positive aspects of idleness; our manic work ethic can leave us with:

> A poor life this if, full of care,
> We have no time to stand and stare. (from *Leisure* by William H. Davies)

We also need time to do what we choose, including contributing thought and work to improve our communities.

What follows in this section is a general presentation of three policy routes to the redistribution of work that follow on from the three chapters in Part III which present these alternatives. The first is some form of citizens' income scheme which - in guaranteeing some level of basic income to all - could facilitate more personal choice over hours worked than the predisposition to enforced choice provided by insecure labour markets. This can be characterised as the 'right to idleness'. In contrast, policies to control working hours might be seen in terms of a 'right to personal and family time'. The last policy route - promoting third sector employment - tackles the issue of job deficits directly, underpinning the 'right to work', even of those on the low road.

In the subsections which follow we draw attention to the differences between a progressive and a conservative approach to work redistribution for each of these policy routes. An emancipatory approach to work redistribution is one that is socially negotiated and fosters individual autonomy and equality; conservative approaches are driven by economic imperatives, rely on compulsion and unilateral imposition to shift individual behaviour, and have no impact on the inequities of gender power. As an example, a redistribution of work could conceivably be organised around the exclusion of certain groups (women, ethnic minorities, youth) from the labour market and the redistribution of job opportunities among the remaining population (men, ethnic nationals), as Switzerland practised so methodically in past decades. (Glyn and Rowthorn, 1990) That such a policy could succeed in its redistributive goals should not blind one to the fact that it was premised on an inegalitarian and exclusionary bias and therefore should not be considered an appropriate instrument of policy making.

Basic income: the right to idleness?

Although the origins of a case for a basic income can be traced as far back as Tom Paine (Van Parijs, 1992), the contemporary resurgence in interest is tied to the profound changes in both the labour market and household highlighted above. On the one hand, millions of people who desire paid work are unable to find employment in the current economy no matter how low they are prepared to set their wages. When the millions in work who do not earn a decent living wage are included, it is no surprise that poverty rates have skyrocketed across Europe and North America. The demise of full employment and the sharp incidence in poverty has led many to argue that the time has come to sever the link between income and the labour market entirely.

Changes in family life in tandem with women's increased participation in the labour market are the other part of the story. The dual burden which women disproportionately shoulder - primary responsibility for household tasks and caring activities in the home as well as paid work in the labour market - shows only minimal signs of dissipating and with more and more women working in the labour market, a distinct 'caring' deficit has arisen because of men's unwillingness to make up the shortfall. (See the chapters by Rachel Woodward and Irene Bruegel and her colleagues) Is it possible for social policy to find a way to link up these two objectives: to uncouple income from work and thereby assure a decent income for every citizen and to reorganise the realm of social reproduction on a more egalitarian footing?

Proponents of basic income argue this is precisely the attraction of their programme. Basic income would be an unconditional grant paid to every citizen on an individual basis without any means test or requirement for past or current work performance, or for that matter any requirement to accept paid work in return for the grant. There is no preordained level of entitlement and the grant would not be constrained by any a *priori* notion of what constitutes a basic need. Most advocates assume it would be set at a relatively low level and individuals would be free to choose whether they wanted to add to this subsistence income by taking on paid work. Basic income would be funded out of general taxation and all other welfare transfers would be gradually eliminated in favour of the grant. The unconditional nature of the grant would mean that the gigantic system of record keeping and files of the welfare Leviathan, largely 'devoted to establishing the fact that the unemployed are indeed idle' (Walter, 1989; 123) could be happily dismantled.

The advantages of such a system to realise the objectives above are quite far reaching. Basic income would have an immediate impact on providing greater income security to poorer households and would eliminate the stigma of welfare 'dependency' that results from selectivity. Basic income would abolish the employment trap that plagues so many transfer systems where individuals are irrationally penalised for taking up paid work because of the dire consequences on their grant income if they chose to do so. Because it is an unconditional grant with no such restrictions, people would have much greater autonomy and choice in deciding what kind of employment they took on. Wage earners generally would have more bargaining power to negotiate with low paying employers and more freedom to walk away from dead end jobs. This would contribute to more flexible patterns of work that were more about employee choice and less about employer compulsion.

Women in particular would have greater opportunity to choose an appropriate combination of paid and unpaid work. As David Purdy is arguing, they would enjoy greater material power to persuade their partners to take on a greater role in domestic responsibilities. The quality of life for individuals would improve immeasurably: the constant insecurity of making ends meet would be eliminated and people would be free to devote time to pursuits of their own choosing. The 'right to idleness' could entail a renewed focus on personal relationships, the development of new skills and projects, participation in community activities, as well as doing absolutely nothing at all. 'It is the real freedom', writes Phillipe Van Parijs of basic income, 'to choose among the various lives one might wish to live'. (Van Parijs, 1995).

This vision of the transformative potential of basic income can be contrasted with proposals for a negative income tax that have been associated with the libertarian right for years. Although in many ways the distributional consequences of a negative income tax may be considerably more progressive than what currently exists in many welfare regimes (Block, 1996), it does not embody the emancipatory values which we suggested earlier should be used to differentiate between approaches. The different modes of operation can be summarised as follows: whereas basic income is granted to individuals, a negative income tax is awarded to households; basic income is given to all citizens without any strings attached while negative income tax is paid selectively to those who are in financial need and with a presumption that it is linked to paid employment; basic income is a transfer that would be received every month like clockwork while a negative income tax would be granted only after a certain period had elapsed. Because a negative income tax assumes that the financial award would be received by the head of the household (a dubious premise from the start) and then would trickle down to all other dependants, it avoids any recognition of - and does nothing to alleviate - the way in which power relations within the household are asymmetrical and shaped by gender relations. The 'dependency' stigma that so often permeates traditional transfer systems would not be challenged and because it does nothing to eliminate the poverty trap for recipients, the greater flexibility and autonomy of a basic income system would not be present.

Working hours: the right to personal and family time?

It has been a long standing aspiration of workers everywhere to control how long and when they work. Indeed, some of the most stirring battles fought by the international labour movement have concerned the issue of working time: working class struggles over the eight hour day which led to the May day celebrations and the Popular Front battles in France in the 1930s for a second day of rest and longer holidays are but two prominent examples. Today, calls for a transformation of working time have again resurfaced and are being widely supported by trade unions and politicians throughout Europe and North America[6]. The impetus for this resurgence, argues David Purdy in his contribution, is related to the twin problems of mass unemployment and the fact that women continue to bear disproportionate responsibility for unpaid domestic work. He writes: 'Here one might suppose, are two problems with a common solution. Reducing hours of work in full time employment would simultaneously help to create more jobs in the formal economy and facilitate a redistribution of unpaid caring work in the home'.

Proposals for a rethinking of work time include a remarkably different number of approaches: reducing overtime hours worked; longer holidays; early or gradual retirement; increasing part-time employment in relation to full time work; parental or caring leaves; sabbaticals; job sharing or job rotation; short time; and reductions in the standard work week (or days/month). Each of these measures corresponds to different sets of interests on the part of employers and workers; have different consequences in their ability to aid job creation, fight social exclusion, and reorient the sexual division of labour; and have different distributional and macro level consequences as well. As an example, leaves or sabbaticals can have very beneficial consequences for social reproduction with a greater likelihood that men will use this time to take on domestic responsibilities; yet its potential for employment creation is limited given that fellow workers are usually asked to take up part of the duties. Employers like it for these very reasons yet workers may not support such programmes for fear that if an employer can generate an equal amount of output or service delivery with fewer workers they have an incentive to forego hiring workers who want to return from leaves (hence the rather lukewarm attitude which many trade unions have taken on the question) (Hinrich, *et al*, 1991). In a similar vein, gradual retirement is likely to prove attractive to management: they can continue to monopolise valuable knowledge and experience of these workers and utilise them in a mentoring/training role. Many workers may likewise appreciate a more measured transition into retirement but the overall effect on either job creation or the sexual division of labour is bound to be minimal (see Geneviève Reday-Mulvey's contribution).

The idea of moving to a four day week, or a 35 hour work week, has great personal appeal to most workers who can readily see the personal advantages of such a proposal and the idea of spreading the limited pool of hours worked in order to increase employment has an attractive intuitive appeal to most people. Still it is necessary to distinguish between the individual and collective benefits of a redistribution of working time. A release from the world of work provides immediate advantages in extra leisure time which workers can use in a variety of ways: to recover from the soul crushing drudgery of work, to invest in education and training for new skills, to develop personal projects of self realisation. Yet the possibilities for greater self realisation has to be balanced with a greater understanding - by men that is: women rarely require such stimulus - that this reward of free time has a collective element as well: of the collective responsibility and societal importance of caring labour and domestic responsibilities. The redistribution of work cannot be limited to the sphere of paid work: it must result in a fundamental reordering of domestic work as well.

The gains of autonomy and equality and solidarity that are the hallmark of a concern for working time rarely extend to the neo-liberal variants of work time flexibility. The entire issue of part-time work is a minefield of contention and rife with ideological posturing masquerading as objective analysis. Should we see part-time work as a welcome opportunity for those employees who want to work on non standard schedules and are willing to accept lower compensation in return for their flexibility (Hakim, 1996b). Or is it largely a drive by employers, dictated by the imperatives of the global environment, 'to make labour power as available as electricity by a switch or water from a tap?' (Tilly, 1996) An entire revolution away from the standard work week and the continuous career model is now underway: the extension of weekend hours and night work, atypical work hours, staggered start times, so called flexi-time[7]. Chris Tilly and other writers argue this drive for flexibility is largely dictated by employer preferences: it has given them a handy tool to beat up on organised labour; it has allowed them to deepen the dual labour market which has reinforced social divisions and inequality; it has actually widened the dispersion of working hours, with employers lowering the hours of their part-time staff (predominantly women) to avoid paying social security contributions or having to face industrial relations guidelines while expecting full time employees to put in extra hours as a sign of loyalty to the firm.

Even the most enthusiastic proponents of flexible time initiatives are loath to consider the gendered assumptions of their programmes. 'Mommy track' programmes which are directed at women in full time paid employment who would like to combine both career and family rarely offer the same opportunities to men who may seek the very same goal. Indeed, they obscure the male career model which allows men to build up their career through long hours of work while ignoring domestic responsibilities altogether. These programmes also have to be viewed against the backdrop of the endemic job insecurity of the contemporary labour market: few men or women are likely to take advantage of flexitime if they feel it will jeopardise their chances of promotion or if they fear that the long hours they currently enjoy will disappear in the not too distant future.

Third sector: the right to work?

As Hilary Wainwright and Paul Gosling describe in their contribution, the third sector (or social economy) typically embraces campaigning and advocacy organisations, non profit and voluntary sector organisations, charities, community trusts, co-operatives, housing associations, self help programmes and local exchange programmes (LETS). Although they criticise the concept of the third sector for its lack of analytical clarity, the unique status of the social economy can be highlighted first by emphasising its non profit rationale which clearly demarcates it from the profit maximising market; and second that its core principles do not include formal coercion as is a hallmark of the state. The third sector is conceived of an arena of social life which is motivated by values of solidarity and reciprocity, where membership is based on an ethic of caring and inclusion rather than market purchasing power. Third sector organisations help create an active and informed citizenry, develop entrepreneurial talents and skills, strengthen an ethic of service and sacrifice, and represent valuable 'social capital' that enrich the fabric of the community and polity. (Putnam, 1995).

The contribution of the third sector to employment goes beyond the existing weight which this sector currently occupies in national economies to consider how it could be utilised as the focus of new job creation. Third sector job creation is a species of employment policy which Andrew Glyn describes as 'demarketisation'; typically, this has involved the release of employment from the market sector and its absorption in public sector employment. (Glyn, 1992). One advantage of creating growth in the non traded sector is that the macro-economic problem of import leakages and the resulting balance of payments difficulties can be minimised. Another is that the services provided by this new employment can be used to address a whole series of critical social needs (in education, heath, community care, etc.) that are typically undersupplied because the value of these services far exceeds the profits that could be captured if left to the market to supply. (Kuttner, 1997) Finally, growth in the non market sector can provide a sustainable, ecologically sensitive alternative to the productivist orientation of market led accumulation.

But Glyn is careful to note that programmes which target greater public spending on infrastructure or social services are generally neutral about where the employment growth takes place or who conducts the services: 'the benefits of increased public expenditure programmes do not depend on the output being provided directly by the public sector'. (Glyn and Rowthorn, 1990; 232) Non profit groups already provide services that are paid for in large part by the government: in health care, social services, and education, the third sector is a major provider of services. This has been consistent with neo-liberal privatisation initiatives but while the impetus for third sector job creation may share similar concerns of delegating service provision to the local level to respect local needs and values, it by no means accepts the rationale that government services are by their very nature illegitimate on grounds of either efficiency or accountability. Third sector initiatives should be seen as a complement to rather than as a substitute for state sector employment growth.

The emphasis on the third sector's contribution to job creation is rooted in both the potential flexibility of its labour policies and the competitive advantage it enjoys over state bureaucracies as result of its organisational structure. (Rustin, 1994) The ability of organisations in the social economy to target employment to those who are most in need of it is an important factor: disadvantaged populations - youth, ethnic minorities, disabled, women, elderly - are systematically excluded from the labour market and face severe obstacles in finding work (Part II). These are the people who would clearly benefit from productive work that could be provided by the third sector. Careers in the social economy can provide a critical ladder out of poverty and social exclusion; as agents of social cohesion and civic responsibility, associations have an integrative potential that state agencies can not match. Finally, because these associations are premised on high levels of altruism and trust, there is an intuitive understanding that social services that rely on these values are best delivered by organisations that are committed to them (Rustin, 1994).

As a last point, the progressive elements of a third sector approach need to be carefully differentiated from 'welfare to work' programmes that have become the current vogue among the Anglo-American centre-left. One key difference to highlight is the way in which these programmes are used consciously as a means of social control. Coercion is an integral feature of their operation: in the welfare legislation recently implemented in the United States (and in the New Deal welfare to work programme in Great Britain) benefits can be withheld from any welfare claimant who refuses to participate in a job programme. This element of compulsion is an unmistakable indication that these programmes are as much about disciplining the less advantaged as they are about helping them. The devastating consequences of this approach on the lives of welfare recipients have been widely noted. Tensions likewise exist regarding what range of activities is deemed to constitute 'work'. As David Purdy notes, the scope of workfare is currently quite narrow: there is no recognition of the extent and significance of the amount of unpaid work already performed or for that matter a realisation that there are a multitude of ways in which people could contribute to the common good that go beyond the restrictive definitions currently in operation. Third sector employment should be able to avoid both of these traps: by offering a range of jobs that are intrinsically satisfying and challenging, there should be sufficient incentive for people who want paid employment to take up positions without resort to coercive means of any kind.

In this introduction we have argued that growing insecurity in labour markets has unbalanced the lives of an overwhelming majority in our society. It has led to invidious contrasts between those who are working 'all the hours that God sends' and those who sit idle, with no job to go to. It has divided us into the 'time burdened' surviving on poverty level incomes, and the 'time pressed' who may lack even the time to care for their children or the elderly. How can we get beyond the 'new individualism' that is the legacy of nearly two decades of the cult of the market and find a radical vision for our collective future? A debate about the redistribution of work and employment is long overdue. As individuals, we need to ask ourselves how we want to combine reasonable hours of paid work with caring work at home and voluntary work in our communities. As a society we need to ensure that time in employment and time to give and receive care is reasonably shared out to the benefit of all. A redistribution of work can provide us with the possibility of something much more desirable than the right to full employment. It could give individuals and society the right to full work and full care, now and in the future. We hope that when you have read this book, you too are convinced that a radical social imagination can indeed be combined with political feasibility. In the conclusion, John Vail investigates just how feasible policies for a redistribution of work may be as a response to the end of full employment.

Notes

[1] Jospin's remarkable electoral victory itself followed on the heels of a convulsive strike by the French truck drivers in November 1996 that revolved around the issue of early retirement at age 55. The truckers' victory sparked other sectors of the French workforce to take up the fight for a change in work time policy. Indeed, the case for working time has been widely debated in the French media: Alain Lipietz argues that 'no other economic policy ... will have spurred so much public debate, surveys, controversies and experiments, before its actual implementation'. (Lipietz, 1997)

[2] The argument provided here draws on a forthcoming book edited by John Vail, Jane Wheelock and Michael Hill provisionally entitled *Insecure Times: insecurity in modern society* to be published by Routledge in 1999.

[3] Part II should have contained a chapter on the problems faced by blacks and Hispanics in the US, but two successive authors withdrew. We regret this omission.

4 It should be noted that the rise in self-employment - in contrast with other labour market trends - is giving rise to some decommodification of labour. In drawing on the services of family members, micro-businesses are reducing reliance on the market. They may of course be exploiting the family in doing so. (Baines and Wheelock, forthcoming).

5 See endnote 2, especially Jane Wheelock's chapter on 'Insecurity in Employment'.

6 Campaigns for working time may be offensive or devensive. The 1980s working time campaigns and the Jospin government's initiatives were proactive attempts to redistribute work opportunities across an entire sector or economy Work sharing in the 1990s on the contrary have generally been last ditch efforts to avoid redundancies at firm level: plant time agreements, such as those agreed in Volkswagen in late 1993, promote a work sharing alternative where all workers are placed on reduced hours (at reduced wages) in order to prevent any lay offs. Employers derive an advantage because they are in essence creating a reserve of highly skilled, experienced workers who can be brought back on once conditions permit; workers are able to keep their jobs, albeit at reduced wages, but avoid the high costs associated with being unemployed. In essence, these agreements can be seen as less an encouragement of a new redistributive regime and more as an extended form of concealed partial unemployment. (ETUI, 1994).

[7] Workers and trade unions had good reasons to support fixed time standards (albeit within a desire to limit the time worked). The first, most essential function as noted by Marx, Polanyi and others, was to prevent workers from being worn down under the strain and toil of work to the extent that they damaged their very capacity to work. Fixed norms also reduced competition among workers and gave unions an important weapon with which to restrict labour supply. Finally, it prevented employers from attempting to increase the working day in order to make up for wage increases.

PART I

THEORIES OF FULL EMPLOYMENT

CHAPTER 2

A KEYNESIAN VIEW OF THE REDISTRIBUTION OF WORK

John Wells

Introduction

The task of reconciling full employment with relatively low inflation was achieved in most industrial countries with reasonable success during the immediate post-war decades. However, the emergence of 'stagflation' - simultaneous increases in unemployment and inflation - in the 1970s under the impact of oil price shocks ushered in 'monetarist' policies, which assigned inflation-reduction a higher priority than full employment. The ensuing monetary shocks resulted in unprecedented mass unemployment throughout the world. Whilst the United States has created near full employment conditions, in the EU, unemployment, albeit cyclical, has persisted at high levels and co-exists with often excessively long hours worked by those in employment. Solutions to European unemployment divide between a neo-liberal orthodoxy which advocates the introduction of more 'flexible' labour markets in an attempt to ape what is thought to explain the US success and a heterodoxy which advocates demand reflation as well as a redistribution of working time, involving hours-reduction and work-sharing. This paper analyses the causes of unemployment and its solutions, including a redistribution of work, from a Keynesian perspective.

Keynesian economics and unemployment theory

In order to appreciate the contribution of Keynesian economics to unemployment theory, a short exposition of orthodox, equilibrium or 'natural' rate theories is required. (See also Chapter 3). In the simplest competitive version, the labour market is assumed to function just like a goods market characterised by free competition. Labour demand is a continuously decreasing function (downward-sloping) in the real wage, and labour supply a continuously increasing function (upward-sloping) in the real wage. Demand and supply curves intersect at a *unique* real wage-employment combination: an equilibrium *exists*, which 'clears' the market and, since workers are on their supply curve - supplying just that amount of labour given their work/leisure preferences - a full employment equilibrium can be achieved. Any residual unemployment, observed from household surveys, must be either 'frictional' (i.e. workers moving between jobs) or 'voluntary' (such that the real wage does not compensate for the disutility of lost leisure). This equilibrium is not completely static and can change through time in response to small underlying changes in demand or supply. When shocked by shifts in either demand or supply, the labour market is capable of converging rapidly on a new equilibrium, but only for so long as the real wage is "downwards flexible" (as a result of workers being willing to compete with each other and bid down the wage); workers can price themselves into work, moving down the demand curve until a new equilibrium is established. Indeed, virtually continuous full employment can be achieved so long as real wages are sufficiently flexible downwards. Any 'involuntary' unemployment (i.e. an excess supply of workers willing to work at the going rate) is at worst temporary[1]. Given the strong self-equilibrating properties of competitive markets, the 'natural' employment/unemployment rate of such a model is a centre of gravity in the system and unemployment should at most show cyclical fluctuations reverting to a low level of frictional unemployment.

Labour market models incorporating imperfect competition features, with monopolistically competitive price-setting firms and labour unions bargaining over wages (Layard, Nickell and Jackman (1991))[2], yield an equilibrium, a 'natural' rate of employment/unemployment which, nevertheless, coincides with the existence of involuntary unemployment. The reason being that, in such models, the real wage may be set above market-clearing levels, as a result of, for example, 'efficiency' wage considerations by employers or the exercise of labour union or 'insider' power, which causes job rationing and involuntary unemployment in the primary sector of the economy[3]. The cause of involuntary unemployment lies not with the individual worker herself but with structural features of the labour market.

Introducing dynamics and price and wage expectations leads on to a so-called 'expectations-augmented' Phillips-type inverse relationship between changes in inflation and unemployment[4], with the 'natural' rate of unemployment being a point of balance, above which inflation decelerates and below which it accelerates. This NAIRU (non-accelerating inflation rate of unemployment) becomes the focus of both macro- and micro-economic policy. Macro-policy focuses on trying to keep the economy as close as possible to the NAIRU, whilst reducing inflationary expectations; the aim of micro-policy is to minimise the NAIRU. Such so-called 'structural' labour market reforms consist basically of removing 'impediments' to the operation of freely-functioning market forces, thereby enhancing real and nominal wage flexibility: reductions in labour union power, diminution of employment protection (with the aim of reducing firing costs and, according to the theory, encouraging hiring), reducing out-of-work benefit levels and benefit duration (in order to encourage more effective 'job search' by the unemployed), diminishing the 'wedge' between employer wage costs and take-home pay, increasing product market competition (in order to bid down rents which may contribute to non-market clearing wages).

The 'scientific' basis for such measures is econometric work (Layard *et al*, (1994), Nickell (1997)) confirming that such 'structural' labour market (or 'supply' side) variables, together with a demand side variable, account statistically for a large proportion of the variation in unemployment between OED countries and can also explain the time series behaviour of unemployment in individual countries[5]. The predictive power of such models has not, however, been impressive. Thus, the UK NAIRU is thought to have risen between the 1970s and 1980s - despite the Thatcher government's success in reducing trade union power, curtailing benefits, and encouraging the unemployed to engage in more active job search. Also surprisingly, the NAIRU, as modelled by Layard *et al* is not affected by investment in machinery equipment, which might be expected to lower the NAIRU (Rowthorn, 1996), nor do Layard *et al* believe that labour market 'mismatch' (i.e. supply-demand imbalances) by skill, sector or region have contributed to raising the UK NAIRU - despite the fact that the emergence of such imbalances and the inflationary pressures to which they give rise has foreshortened cyclical recoveries in the UK.

The Layard *et al* model allows (adverse) demand and supply shocks to give rise to substantial unemployment which, rather than subside quickly (as in the perfectly competitive model), may persist through time, a phenomenon termed unemployment 'hysteresis'. Thus, the 'natural' rate, rather than being the centre of gravity of the labour market, contradictorily from a methodological point of view, tracks actual unemployment. Such unemployment persistence is, in the model of Layard *et al*, as might be expected, real and nominal wage rigidity, to be addressed by supply side reforms e.g. encouraging the long-term unemployed, whose attachment to the labour market may have become attenuated, to engage in more effective job search, thereby exerting greater downward pressure on wages. Thus, what starts out as demand-deficient unemployment becomes, under this interpretation, 'structural' in character and the object of labour market 'reforms'. Accordingly, high continental European unemployment, though self-evidently resulting from aggregate demand deflation consequent upon pursuit of the Maastricht criteria for EMU, is treated in recent IMF and OECD publications as almost entirely structural.

The bottom line in orthodox models is that capitalist economies have an inherent, self-equilibrating tendency to full employment - provided competitive market forces are allowed to prevail. State policy should be directed towards ensuring: (i) that the 'natural' rate is as close as possible to the full employment rate and (ii) that actual unemployment converges rapidly on the 'natural' rate. Both involve the intensification of competition and increased flexibility. Such labour market 'reforms' go hand in hand in current orthodoxy with a conservative macro-economics which grants aggregate demand management (monetary and fiscal policy) little scope for reducing unemployment compared with 'structural' labour market policies[6]. Orthodoxy views the Phillips curve as vertical at the NAIRU, implying no scope for exploiting any possible inflation-unemployment trade-off in the medium- to long-run; as a result monetary policy is neutral with respect to the real economy (output and employment)[7] when the economy is at its full capacity (determined by the NAIRU) trend growth path. Since the NAIRU is the best that can be achieved on a sustained basis, monetary policy should focus on targeting the NAIRU (i.e. trying to stabilise the economy at the NAIRU) and reducing inflationary expectations, thereby achieving the over-riding objective of monetary policy which is price stability. Since politicians have an incentive to spring inflation 'surprises', they are considered a major source of instability in capitalism, and monetary policy is best placed in the hands of conservative central bankers and technocrats. Nevertheless, current orthodoxy, by recognising that adverse demand shocks can give rise to persistent unemployment (which mark-one monetarism denied), recognises (see Bean, 1994; 615) that aggregate demand should be managed in a way conducive/supportive of employment[8].

Keynesian economics challenges all the theoretical underpinnings of orthodox views: its assumptions regarding the capacity of freely-operating market forces spontaneously to achieve full employment, its vision of the labour market as little different from a market for commodities, its views regarding the state's role in a capitalist economy as well as the role of broader economy-wide forces in determining employment. Keynesian economics contests both the *existence* of a *unique, stable* full employment equilibrium as well as the assumption that even a fully flexible, competitive labour market has an inherent tendency to revert to that equilibrium. Thus, a bad, high unemployment position, which arises as a result of an adverse demand shock (i.e. an autonomous reduction in consumer or investment demand), may persist and even be accompanied by accelerating inflation. And this may be an equilibrium, in the sense that the forces tending to push the system towards lower unemployment may be weak or non-existent; indeed, there may be a cumulative departure towards ever higher unemployment. Thus, there exists the possibility of *multiple* equilibria (Solow, 1990; Blanchard and Summers, 1990) or none (with the system oscillating wildly between mass unemployment and over-full employment).

The explanation for unemployment persistence in Keynes' system of thought is the source of some controversy. Some 'fixed price' interpretations of Keynes, which stress real wage and price rigidities as the source of non-market clearing, focus on features of the labour market, namely its role as a 'social institution' in which non-market relationships such as trust, co-operation, norms and solidarity can predominate. For example, employers often seek to establish long-term relationships with their employees, whilst solidarity amongst employees inhibits the completely free play of market forces (in particular, the undercutting of wages by the unemployed). A rich seam of recent research by US Keynesians has been devoted to such features, some with the aim of demonstrating that contraventions of the assumptions of pure competition in the case of the labour market often have a basis in rational, self-interested, maximising behaviour[9]. Keynes himself certainly thought real wage rigidity, arising, for example, from the exercise of trade union power, could constitute an obstacle to the achievement of full employment; labour market flexibility was seen as an inevitable requirement for economic success in an era of rapid technological and structural change of all kinds. However, since such accounts constituted the orthodoxy of his day, his contribution to revolutionising economic thought, must be seen to have superseded such 'fixed-price' interpretations.

On the one hand, Keynes challenged the contemporary orthodoxy that wage and price flexibility would ensure full employment. Not only would nominal wage cuts be politically disruptive and, hence, economically damaging, but he adduced a whole host of reasons why flexibility would be economically damaging in itself: nominal wage cuts would induce price cuts, leaving real wages (the cost of labour) unchanged; price deflation would likely redistribute income from debtors (enterprises) to creditors, thereby damaging the propensity to invest; the expectation of falling prices would dampen 'animal spirits', causing investment to be postponed. Recent formal modelling undertaken by Hahn and Solow (1996) confirms Keynes' intuition. In these models, flexible nominal wages do not, generally, ensure convergence to full employment, whilst the intermediate path can be extremely unstable. This is confirmed by historical evidence from the pre-World War One era of relatively competitive labour markets, when unemployment exhibited big fluctuations and a mean level was far from zero.

In addition, Keynes, whilst accepting real wage rigidities as a source of non-market clearing, was uncomfortable with policies involving a full frontal attack on the organised power of the working-class (such as that undertaken by successive Conservative governments in Britain between 1979 and 1997), preferring instead a solution to unemployment which accommodated the existing balance of social forces[10]. Keynes' important insight was that developments in employment and unemployment cannot simply be viewed through the prism of factors directly impinging on the labour market, such as employer and workers' organisations or the benefit regime, but must be seen in the context of developments in the economy as a whole (the macro-economy), in particular the evolution of aggregate demand and its components (consumption, investment and exports), and in the economy's capacity to grow and absorb new technology. For example, high levels of equipment investment can reap positive employment effects, on account of both direct job-creation benefits as well as its capacity to sustain economic growth through the creation of new products and processes, and their absorption and diffusion.

The state's role in Keynesian economics is thus qualitatively different from that assigned by orthodox theory. If the market economy cannot spontaneously generate full employment, then scope exists for state action to improve on this outcome: by supporting high levels of demand, by countering the economic cycle and by trying to improve the trend rate of growth. In the short-run, policy-makers have little option but to target the NAIRU, but the fact that the NAIRU appears to track actual unemployment supports the case for an expansionary bias to monetary and fiscal policies which pushes down unemployment as far as it will go before inflationary pressures are triggered (Stiglitz, 1997). Meanwhile, the risk of moderate inflation exploding into uncontrolled inflation appear to have been exaggerated (Stiglitz, 1997)[11], whilst modest inflation (in the single-digit range) appears beneficial for growth. The case for attempting counter-cyclical fine-tuning of the economy, albeit exceptionally difficult in practice, remains important in an increasingly global economy where national economies are subject to external shocks. Finally, if the state mobilises the whole range of policy instruments at its disposal, including industrial policy, incomes policy, and increased borrowing then better states of the world can be achieved.

Current orthodoxy of conservative macro-economics combined with enhanced labour market 'flexibility' cannot possibly, from a Keynesian perspective, deliver improved economic performance. Subordinating all policy objectives, including full employment, to the over-riding goal of inflation-reduction risks trapping the economy into a low investment, low growth path, whilst reliance on a single economic tool (monetary policy and interest rates) to achieve short-run stabilisation, risks excessive fluctuations in the real exchange rate with adverse consequences for exports and manufacturing and, hence, the structural balance of the economy. Meanwhile, increased labour 'flexibility' can have very undesirable effects: a 'hire-and-fire' culture which makes employment more sensitive to output (in recessions as well as recoveries), thereby discouraging both employers and employees from investing in human capital through the cycle; the proliferation of poorly-paid, low-tech jobs, whose social productivity, as in the case of many private and domestic services, is derisory and which accentuate inequality and reinforce the low growth trajectory.

Finally, the importance of a country's social institutions in assessing its labour market performance (in respect of employment/unemployment and inequality) needs stressing. Keynes' definition of 'involuntary' unemployment, as occurring when workers cannot find work at the going wage for their particular skill and experience, has been the object of much criticism. Lucas (1978), for example, argued that, if people really want to work, they should be prepared to accept a real wage cut, to price themselves into work by moving down the labour demand curve. People have choices, even if those forced to downgrade face unfavourable ones. Just how unfavourable can be seen in less developed capitalist countries, where in the absence of state income support schemes, measured open unemployment is minimal: those unable to find work in the relatively high-paying 'formal' sector of the economy have to eke out a living in poorly-capitalised, low income jobs in the 'informal' sector, whose social productivity, as in domestic services, is typically low. And the resulting inequality is extreme. Indeed, Keynes' colleague, Joan Robinson, noticing the re-appearance of petty traders in the 1930s in response to the crisis of mass unemployment, coined the term 'underemployment'.

Does, therefore, the existence of 'involuntary' unemployment in industrial societies simply reflect the existence of real wage norms, supported by social consensus and reinforced by mechanisms such as minimum wages and out-of-work benefits? To a large degree: yes. Societies which dispense with social safety nets and are not inequality-averse probably have less open unemployment. But, the only 'choice' confronting the unemployed worker in such countries is that between starvation and poverty wages, hardly a civilised choice when urban workers have few assets to fall back upon. Thus, poor economic and employment performance can be reflected in some combination of increased open unemployment and/or greater income inequality, depending on a country's values as reflected in its social and political institutions. Thus, the US success in rapid job-creation and avoiding any trend rise in unemployment, albeit at the cost of growing inequality and absolute wage declines for low-paid workers, is not necessarily a superior outcome to that of continental Europe, where, by contrast, job growth has been sluggish and unemployment has trended upwards, albeit inequality has not increased and the social security system is intact. Macro-economic performance comparing the US and EU, as measured by the trend growth rate, has been equally poor: the differing labour market outcomes reflect competing social beliefs and institutions[12]. Of course, assuming the existence of a continuous and downward-sloping demand curve for labour as a function of the real wage, the labour market may only clear at a real wage which is less than the conventional subsistence minimum. The case for state-financed 'in work' benefits appears compelling - albeit the state risks assuming an open-ended commitment to subsidise the wage bill and helps to sustain low-tech, low-productivity jobs - neither of which seems desirable.

Mass unemployment and increased inequality in the UK: a statistical picture

Different OECD countries have had widely varying employment/unemployment performance in recent years. At one pole stands the US, where unemployment has fluctuated along with the economic cycle but has exhibited no long-term trend upwards. The NAIRU, considered as an empirical category, has varied pro-cyclically, although within comparatively narrow bands (Gordon, 1996) and the US currently (1998) combines exceptionally low unemployment with low inflation. Employment growth has been rapid, employment rates amongst both men and women of working-age are high and increased labour supplies (from immigration and new female participants) have been absorbed - albeit earnings of low-paid, male manual workers have decreased in real terms (Gottschalk, 1997) and earnings and wealth inequality have risen sharply. Orthodox economists ascribe the US successful employment/unemployment record to its labour market 'flexibility' (e.g. weak trade unions, plant-level bargaining, scant employment protection and short-duration unemployment benefits), although the commitment of US policy-makers to maintaining economic expansion is often ignored.

In continental Europe, by contrast, unemployment has been cyclical, but around a sharply-rising trend[13]; employment growth has been slow and participation rates low, although inequality has barely changed (Atkinson, 1997). Following adverse shocks, unemployment in Europe exhibits greater persistence than in the US, and this is increasingly attributed to an absence of 'flexibility'[14] requiring structural labour market reforms, although this view seemingly ignores the succession of adverse demand shocks visited on the EU economy, including, most recently, the fiscal tightening involved in meeting the Maastricht criteria for EMU.

The UK seemingly stands between these polar cases. Unemployment shot up to unprecedented levels (by post-World War Two experience) in the wake of the oil price (supply side) shocks of the 1970s and the demand shocks of the deep recessions of the early 1980s and 1990s. But, employment recovered and unemployment declined during the cyclical recoveries of the late 1980s and mid-1990s. The NAIRU appears to have risen during the 1980s and then fallen during the 1990s. The rapid decline in UK unemployment during the 1990s is attributed by some to enhanced labour market 'flexibility': the product of Thatcherite labour market reforms involving *inter alia*: reduced union membership, the weakening of collective bargaining and employment protection, the abolition of a minimum wage. UK inequality has increased very sharply - by more even than in the US - but employment creation has been only a little less disappointing than in Europe. In the context of these very divergent national experiences, the UK, as an intermediate case, constitutes a useful case study to illustrate the Keynesian approach as both an explanation for unemployment and as a remedial policy measure.

Following three decades of near full employment after the end of World War Two, when unemployment fluctuated in line with the stop-go output cycle but around a low average level, mass unemployment in the UK emerged in the late 1970s and has blighted the scene ever since. Unemployment rose sharply and the variability of unemployment increased in line with the greatly accentuated economic cycle. The internationally-comparable ILO unemployment measure[15] shot up to 3 million (10 per cent of the labour force) during the recessions of the early 1980s and early 1990s but did not fall much below 2 million during the so-called Lawson boom of the late 1980s and the recovery currently under way. A further 2 million people would like to work but are excluded from the ILO measure. This massive reserve army of labour is a measure of the British economy's failure to meet people's desire for paid employment. Unemployment has been higher amongst men than women, especially recently (see Figure 2.1), and higher amongst those with the least formal education, amongst former manufacturing and construction workers, amongst the young and the old and amongst ethnic minorities. Amongst older working-age males, employment rates have declined sharply (see Figure 2.2), many having been forced by labour market conditions to spend the twilight of their working life on sickness benefit and/or in involuntary early retirement[16].

The rise of mass unemployment is, from a Keynesian perspective, wholly undesirable, representing a huge waste of resources and a massive human tragedy as well as contributing to an accentuation of the fiscal crisis (through enhanced spending on benefits and law and order *inter alia* and reduced revenues). Moreover, as unemployment has been used as a weapon in the war against inflation, the long-term unemployed, an increasing proportion of the total, have borne a disproportionate share of the cost (Summers and Clark, 1979). Accompanying the rise in mass unemployment has been an increased polarisation of income and employment opportunities amongst working-age adults. At one extreme, amongst better-off households, increased female participation has mostly occurred in households where her partner is already in work (see Figure 2.3)[17]. As a result, the number of 'work-rich' households, i.e. those with more than one adult in work, increased from 56.1 per cent of all (non-pensioner) households in 1975 to 59.9 per cent in 1994. Meanwhile, the numbers working abnormally long hours is on the rise: the number of employees working more than 48 hours per week in Great Britain increased from 2.7 million in 1984 to 3.8 million in 1996. In 'work-rich' households, adults are devoting ever more time to working in the external labour market, in may cases leaving them insufficient time to enjoy family life. At the other extreme, many households, constrained in their ability to find paid work, are condemned to extreme poverty and find themselves with 'time on their hands'. Thus, the number of 'work-less' households, i.e. where no adult member works, rose from 902 thousand in 1975 (6.5 per cent of all non-pensioner households) to 3.3 million (or nearly 1 in 5 households) in 1995[18].

Thus, more than ever, those in work (79.4 per cent of them) are concentrated in households where everyone is in work, and more of the work-less (52.4 per cent) live in households where everyone else is out of work[19]. This polarisation of work has contributed to the sharp increase in household income inequality since 1979. Overall, the British economy has failed to adjust even remotely successfully to increased female participation. Two million more women are now at work than in 1979, with female employment of all types (full- and part-time waged and self-employment) having increased. But, one million fewer men are in work compared to 1979, and this is reflected in higher unemployment and sickness, early retirement and longer schooling. Male waged employment has declined (the fall in full-time not offset by an increase in part-time), whilst self-employment, both full- and part-time, has increased. The one million increase in total employment misleads, however, as to true job-creation in the economy; by weighting everyone equally, it overstates employment growth in an era of increased part-time working. The trend in total number of hours worked has remained virtually unchanged during the past 20 years, despite very pronounced cyclical fluctuations. (See Figure 2.4).

Herein lies the cause of the British economy's failure to adjust to increased female participation. Unchanging total hours may reflect the shortcomings of monetarism and *laissez-faire* and, therefore, point to the need for changed policies to improve economic performance and increase total hours worked. However, if unchanged hours is the unavoidable consequence of economic 'maturity' and international constraints, then this points to the need for work-sharing to redistribute working time to enable the unemployed to participate in society.

A modest redistribution of working time, between the sexes, has already occurred as a result of rising female employment. Women now account for 45 per cent of all paid jobs: 11.5 million compared with 14.1 million men, and women's share in total hours worked has risen from 32.2 per cent in 1983 to 35.5 per cent in 1996 (see Figure 2.5), although women still constitute, measured on an hourly basis, well under 'half the labour force' with which they are sometimes credited. There has also been a redistribution of working time - from full- to part-time - as a result of the rapid growth of part-time, mainly female, employment. Part-time work now accounts for 10 per cent of total hours (up from 8 per cent in 1979). (See Figure 2.6). However, full-time work still dominates the economy - the main shift since 1979 being from waged work to self-employment. Average weekly hours actually worked by different categories of worker have changed surprisingly little since 1984 (see Figure 2.7). However, unchanging average hours conceals the increased incidence of long hours worked in the economy (see Table 2.1) - because increases in the incidence of long and short hours are roughly off-setting. 6.7 million people or 26.2 per cent of the labour force usually work 46 hours a week or more - up from 5.4 million (22.8 per cent of workers) since 1984. It is mainly men who work long hours: with 37.3 per cent of male employees and 51.0 per cent of male self-employed usually working 46 hours or more.

Mass unemployment and increased inequality in the UK: a Keynesian account

The rise of mass unemployment and increasing inequality in the UK since the mid-1970s represent a sharp discontinuity with the preceding 30 year so-called golden age of international economic development. Between the end of World War Two and the mid-1970s, Britain, along with other advanced economies, succeeded in achieving simultaneously: full employment, low inflation, rapid economic growth and increasing equality. British economic growth, whilst slower than that of her European neighbours - reflecting factors such as her greater economic maturity, a legacy of low investment in fixed and human capital and, perhaps, a certain institutional continuity (class structure) through the war - was, nevertheless, remarkable and resulted in large and equally distributed increases in living-standards.

Keynesian explanations for this good 30-year economic equilibrium in the UK emphasise the interaction between domestic and international factors. Domestically, there was the emergence after World War Two of a political consensus on the desirability of high and stable levels of employment to be achieved through state economic policy activism: e.g. high levels of public expenditure on investment and social spending to be financed from redistributive taxation, low interest rates to foster investment and counter-cyclical fiscal and monetary policy to try to stabilise the cycle. This consensus was the product of many factors: a desire to avoid a return to the mass unemployment and poverty of the 1930s, successful cross-class collaboration during World War Two, a strong labour and trade union movement and the ascendancy of enlightened, Keynesian ideas on the beneficial role of state intervention. Despite the enhanced role of the state, the so-called 'stop-go' cycles persisted, and fiscal and monetary 'fine-tuning' appear to have been slightly de-stabilising (e.g. stimulating the economy when recovery was already underway). Nevertheless, the full employment commitment and high levels of government spending probably provided a firm anchor for business expansion.

Important as domestic developments undoubtedly were, the exceptional international economic prosperity and technological progress of the golden age era must be the foremost factors accounting for Britain's prosperity during post-war decades: a rising tide lifts all boats - even the weakest international competitor. International prosperity was hardly at all due to the explicit adoption of Keynesian policies in individual industrial states, although the new post-war international institutions - the IMF, World Bank, OECD - the products of a desire to avoid any return to the international economic nightmare of the 1930s, monitored the health of the global economy and took some responsibility for ensuring stability and growth. The Golden Age of international prosperity mainly resulted from: the enormous scope for relatively easy 'catch-up' growth with the US (in terms of industrial productivity and consumption patterns) in Europe and the Far-East; rapid rates of industrialisation and associated structural change stimulating high investment levels; the growth of direct investment flows (initially by US multinationals) and rapid trade growth, fuelled by trade liberalisation. The US also was a successful world hegemon in terms of its international economic obligations, pursuing moderately expansionary policies at home (at least until the Vietnam War), committed to trade liberalisation (in particular, an 'open' door policy to the exports of late-industrialising countries, like Italy or Japan), massively transferring resources to the rest of the world (through aid, military spending, and investment) and fuelling the growth of liquidity through the expanded use of the US dollar as an international reserve currency.

Briatin's comparatively slower rate of growth than its neighbours, reflecting the weak competitive position of the internationally-exposed manufacturing sector, resulted in gradually increasing state intervention in the economic structure in the form of regional and industrial policies. Meanwhile, difficulties of reconciling full employment with low inflation (arising from prolonged full employment and a strengthened labour movement) led to the adoption of prices and incomes policies and increased corporatism - tri-partite deals between the state, employers and the trade unions. Fledgling UK corporatism, revisionist (and inaccurate) critical interpretations of history from Thatcherites and New Labour notwithstanding, was not without its successes both within the industrial field and in countering inflation. The 1970s, however, witnessed a sharp discontinuity in the international economy and the abandonment of the domestic political commitment to full employment - and both developments lay behind the emergence of mass unemployment in Britain.

The international economic crisis of the 1970s can be interpreted as one of 'overheating' following several decades of sustained expansion which had increased the bargaining power of both commodity producers and advanced industrial workers. Oil and other commodity price shocks collided with the real wage resistance of advanced country workers. The ensuing 'stagflation' signalled a break in the tempo of world economic growth and provided a fertile breeding-ground for a conservative counter-revolution in macro-economic theory and policy, spearheaded by Friedman and his Chicago school. Placing fighting inflation at the top of the policy-maker's agenda, to which all other objectives (full employment, growth) were subordinated, the adoption of restrictive monetary and fiscal policies and curbs on state intervention in economic life can be viewed as an attempt to re-impose discipline on a world order made inflation-prone by prolonged expansion. Keynesians, whilst accepting that prosperity had enhanced worker and producer militancy, rejected the deliberate creation of recession as a barbaric way to run a modern economy - preferring, instead, the path of negotiation and conciliation with worker and producer representatives.

The UK, the slowest ship in the international convoy, departed from full employment under the combined impact of the deflating international economic environment and the first steps towards domestic monetarism under Labour Chancellor Healey (so-called 'punk' monetarism involving the targeting of domestic credit expansion). The election of the Conservative Thatcher government in 1979 and the resulting adoption of an unprecedently severe monetary and fiscal squeeze further shocked the UK economy; additionally, the interaction between high interest rates and the coming on stream of North Sea oil and gas pushed the pound sterling to new heights as it acquired petro-currency status with devastatingly adverse impacts on internationally-exposed sectors of the economy particularly manufacturing which experienced massive losses of output, capacity and employment. Internationally, the targeting of inflation by resort to an active interest policy by the US Federal Reserve under Chairman Volcker also shocked the US economy - whose deflationary effects were quickly transmitted to the global economy resulting in the eruption of the Third World debt crisis. The importance of adverse macro shocks to the initial emergence of mass unemployment, and the need to avoid them - especially where labour markets display weak self-equilibrating tendencies resulting in unemployment persistence - is now a consensus amongst even mainstream economists[20].

There are a number of additional explanations that have been put forward by economists to explain the persistence of unemployment. The poor performance of UK-based producers relative to international competitors, whether in the North or the South of the world economy, has contributed to Britain's endemic economic weakness - a situation aggravated as the struggle for markets at home and abroad intensified under the impact of global trade liberalisation since World War Two. However, globalisation - or the growing liberalisation of international trade and capital flows - was not uniformly bad news. Job losses due to increased import-penetration of the home market by Northern and Southern producers need to be placed in the balance alongside job gains due to increased sales abroad, whilst inward direct investment has modernised large sectors of manufacturing industry and the City reaped huge benefits from its position as an international financial centre.

Technological unemployment, due to a presumed acceleration in labour productivity growth, resulting from the electronics revolution, is likewise thought by many to be the cause of recent high unemployment despite the fact that, notwithstanding huge strides in labour productivity since the Industrial Revolution, capitalism has exhibited full employment for long periods of time. In fact, although UK manufacturing labour productivity growth has accelerated somewhat since 1980 due, in part, to the electronics revolution but mainly to dramatic labour shedding consequent upon the Thatcher macro shock, exchange rate over-valuation, privatisation and the weakening of trade union power, economy-wide productivity growth, measured per hour of labour performed, has probably slowed somewhat as the composition of employment has shifted dramatically towards the services, characterised by a slower average productivity growth than manufacturing (Oulton (1995), Table 2). This is in line with US and EU experience, where the employment-intensity of output - the inverse of labour productivity growth - has also risen in recent years (EC 1993; 45).

Structural unemployment, defined as labour market rigidities resulting in the simultaneous existence of excess labour supply (unemployment) in certain sectors/regions/occupations and excess demands (vacancies) in others, does appear to have contributed to the rise in UK unemployment. Job-shedding was concentrated amongst full-time, male, manual workers in heavy manufacturing and mining in regions outside the south-east. Job creation was focused on the services reflecting changes in the composition of final demand, including increased international specialisation in financial services and tourism, as well as differentially slow productivity growth, and in non-manual occupations with regional concentration in the south. Evidence for mismatch can be seen in the fact that male, manufacturing workers constitute a quite disproportionate share of the long-term unemployed[21]. Quite why former male industrial workers failed to take up the opportunities available locally in the service sector - and, in consequence, experienced such high unemployment - is not fully understood, but male inertia in respect of occupation, sector and wage as well as increased female participation are contributing factors.

Having accounted for the emergence of mass unemployment, several conundra appeared in the 1980s. First, why did high unemployment persist even after aggregate demand recovered? The answer lay in expansionary factors in labour supply, demographic developments and an increase in female participation. Second, although nominal wage inflation decelerated in response to high unemployment, why did real wages of the employed increase quite rapidly in the 1980s? The answer lies in the 'productivity' deals struck with employers as the price for 'de-manning' where insiders who kept their jobs shared part of the productivity gains with capital - a development encouraged by government support for a move away from centralised to more de-centralised bargaining. Finally, why did money and real wages accelerate so rapidly in the late 1980s boom when, despite falling unemployment, large labour reserves remained? The answer lay in the excessive tempo of demand expansion (Rowthorn 1996) (fuelled by financial liberalisation) as well as its regional imbalance (in the south-east) - both factors tending to exacerbate short-run demand-supply imbalances. Certainly, the conventional factors held responsible for an apparent rise in the NAIRU - trade union strength, the benefit regime - had moved in the opposite direction under the Thatcher regime.

Unemployment and the polarisation between households in access to paid employment

The final section of this paper considers a number of possible solutions to the twin problems of continuing mass unemployment and inequality in the distribution of paid working time between households.

Increasing the size of the economic cake

The standard solution to the problem of a shortage of paid employment is to create the conditions to permit an increase in the total output of goods and services and, therewith, the total hours of paid work. Increasing total output addresses the substantial unmet needs for goods and services of all kinds - ranging from necessities for low income households (sufficient nutrition, adequate housing, clothing, furniture) through to manufactured consumer durables and education and health services for the great mass of society and including an improved social infrastructure, such as transportation, and increased provision of caring services for both the very young and very old. Increasing the total economic cake gives society the capacity to meet the material aspirations of both the poor and better-off. Increasing hours of paid work is a vital factor of production in achieving an increase in total output - and, simultaneously, generates the income with which workers can purchase higher personal consumption standards and the state, through taxation, can increase provision of collective consumption goods and cash transfers.

The main objections to relying on growth as a means of addressing the needs of the unemployed, poor or workless are: (i) national economic performance may be so weak as to preclude an expansion in total output; (ii) the character of capitalist development may be such that the gains from growth may accrue disproportionately to the haves rather than the have-nots (the 'trickle-down' effects of growth are weak) - indeed, the expansion of output may be predicated upon increased relative immiseration (wage cuts, weakening of trade union power); (iii) expansion of material production may result in increased pollution and environmental degradation which, if it were properly accounted for, leaves welfare unchanged - or increases demand for scarce global resources thereby inhibiting successful development in poor countries.

These objections to the growth paradigm, whilst important in principle, are not decisive in practice - though (ii) points to the need for growth to be accompanied by strong distributive mechanisms ('redistribution with growth') and (iii) for policy instruments which lead economic agents continuously to economise on the input of scarce and environmental resources per unit of output. In respect of (i), Britain's experience during the recent cyclical recovery since 1992 indicates that even a weakly-performing economy can expand and generate employment - provided a conducive macro-economic framework is in place. In fact, good macro-economic policy is a necessary condition for addressing the unemployment problem - albeit possibly not sufficient. It is worth examining in detail Britain's output and jobs recovery since 1992 to see both the benefits as well as the shortcomings of relying on a macro-economic expansion alone.

Since Britain's ejection from the ERM in September 1992, whereupon both the value of the pound sterling and domestic interest rates fell sharply, the country has enjoyed a near perfect cyclical recovery in terms of conventional macro-economic and structural indicators: output growth was fuelled initially by increased net exports and rising manufacturing output, although consumer demand and services have subsequently come to the fore, and the economy has achieved the simultaneous triple of: sustained output growth, non-deteriorating external balance and a non-increasing, low rate of inflation.

What has been the impact of recovery on employment, unemployment and the distribution of paid work between households? (See Table 2.2) Employment has risen by 0.813 million, whilst unemployment on the ILO definition has fallen by 0.623 million. The extra jobs were shared more-or-less equally between men and women, but ILO unemployment has fallen more sharply amongst men. Surprisingly, activity rates for men have continued to drift downwards and inactivity has risen - the opposite being the case for women. Of the additional jobs, a disproportionate number are part-time in the case of both men and women, and the persistent weakness of the jobs outlook for men is shown by the fact that the increase in part-time jobs substantially outstrips that of full-time. (See Table 2.3) The increase in the number of people with a second job (up from 978,000 to 1.231 million) confirms that, in the absence of sufficient growth of full-time jobs, increasing numbers are having to assemble a portfolio of part-time jobs to survive.

The numbers of long-term unemployed have fallen during the recovery - but only at the same rate as unemployment overall, so that the share of the long-term unemployed in the total has remained about the same. (See Table 2.4) A curious feature of the decline in ILO ('search and availability') unemployment - the internationally comparable measure - is that it has been concentrated amongst ILO unemployed who are also claimants. (See Table 2.5). Meanwhile, the numbers of those unemployed on the ILO definition but who are ineligible to claim benefit have risen. This may indicate that new jobs have gone to those on benefit, whilst the recovery may have encouraged new entrants into the labour market who are not eligible for benefit; but, the increased numbers of ILO unemployed non-claimants may also reflect the tightening of the benefit regime. The unemployment measure which is the combination of ILO and claimant unemployment (i.e. including those unemployed according to either definition) fell from 3.745 million to 3.014 million (a fall of 731,000) of which men: 2.12 million to 1.464 million (fall of 656,000); women: 0.643 million to 0.464 million (fall of 179,000). The extent of unemployment is certainly understated by the exclusion from the above measures of people without a job who say they would like to work but who are treated as 'inactives' - either because they have not sought work or, if they have, are not available to start[22].

The numbers of semi-unemployed - those on the margins of the labour force who would like to work but have not engaged in active job search - have increased sharply during the recovery from 1.7 million in 1992 to 2.1 million in 1996. (See Table 2.6). For both men and women, the largest increase is amongst the 'long-term sick/disabled' - a category which must include disguised unemployed on an alternative benefit regime.

To conclude: the recovery has generated many additional jobs and made substantial inroads into unemployment and long-term unemployment. However, considerable labour reserves exist - both on the officially-defined measures of unemployment and long-term unemployment and the large numbers of semi-unemployed. A worrying feature of the recovery has been the weak record in terms of male full-time job creation. Moreover, the latest available data suggests that the number of work-less households (and the total number of individuals in them) has continued to rise[23] - implying that the jobs recovery has by-passed those most in need of work. Further, there are concerns that a disproportionate number of the new jobs are temporary rather than permanent - and, by paying low wages, are doing nothing to reverse the increase in inequality. The increased numbers in receipt of so-called 'in work' benefits i.e. state subsidies to poverty wages, confirms the proliferation of low-paid jobs.

What seems clear is that, if further inroads into unemployment are to be made, then it is necessary both to sustain the recovery in the macro-economy as well as intensify the economy's job creating capacity - in order to reach those parts of the unemployed pool which economic expansion alone cannot reach. Maintaining a stable macro-economic recovery will not be easy - bearing in mind the British economy's post-World War Two record of cyclical instability summarised in its 'stop-go-stop' record as well as more recent de-stabilising developments, such as increased liberalisation and de-regulation, increased international openness, reduced participation of the state in economic life and the unwillingness of politicians to deploy the full range of policy instruments, especially fiscal tightening, in their Gadarene rush to diminish the tax burden. Earnings may be accelerating and skill shortages appearing at a time when ILO unemployment remains above 2 million confirming the NAIRU pessimists. This may call for some dampening of the pace of expansion, although a sudden juddering 'stop' must be avoided at all costs. Measures to increase the supply of skilled labour are also necessary. In addition, it is necessary to increase the employment-intensity of output growth. This can be done either through producing existing output in a more labour-intensive way and/or encouraging the growth of sectors which make particularly intensive use of labour e.g. services.

To achieve the former would require the deployment of micro-policy instruments such as: reduction in employment or payroll taxes (with compensating revenue-raising increases in taxation of pollution, fossil fuels and environmental resources) and increased use of wage subsidies to employers, targeted on the long-term unemployed and young unemployed. Both measures work with the grain of market forces. The most obvious way of increasing the output of labour-intensive services would be through public employment programmes, financed from increased taxation of corporate and high personal incomes - the size of fiscal deficits in most advanced countries, the UK being no exception, precluding increased resort to deficit finance. Net employment generation would be positive to the extent that the tax burden fell on savings or on personal sector expenditure with a lower employment and/or higher import content. Increased public service provision of this kind could address a whole range of important human needs - from environmental clean-up to caring for the young and the old through to the increased supply of leisure facilities, to give just a few examples - certainly by comparison with the low tech jobs generated by market forces (with the assistance of 'in work' benefits), many of which meet low priority needs. Contrast the provision of 'meals on wheels' for the elderly in their homes with the growing army of telephone salespeople (estimated at 1 per cent of the UK workforce).

The redistribution of working time

The redistribution of working time or work-sharing as a means of addressing unemployment and inequality in access to paid employment has shot up the agenda in recent years (EC 1992). If work-sharing were to be advocated as the sole solution to these problems, then it would, to my mind, be a counsel of despair. Because it would amount to assuming that there exists a fixed volume of goods and services - as a result of which unemployment and poverty can only be addressed through a redistribution of labour time and a sharp redistribution of goods and services. We would in the British economy be in a zero-sum game - a situation which, were a serious attempt made to address unemployment and poverty, would involve such intense social conflict as to preclude a satisfactory solution.

Certainly, some will argue that zero growth is a desirable objective for the British economy: the country has achieved a high level of economic development and the mean per capita income attained, were it to be equitably distributed, could easily provide a civilised standard of living for all. And zero growth would mean making no new demands on scarce environmental or global resources - making space, as it were, for the economic development of Third World countries. However, it is far from clear that capitalism is compatible with zero growth - and any implied lessening of the forces of global competition and technical progress might result in economic regression. Growth certainly makes it easier to reconcile redistributive objectives with economic and political stability - and, if policy were directed to economising on scarce environmental and global resources, could be made compatible with saving 'lifeboat' earth and fostering the development of the Third World. Even if it were thought that total consumption of material goods and services was high enough in our society, there would be a case for trying to mobilise the additional labour resources represented by the unemployed in producing goods and services for the Third World and transferring them free-of-charge! Thus, work-sharing, to my mind, only has a contribution to make to solving unemployment as part of a broader policy-set.

The main issues connected with work-sharing seem to be as follows[24]. First, is it to be introduced compulsorily by government *fiat* or voluntarily negotiated between employees and their employers - and, if the latter, what policy instruments might government deploy to encourage work-sharing (e.g. higher taxation of additional hours)? Second, would hours' reduction leave an individual's total pay unchanged, thereby increasing the hourly wage - or result in a pay cut, leaving the hourly rate unchanged? Trade unions demands for a shorter working-week have traditionally opposed any reduction in weekly pay. But, such an approach risks prejudicing the job-creating potential of the scheme (to the extent of about 50 per cent) (Gregg, 1994) by encouraging firms to increase hourly productivity to match the rise in hourly pay rates; workers are, in any case, likely to work more intensively during their shorter hours. Empirical evidence for the UK on the effect of reductions in basic hours in manufacturing industry in the late 1970s/early 1980s indicates that it generally resulted in an increase in labour productivity (helping to offset the cost to employers) but there was no widespread increase in employment (Watson, 1992). White and Ghobadian (1984) reported that, following the introduction of reductions in basic working time, overtime working increased, though the link between the two was by no means straightforward. Richardson and Rubin (1991) report that reductions in the basic working week in the engineering industry did not result in job creation. There is also the possibility that constraining labour input and encouraging forced capital-for-labour substitution could result in a fall in total factor productivity (i.e. total efficiency) thereby compromising enterprise profitability. If one national economy acts unilaterally there are possible adverse macro-economic effects through lower profitability and investment, higher inflation and reduced international competitiveness with adverse trade balance consequences. As a consequence of all these considerations, the general outcome of hours reductions is therefore unclear and difficult to measure even at the level of then individual firm. For the economy as whole, positive employment effects seem unlikely.

Notes

---

[1] Lucas (1978) argued that people have choices, albeit those forced to accept wage cuts to obtain work face unfavourable choices; thus, any measured unemployment must be voluntary. Meanwhile, 'inter-temporal substitution' theory seeks to explain statistical fluctuations in employment and unemployment in terms of workers willingness to work harder in years when the real wage or interest rate are unusually high (making it worth working more now to consume more later).

[2] Rowthorn (1997) made the seminal contribution to modelling inflation and unemployment in this way.

[3] Layard *et al* also posit the existence of a (comparatively small) secondary labour market (in e.g. construction, retail, self-employment, domestic service), where market-clearing occurs. Failure to take such jobs would be indicative of voluntary unemployment. Thus, in this model, unemployment is both involuntary and voluntary (*sic*).

[4] With the 'stagflation' of the 1970s came the recognition that the Phillips inverse relationship between inflation and unemployment was not stable but could shift outwards in function of inflationary expectations. Inflation, then, can be modelled as a function of both excess demand pressures in the labour market and expected inflation.

[5] Note that the desire to push the UK (and now EU) labour market with its Social Democratic institutions in the direction of the enhanced 'flexibility' of the US ignores the econometric result that a low unemployment-low inflation outcome is equally possible with full-blooded Social Democratic institutions i.e. powerful unions and centralised bargaining ('corporatism') as formerly exhibited by the Nordic model.

[6] For example, Layard (1996) argues that the dis-inflationary Maastricht criteria (for membership of the European single currency) can have no impact on unemployment in the long-run: 'a non-inflationary reduction of unemployment in all the countries of Europe is essential, *and there are labour market policies that can achieve it.'*

[7] Orthodoxy concedes that monetary expansion can exploit the inflation-unemployment trade-off in the short-run, so long as it is unanticipated - with 'surprise' inflation eroding real wages and moving the economy down the labour demand curve, although this is not a very realistic story. In a cyclically-depressed economy, monetary expansion can also raise output and employment.

[8] The formulation by the UK Treasury under New Labour is that macro-policy stability and active labour market policies are both necessary but neither is sufficient on their own to produce good outcomes.

[9] It is sadly ironic that, whilst US Keynesians were devoting immense intellectual energy to exploring the institutional basis for wage and price rigidity, real earnings of US male manual workers declined from 1973 onwards under the impact of: de-industrialisation, import-penetration from low-wage countries, immigration etc. (Gottschalk, 1997; Topel, 1997; Fortin and Lemieux, 1997). Meanwhile, such labour market flexibility accounts, in the eyes of orthodox economists, for the US economy's apparent ability to reconcile price stability with ever fuller levels of employment during the 1990s.

[10] Note that the existence of strong, working-class organisations was perfectly compatible with full employment and price stability for the 25 years after World War Two (Boyer, 1997).

[11] Solow (1990) suggests incomes and prices policy may be a temporary necessity in the transition from high to low unemployment states.

[12] GDP grew more rapidly in the US, but the superior employment creation record is due to superior intensity of employment per unit output.

[13] Due to halving in the probability of an unemployed person leaving unemployment - not to any change in the probability of becoming unemployed (Bean, 1994 Table 2).

[14] This 'rigidity' is reflected in: lower responsiveness of real wages to unemployment and lower elasticity of labour demand to real wages in continental Europe relative to US.

[15] Defined as those without work and would like to work and who have engaged in job search in recent weeks and are available to start work.

[16] The numbers in receipt of invalidity benefit equalled the number of 'claimant' unemployed (i.e. those unemployed and in receipt of benefit) during early 1997 (*The Guardian*, 20 March 1997).

[17] The reasons for this are not fully understood as yet but the most plausible explanation is that the unemployed and their partners are caught up in the 'benefits trap' from taking low-paid jobs. See Dex *et al* (1995).

[18] The polarisation of households between 'work-poor' and 'work-rich' categories has resulted in a corresponding hollowing-out or reduction in the proportion of 'mixed' households i.e. those where one adult is in work and the other(s) are engaged full-time in household work.

[19] The latter contain 4.5 million workless individuals. Data from the pioneering work of Gregg and Wadsworth (1995). The rise in lone parenthood has contributed to the rise in the number of 'work-less' households, accounting for a quarter of the rise between 1981 and 1994. The erosion of the nuclear family and the increasing number of single adult households (who have the highest propensity of all household types to be workless) has contributed - but single households account for an unchanged proportion 'work-less' households over time.

[20] 'it may be difficult to get unemployment down once it has been allowed to rise, and there is a large pay-off to prevent unemployment rising in the first place'. (Bean, 1994; 615).

[21] The standard reference on the subject Jackman & Roper (1987) is frequently referred to as constituting an empirical refutation of the 'mismatch' hypothesis. In fact, the paper which only contains data up to 1982, concludes 'that there has not been much change in structural imbalance over the past 20 years, with the exception of a sharp increase in industrial balance since 1979.' (p.22) and goes on to refer to 'the sharp increase in industrial mismatch in Britain' and 'the UK's experience of exceptional structural shifts in the 1980s' (p.25).

[22] Those who want a job, have sought work but are not available to start (some 169,000 in total) are not included in the Table.

[23] Employment Policy Institute (1997), Table 14. This is disputed by Ministers on the basis of access to more recent data not available to independent researchers.

[24] These comments owe much to reading Gregg (1994).

Figure 2.1: GB: unemployment (consistent definition) as % labour force (employed plus unemployed), aged 16-59/65, men and women compared, 1975-96

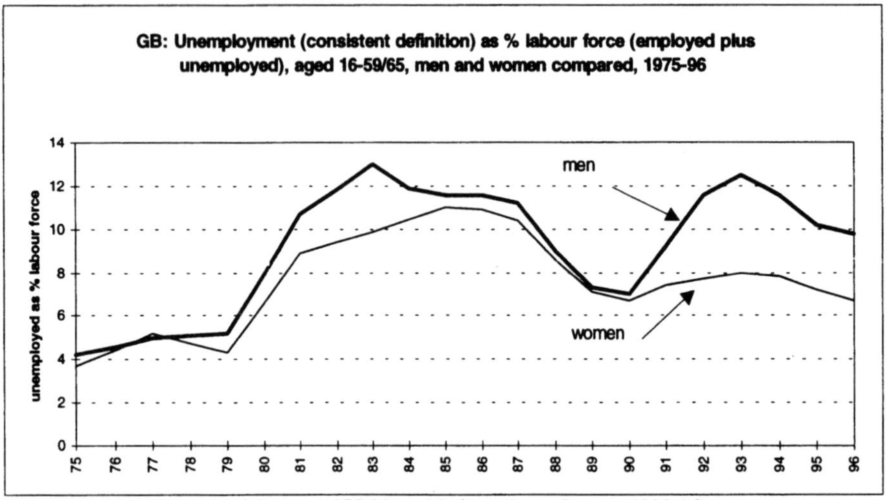

Source: General Household Survey (1975-90) and *Labour Force Survey (1990-96)*

Figure 2.2: GB: Employment and unemployment as % male population, aged 60-65

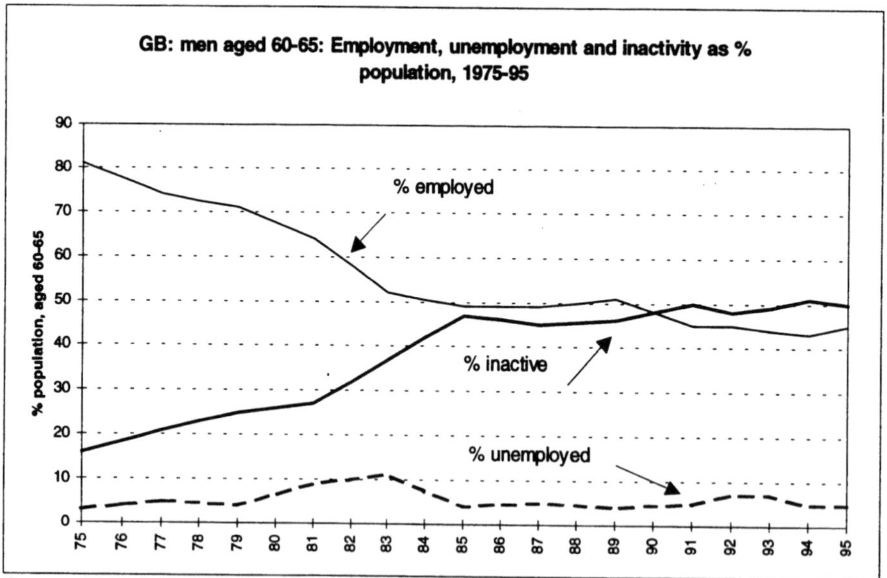

Source: General Household Survey (1975-90) and *Labour Force Survey (1990-96)*

Figure 2.3: GB: full-time and part-time work for men and women, Autumn 1992 and 1996 compared

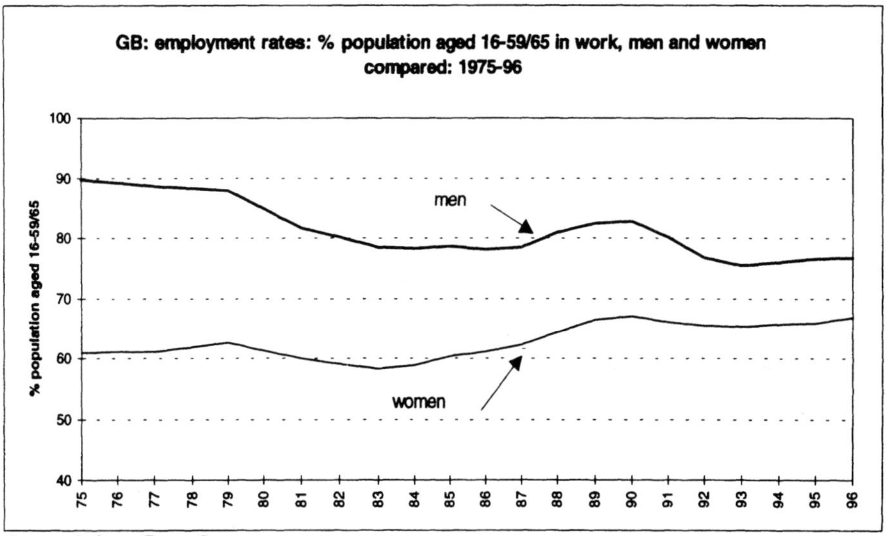

Source: Labour Force Survey

Figure 2.4: Great Britain: total number of hours actually worked (millions) and total number of persons employed, Spring of each year, 1979-96, seasonally-adjusted

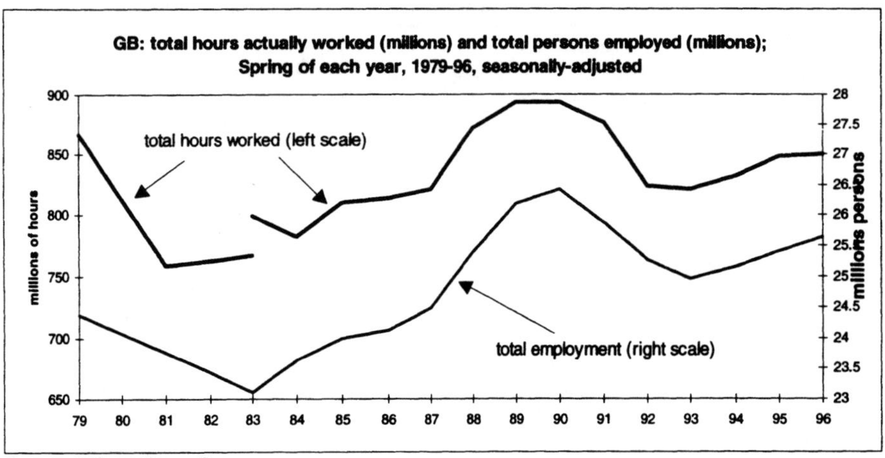

Source: Labour Force Survey

Figure 2.5: Great Britain: women's % share of total hours actually worked, Spring, 1984-96, seasonally-adjusted

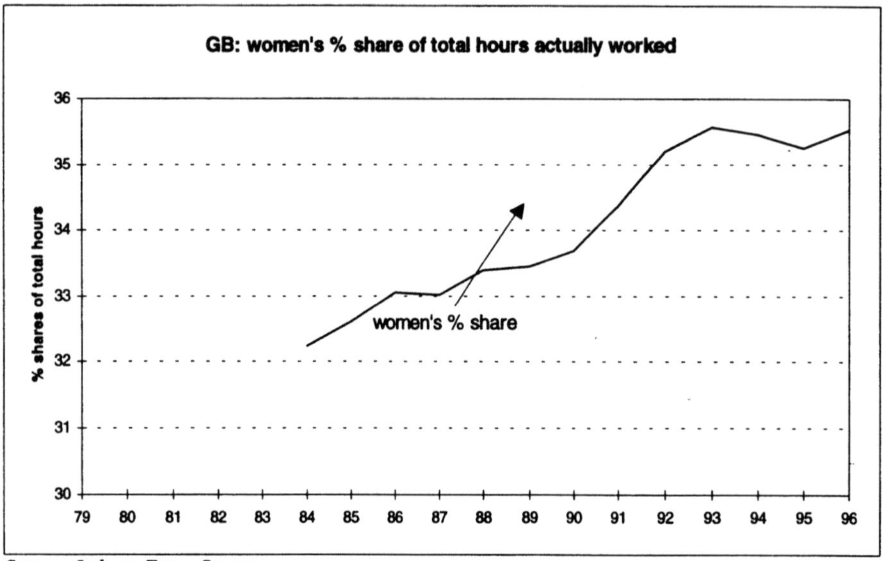

Source: Labour Force Survey

Figure 2.6: Great Britain: % distribution of total hours worked in main job between full-time and part-time work, Spring, 1979-94

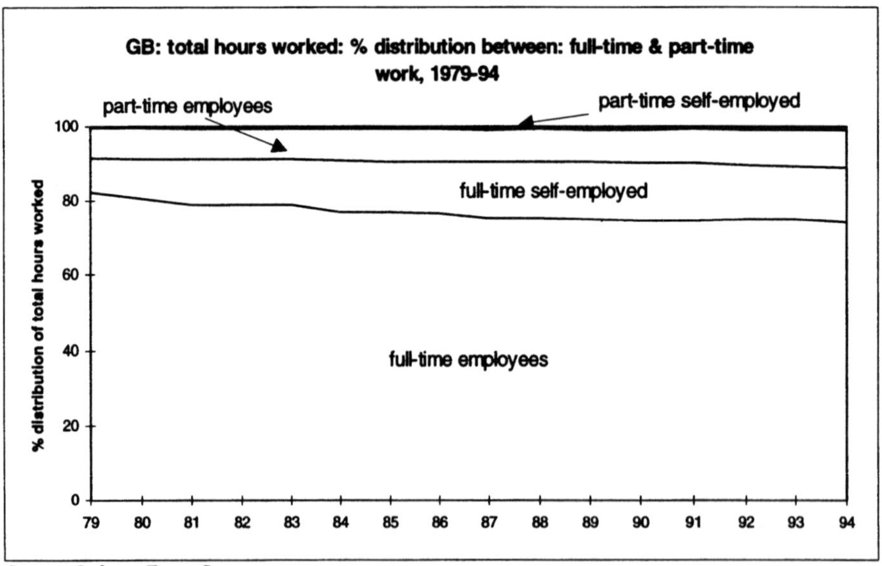

Source: Labour Force Survey

Figure 2.7: Great Britain: average weekly hours actually worked by different categories of worker, Spring, 1984-96, not seasonally-adjusted

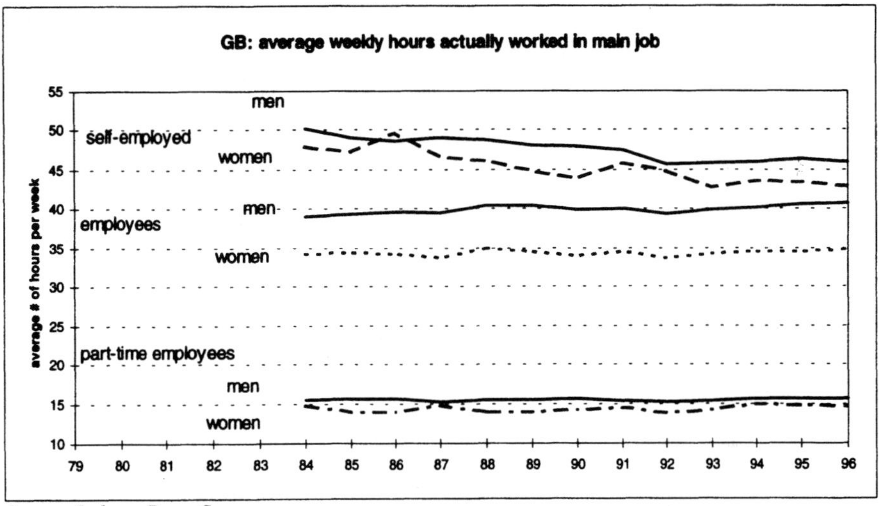

Source: Labour Force Survey

Table 2.1: GB: persons working 46 hours or more, Spring of 1984 and 1996 compared

	employees *000s*	**% employees**	**self-employed** *000s*	**% self-employed**	**total** *000s*	**% total**
Men						
1984	3473	30.0	1170	59.1	4665	33.9
1996	4300	37.3	1219	51.0	5530	39.2
Women						
1984	275	3.1	178	27.9	688	7.1
1996	972	9.3	183	22.5	1166	10.2
All						
1984	3971	19.4	1348	51.5	5354	22.8
1996	5271	23.9	1404	43.8	6695	26.2

Source: Labour Force Survey

Table 2.2: GB: employment, ILO ('search & availability') unemployment, activity and inactivity for working-age population, age 16-59/65, Autumn 1992 and 1996

	All		Men		Women	
	000s	*% population*	*000s*	*% population*	*000s*	*% population*
Employment						
1992	24285	70.9	13573	75.8	10712	65.5
1996	25098	72.5	13989	77.2	11109	67.3
change	+813		+416		+397	
ILO Unemployment		*(% econ active)*		*(% econ active)*		*(% econ active)*
1992	2828	10.4	1907	12.3	921	7.9
1996	2205	8.1	1431	9.3	774	6.5
change	-623		-476		-147	
Econ Active						
1992	27113	79.1	15481	86.9	11632	71.1
1996	27303	78.8	15420	85.1	11883	72.0
change	+190		-61		+241	
Econ Inactive						
1992	7157	20.9	2434	13.6	4722	28.9
1996	7326	21.2	2698	14.9	4628	28.0
change	+169		+264		-94	

Source: Labour Force Survey

Table 2.3: GB: full-time and part-time work for men and women, Autumn 1992 and 1996 compared

	Full-time employees *000s*	**Full-time self-employed** *000s*	**Part-time employees** *000s*	**Part-time self-employed** *000s*
Men				
1992	10604	2125	640	194
1996	10694	2215	931	248
change	+90	+90	+291	+54
Women				
1992	5769	407	4401	361
1996	5955	409	4660	419
change	+186	+2	+259	+58

Source: *Labour Force Survey*

Table 2.4: GB: long term (>12 months) ILO unemployment, men and women, Autumn 1992 and 1996 compared

	All *(000s)*	**% all LTU**	**Men** *(000s)*	**% all LTU**	**Women** *(000s)*	**% all LTU**
1992	1121	39.4	837	44.2	284	29.8
1996	843	37.9	634	44.8	209	25.8
change	-278		-203		-75	

Source: *Labour Force Survey*

Table 2.5: GB: Alternative unemployment definitions (ILO and claimant unemployment) compared, men and women, Autumn 1992 and 1996

	ILO unemployed claimants	Non-claimant ILO unemployed	Total ILO unemployed	Total claimant unemployed	*(of which)* ILO unemployed claimants	Inactive claimants	Working claimants
Men							
1992	1479	440	1919	2120	1479	381	260
1996	890	554	1445	1464	890	342	231
change	-589	+114	-474	-656	-589	-39	-29
Women							
1992	398	541	939	643	398	166	79
1996	253	533	786	464	253	129	81
change	-145	-8	-153	-179	-145	-37	+2

Source: Labour Force Survey

Table 2.6: GB: persons wanting a job but not searching, according to whether available to start or not, and reasons for not searching, men and women of working age 16-59/65, Autumn 1992 and 1996

				reasons for not seeking work				
	total	**available to start work**	**not available to start work**	**discouraged**	**long-term sick/disalbed**	**looking after family**	**student**	**other**
Men								
1992	495	221	274	53	184	36	106	116
1996	810	280	530	55	416	63	125	151
change	+315	+59	+256	+2	+232	+27	+19	+35
Women								
1992	1169	544	625	60	136	690	80	203
1996	1270	515	756	35	238	657	110	231
change	+101	-29	+131	-25	+102	-33	+30	+28

Source: Labour Force Survey

CHAPTER 3

NEO-CLASSICAL PERSPECTIVES ON UNEMPLOYMENT AND LABOUR SUPPLY: THE MACRO ENVIRONMENT AND MICRO RESPONSES

Tim Barmby and Martin Robson

Introduction

To an economist a neo-classical view of the world rests primarily on the idea that agents making transactions on various markets do so in such a way as to further their own self interest. This idea is central to both macro and micro views of the economy. Macro-economics is concerned with attempts to explain the movements in aggregate economic quantities, for example the total number of unemployed at a particular date. Microeconomics, on the other hand, focuses on the ways in which a single household (or individual) might respond to the economic environment they are in.

This chapter is organised as follows: firstly, we look at a macro-economic perspective on the determinants of unemployment and, in particular, examine reasons for its persistence over time. Secondly, we look at a view of the micro behaviour of households, concentrating specifically on recent theories which examine the way in which individuals within households interact, and then we consider how we might expect households to react to constraints from the demand side of the market, one of which may be the unemployment of a household member.

A macro-economic perspective on the causes of unemployment

Since the pioneering work of Friedman (1968) and Phelps (1968), the dominant framework for the analysis of unemployment, among economists brought up in the neo-classical tradition, has been the natural rate hypothesis. Under this hypothesis, mistakes in the pricing and labour supply decisions of firms and workers caused by their failure to correctly anticipate the rate of inflation, lead to temporary fluctuations in unemployment around an essentially constant equilibrium or 'natural' rate. In recent years, however, the experience of persistently high rates of unemployment in the countries of the European Union and the contrast with the relatively low rates of unemployment experienced in Japan, the USA and the countries of the former

European Free Trade Area, has led many economists to re-think their approach to the analysis of unemployment.

A significant development in this process has been a recognition that markets for both goods and labour may be characterised by elements of imperfect competition. Firms and workers, rather than being simple passive respondents to market-determined levels of prices and wages - as is assumed in the traditional paradigm of perfectly competitive markets which has under-pinned most variants of the natural rate hypothesis - may instead be able to exert some influence over these variables through their own actions. An implication of the existence of such 'market power' in the price and wage-setting process is that the economy may settle at an equilibrium in which markets fail to clear; an equilibrium in which there is an imbalance between supply and demand. In particular, there may be unemployed workers who would be willing to work at the prevailing level of real wages - at least, those prevailing in the 'primary' sector of the economy - but who are unable to obtain employment. In addition, the economy may take some time to return to an initial equilibrium from which it has been disturbed by a 'shock' to demand or supply. Indeed, in extreme circumstances, the economy may exhibit no tendency at all to return to its initial equilibrium, so that a one-time 'shock' to demand, for example, may have a permanent effect on the rate of unemployment. As we shall see, the key factors which determine the degree of persistence in an economy's unemployment rate in response to shocks are the speed with which wage and price-setting behaviour respond to changes in unemployment.

An accessible exposition of this new approach to the analysis of unemployment may be found in the books by Layard, Nickell and Jackman (1991, 1994). They put forward an analytical model of the labour market which they claim (with some supporting evidence) is capable of accounting both for changes in the rate of unemployment through time and for differences in unemployment rates across the member countries of the OECD. In this part of the chapter, we set out a simple macro-economic model of the labour market which draws heavily on the analysis of Layard, Nickell and Jackman, and show how this may be used to try to understand variations in unemployment both within and between developed market economies. We then use this framework to briefly consider, from a macro-economic perspective, the types of policies which might be employed to successfully combat the problem of high and persistent unemployment.

The model

Reflecting the current emphasis on the role of imperfect competition in the product and labour markets, the basic building blocks of the model are two equations describing price and wage-setting behaviour. These replace the aggregate labour demand and labour supply schedules of traditional models based on the assumption of perfectly competitive markets. The price-setting schedule captures the behaviour of firms in the product market and determines the mark-up of (value added) price over expected wage costs as an increasing function of the level of aggregate demand in the economy. Using the aggregate unemployment rate as an (inverse) proxy for the level of demand, the equation may be written as:

$$p - w^e = \alpha_1 - \alpha_2 u \quad \alpha_2 \geq 0 \tag{1}$$

where p is the natural logarithm of price, w^e is the log of the expected wage and u denotes the log of the unemployment rate. Empirical evidence indicates that the relationship between product prices and demand may be rather weak (for UK evidence, see Geroski, 1992; Geroski and Hall, 1995) and therefore we assume α_2 to be weakly, rather than strictly, positive in equation (1). This equation may in a sense be thought of as determining the 'feasible' real wage - that is, the real wage which firms are prepared to concede to their employees (at a given level of productivity).

The wage-setting equation shows how nominal wages are set as a mark-up on the expected price level. This mark-up - which may be thought of as the 'target' real wage intended by wage-setters - is assumed to be a declining function of the unemployment rate. In addition, we may suppose it to depend on a vector of 'wage pressure' variables, Z, so that an increase in 'wage pressure' leads to a higher target real wage at any given rate of unemployment. As we shall shortly see, an understanding of the factors which create pressure for higher wages at a given rate of unemployment is a key to understanding the determinants of an economy's equilibrium rate of unemployment and we consider the type of variables which might enter the vector Z below. For now, we note that the wage-setting equation may be written as:

$$w - p^e = \beta_1 - \beta_2 u + Z \qquad (\beta_2 > 0) \tag{2}$$

Equation (2) is consistent with a variety of models of labour market behaviour, including, for example, models of employer-trade union bargaining and efficiency wage models in which firms are assumed to set nominal wages with the aim of raising labour productivity or aiding worker recruitment and retention[1].

In equilibrium, prices and wages are equal to their expected levels, and the unemployment rate adjusts to ensure that the 'target' and 'feasible' real wage are brought into line with one another. With $p = p^e$ and $w = w^e$, the equilibrium unemployment rate may be determined by adding equations (1) and (2) together:

$$u^* = \frac{\alpha_1 + \beta_1 + Z}{(\alpha_2 + \beta_2)} \tag{3}$$

Equation (3) tells us that the equilibrium unemployment rate will be higher: (a) the less responsive are prices and wages to changes in the rate of unemployment (i.e., the lower the degree of price and wage 'flexibility'); and (b) the greater the degree of 'wage pressure' at a given rate of unemployment. In principle, the equilibrium unemployment rate might also be affected by factors which create pressure for a higher mark-up of prices over wages at a given unemployment rate, such as the degree of collusion in the product market. These could be incorporated in the model through the introduction of a 'price pressure' term, analogous to the vector Z, in the price-setting schedule. However, such factors have tended to receive relatively little attention in the literature.

Figure 3.1 Determination of equilibrium unemployment and the effects of an increase in 'wage pressure'

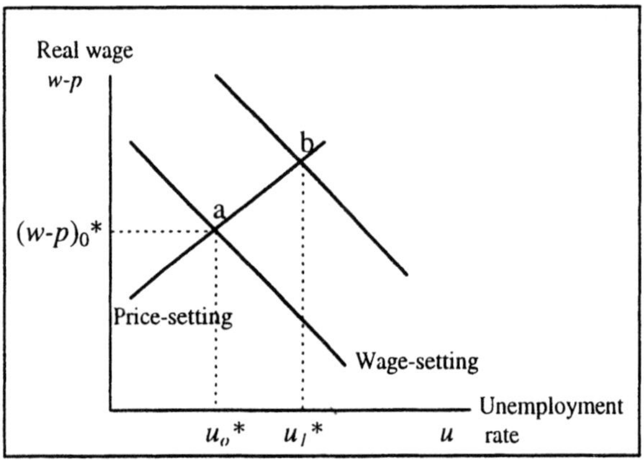

Figure 3.1 shows the determination of the equilibrium unemployment rate graphically. The price and wage-setting schedules are drawn for the situation where prices and wages are equal to their expected levels (i.e. $p = p^e$ and $w = w^e$) and their intersection determines both the equilibrium level of real wages $(w - p)_0^*$ and the rate of unemployment u_0^*. An increase in the degree of 'wage pressure', Z, shifts the wage-setting schedule upwards, leading to an increase in the equilibrium rate of unemployment, to u_1^*.

Unemployment and inflation

Before we consider the type of factors which might influence the degree of wage pressure and wage and price flexibility in an economy and hence determine the equilibrium rate of unemployment, it is useful to consider what happens when wages and prices deviate from their expected values. In this case, by adding equations (1) and (2) together we find that:

$$u = \frac{\alpha_1 + \beta_1 + Z - (p - p^e) - (w - w^e)}{(\alpha_2 + \beta_2)}$$

$$= u^* - \frac{(p - p^e) + (w - w^e)}{(a_2 + \beta_2)} \qquad (4)$$

If either prices or wages exceed their expected value, the unemployment rate will therefore be below its equilibrium level. Layard, Nickell and Jackman suggest that both $(p - p^e)$ and $(w - w^e)$ may be reasonably proxied by changes in the rate of price inflation, i.e. by $\Delta^2 p$, (where $\Delta^2 p = \Delta p_t - \Delta p_{t-1}$). In this case, it follows that equation (4) may be rewritten as:

$$u = u^* - \frac{1}{\phi} \Delta^2 p \qquad (5)$$

where $\phi = (\alpha_2 + \beta_2)/2$.

From this relationship, we can see that unemployment will be below (above) its equilibrium rate if inflation is rising (falling), as a result of mistakes made by workers and firms in their perception of the true levels of wages and prices. It follows too that u^* may be thought of as the non-accelerating inflation (or more correctly, the non-changing inflation) rate of unemployment, or NAIRU.

Explaining unemployment differences across countries and over time

Equations (3) and (5) provide a useful framework for understanding differences in the rate of unemployment across countries and over time, at least over reasonably long periods. They suggest that in analysing the causes of such differences, we need to focus attention on identifying the factors - which are likely to be primarily supply-side in nature - which influence the degree of wage pressure and wage and price flexibility in an economy. Layard, Nickell and Jackman identify three such factors as being important to an explanation of cross-country differences in unemployment between members of the OECD, namely: (i) the unemployment benefit system; (ii) the framework within which wage bargaining is conducted; and (iii) the scale of government spending on active labour market programmes to help the unemployed into jobs. Within the first, they show that what matters is not only the scale of unemployment benefits relative to wages when in work, but also the length of time for which benefits may be claimed[2]. Countries with relatively generous benefit systems, on either or both of these measures, will tend to have a relatively high equilibrium rate of unemployment, other things being equal.

A key consideration in the wage bargaining framework is the degree to which bargaining is centralised or decentralised. In terms of minimising the degree of wage pressure and maximising flexibility, it seems that either highly centralised systems - in which trade unions and employers negotiate with one another at the national level - or highly decentralised systems - where bargaining occurs either at the workplace level or between employers and individual employees - work best. Countries, such as the United Kingdom, in which bargaining takes place at an intermediate level will tend to perform relatively poorly in this respect (Calmfors and Driffill, 1988)[3] .

Spending on active labour market programmes embraces measures ranging from the provision of placement and counselling services for the unemployed, the provision of training programmes, to direct subsidies to job creation and recruitment. The key to the effectiveness of such measures in reducing unemployment is the degree to which they increase the effectiveness of the unemployed as competitors in the market for jobs and hence restrain wage pressure and raise the responsiveness of wages to changes in unemployment[4] . Layard, Nickell and Jackman show that the three factors identified above, together with the change in the rate of inflation, can account for over 90 per cent of the variation in the average rate of unemployment over 1983-8 for a sample of 20 OECD countries[5] . Other factors may also be relevant to an explanation of variations in the equilibrium unemployment rate, particularly within individual countries over time. Increased taxes (including payroll taxes) or import prices for example, which drive a wedge between the real wages received by workers and the real cost of labour to employers, could serve to increase the degree of wage pressure and hence raise the equilibrium rate of unemployment. A deterioration in the degree to which the unemployed are 'matched' to available vacancies - either in terms of their geographical location or their skill requirements - might have similar effects[6] .

In practice, changes in taxes appear to have only a small effect on the equilibrium rate of unemployment: in the long-run, their effect is fully absorbed by changes in the nominal wage. However, the short-run effects of changes in taxes may be quite large and persist for some time (Jackman, Layard and Nickell, 1996). Changes in real import prices appear to have a more significant long-run effect on unemployment - Layard, Nickell and Jackman, for example, calculate that higher real import prices accounted for something like 80 per cent of the estimated increase in the equilibrium rate of unemployment in the UK between 1967-73 and 1974-80, with a further significant contribution in the period 1981-87 (Layard, Nickell and Jackman, 1991; 446.). On the face of it, this might appear to suggest that national authorities may be able to engineer a permanent reduction in the rate of unemployment in an economy through an appreciation of the external value of its currency. However, such a strategy would lead to a deterioration in the country's international competitiveness and an eventual collapse of its balance of trade, and could not therefore be sustained in the long-run.

Evidence on the effect of mismatch between labour supply and labour demand is - with one important exception, which we discuss below - somewhat mixed, depending in part on the dimension of mismatch under consideration and the measure used. For example, using information on relative unemployment rates in different industry sectors, occupations and regions for a number of countries, Jackman, Layard and

Savouri (1991) find that only in Sweden is there evidence that the degree of mismatch increased significantly between the 1970s and the 1980s[7] . Nor do they find any evidence of an increase in the degree of mismatch between the unemployed and available vacancies. On neither measure, therefore, does increased mismatch appear to be a significant factor behind the increase in unemployment experienced in most countries between these two periods. In contrast, Layard, Nickell and Jackman find that an increase in the degree of employment 'turbulence' (measured by the absolute change in the proportion of employees in production industries) has contributed significantly to an increase in the equilibrium unemployment rate in the United Kingdom, particularly in the period between 1974-80 and 1981-7.

One aspect of mismatch which has attracted increasing attention in recent years as a potential explanation for the rise in unemployment is that associated with changes in the relative demand for skilled labour. It is increasingly recognised that in the last twenty years there has been a significant decline in the relative demand for unskilled labour in the OECD economies. The causes of this are as yet unclear. Some have pointed to the effects of increased import competition due to the growth of international trade (e.g. Wood, 1994). The most likely source, however, is technological change - in particular the spread of computerisation - which, it is argued, has led to a growth in the demand for skilled at the expense of unskilled labour (e.g Berman *et al.*, 1994, Machin; 1996). Because the relative supply of unskilled labour has failed to shrink as quickly as the decline in relative demand, this has led in a number of countries to an increase in the absolute and relative unemployment rate of unskilled workers[8]. Such an increase in relative unemployment rates can be shown, under certain circumstances, to lead to an increase in the degree of wage pressure at a given rate of unemployment (see Manacorda and Petrongolo, 1996, for example, for details). Hence, a higher aggregate rate of unemployment is needed to restrain the growth of real wages. Both Nickell and Bell (1995) and Manacorda and Petrongolo (1996) identify strong effects on the aggregate rate of unemployment in the UK arising from changes in the relative demand for skilled labour. The former suggest that around 20 per cent of the increase in the rate of unemployment in the UK between the 1960s and the 1980s may be accounted for by a decline in the relative demand for unskilled labour, whilst the latter suggest that between 1975 and 1992, around half the increase in UK unemployment may be attributed to the imbalance between the supply and demand for skills.

Within the model presented here, technological change may therefore have an effect on the equilibrium rate of unemployment if it leads to changes in the relative demand for different types of labour. However, technological change which is neutral in this respect would not be expected to affect the unemployment rate in the long-run. This is because neutral technological change leads to increases in the real wage which are 'warranted' in terms of higher labour productivity and which employers are therefore willing to concede to workers[9] . Evidence in support of this proposition comes from an inspection of long runs of economic data, which show no tendency for the rate of unemployment to increase as productivity has grown.

Why does unemployment persist?

It was noted earlier that one of the puzzles which has led economists to re-think their approach to the analysis of unemployment is the question of why unemployment - particularly in the EU countries - has continued to remain at historically high levels even though inflation has fallen. One reason, of course, may be that the equilibrium unemployment rate has increased. An alternative - though not necessarily mutually exclusive - explanation is that once unemployment has risen above its equilibrium rate, perhaps because of a negative shock to demand, it may be slow to return to its initial equilibrium. In order to see how such a situation might come about, suppose we modify our original price and wage equations as follows:

$$(p - w^e) = \alpha_1 - \alpha_2 u - \alpha_3 \Delta u \qquad (1a)$$

$$(w - p^e) = \beta_1 - \beta_2 u - \beta_3 \Delta u + Z \qquad (2a)$$

so that prices and wages now depend on the change in the unemployment rate as well as on its level. It can be shown that this leads to an equation for unemployment of the form:

$$u = \frac{\gamma_1}{\gamma_1 + \gamma_{11}} u^* + \frac{\gamma_{11}}{\gamma_1 + \gamma_{11}} u_{-1} - \frac{1}{\gamma_2} \Delta^2 p \qquad (6)$$

where u^* is as defined before, u_{-1} denotes the previous period's rate of unemployment, $\gamma_1 = (a_2 + \beta_2)$, $\gamma_{11} = (\alpha_3 + \beta_3)$, and $\gamma_2 = (\gamma_1 + \gamma_{11})/2$. The presence of u_{-1} on the right-hand side of equation (6) implies that the unemployment rate exhibits a degree of persistence in response to shocks and the equation parameters indicate that this degree of persistence will be greater, the more responsive are prices and wages to the change in the unemployment rate (γ_{11}) rather than its level (γ_1)[10] .

The relative size of the parameters γ_1 and γ_{11} is likely to be determined by factors similar to those discussed above in relation to the size of γ_1. In particular, one would expect the degree of unemployment persistence to be greater in countries characterised by relatively generous unemployment benefit systems - particularly in relation to the length of time for which benefits may be claimed - and in which wage bargaining takes place at an intermediate level of centralisation. One particular aspect of this issue which has attracted attention in this respect is the degree of 'insider' influence in wage determination. Blanchard and Summers (1987), Lindbeck and Snower (1988) and Robson (1989) amongst others, suggest that once employment has stabilised in the aftermath of a downward shock, those workers remaining in employment - the 'insiders' - may perceive relatively little further threat to their job security and, focusing solely on their own interests, may press for wages which preclude the re-employment of those thrown out of work by the initial employment shock (who have now become 'outsiders' in the wage determination process). The implication of this is that whereas *changes* in the unemployment rate (representing employment shocks) may have a relatively strong restraining impact on real wages, the *level* of the unemployment rate may exert relatively little effect. In the extreme case, wages may be completely independent of the level of the unemployment rate - only changes matter[11].

The importance of such 'insider' effects is likely to depend on the degree of centralisation in wage bargaining. In highly centralised (or 'corporatist') systems, one would expect the interests of 'outsiders' to receive a relatively high weight in the wage determination process. Similarly, in highly decentralised systems one would expect 'outsider' effects to dominate as 'insiders' will have only a relatively low degree of bargaining power. Conversely, 'insider' effects are likely to be greatest in systems with an intermediate degree of centralisation and, in addition, where job security regulations (e.g. measures to protect workers against the threat of unfair dismissal) provide the 'insiders' with a relatively high degree of protection against competition from 'outsiders'.

Policies to reduce unemployment: a macro-economic perspective

This is not the place to engage in a detailed assessment of alternative policy proposals for addressing the problem of high and persistent unemployment (for a more detailed consideration of some such proposals see the contributions to Part III of this book). However, it may be useful to take a little time to briefly consider the type of measures which the framework outlined in this part of the chapter suggests may or may not be successful in combating high unemployment.

It should be fairly clear that within the framework discussed above, the type of measures which are most likely to be successful in combating unemployment are those which have the effect of reducing wage pressure and raising the flexibility of real wages in response to variations in the rate of unemployment. Such measures might include a shift away from what, in the UK at least, have traditionally been 'passive' measures of support for the unemployed (in the form of the payment of unemployment benefit, for example) to more active measures designed to help the unemployed to more easily make the transition into work. The Restart Programme, introduced in the UK in 1986, can clearly be seen to represent a step in the right direction in this respect, but bolder measures such as the guarantee of a job or a place on a re-training programme for the long-term unemployed might also be effective. Elsewhere - in spite of the reservations expressed by the OECD (OECD, 1997) - the recent moves towards greater decentralisation in wage determination should also have beneficial effects on the long-run rate of unemployment in the UK; though as we have seen, a movement in the opposite direction, towards greater centralisation, might have been equally effective.

Amongst the many measures which are less likely to be successful in reducing unemployment are those aimed at encouraging early retirement and greater work-sharing. Whilst there may be sound micro-economic arguments for the introduction of policies which aim to redistribute work - in terms of market failure in the provision of short-hour jobs, for example (see the discussion in the next section) - such schemes can only be expected to have a limited impact on the rate of unemployment. In the long-run, as we have seen, the equilibrium rate of unemployment is determined by the degree of wage pressure and the degree of wage and price flexibility. None of these variables is likely to be significantly affected by a reduction in the size of the labour force (induced by greater early retirement) or by a reduction in the level of hours worked per worker.

Household responses to unemployment

The preceding analysis considered the determination of unemployment at the level of the macro-economy. At the micro-level, variations in unemployment may be expected to influence the consumption and labour supply decisions of households. In the remainder of this chapter, we use the tools of neo-classical economics to examine the possible responses of households to the experience of unemployment; in particular, we consider how household labour supply decisions may be influenced by the unemployment of an individual household member.

A neo-classical view of household labour supply decisions

A neo-classical view of the way households make their labour supply decisions would, at its simplest level, say that a household, as a unit, gains satisfaction (or utility) from market goods, q, and non-market time, l, of its various members. This idea is encapsulated by writing down an objective function (or utility function) $U(q, l_f, l_m)$, where subscripts f and m, indicate two household members who can be thought of as being male and female. It is then assumed that the behaviour of the household can be described by imagining that it is maximising this function, it chooses actions which gives the highest value for this function, and in doing this is said to be maximising utility. How non-market time is viewed is important for the interpretation of micro-theories of household behaviour. In the presently stated formulation, households obtain utility from consumption of goods and non-market time in their 'raw' state; alternatively the household can be viewed as combining goods and time at an intermediate stage to 'produce' household specific consumables. This idea of household output allows a productive interpretation to be given to non-market time. Some interpretations of gender divisions within the household are given later on in the discussion of the Pareto optimal labour supply model.

There are a number of things which need to be made plain at the outset. Firstly, describing behaviour in this way is, in a sense, circular, since any observed action can be rationalised as being that which gave the maximum available utility. Gorman (1976) describes the economic anthropologist, Mary Douglas's conclusions about choice theory as being 'utility is empty, so we can fill it'. There is no need to ask why people like certain things. Just as long as they do, and their preferences are sufficiently consistent over time, then the above way of analysing behaviour gives predictive power. It allows us to say how the behaviour of a group might change as the constraints which act upon them change.

The constraints which are relevant for a household's labour supply are simply that, in the absence of any unearned income, households cannot buy market goods unless they receive earned income. So earned income plus unearned income must equal the consumption of market goods. (In what follows it is assumed that there is no saving or borrowing). This constraint can be written simply as, $pq \leq w_m h_m + w_f h_f + \mu$ where p is the price of market goods, q, h is hours of work and μ is unearned income of the household. It is assumed that the essential time allocation decision is between market and non-market activities, and that each individual has only a fixed amount of time, T, in hours, to allocate between the two. If the analysis was at the weekly level then T=168, if daily T=24. The structure of this model can be seen in a diagram.

Figure 3.2 The Labour supply Decision

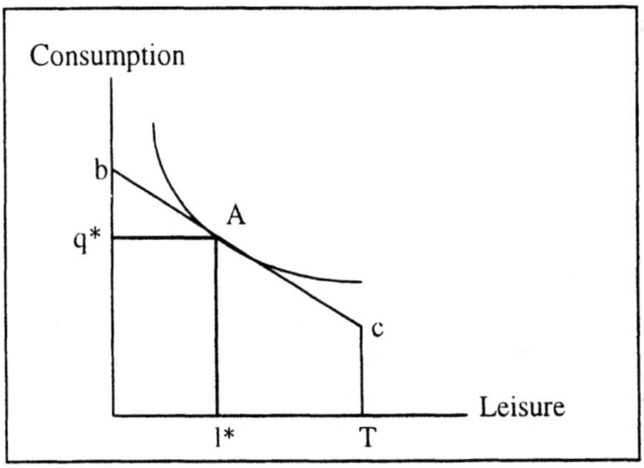

The budget constraint is given by the line bc which has slope -w meaning that moving along the line from c to b hours of leisure are being traded on the market at price w, which is the market valuation of an hour of the individual's time. The curved line gives all the levels of q (goods) and l (non-market time) at which there is equal utility - the leisure-consumption bundles between which individuals would be indifferent. There is a whole map of these curves representing higher levels of utility as they move in a north-easterly direction. The lines are convex which indicates that as you have less of something, say, leisure time, then it becomes more valuable to you, so you would need more consumption to induce you to give it up. The slope of the indifference curve as we move back along the horizontal axis therefore represents the value of leisure time to the individual agent. The individual will not be able to do better, given the constraints, than at the point where the budget constraint just touches the highest indifference curve, which is the point A drawn in the diagram.

The important message of this analysis is that at point A the individual's value of time will be the same as the market's valuation. This is the basic tenet of the neo-classical view of households' micro labour market behaviour, that households will attempt to allocate time such that it has equal value in each of its uses.

While, of course, this is a simplification of the real world, it contains an important guiding principle in interpreting behaviour. It allows us to interpret why high earning couples tend to employ nannies for example, why high earning individuals won't tend to engage as much in time-intensive home production, and in general why individuals will try and seek out better paid jobs. There are a number of ways in which the degree of simplification can be reduced, making the model more realistic but staying within the same neo-classical perspective. We will look at two such directions here, firstly whether it is sensible to regard the household as a single entity with regard to decision making , or whether there is useful mileage in modelling the dynamics of household decision making. Secondly we will consider how the actions and objectives of firms, or the demand side of the market, affect what individuals on the supply side are able to do.

Inside the black box of the household

Neo-classical theory is essentially a development of the idea that individuals are optimisers. It might seem strange, therefore, that the model described in the last section took the household, which will typically comprise more than one individual, as the optimising unit. This observation has generated some recent research to try and develop models which don't have this characteristic. Chiappori (1992) develops a general 'collective' model of household behaviour, in which individuals within the household have their own preferences. This section will examine some ways in which the potential interactions of individuals within households can be modelled and look at empirical support for these approaches.

Individuals within households will typically be different, that is to say their behaviour can be represented by different utility functions. If a household has two members (which can represent male (M) and female (F) partners) who pool their resources, then there is potential for a type of conflict within the household as the behaviour of the individuals (as described by their utility functions) might not give the same outcome. We can think about this conflict in the following way: consider the action of one individual, M, his utility maximising labour supply h_m will depend on the labour supply of his partner F as the level of her labour supply, h_f, will determine the budget constraint which M will make his decision under. This will describe a conditional labour supply function a-b depicted in Figure 3.3; F's conditional labour supply function is similarly defined and appears as c-d in the same figure. This is referred to as the duopolist model (see Killingsworth, 1983). The conditional labour supply functions are each individual's utility maximising response to the behaviour of the other. Their responses are consistent and define an equilibrium at C^*, which is referred to as a Cournot equilibrium. Common sense suggests that this model will not really be a very good description of reality, and indeed economic theory would suggest that co-operating individuals could do better.

Figure 3.3 Pareto optimal labour supply

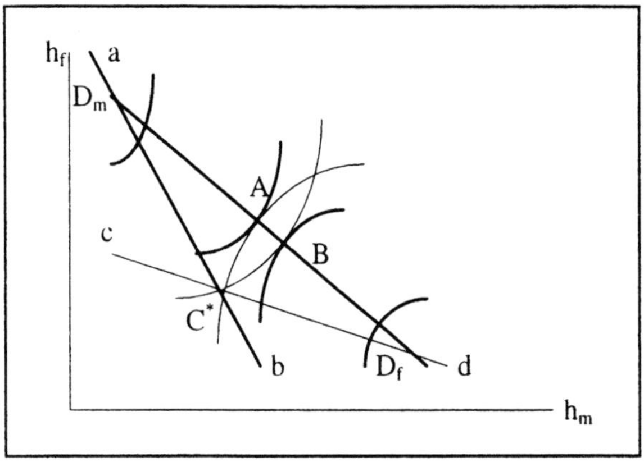

They will do this in the following way. Since the schedules a-b and c-d represent utility maximising responses to the labour supply of the other there will be points on the curve which are the global maximum, these are D_m and D_f (D can be thought of as standing for dictator, as they would be the outcomes if one of the individuals dictated the behaviour of the other). Contours representing diminishing levels of utility can be thought of as emanating from these points, and their tangencies will define what is termed a contract curve between D_m and D_f which will represent the set of Pareto optimal allocations of work time. Pareto optimal allocations have the characteristic that no reallocation can be made without making one of the parties worse off. It is also the case that allocations off the contract curve, like C^* for instance, can always be improved upon, in the sense of making one, or both, of the agents better off. This is achieved simply by a movement on to the contract curve. Indeed by drawing the utility contours for both F and M which pass though C^* it can be clearly seen that both will be better off along the segment of the contract curve AB. We would expect co-operating individuals to find these allocations.

Another way of viewing this situation is to think of a household having a utility possibility frontier as illustrated in the following diagram, Figure 3.4. Points on the curve represent maximum attainable levels of utility for the two individuals within the household. Note that on the boundary there is a trade-off between U^f and U^m, as one individual does better within the household, the other must do worse. This characteristic of the model has made this an attractive framework within which to analyse the issue of resource distribution within households. Thinking about this trade-off it is not surprising that Pareto optimal models can be represented as the maximisation of a household welfare function that gives a relative weighting to each member's utility, so the objective of the household is a balance of the interests of the two individuals within the household. Barmby (1994) discusses the estimation of these models. One interesting interpretation of these models is to view the relative weight as a measure of the power or influence which an individual has within the household in influencing allocation decisions. Barmby (1994) finds, using data drawn from the 1984 Family Expenditure Survey, that as the male wage rate increases, relative to female, then females' utility receives less weight in household decisions.

Figure 3.4: Utility possibility frontier

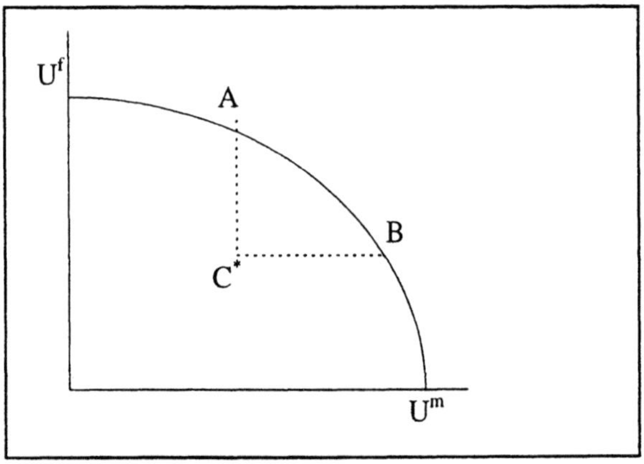

Another strand of research in this area has focused on the way in which individuals' options outside the household influence household behaviour itself. McElroy (1990) sets this idea into the framework of households maximising what are referred to as Nash products.[12] The difference in the structure of these models is that the outcome in terms of the allocation the household chooses is influenced by the utility the individual can receive outside the household. Barmby (1996) discusses the estimation of this type of collective model. A characteristic of this model structure is that unearned income, and who receives it, directly impacts on household behaviour. This clear empirical regularity has been studied in a number of contexts. Using survey data from Brazil, Thomas (1990), finds that unearned income in the hands of the mother has a bigger impact on the health of her family (measured in a number of ways including nutrient intake and child survival probability) than income attributed to the father.

Demand side effects and the impact of unemployment on household labour supply decisions

The previous section essentially described households' supply side behaviour. Given that households face certain wage rates and receive some amount of unearned income they will desire to supply certain levels of work to the market. The demand side will be made up of the set of employers offering a range of job contracts. An individual worker from one of the households might not be able to match their desired hours to contracted hours offered on the market exactly. Typically, workers will try and match their desired hours to contracted hours offered by some firm in the market, and will search over offers until as close a match as possible is achieved. However, search of this type is costly and workers will typically stop searching when the benefits from continuing search fall below the costs. We will look at the motivation of firms in setting the contracted hours which they offer to the market. In addition workers may not be able to find a job at all, and will be unemployed. We will examine this second demand restriction first.

There have been a number of studies which have examined the labour supply behaviour of married women in response to their husbands' unemployment. A neo-classical model of family labour supply would, in general, predict that the unemployment of one member of a household should increase the likelihood of employment of the other; the reason being that the unemployment represents a loss in income to the household. This is termed the 'added worker effect' where it is the male spouse who experiences the unemployment. Lundberg (1985) in an analysis of transition rates for US households finds that, on average, white married women are more likely to enter the labour force in response to the unemployment of their spouse, though for other groups this is not the case. Maloney (1990) finds no evidence for the added worker effect for married couples in the US. On the face of it this represents weak evidence for the view of household labour supply just developed, but there are a number of good reasons why this would be expected. Unemployment is often caused by a shock in the local labour market which would also negatively affect the spouse's chance of getting a job. Here the event of the husband's unemployment is correlated with the state of the local labour market, which impacts on the wife's labour supply decision. There is a more direct link when the eligibility level for household benefit payments with an unemployed husband depends on the level of other income in the household. This would act as a fixed cost on the wife's labour supply and tend to discourage participation. Lundberg additionally conjectures that sorting mechanisms in the formation of households (Becker 1991) bring together individuals with low human capital, so that those individuals whose husbands experience unemployment are also those whose potential market wage is low. It is generally felt that the mechanisms which will tend to act against the spouse increasing participation can often outweigh the added worker effect, especially when the shock is perceived to be transitory.

The effect that the demand side of the market has on households and their working experiences can be felt in more subtle ways. One way in which this might be seen is though the setting of contractual hours by firms. In very simple views of the way that the labour market works, it will pay firms to elicit the desired hours of prospective workers as this will minimise costs (through potential future absenteeism and other ways), and workers will have the incentive to reveal their preferred hours to employers. Now consider two aspects of labour markets which are likely to more closely characterise reality. Firstly, there is unemployment, so that if a worker loses his or her job then there are substantial costs in finding another one. Secondly, the willingness of workers to work long hours might be an indicator of their responsiveness to other work incentives. If this is the case then firms might set contracted hours 'high' to select out from a pool of prospective employees those who will be generally more responsive, and in addition workers will, knowing this, not reveal their true preferences (see Rebitzer and Taylor, 1991). If this is the case then there will be a market failure which will result in an under-supply of short-hour jobs.

This mechanism could help us to resolve the recent puzzle of why British workers (in particular men) are working longer hours. Stewart and Swaffield (1997) using data from the British Household Panel Study, report that typically more than a third of British men are working more than they would prefer to at the wage rate they face (meaning that they have taken into account the loss of income this would involve). In the same paper Stewart and Swaffield construct an empirical model in which firms set a lower limit on the number of hours worked by the worker. An interesting finding is that the lower limit on hours is positively related to the unemployment rate. This gives an interpretation of recent developments in the labour market where, against a background of persistent unemployment, those in work are working longer. It also suggests that if there are benefits for firms in setting contracts in this way it will not encourage the job sharing policies referred to in the previous section, and might be part of the explanation of why more job sharing has not been observed.

Notes

---

[1] See Chapters 2 and 3 of Layard, Nickell and Jackman (1991) for a review.

[2] Also relevant will be the ease with which benefits may be claimed, i.e. the severity of any 'work test' which the unemployed must satisfy to be eligible for benefit.

[3] There is evidence to suggest that wage bargaining in the United Kingdom, and in a number of other OECD countries, has tended to become more decentralized in recent years. See Beatson (1995) for a review.

[4] Calmfors and Forslund (1991) point out a potentially offsetting feature of active labour market programmes, which is that by reducing the expected duration of unemployment for job losers they may actually serve to increase the degree of 'wage pressure'. They show further that, in Sweden, spending on active labour market programmes has had a strong positive effect on the level of real wages.

[5] In more recent work, Jackman, Layard and Nickell (1996) extend this analysis to cover the period 1989-94.

[6] Much attention in the literature has focused on the role of the share of the long-term unemployed in the unemployment stock as a potential contributor to increased 'wage pressure' and a reduction in the flexibility of wages in response to changes in unemployment. In practice, however, the proportion of long-term unemployment is not an exogenous variable but is itself determined by more fundamental features of the labour market such as the generosity of the benefit system, the structure of wage bargaining and the scale of spending on active labour market programmes (see Heylen, 1992).

[7] The other countries examined include the UK, the USA, Australia, Canada, West Germany and Spain

[8] Though the relative unemployment rate of unskilled workers fell significantly in many countries during the early 1990s recession (Nickell and Bell, 1995).

[9] Grubb, Jackman and Layard (1983) investigate the possibility that the productivity slowdown of the early to mid 1970s, associated with the OPEC induced rise in oil process, may have had a temporary effect in raising unemployment as workers continued to press for wage increases in line with previous levels of productivity growth.

[10] Equation (6) also implies that even if the inflation rate is constant, unemployment may deviate from u*, so that, strictly speaking, u* may no longer be thought of as the NAIRU. Layard, Nickell and Jackman suggest, however, that u* may be thought of as the long-run NAIRU, whilst the unemployment rate given by equation (6) when the inflation rate is constant may be interpreted as the short-run NAIRU.

[11] As long as price-setting behaviour is influenced by the unemployment rate, unemployment will still exhibit a tendency to return to equilibrium. However, as we have already observed, the relationship between prices and unemployment may be relatively weak, so that deviations from the equilibrium rate of employment are likely to be highly persistent.

[12] These have the form $(U^f - V^f)^{\lambda}(U^m - V^m)^{1-\lambda}$ where the Vs represent the outside options of the individuals. Often these are thought of as being the utility attainable as a single individual. Again the weighting parameter λ can be seen as a power parameter

CHAPTER 4

WHOSE FULL EMPLOYMENT? A FEMINIST PERSPECTIVE ON WORK REDISTRIBUTION

Irene Bruegel, Deborah M Figart and Ellen Mutari

Introduction

Contemporary profitability strategies pose powerful obstacles to progressive demands for full employment as we have known it. The formerly hegemonic ideal of the nuclear family supported by a male breadwinner wage is under question, as advanced industrial economies wrestle with the integral role of women's paid employment in the process of restructuring. These dramatic changes require rethinking traditional concepts of full employment, as embedded in the dominant schools of economic theory. Gunther Schmid, for one, refers to our traditional notion of full employment as outmoded;

> If we understand by 'full employment' continuous full-time employment for all - 8 hours a day, 5 days a week, 48 weeks a year and for 45 years of our lifetime (possibly restricted to men as the so-called 'breadwinners of the family') - then ... by this definition, full employment is not only a utopian but also an old-fashioned goal (Schmid, 1995a; 429).

Our argument is that work redistribution policies that combine a shorter standard work week with shared responsibility for reproductive labour are not only more equitable than post-war definitions of full employment, but also more promising. Work redistribution embraces a progressive approach to the contemporary quest for flexible employment conditions, while providing an institutional framework for a reformulation of gender relations.

This chapter summarises theoretical developments in feminist political economy and explores their application to full employment and work redistribution policies. Feminist political economists have brought the insights of feminist analysis to a critique of economic theories. Among the most crucial tools of feminist analysis is the concept of gender. As elaborated by Joan Scott (1988), gender is an analytical category used to reject both biological determinism and the tendency to naturalise a socially constructed gender order. She emphasises that gender is concerned with 'social relationships based on perceived differences between the sexes' and that it is about power (Scott, 1988; 42). In common with other schools within political economy, feminist perspectives recognise that social institutions, among them gender relations, are historically contingent, human constructs.

To varying degrees, feminist thought analyses the material bases of the dominant gender order (patriarchy) as well as the cultural and ideological dimensions of gender that inform and provide meaning to social interactions. Many recent feminist theorists focus on consciousness and language as ways in which power relations are constituted and perpetuated. Our sense of ourselves as gendered beings (masculine or feminine) is created through language and other social processes, and influences how institutional arrangements are constructed. The strength of this approach is its reading of gender in a myriad of social institutions. In Eileen Boris's words:

> An identity experienced by individuals, gender also constitutes a symbolic system, one with sexual difference at the center.... As a cultural force, gender goes beyond the relations between the sexes. It permeates society, modes of thought, economic life, and political praxis. Gender exists in the home and other workplaces, in the union hall and the courts, in the legal brief and social survey. Gender is not class, or a cultural and social relation to the means of production, but class is gendered and both are racialized (Boris, 1994; 4).

In this view, the gender order can not be limited to the confines of 'the family', 'the household', or 'reproduction,' but is fully implicated in the dynamics of production.

Central to this feminist perspective is the recognition that systems of production and reproduction do not operate autonomously; labour markets and households interconnect continually. Thus, feminist thought presents a challenge to analyses in the dominant economic paradigms that either accept gender relations in the household as exogenously determined or ignore the cumulative causation which results from the interaction of the two spheres. Attraction to gender has also opened up feminist scholarship to critically analysing men's experiences as well as women's, masculinity as well as femininity. Yet gender alone is also insufficient. Class, race, sexuality, nationhood and other intersecting analytical categories (or what Nancy Folbre, 1994, refers to as 'structures of constraint') operate within economic institutions.

From this perspective, feminist political economy transcends issues of gender equity and the problems posed by the entrenched gendered division of labour. More broadly, it is a vision about the kind of economy we want. Women's lack of economic power combined with a division of labour that assigns to them the care of other people leads feminist political economists to address the processes by which needs are met and to question why issues of the quality of relationships have been taken out of the economic sphere. In its emphasis on the quality of relationships, on processes and on values, feminist political economy contests the prospect of a technical 'fix' to the problem of unemployment. Instead, a feminist perspective calls for a fundamental revaluation of the categories used by economists. Among them is the distinction between 'work' and 'idleness,' so central to orthodox labour economics. Thus, a feminist approach to full employment involves a radical reappraisal of the nature of work as well as the domestic division of labour and the current form in which jobs are gendered.

In relation to employment and unemployment, a feminist analysis focuses on time, specifically on the distribution of time between all the activities - production, consumption, learning, enjoyment, relating, planning, and decision making - that fulfil the complex set of human needs. At the centre of this analysis is the question of the distribution of hours of paid and unpaid work across the population. Thus, feminism from a political economy perspective is not simply concerned with the relative position of women *vis à vis* men, rather reductions in working hours are conceived as an essential means of reconciling feminist demands with economic and environmental concerns.

Three streams of research in feminist political economy are incorporated into the argument for work redistribution as a means to achieving full employment. This research addresses (1) the gendered division of labour within heterosexual households between paid labour and unpaid domestic labour; (2) the processes of job segmentation and occupational differentiation that characterise paid jobs as male or female; and (3) the valuation of unpaid domestic labour. First, historical analyses of the sexual division of labour and the evolution of the male breadwinner identity shed light on the social construction of the concept of full employment and barriers to redistributing work along gender-neutral lines. Second, the literature on the gendering of paid jobs underlies feminist analyses of contemporary employer strategies regarding working time. Managerial strategies to achieve numerical flexibility in labour markets are gendered, with feminised part-time employment presented as a 'family-friendly' policy; in male employment sectors, overtime is the dominant means of achieving flexibility. Third, feminist analyses of the economic value of domestic labour highlight the public interest in providing for social reproduction. During the post-war era this was accomplished through the more extensive institution of the family wage. Contemporary economic restructuring has undermined this provision without providing a new set of hegemonic social institutions to facilitate reproduction. Each of these contributions by feminist analysis is discussed in the following three sections.

Drawing on the work of Irene Bruegel and Diane Perrons (1995), we contend that there are economic costs to the prevailing gender order, and these costs go well beyond the costs of discrimination to individual women. Further, the process of restructuring has intensified the contradictions between the post-war gender order and managerial strategies. We conclude that the contemporary period may provide an opportune moment for redefining gender relations, as these contradictions bring traditional gender relations into question. Since public policies to boost employment can be structured to either reinforce or challenge this gender order, it is crucial to incorporate policies such as work redistribution into progressive political agendas.

Whose full employment? Gender in the post-war order

What is full employment? More specifically, what does it mean to be employed, and who must meet this criterion? The traditional socialist demand for full employment embodies a conception of paid work as a necessary means of existence and the basis of working class organisation. Typically, neo-classical economists seek to quantify a 'natural rate of unemployment' (a non-accelerating inflation rate of unemployment or NAIRU) that defines a specific level of unemployment as 'full employment'. Post-Keynesian analysts view full employment as low involuntary unemployment and harken back to the days of the post-war period when full employment was a macro-economic policy objective.

Each of these socially constructed concepts of full employment is grounded in a belief in conceptually separable spheres of human activity. Over the course of the nineteenth century, as the economics discipline solidified many of its basic concepts, a gendered division of market and non-market spheres became entrenched in middle-class norms and working-class ideology (Rose, 1992; Davidoff, 1995; Horrell and Humphries, 1995; Frader, 1996). In international statistical publications, the terms 'labour force,' 'economically active population,' 'economic activity,' 'gainful employment,' and 'economic participation' are all concepts that differentiate those who 'work' from those who do not. This division between 'work' and 'non-work,' or more explicitly in many labour economics texts, between 'work' and 'leisure,' is deeply gendered. As Marilyn Waring (1988) and others have demonstrated, the productive and reproductive activities of 'housewives' are not considered economic activity. Women everywhere retain the primary responsibility for unpaid household labour, especially cleaning and caring for children (UN, 1991; Table 7, 101-102). Because only transactions subject to monetary exchange are counted, housework, as well as barter and informal sector work, is defined out of the sphere of economic analysis.

The standard definition of economic activity has been broadened over the years but it still excludes unpaid housework such as cooking, cleaning, shopping, and taking care of children and other family members (UN, 1991; 85). The gendered assumptions underlying these basic economic categories appear as natural, or at least eminently rational, to those inside the dominant paradigms, Folbre (1991) traces the gradual disappearance of household labour from the measurement of Gross Domestic Product, reflecting the consensus of the economic discipline. While Simon Kuznets acknowledged that non-market labour was important to economic welfare, he questioned its relevance to the measurement of growth (Folbre and Wagman, 1993; 277). Similarly, Stanley Lebergott, one of the foremost experts on historical labour force statistics in the United States, argues that although women's domestic labour is vital: 'there would be little analytic value to measures that always showed about 100 per cent of women in the labour force, varying not at all through the business cycle or through time' (cited in Ciancanelli and Berch, 1987; 247).

Martha MacDonald asserts that 'A unifying theme of feminist work is to challenge the distinctions made between the formal and informal economy, paid and unpaid work, market and non-market activities, productive and reproductive labor' (MacDonald, 1995; 163). Thus, the goal of many feminist economists concerned with establishing the economic value of women's non-market contributions has been the redefinition of productive economic activity. From this perspective, the concept of full employment is apparently meaningless, since women (and men) would be 100 per cent employed in productive economic activity, both market and non-market. The danger is that this perspective downplays the concrete material benefits derived from having a job in a market economy, as well as the social power conveyed by being employed. These material and psycho-social benefits are linked to socially constructed concepts of masculinity.

Within this historical context, the extension of paid employment can be a meaningful feminist demand. High employment levels during the 'boom' years played a critical role in achieving a better standard of living for women; conversely, there is some evidence that high levels of unemployment disproportionately impact on women (see, for example, Rubery, 1988). Unless and until full employment policies actively challenge the division of labour between the domestic sphere and the sphere of 'productive' economic activity they will remain partial and male-centred. In order to elaborate this argument, we focus on the process by which the gendered division of labour was institutionalised during the post-war period.

One of the institutional hallmarks of the post-war political and economic order in the industrialised countries of Europe and the United States was a policy commitment to full employment (Singh, 1995; Eatwell, 1996). The so-called Fordist regime of the post-war period is typically defined as having two components: an economic regime founded on mass-production-for-mass-consumption and a political regime or mode of regulation founded on the Keynesian welfare state (Burrows and Loader, 1994). Depictions of the stability of this golden age focus on the concept of a 'virtuous circle' that enabled Keynesian policies to flourish during the post-war period. With domestic markets for manufactured goods expanding, growth in worker productivity and in employment went hand-in-hand, permitting increased consumption with stable prices. If employers shared the benefits of increased productivity with workers in core industries - through wage increases, fiscal policy, or welfare state provisions - the resultant increase in demand would fuel profits (see Appelbaum, 1995).

Feminists have drawn attention to the existence of a stable, but not immutable, gender order that also supported macro-economic stability during the post-war period (McDowell, 1991; Williams, 1994; Bruegel and Perrons, 1995; O'Hara, 1995; Bakker, 1996). One pillar was the male breadwinner earning a family wage; the second pillar was married women's unpaid domestic labour, not necessarily full-time. Though its roots can be traced to nineteenth century industrialisation, the family wage was most extensively institutionalised for the working class during the post-war period, as families no longer relied upon the wages of children, young adults, and other extended family members. The central significance of the breadwinner identity to masculinity contributes to economic stability by constructing social relations where not being exploited is worse than being exploited. In addition to the material benefits that having a job brings, paid employment provides breadwinners a degree of power and autonomy. The psychological costs of job loss are intimately tied to the construction of male identity in capitalist society.

The racialised nature of this definition of masculinity is evident both in the United

States and the UK where unemployment rates for ethnic minority men are generally twice the white male unemployment rate (Shulman, 1991; Wilson, Tienda and Wu, 1995; Jones, 1993). Even during the period when a policy commitment to full employment was a social norm, a substantial black/white unemployment ratio persisted in the USA. Economists and sociologists have put forward a variety of hypotheses to explain this gap, including skills mismatch, spatial mismatch, culture of poverty, and skill-biased technological change (Skinner, 1995). As William Darity (1989) notes, culture has largely displaced discrimination as the dominant 'story' in these accounts. But the two are not inseparable; culture for Darity is 'an instrument that mobilises discriminatory action' (Darity, 1989; 365), not an alternative explanation for racial inequality. Therefore, the term 'worker' has come to have a racialised as well as a gendered meaning; the average worker is perceived to be white as well as male (Roediger, 1991).

Just as race delineated concepts of masculinity, it also differentiated women's economic roles. As Glenn (1996) has noted, responsibility for reproductive labour was historically constructed by race as well as gender. Minority ethnic women perform paid reproductive labour, historically as servants in the USA and the British Empire and increasingly in commodified service industries. Minority ethnic women are more likely to work full-time and are frequently primary breadwinners, especially as male manufacturing jobs have left urban areas (Bruegel, 1989; Woody, 1989).

Thus, post-war full employment was conceived almost entirely as full employment for white male breadwinners. The expectation that paid work was a secondary activity for women as distinct from men, or at least for the vast majority of women as distinct from the vast majority of men, placed white male unemployment at the centre of policy debates. Each of the theoretical perspectives on full employment presented at the outset of this section accommodated itself to the dominant gender order.

The socialist movements of Europe embraced the ideal of the male breadwinner household through active pursuit of family wage policies. However, this commitment shared a tense coexistence with the concept of wage labour as emancipatory for women. Through proletarianisation, women could be incorporated into the central class struggle. Hence, in theory, socialist discourse could include women in the concept of full employment. In reality, full employment as it existed in self-proclaimed socialist societies of Eastern Europe was clearly patriarchal, with women undertaking a grossly disproportionate amount of the reproductive labour of society as a whole. Further, Eastern European states vacillated between long term demographic concerns and problems of immediate labour shortage and were rarely driven by avowed equality principles (see, for example, Aslanbeigui, Pressman and Summerfield, 1994).

Neo-classical perspectives that regard most unemployment as voluntary or frictional, also incorporate gender bias. For example, several defenders of the concept of a natural or non-accelerating inflation rate of unemployment argued during the 1980s that married women's increased labour force attachment was partly responsible for increasing the natural rate (see Gordon, 1987 for a summary of this literature). Adult women, ethnic minority men, and young workers, as recent labour market entrants, are all presumed to have lower skills than white male adult workers.

As employers bid up the wages of experienced males, the non-inflationary level of unemployment creeps upward. The higher unemployment rates of the, 1980s, according to neo-classical analysis, reflected not a failure of economic policy, but a slow adjustment process to changed preferences on the supply side of the labour market. Yet, as David Gordon has pointed out, this analysis reverses causation; it is more reasonable to see married women's increased labour force participation as reflecting inflationary pressures and declining real wages rather than as the cause of these economic problems (see also Krashevski, 1988; Michie and Wilkinson, 1992). Even post-Keynesian analysis has frequently ignored the gendered and racialised nature of post-war prosperity. As Bea Campbell (1976) noted, women never had full employment. Even when full employment is defined most broadly, as the provision of jobs for all who *want* them, the essence of the feminist objection is usually missed; namely that the gendered division of labour frames the expectations of women. So long as women see themselves as secondary workers, they are less likely to express a desire for paid work, though they may nevertheless take up a job, if it becomes available. Further the relationship between full employment and job segregation in the post-war era has been under-theorised. It is possible that job segmentation limited the inflationary impact of full employment regimes by reducing the costs of labour-intensive services, both public and private. Wage discrimination against women helped contain wage-push inflation in female employment sectors, providing a cushion that enabled 'primary' sectors to continue a degree of employment growth. While full employment does not necessarily imply gender segregation, prior gender differentiation may be viewed as a way of managing the contradictions full employment poses for capital.

Although the post-war vision of the fully employed welfare state was built upon the expectation that married women remain in the domestic arena, this was never completely accomplished. Despite the link between productivity and real wage increases in Fordist manufacturing industries, increasing consumption standards racheted up target levels of family income. In reality, married women of all ages and ethnic backgrounds deepened their labour force attachment during the post-war period, putting pressure on the validity of the family wage system. However, they have done this within the context of a gendered order of employment in which the household division of labour interacts with segmented labour markets to define a space for women's employment. For many married women, especially white women, part-time work has been promoted as a flexible strategy for reconciling their 'special needs' as workers, with their assumed domestic responsibilities. This meant the creation of a distinct labour force of part-time workers with a contradictory relation to conceptions of full employment[1]. In the following section, we explore gendered employment structures and practices, especially regarding working time, as they have evolved in advanced industrialised countries.

Gendered work time and flexibility strategies

During the, 1980s, the Organisation for Economic Cooperation and Development and other international agencies put the United States forward as a model of labour market flexibility for European countries to follow. The US model was based upon wage employment (that is, numerical) flexibility. These forms of flexibility re-assert the central role of supply and demand forces in external labour markets, signalling a return to classical notions of free market equilibrium. European governments, especially the United Kingdom, have indeed pursued deregulation and privatisation, along with the dismantling of welfare provision, nominally as a means of reducing unemployment (Standing, 1991; Curry, 1992; Howell, 1992; Brodsky, 1994; Mishel and Schmitt, 1995).

Through the 1990s, a third form, functional (or internal) flexibility, has increasingly been sought (Pollert, 1991). The focus is on flexibility within the production process itself. One element of functional labour flexibility is multi-skilling, that permits employers to reassign workers to various tasks in the production process, consolidating the number of job categories in a firm. Under these systems, job descriptions are relatively open-ended, the length of the working day varies, and team work is emphasised. Thus, non-standard working time (also described as 'internal numerical flexibility') is one dimension of functional flexibility strategies. Whether or not these archetypes precisely capture divergent managerial strategies, they have considerable ideological sway (Pollert, 1991; Wheelock and Oughton, 1996).

Although few industrialised countries went beyond legislating maximum daily and weekly hours, a standard week of 37-40 hours was generally institutionalised in line with the industrial relations systems in each country[2]. In the view of flexibility advocates, this 8-hour day and 40-hour week represent institutional rigidities. The OECD (1989), for example, depicted the proliferation of 'non-standard' forms of work as removing institutional impediments to labour force participation by a broader population.

Growth of part-time employment, defined in various ways, is the most evident dimension of the increased diversity of working time arrangement within OECD countries (OECD, 1990; 25). Although there is no simple correlation between women's activity (or labour force participation) rates and part-time work, there is a strong cross national relationship between the two trends (Maier, 1994)[3]. High proportions of working women were in part-time jobs in most of those industrialised countries with relatively strong female activity rates. In Norway, the United Kingdom, Sweden, and Australia over 40 per cent of working women were employed part-time. Less than 12 per cent of working women in Spain, Portugal, Italy, Finland, and Greece worked part-time in 1991; those women who were in the labour force were primarily full-time workers (Freemen and Soete, 1994). Nevertheless, in every OECD country women undertook a disproportionate share of part-time work, ranging from over 90 per cent in the UK to almost two-thirds in Greece (Beechey and Perkins, 1987; 43). In all OECD countries, less than 12 per cent of employed men worked part-time (OECD, 1989; 25).

In contrast, male workers in male-dominated manufacturing industries increasingly work overtime to provide employers with internal numerical flexibility, especially in the UK and US (Beechey and Perkins, 1987; Horrell and Rubery, 1991; Picchio, 1992; Rosenberg, 1993; Marchand, 1993; Golden, 1996). David Purdy (1988; 153-154) found that approximately half of full-time male workers in Britain worked overtime either periodically or regularly. They averaged ten hours of overtime per week. As shown by Sam Rosenberg (1993; 552), US manufacturing production workers averaged close to four hours of weekly overtime, less than their British counterparts but more than a decade earlier. Male workers also tend to have longer basic working weeks than full-time women workers, as well as longer travel times. These long working hours help limit men's involvement in domestic work within work within households (Christopherson, 1991; Humphries and Rubery, 1992; Gardiner, 1997).

The rise of both part-time and overtime are gendered manifestations of contemporary managerial strategies to promote employment flexibility from the demand side. This contrasts with the 1960s in the UK and the USA, when the growth of part-time work reflected changes in labour supply, principally the increase of married women seeking employment. In the 1970s, such demographic shifts explain at most half of the increase in the rate of part-time employment. Since 1979, none of the increase is explained by demographic factors; further, involuntary part-time work has increased relative to voluntary part-time work, with a shift towards male part-time work in many cases (Tilly, 1996; see also Blank, 1990; Appelbaum, 1992; Larson and Ong, 1994; Maier, 1994). The impetus for the expansion of involuntary part-time jobs is the growing demand by employers for flexibility though the long run growth in unemployment has also put pressure on people looking for full time jobs to take part time work (Bruegel and Perrons, 1997)[4 5].

Neo-classical analysis regards involuntary overtime or over-employment in our terms as a way of limiting fixed labour costs; employers prefer paying overtime to hiring additional workers (see also Ehrenberg and Schumann, 1984; Hart, 1987; Coleman and Pencavel, 1993). However, this explanation sits uneasily with the simultaneous growth of under-employment in the form of involuntary part-time work since this increases fixed costs to employers (Golden, 1996). In contrast to the neo-classical approach, Lonnie Golden proposes an eclectic framework based upon post-Keynesian, institutionalist, and radical political economy models. These models suggest that current working time arrangements reflect bargaining power of capital over labour, work-intensification strategies and employer hegemony over work rules. Employers' preferences dominate those of employees. Golden's eclectic model leads him to an 'efficiency hours' hypothesis, that flexible working arrangements can potentially generate increased productivity from employees. This form of flexibility would accommodate the varied preferences of individual workers and the different constraints they face. Golden advocates public policies to foster such flexible working arrangements. Nevertheless, his analysis, like neo-classical theory, neglects the implicit gendered division between under-employment and over-employment, as gender shapes both labour supply and labour demand.

Feminist analyses fill this void. While Veronica Beechey and Tessa Perkins focused on the gendered construction of part-time work, they argue that 'full-time work needs to be treated as problematic' as well (Beechy and Perkins, 1987; 181-182). Working hours are defined within the context of both the gendered division of labour between paid and unpaid labour and a system of labour market segmentation by gender (see also Purdy, 1988; Horrell and Rubery, 1991; Hewitt, 1993; Negrey, 1993). In their study of part-time work in Britain, Beechey and Perkins found that 'employers have gender-specific ways of organizing their labour forces' (1987; 8).

Thus, in feminised sectors, numerical flexibility is accomplished through the use of part-timers; in male-dominated sectors, over-employment is characteristic. Within the dominant gender order of industrialised countries, working time is increasingly a marker for masculinity and femininity.

The dichotomy between part-time and full-time employment reflects the shift from manufacturing to service employment and reinforces occupational and industry segmentation. It accentuates earnings differentials, especially gender differentials in weekly earnings. Further, there are social costs beyond those borne by women workers themselves. The expansion of part-time and contingent labour contributes to the under-utilisation of women's potential. Employers are less likely to invest in training and skill development for workers perceived as marginal (Bruegel and Perrons, 1995). Since insufficient 'competitive capacity', that is, a shortage of skilled workers, has been identified as one reason for sustained unemployment in advanced industrial countries such as Britain (Eatwell, 1996), employer strategies to minimise private costs are 'costly' at the macro-economic level. Thus, these gendered forms of employment are one dimension of what has been termed the 'low road' to flexibility, that entails relying upon a cheap and disposable labour force in a deregulated environment[6].

In contrast, the 'high road' would provide both workers and employers with a degree of flexibility and a share in prosperity. Current strategies for flexible work time offer shorter hours to married women at the cost of full participation in the public realm. Rather than accepting the accommodation of working time to the gendered division of labour, work redistribution policies could provide an institutional basis for the reallocation of reproductive labour within the household.

The emerging crisis of caring

Probably the most consistent theme in feminist political economy over the past few decades has been the economic significance of reproductive labour in the household, designated as women's work within the gendered division of labour. Starting with the domestic labour debate of the early 1970s, socialist feminists have sought to analyse the contribution of domestic labour in the production of use value and the reconstitution of labour power. Implicitly and explicitly, these discussions have addressed the role of women's unpaid labour in the perpetuation of capitalism. These early Marxist-feminist debates tended toward reductionist arguments over who benefited from women's unpaid housework; men as husbands or capitalists who needed their workers nurtured and sustained. They also were weighted down by arcane interpretations of Marx's value theory. Nevertheless, this groundbreaking theoretical work raised issues that have been the foundation for subsequent feminist research on the household. From these pioneers has emerged an ongoing stream of research which stresses that production cannot be sustained without social reproduction and that women's unpaid domestic labour is systematically undervalued. This is the heart of the feminist challenge to the dichotomy between 'work' and 'leisure'. More recently, a number of feminist economists have criticised the omission of household production from national income accounts (Ciancanelli and Berch, 1987; Waring, 1988; Folbre, 1991; Beneria, 1992; MacDonald, 1995).

There have been some attempts to quantify this uncounted production, generally using the market wage in comparable work as the measure of value, despite the probable market under valuation of women's labour (see, for example, Folbre and Wagman, 1993; Ironmonger, 1996; Aslaksen and Koren, 1996; Cloud and Garrett, 1996)[7].

By incorporating domestic labour into official statistics, feminists hope to gain symbolic acknowledgement for women's unpaid work, as well influence the development of economic policy. Feminist economists argue that by recognising the economic contribution of domestic labour, the gendered impact of various macro-economic policies can be assessed. For example, the trend towards taxing consumption rather than income disproportionately affects women in their role as household managers. Structural adjustment policies that reduce welfare state expenditures generally presuppose the absorption of these social costs by the unaccounted-for household sector (Bakker, 1994; Beneria, 1992).

However, counting household labour is not the same as providing support and even remuneration. By relegating household labour to a matter of women's personal choices, dominant ideology denies either the necessity for, or justice of, payment for reproductive labour. Therefore, in addition to measuring housework, feminists have investigated the organisation of reproduction in different historical, regional, and cultural contexts. Folbre has posed this question as 'Who pays for the kids?' and noted that 'This is the short version of a larger question; how are the costs of caring for ourselves, our children, and other dependents distributed among members of society?' (Folbre, 1994; 1).

The family wage system provided one type of institutional mechanism for social reproduction, one based on the two pillars of the male breadwinner and the unpaid female homemaker. Under this system, the costs of social reproduction were absorbed by capitalists who (theoretically) paid a male breadwinner a wage adequate to support himself and 'non-working' members of the household. One of these pillars, the male breadwinner wage, has been undermined by changes in economic and social institutions. The second pillar is worn but standing. Despite their increased role as waged workers, women's responsibility for unpaid reproductive labour has not generally declined (Schor, 1992; Picchio, 1992; Hewitt, 1993; Folbre, 1994; Leete and Schor, 1994)[8]. According to a United Nations report on the world's women, time-use statistics considering all work, paid and unpaid, reveal that women spend more of their time working than men in all developed and developing regions except Northern America and Australia, where hours are nearly the same (UN, 1991; 80-81).

Yet Folbre (1994) and others argue that this double day has limits. As women's labour force participation continues to escalate, the amount of time devoted to domestic labour will eventually decline. The welfare state alternative to the intensification of women's double day has been under severe attack across the world, leaving the relocation of domestic labour to the market economy as the only politically acceptable alternative. As a result, unpaid domestic labour has been increasingly commodified, in service sector jobs segmented by gender and race[9].

Feminist political economists such as Folbre (1994; 1995) and Susan Himmelweit (1995) have suggested that this commodification process is problematic rather than emancipatory. A crucial aspect of women's unpaid labour is that it is involves caring work. Folbre defines caring labour as 'labor undertaken out of affection or a sense of responsibility for other people, with no expectation of immediate pecuniary reward' (1995; 75). The supply of caring labour is independent of price, at least in the short run[10]. Himmelweit (1995) emphasises that caring, unlike traditional concepts of work, does not entail a separation between producer and product. Women perform caring labour not because they are naturally altruistic but because of historically developed social relations. However, social norms, preferences, and values have devalued all forms of caring labour. Within this gender system, the wage conferred upon men a degree of bargaining power within the household and the public sphere (see Seiz, 1995; Wheelock and Oughton, 1996). The male breadwinner identity was also related to the avoidance of caring work, and the development of a very specific subjectivity.

Within a market economy the generation of exchange value/profits are the motive force of much economic activity; work is a means rather than an end in itself. As reproductive labour is commodified, society faces a net loss of 'caring' which is undervalued within the market paradigm. Further, Himmelweit notes that market substitutes more readily satisfy certain needs than others. 'Non-consumption' needs may be rendered invisible if they are not easily translated into marketable commodities. Women's increased labour force participation and attachment intensifies this process of commodification of reproductive labour. Therefore, the expansion of market relations intensifies the distinction between work and non-work, that is, between activity which is a means to an end and that which is an end in itself, in such a way that the former encroaches on the latter.

The concept of caring labour and its diminishing supply provides the basis for a different understanding of work, and thus of full employment. The process of economic development, especially as it generates increased labour productivity, offers two alternative prospects. The first is a continued expansion of output and consumption; the second is the reduction of human toil and an increase in self-fulfilling activity. Purdy (1988) presents an argument that capitalism has a structural bias toward the former. The gender system also poses barriers against the latter possibility since masculinity is constructed on the basis of bringing home the bacon. In order to redirect ourselves toward the path of toil-reduction, an alternative concept of full employment must be developed that creates a space for those economic activities that are neither work nor non-work, the type of activity that feminists term 'caring labour'.

What is needed is an alternative set of institutional arrangements providing for social responsibility for reproductive labour - alternative pillars on which to construct gender relations. A more equitable future could be built on the concepts of a living wage and work redistribution. In the United States, the labour movement has recently embraced the discourse of a 'living wage'. These campaigns de-gender the concept of the family wage as a movement to ensure that all workers can support their families, embracing a diversity of family forms. Efforts to create a fair wage and a living wage for all workers, including those in predominantly female and disproportionately minority jobs and occupations, will be critical in the 1990s and beyond. Policies that facilitate work redistribution, including a movement to shorten the standard work week, similarly provide an institutional basis for redefining gender relations. The final section of this chapter explores the prospects for and obstacles to such policies.

Prospects for a new vision of full employment

A feminist perspective on full employment looks beyond aggregate measures at the differential impact of economic fluctuations and change on segments of the population. The issues it addresses include the quality as well as the quantity of jobs, and the quality of life that these jobs can sustain. Full employment should not be understood solely as whether or not everyone is employed, but rather must address the hours, conditions, and pay of available jobs. It must also address long-term issues such as an economy's ability to sustain and reproduce itself and the extent to which market relations permeate human activity. Broad statistical measures of full employment and blunt policy instruments that stimulate aggregate demand overlook these concerns. As Jane Wheelock (1992) has noted, the household is at the heart of *total economic activity*. Gender thus provides one lens for focusing in on the relationship between productive and reproductive economic activity and the institutional context in which this measured and unmeasured activity occurs.

As demonstrated in the preceding sections, a gender perspective points to several limitations in current analyses. The gender division of labour between paid and unpaid activity remains a fundamental assumption behind economic theory, statistical measures, and public policy. This model has disadvantaged women since it reduces their access to the resources that provide empowerment within a market economy. This gender division of labour, in interacting with capitalist accumulation strategies, has given rise to segmented labour markets in which women's paid employment is also undervalued. The post-war period of relative economic growth and stability - of so-called full employment - was a period in which women remained simultaneously an over-exploited and an under-utilised resource. The contemporary period is one where much of the institutional framework for post-war accumulation is being reformulated. Gender is once again at the heart of the process. One crucial dimension of contemporary economic restructuring in advanced industrialised countries has been the feminisation of employment. Deregulation and flexible employment strategies foster jobs that do not have the characteristics of male breadwinner jobs, and are therefore gendered 'female' regardless of the biological sex of the incumbents.

While these trends have some benefits for women as they open up opportunities for access to paid employment, these benefits are not equally distributed (Wagman and Folbre, 1988; Humphries and Rubery, 1992; Bruegel and Perrons, 1997). Some women's class and educational backgrounds have enabled them to prosper in the context of rising overall inequality. These better-paid women are generally committed to traditional concepts of full-time labour force participation. They either have access to 'family friendly' policies at the workplace; have sufficient individual resources to purchase commodified forms of reproductive labour; or have eschewed traditional nuclear family structures. Nevertheless, gender (and race) segmentation in low-wage labour markets has continued to define most women's paid employment. This is vividly illustrated by the expansion of part-time employment in female-intensive industries. These part-time jobs are not only low-paid, they exclude women from access to training and skill development over the life cycle. They are structured on the expectation that women continue to define themselves in terms of their reproductive labour.

We maintain that policies to redefine the concept of full-time work need to be articulated as part of an overall competitiveness strategy that takes the high road to flexibility. But who will travel on the high road? Work redistribution has the potential to cut to the heart of contemporary managerial strategies to promote flexibility via feminisation - if gender inequality in the household is directly confronted. By stressing that productive economic activity occurs outside the market nexus, feminism provides an alternative conception of how the benefits of work redistribution will be reaped. A new paradigm is needed, one that allows time outside paid work to be fulfilling and which stresses the possibilities of individual self-realisation. A feminist vision accentuates collective responsibility for social reproduction, best achieved through caring labour. Shortening the work week can institutionalise a commitment to non-market forms of economic activity rather than to consumption. This is where feminist analyses add a new dimension to other work redistribution advocates.

This social vision of the purpose of work redistribution is not easily achieved. Public policies and workplace institutions are only one step in the process. Unless collective responsibility, male and female, for the work of reproduction becomes a social norm, there is no assurance that shortening time in paid employment will achieve the goal of work redistribution between men and women. Changes in structures and changes in hegemonic ideologies must reinforce each other. As Picchio warns, 'The division of labour between the sexes is too deeply rooted in the structure of the social system to be transformed by a simple rationalisation of individual working times' (Picchio, 1992; 113). Women must make demands upon men as well as the state and employers. Work redistribution policies have the potential to redefine the gendered context of full employment, but only if they are accompanied by direct confrontation with the gender ideologies of masculinity and femininity that continue to constrain our visions.

Notes

---

[1] In Britain in the 1980s, part-timers were included in the calculation of numbers in work, but excluded from the unemployment statistics.

[2] In both the United States and the United Kingdom, working time policies aregendered. Protective legislation has left a legacy of limitations on the working hours of women and young people

[3] Full-time employment for women has also increased in most OECD countries. The ratio of female full-time employment to population declined between 1973 and 1988 in only four countries: Germany, France, Belgium, and the Netherlands. However, part-time work for women has expanded at a faster rate than full-time work (OECD, 1989).

[4] The contrast between the full-time employment of black women with children versus part-time employment for white women with children is further support of the importance of differentiated opportunity structures in determing work hours (Bruegel, 1989). Further, Horrell and Rubery (1991). point out that women's shorter hours are not necessarily accommodated to their domestic responsibilities. For example, women may be asked to work evenings and weekends.

[5] For a feminist analysis of part-time work and other 'family friendly' policies as a form of efficiency wage, see Bruegel and Perrons (1995).

[6] For a contrast between the 'low road' or 'mean' versions of flexibility and more progressive alternatives, see Appelbaum and Batt, 1994; Harrison, 1994;Babson, 1995; Gordon, 1996.

[7] Nevertheless, there is some dissention among feminist economists who express concern that these efforts reinforce the gender division of labour by glorifying activity which disempowers women. See Folbre (1995). and Nelson (1995). for a discussion of this position by feminist economists such as Barbara Bergmann.

[8] Folbre (1994). suggests that the development of welfare states represents a socialisation of the family wage concept when it failed to be extensively adopted within private market economies.

[9] Service sector jobs involving cooking, cleaning, or childcare embody women's domestic skills that are undervalued by society. This work is generally low-paid with few promotional opportunities (see for example, Woody, 1989; Glenn, 1996).

[10] Some wage labour may in fact be caring labour since workers may bring caring motives to the labour process.

CHAPTER 5

A GREEN APPROACH TO WORK AND IDLENESS

Christer Sanne

Introduction

Today everyone claims to be in favour of the environment. The battle is won in the sense that nature's limits are recognised in principle, and environmentalism has gained a definite place on the political agenda. All the major political parties have 'stitched a green stripe into their respective flags' (Dobson, 1995; 201) and politicians of all shades are compelled to provide at least rhetorical support to sustainable development. But by and large, the ingrained habits and structures of industrial society in regards to work and leisure remain deeply rooted. Work is still seen as the highest value in society and our political goals remain those time honoured projects of maximum economic growth and employment. All evidence on 'sustainable development', however, suggests that industrial production must be curtailed, at least in the rich West. Thus a green approach to work is a delicate endeavour, yet it remains undeveloped.

This chapter suggests that a green agenda for work in the developed world is long overdue, and that to be comprehensive, it has to concern work at three levels. First, how do we perform those daily activities called work to take account of their environmental impact? This not only includes paid work – which political discourse and daily speech normally mean when they refer to 'work' – but also unpaid work in the household and neighbourhood. Unpaid work has been highlighted by feminist theory (see Chapter 4) but it has an equally important focus in green theory as well. Second, what type of (paid) work should we favour in society? Some activities, processes and products are evidently more harmful to the environment than others. Greens would wish to promote those business and public sector activities which have the least impact on the environment while doing the most for our welfare. Lastly, how much of our time – our life – should we devote to (paid) work, given that this supports the consuming lifestyles responsible for global threats to our common future, like acid rain, global warming and the exhaustion of natural resources?

A key element of a comprehensive green approach to work is the reconception of the social order of work and the 'work-and-spend' character of our society. The emphasis in this chapter is on working time. The most effective strategy for saving resources and limiting pollution may be to work less in the already 'overdeveloped' parts of the world. In support of such an approach, this chapter discusses what is meant by 'green', and follows this up with asking how a green approach relates to work. These sections embrace cautious as well as radical approaches, lay opinions as well as expert views.

The first section of the chapter deals with the emergence of 'green' concerns and values related to production and consumption. These create an evident tension within the green camp. At one end, an 'environmentalist' position largely co-opts green concerns into the current economic structure, positing a 'green capitalism' which can satisfy both the needs of the environment and economic growth. At the other end, an 'ecologist' stand asserts that any truly sustainable development requires a radical reorganisation of production and society. This chapter endorses the ecological position and reviews the green critique of 'productivism', which Alain Lipietz defines as 'the whole set of socio-economic structures and mentalities which push people to "produce for the sake of producing", with no care for the real needs of people or the sustainability of the production regime' (quoted in Sanne, 1995).

The next section focuses on the varying green approaches to work. These are rarely clear-cut, but rather are mediated by views on what production does to nature, and how work organises society. Modern industrial society seems to be caught between the Scylla of efficiency and the Charybis of increasing volume: increasing labour productivity spells unemployment, while environmental costs rule out expanding production. The mainstream political debate struggles with this dilemma, so far seemingly in vain, while the greens have questioned the very foundations of the debate.

The last section attempts to distil a systematic green approach to work in the form of three golden rules based on the three levels described above. How to go about the work we do, including activities in the 'informal sector'; what sectors of production should be favoured in the light of their environmental impact; and finally how much of our lives should be devoted to work? Do we need to join forces with those radicals who have fought for a hundred years for more free time, for idleness, as the basis for true human development? None of these questions can be addressed in a straightforward manner because a green approach to work necessarily presupposes political conflict at a variety of levels. Closing polluting workplaces may have a positive effect on the environment yet intensify job insecurity for many workers. Likewise, in a globally interdependent world, where environmental degradation routinely violates national borders, policy making to reduce environmental hazards necessarily involves extremely complex trade-offs between various national governments and transnational institutions where the potential for disagreement is quite high.

Green views of the productive environment

'Green' philosophy is many-sided but its essence is responsibility for nature and a sense of nature's limits. It is a recognition that people are ultimately dependent on nature for survival and well-being – in recent economic parlance 'nature's services'. It is a call for a more respectful attitude to nature. This is a denial of much of the inheritance of the project of modernity, in particular the attitude of conquering and utilising nature that is traditionally ascribed to Western philosophy (White, 1967; Newman, 1997). Greens do not trust that there are 'technical fixes' for all problems, or embrace the faith in unlimited economic growth.

An ecological perspective seeks to broaden the concerns of political economy to encompass the distribution of environmental goods and bads (Guha and Martinez-Alier, 1997; Dobson, 1995). I would argue that a green ecology is based on three tenets: responsibility, sharing with future generations, and a sense of the limits to economic growth. Alain Lipietz has proposed responsibility as a key value of 'political ecology'. In most green thinking, a sense of responsibility implies a set of reciprocal obligations which we undertake with nature, a recognition that our actions have a determining impact on the natural world, and this in turn shapes and constrains our actions. Responsibility, autonomy and solidarity go together, argues Lipietz, but responsibility is 'ecology's "patent", its contribution to the long history of human consciousness' (Lipietz 1995; 44). Individual autonomy is a prerequisite for taking responsibility. Solidarity – with present fellow beings – is a natural consequence of taking responsibility for nature and its capability to serve future generations of humans.

Such responsibility is at odds with the capitalism of Fordist production. Fordism represented a 'grand compromise' between the major social groups, a left-to-right shared understanding 'of what humanity can best expect from economic activities' (Lipietz, 1992; x). Although this system remained viable for many decades, it comprised a Faustian bargain, a subordination of workers in return for the right to a share of the productivity gains. The deal fell apart once trade unionists began to revolt against deteriorating working conditions in the late 1960s. Eventually, the vitality of the Fordist system faded because of the strict Taylorist allocation of responsibility between workers and management: management sought to increase productivity through mechanisation and automation rather than by the active involvement of the workers themselves in the production process. Solidarity was cast narrowly on both sides of the class divide, and without the collective goods of trust and co-operation the success of the Fordist firm could not be guaranteed in the new economic environment. Where a tacit, if largely unspoken, agreement existed was in the mutual denial of the responsibility of Fordist productivism for a general environmental crisis: while they lasted, the reciprocal benefits of growth were enough to drown out any possibility of ecological sentiment on behalf of either management or unions.

The second basic Green tenet is sharing with future generations, embodied in the familiar green slogan is 'there is only one earth'. The resources of the earth are finite and precious to all humans: they cannot be recklessly squandered and pilfered by the current generation without fundamentally destroying the common birthright of all the generations that will follow. In Boulding's terms, we need a 'spaceship economy', rather than the still pervasive 'cowboy economy' inspired by thinkers like the seventeenth century British empiricist, John Locke (Boulding, 1966). Dobson takes the moral tone even further, when he refers to 'the spiritual asceticism that is so much a part of political ecology' and the '[deep]green contention that the sustainable society would be a spiritually fulfilling place in which to live' as an advertisement for frugal living (Dobson 1995; 19). But what of the sacrifice that reduced consumption may require of some? Do the positive effects accrue to the individual through a more genuinely satisfactory life, or are individuals losing out for the sake of the public good, and the preservation of an environment for future generations? Dobson remains unclear whether the effects will fall on the individual or humanity at large.

A third, crucial issue - sometimes regarded as a watershed for correct ecological thinking - is the attitude to economic growth. Capitalism has an inherent bias towards ever expanding growth: companies must continually seek out new innovations, new products, new markets in order to safeguard their profits. Constant growth is inextricably linked with the constant expansion of environmental degradation. As the greens have always highlighted, these problems have an exponential character: risks which appear to have a limited impact in the short run can very quickly lead to massive danger.

Capitalist economic growth is premised as well on a model of ever expanding consumption. Firms derive profits from increasing their sale of goods so the creation of new needs and desires for products is essential for keeping the profit mechanism functioning. Endless consumption is equally associated with endless toil: this fantasy world of consumption can only be guaranteed if people expand their capacity to work. The belief in the magical powers of consumption is matched only by the pervasive embrace of paid work as the root of all happiness. This work ethic has a material basis as Juliet Schor explains with an inversion of the normal perspective on economic 'logic'. Generally the idea of 'revealed preferences' is used to demonstrate that people appreciate the prevailing order, but this disregards the importance of institutional bonds. Schor argues that working hours, and hence the extent of work, are not freely chosen, in contrast to what the term labour 'market' implies. Put simply, she suggests that we do not work to be able to consume, as much as we consume because we have worked (and earned an income) (Schor , 1992).

Green theorists have argued that the acquisitive ethic leads to a one sided development of human personalities with the spiritual, intellectual and interpersonal side conspicuously ignored. A green position insists that the dominant notions of what constitutes human needs and desires, of what constitutes success and failure, will have to be systematically rethought. It also maintains that the never ending spiral of consumption is unsustainable and can not be extended to the non developed world; to raise the rest of the world up to the level of the average Western living standards would basically make the planet uninhabitable. The greens' insistence that consumption levels will have to be reversed represents a decisive break with the modern era and with the objectives of capitalism itself.

One of the most interesting attempts in recent years at theorising the fundamental nature of productivism is the 'ecological Marxism' offered by James O'Connor. He argues that capitalism faces a 'second contradiction' which supplements the original contradiction Marx defined between the forces and relations of production (O'Connor, 1996): there is an analogous contradiction between the forces (and relations) of production and the 'conditions of production'. These conditions – already delineated by Marx – are threefold: external physical conditions (which in present understanding would include ecosystems), labour power (workers' health and social reproduction of the work force) and 'communal, general conditions of social production' which today would include urban infrastructure and other man-made production conditions (as well as conditions for day-to-day life). The analogy suggests that both contradictions lead to crises for capital but of different, even partly opposing kinds: against the crisis of over production of capital in the traditional Marxist account, the problems created in O'Connor's second contradiction can rather be described as an under production due to the rising costs of reproducing the impaired conditions of production. O'Connor provides a long list of modern societal problems which are the result of the ravagings of capital, including generally accepted environmental effects as well as the destruction of urban areas, collapse of social cohesion and political legitimacy.

To resolve crises (of either kind) requires a restructuring of the forces/relations and conditions of production. This requires a growing 'socialisation' which erects social barriers to further capital accumulation. The state (together with capital) may become more involved in planning production (including producing the infrastructure and creating the conditions for reproduction). Historically, the crisis of the 'first' contradiction characterised by labour exploitation engendered the labour movement. Today, O'Connor points to the exploitation of nature as engendering new social movements of environmentalists, women, and so on. This is not to claim that action stems from systemic forces only; there is obviously also a many-sided civil society engaged in the struggle against environmental destruction. (O'Connor 1996).

In almost every country, the problems of Fordism were met with a form of 'liberal-productivism'. In contrast to nineteenth century liberalism, this lacks the moral – utilitarian – justification of societal betterment. It rather feeds on self-amplifying circular arguments for a continued accumulation process – a question, not of winning anything concrete, but of winning in terms of retaining a lead over competitors. Even if this never became an accepted development model – as the Fordist compromise had been – it has still managed to erode the power of governments and trade unions in favour of 'the market'. When corporations rule the world, says David Korten, they dictate the conditions for governments and employees (Korten, 1995). Investors are granted favours by nations or regions eager for 'job opportunities'; laws safe-guarding employees, customers and the natural environment are lifted, and old models of collective wage negotiations are replaced by individual arrangements. One result is a social rupture between winners and losers. The effects on the environment are equally devastating. But from an ecological perspective it is important to acknowledge that not only the new, but also the old Fordist regime relied upon 'productivism' and as such is to be regretted. 'Productivism' takes a slightly different tenor in the pronounced welfare state. Here we meet 'growth mania', and a preoccupation with economic growth and how to achieve it. The rationale is obvious: only with a bigger cake are politicians able to fulfil promises of income redistribution and improved social services. Again, consumption is not an end in itself but a means of making the wheels of production move faster.

A modest environmentalism?

There has been some progress, nevertheless. The concern about the environment has induced many producers in the market economy to turn their products and production (more) 'green' to please customers - though also to save costs. Green-labelled products have been remarkably successful. Consumer pressure has even forced companies to adjust their production methods to satisfy their demands (Lovins *et al.*, 1995). The gains in material efficiency have often reduced per-product resource use and pollution. Statistics indicate that energy use per head has decreased considerably in major industrial countries. But this is a secular trend, not an effect of the green wave. The earliest country to peak was the industrial front-runner, Great Britain, over 100 years ago, while the USA and Germany peaked in the 1920s. And it is equally clear that the savings due to higher efficiency are more than offset by increases in economic growth. Only one country (Denmark) has managed to lower its energy use in absolute terms in recent decades (Turner *et al.*, 1994). Sweden has an excellent record of reducing carbon dioxide, but only at the cost of a very large nuclear energy sector.

All the same, the notion of 'dematerialization' or of a 'decoupling' effect has been used to claim that society is already on a sustainable track (Daly and Cobb, 1994). This, in turn, is used to legitimise a business-as-usual attitude. Advances in cleaner and leaner production also bolster a general 'anti-political' claim of neo-liberal origin. The assertion is that 'green capitalism plus high-tech' offers a faster solution to environmental problems. The 'politician-governed sector' is presumed to only regulate and restrict: in economic parlance, a form of 'control-and-command' (Turner *et al.*, 1994). In support of economic growth, it is often claimed that growing demand leads to faster 'modernisation'; in other words, to the replacement of dirty old production. This argument is used particularly in the case of the former Eastern bloc. But in reality, the higher energy efficiency in modern industrial states is due to structural changes in the economy rather than to technical progress. Gross National Product is constituted by more services than before. Outsourcing of dirty and heavy processes to other countries also improves the statistics for the West, but does nothing to change the overall amounts of pollution.

Below the surface of buoyant commercialism, there is also evidence of a growing scepticism towards consumption. In surveys in the West, people agree – between 80 and 90 per cent of them – that consumption is overblown. Many people claim that needs are being far surpassed, and that we would do just as well, or even better with less. This puts in question the meaning of further increases in a (private) world already saturated with material belongings which no longer yield a growing satisfaction. A recent survey from Sweden gives an amazingly negative view of the social changes over the last 30 years. (It was undertaken by TERMO in 1995, but the newspaper syndicate that commissioned the research never published it). Although it is recognised that the economy has improved (as have working conditions), this by no means makes up for the deterioration of most other aspects of life (including the environment). It seems that income and consumption, although predominant in the general political debate and mass media, fail to determine people's basic judgement about the 'good life'. Movements in the United States around the notion of 'voluntary simplicity', echoed in the relocation to rural areas or the abandonment of high powered career trajectories, denote a growing attitude of 'having enough for one's needs'.

It is indeed remarkable – and a testimony to its strength – that this popular understanding of green issues survives in the normally aggressive atmosphere of commercial marketing, where the media plays a significant role. The media usually conveys the concept of 'economic man' with connotations of (material) insatiability; there is also the tendency to underline discontent, and to perpetuate and normalise a world view of (material) dissatisfaction. In the political process, many interest organisations form a symbiotic relation with the media to this end, since their *raison d'être* is to give voice to discontent. All of this stands in the way of shifting the political course towards the question of sustainability.

A green analysis of work

A green analysis of work necessarily begins with the distinction between paid work and unpaid work. Unpaid work in the household and neighbourhood is often seen as the most environmentally friendly form of work. There are a number of reasons for this. Unpaid work appears to short circuit the work and spend cycle, since it is decommodified. It fulfils the ideal of 'making do and sharing' and promotes the ideal of self dependency and self reliance. It provides opportunities for self fulfilment in answering to needs rather than pandering to wants. Yet an approach that unconditionally promotes this kind of vision of unpaid work should be viewed with caution. For naive or utopian advocacy of decommodifying labour markets ignores the problems that arise from the essential complementarity between paid and unpaid work, and from the uncosted nature of work which does not enter the monetary economy (Wheelock, 1992). Decisions about how to combine paid and unpaid work are usually taken within the household, and are often based on traditionally gendered divisions of labour where women undertake the unpaid work, but where men are joined by women when it comes to paid work. (Anderson *et. al.*, 1994). Such decisions are also shaped by overall levels of household income, where class based levels of pay may necessitate increased hours of paid work simply to allow the household to survive. The household is not merely the institution where decisions about who does what hours of paid and unpaid work, it is also the consumption unit. In this sense, the household is at the core of the work-and -spend cycle highlighted previously.

A more balanced perspective on the contribution that unpaid work can make to environmental concerns needs to take on board the inherent policy problems that can arise. Materialism and individualism can easily lock households into a 'keeping up with the Jones' mentality, while, as the women's movement has shown, caring can become decommodified and isolated drudgery rather than providing self fulfilment. Given the difficulties of breaking down traditional divisions of labour, it is likely that the unpaid work of recycling will fall more heavily on women, who may be easily tempted to use disposable nappies to reduce burgeoning (paid and unpaid) work loads. As long as environmentally friendly products remain more expensive, families or others on low incomes need to make greater sacrifices to purchase them. The constraints of our social and built environment mean that journeys to work, to school, and to out of town shopping make diabolical contributions to pollution; yet these costs are counted as additions to national income (Ekins and Max-Neef, 1992). In all these ways, we are likely to find that choices become locked in to environmentally unfriendly ways of working in a distinctly non-transparent manner, yet in apparent confirmation of individual choice. To achieve an environmentally friendly, yet progressive, balance of paid and unpaid work requires policies to relieve the burden of long hours of both paid and unpaid work Appropriate taxation of employment and consumption goods will not be enough to ease the overall burden of work and to ensure that voluntary work for the community is undertaken by men as well as women in the prime of their lives.

The green position towards work also follows from its critique of the 'industrial-cum-fossil society' society, which presumes that both the scale of production and its methods are environmentally untenable. Immense gains in labour productivity have allowed a very high standard in terms of material goods for rich nations and elites. This has also released a large part of the work force for personal services, not least in the so called 'welfare sectors' in wealthy nations. This has caused two different types of reactions. A fundamental green objection is that gains in labour productivity usually depend on large expenses of energy and other resources; in these respects overall productivity has often gone down. Agriculture is an important case. Even in the West farming was largely solar powered well into this century; today the food energy output is but one tenth of the (fossil) energy input. This is evidently unsustainable.

But the major general political concern of this industrial society, given its social organisational form, is how to provide its members employment. How can everyone remain at work – and remunerated – when the volume of socially necessary work gradually shrinks? This question has long preoccupied politicians and social scientists. Ever since Karl Marx, it has been realised that the volume of necessary work was bound to decrease. To the economist Stanley Jevons a hundred years ago, this was a logical outcome once the marginal utility of consumption eventually dropped below the marginal utility of free time. Alfred Marshall and J. M. Keynes had similar notions. Marshall assumed that the preference for free time would lead to a halt in economic growth. Keynes, in a famous and rather light hearted passage, discusses man's future problem of using his leisure wisely, anticipating a working week of 15 hours. (Cross, 1993).

It was business interests that began to come up with solutions, recognising the importance of 'keeping the consumer dissatisfied' by raising his and her aspirations, so as to maximise throughput - and profits. In the US of the 1920s, it was widely acknowledged that this shift led to a gradual switch from an 'economy of needs' to an 'economy of wants'. It was this economy of wants that stood in the way of transforming rising productivity into more leisure, despite suggestions from many quarters. Even the 'golden' years after World War Two did not usher in an age of leisure. Only a small part of the very substantial productivity gains were cashed out as shorter hours. The industrialised countries adopted a standard contract with 40 hours a week, several weeks of vacation (less in USA and Japan), pensions and other benefits. But of late, as Chapter 2 argues, even this modest increase in non-work time has been reversed. Total family input to the labour market has in fact expanded, as dual earner households became the rule.

So what has happened to the wave of predictions of more leisure put forward in the optimistic 1970s? Twenty years ago, 'workless future scenarios' were first mooted, drawing their inspiration from the technical progress in automation, superficial trend projections and a concomitant increase in unemployment (Toffler, 1980; Robertson, 1985; Rifkin, 1995). Two major societal elements came together to counteract these predictions. Both contain an element of double counting in that they were partly fuelled by a shift in economic activity from the unpaid (and unmeasured) informal or complementary work sector. The first is the transition in the occupational structure already highlighted. As employment in services surpassed that of industrial work, terms like the 'post-industrial society' were invoked, even though it by no means produced fewer material goods. Many of these services were person-to-person services – particularly common in welfare services like care and education – which by their nature were unable to match the continuous productivity gains in material production. That changed the trend, at least temporarily. But it also brought an economic dilemma. If salaries in these occupations were to follow those elsewhere in the economy (a fair presumption), services become more and more expensive. This requires higher taxes and precipitates a fiscal crisis of the welfare state. Private services either become exclusive to the better off, or are substituted by the household's own (unpaid) work. Jonathan Gershuny coined the term 'self service economy' for this latter phenomenon, when cars, washing machines, video-recorders and other consumer durables rearrange the household's activity and consumption patterns (Gershuny, 1978).

The other major change was in terms of advanced information technology and the concomitant globalisation of the economy. This - together with reductions in the public sector - caused a dramatic new wave of job reductions in the 80s and 90s, this time often in white-collar services (Rifkin, 1995). At present, there is little to support hopes of job creation since today's emerging sectors – such as IT and electronic entertainment – have a particular genius for rationalising their functions. The (relative) balance of power towards labour in the Fordist order of the golden years is vanishing as globalisation give employers the upper hand. They can now press for longer hours of work, or demand arrangements of 'just-in-time' and temporary or casual work to increase the burden and the insecurity of the labour force (see Vail, Wheelock, and Hill, forthcoming).

This has created a paradoxical situation. People are forced to work either too little – if they are unemployed – or too much, as Chapter 2 has argued in the case of Britain. There is plenty of evidence for a pent-up demand for free time. Our culture contains a tension between how (most) people are turned into what they are – full-time workers and heavy consumers – and the kind of life they 'really' would prefer. This is brought about by a capitalist-based proliferation of needs, supported by a work-and-spend structure which cancels any effect of growing productivity, and prevents the worker from following his or her preferred balance between consumption and free, disposable time. For the demand for shorter hours is well established in opinion surveys and from assertions in the political debate. Over and over for decades, a majority of people have consistently declared that they would prefer shorter hours for higher pay. But this opinion has largely been neglected in politics and negotiations over work conditions because of resistance from employers, the remains of the traditional work ethic and, of late, a further structural lock-in by the demands for growth by the welfare state block the way.

But perhaps there is a quick-fix solution for both the environment and employment? The view is still established in many quarters, that there can be a virtuous circle established between environmental protection and job creation. It is a well known social democratic theme that jobs can be created through eco-businesses cleaning up 'at the end of the pipe'. Yet studies from the EU and in a variety of nation states cast doubt on the scope for what can be achieved through this route. To date at most 1-2 per cent of jobs have been created for environmental reasons - and even this appears to be with a rather generous definition. Even so, special interests – like employers – warn that environmental protection measures can reduce growth because of a trade-off between growth and jobs. At the national level, this threat is quite clear: countries with stringent environmental rules are likely to lose out in the race for volatile capital. Thus much of the mainstream debate, not least in the EU, is circumscribed by the conditions of the liberal market economy.

A green agenda for work

In conclusion, let me spell out three golden rules, derived from the analysis presented in this chapter, and ranging from the mundane to the almost revolutionary, which together express what might be called a green agenda for work. They are: to work responsibly and carefully, to work in appropriate sectors and to work less.

Work responsibly! Use alternative, truly careful methods of production. Cut down on waste. Assume responsibility for your activities! Such appeals, although often heard, remain highly relevant. We have all been sensitised to the tremendous waste surrounding us – in the work of others and sometimes in our own work. A major difficulty is to set the responsibilities and incentives right. A prime example in the formal economy is modern agriculture which has become a veritable process of 'agro-mining'. In addition to demanding excessive amounts of fossil energy, modern agriculture poisons the environment and destroys the very soil it relies upon. Careful work may mean more labour intensive production, taking the form of lower labour productivity, but being more energy- or resource-productive. A paradigmatic example would be to substitute manual weeding for admittedly labour-efficient but undoubtedly dangerous pesticides. To prescribe or encourage such (economically) 'suboptimal' methods of work is a task for public regulation, where the principle is well established but where many details need to be hammered out.

Work more in appropriate sectors! Produce welfare services, culture and knowledge rather than gadgets, cars and gigantic infrastructures! It is generally assumed that cultural activities and care services carry less environmental load than much of material production. To promote such sectors of society would accord doubly with common political parlance: most people and politicians are likely to agree that these are the most essential kinds of consumption to promote today - and they are labour intensive, and might help to relieve unemployment. But three problems must be faced. To start with, our factual knowledge is limited. The production system is so dominated by intermediate goods and services that the consequences of various activities (or types of consumption) are hard to grasp. Cultural activities require books, buildings, transport and other material inputs; the biggest building in the town may very well be the hospital. It takes a proper input-output analysis to map the real effects. The lack of such analysis may reflect an intuitive resistance among those who regard the market as a proper and sufficient guide to what to produce. This also means that a majority of employees have no way of judging if their individual contribution of work is for the better or worse environmentally. Instinctively, few people would view their own work as harmful; that would amount to a personal loss of meaning. To recommend less work on environmental grounds might even be a dilemma if the unwillingness to repudiate one's daily occupation caused a backlash. The third problem to face is that the environmentally more desirable sectors often rely on public funding or support. This is hard to obtain in a mood of (presumed) tax weariness and tax defiance. A 'post-materialist' turn in the employment pattern is unlikely unless the state is empowered to accept responsibility and raise the funds.

Work less! Reduce the volume of (paid) work, individually and totally, so that production levels off. With continued technical progress, this will mean fewer resource requirements, waste and pollution. This rule is both the most potent one for environmental protection and the most radical since it would *de facto* break with productivism and the dogma of economic growth. Moreover, it illustrates the confluence of green thinking with influential leftist thinking on the 'good life' of work and idleness allowing greater individual freedom to shape one's life. Shorter working hours with less exploitation of nature extends labour's century-long struggle for better living conditions. Kate Soper underlines this point of merger between red and green politics by returning to Marx who:

> reveals socialism as the possibility of idleness; and in this idleness, one may argue, lies one of the most important eco-friendly resources available to human societies at the present time. For it is only if we stop working, in the sense of devoting labour time to the production of resource-hungry material commodities, particularly in the more affluent global regions, that we shall stave off the barbarism of ecological collapse. (Soper 1996; 94)

Similarly Lipietz states that while reforms of working hours in the wake of World War Two have meant a division of productivity gains between higher salary and shorter hours, such progress is not available today and:

> in countries where the needs of a majority are guaranteed, it is absolutely essential that the distribution of productivity gains should have two guiding principles: the fight against social exclusion and non-material growth, i.e. of free time. This is why the reduction of working time is at the core of ecologist macroeconomics (Lipietz 1995;47)

What are the prospects for this triple approach? It may be simple to agree on levying taxes and setting other rules for production. Allocating more labour to services in the welfare state has become more difficult, given that this requires a higher tax rate, but even this might find popular backing once the link is understood. For planning for a more ecologically balanced society may even suit capital's need to confront the crisis of the 'second contradiction'. But the third rule about working less is absolutely crucial. Shorter working hours could have a radical impact on daily life. Opponents of the idea often claim that any reform would be environmentally counterproductive since increased leisure time will simply lead to more of those activities which at present cause much environmental harm. Travel, especially by car, is the prime example since so much travelling - about one half of it - is related to leisure activities. But proponents of more free time (including greens) do not simply anticipate 'more of the same', but a radical change of lifestyle. Shorter work hours would liberate opportunities for a host of alternative activities which are currently denied to those in work for lack of time. Given time, we will be able to develop new relations to people, artifacts and nature. Informal care of family, relatives and even neighbours may grow. More things might be cared for, mended and kept rather than exchanged or scrapped. This could apply all the way from our private cars and houses to our common assets. More free time could mean a boom for preserving neighbourhoods, old buildings, landscapes and other remains of past cultures. This is literally to save the environment, but it also saves resources. This may not lead us to a leisure society: increased responsibility for family, relatives and neighbours as the welfare state steps back, could mean a reappropriation of our time. This is a burden, but many people demonstrate their readiness to shoulder it.

In the same way that the labour movement once changed the world of work, some believe that the Greens will form a 'new social movement' to lead the way to a sustainable society. But they have despairingly little to suggest in terms of forceful actors constituting such a movement. Others put their trust in a change of values to bring change to the way we live and thus to the world. But they have little to say on how to bring it about. Some refer to a crisis to induce a change of course, but that is poor consolation if it means that the environmental damage has already been inflicted. Others believe that raw material shortages will tip the balance in the direction of more work but the sad fact is that resources are often available in poor countries, and given the yawning gap in national incomes, the Lawrence Sumner principle - that the poor will sell cheap to make the best they can of their immediate situation - will always apply. This underlines that the 'global' environmental crisis – existing or pending – does not threaten all of us equally. Economic power is, and will remain, a potent means of keeping it from your own front door.

Rather than rely on a hoped-for major transformation in people's values, I have called attention to what I have shown as a dormant opinion or desire in the public mind. If a majority 'in their best mood' – acting rationally, unaffected by 'keeping-up-with-the-Joneses' and the lure of consumerism - agreed that a slower pace of life – working less, earning (comparatively) less and consuming less – is in their basic interest, it could have decisive environmental consequences. That desire could be harnessed as the basis for a strong environmentally based social movement. If voiced and brought to bear on existing institutions, it could already change the political course. Thus the crisis is perhaps not – or not only – ecological, but is about our democracy, where politicians show contempt for their public when they refuse to face up to ecological conditions. Environmental critics sometimes mock democracy, but more often the demand is that democracy be more radical. Kate Soper has persuasively argued that:

> it is only under a socialist economy that a society is placed in a position to choose the forms of embodiment of its labour time and therefore in principle is able to opt for a more ecologically sustainable pattern of consumption (Soper 1996; 94)

As problematic are those 'demand machines' organised by business interests, which stand in the way of a more contemplative life style. Radical democracy would press them to lend a keen ear to their customers. I see a narrow middle path between the leftist idea of a social class struggle - which few seem prepared to fight - and the liberal appeal to the individual, blind to the fact that she is caught in a web of influencing forces. It is a call for an 'undistorted communication' (as Habermas puts it) to help us arrive at the wise decisions we so desperately need.

PART II

WHO NEEDS WORK?

CHAPTER 6

CRAP JOBS, 'GOVY SCHEMES' AND 'TRAINSPOTTING': REASSESSING THE YOUTH, EMPLOYMENT AND IDLENESS DEBATE

Robert Hollands

Introduction

> 'Choose us. Choose life. Choose mortgage payments; choose washing machines; choose cars; choose sittin' oan a couch watching mind-numbing and spirit-crushing game shows, stuffing junk food intae yir mooth. Choose rotting away, pishing and shiteing yersel in a home, a total fuckin embarrassment tae the selfish, fucked-up brats ye've produced. Choose life. Well, ah choose no to choose life. If the cunts cannae handle that, it's thair fuckin problem.' (Welsh, 1993; 187)[1]

This quote from Mark Renton, the young anti-hero of Irvine Welsh's 1993 cult novel *Trainspotting*, expresses a fundamental contradiction inherent in the debate about work, idleness and the political economy of full employment. The passage graphically reflects the inability of late capitalism to convince a significant number of its young citizens that it can provide them with a sufficiently meaningful, secure and economically productive life. At the same time it conjures up a deep-seated societal fear with a corresponding set of assumptions about the negative consequences of idleness. While certain elements of this concern are genuine and clearly require some form of policy intervention - like the crippling effect unemployment has on poverty levels and alienating people from society - it must be remembered that the root source of such problems comes from an economic system in which inequality and social exclusion are endemic. Finally, Renton's quote hints at people's capacity to begin to understand and unravel these contradictions, actively challenging some of the core tenets - even if that means simply not choosing. This chapter sets out to provocatively examine and extend the work and idleness debate with specific reference to the experiences and social situation of youth.

As a metaphor for social change, the concept of youth is often utilised as a vehicle for the articulation of wider sets of issues and fears in society. It comes as no surprise then, to find that much of the public debate and concern around work and idleness has taken place on the terrain of the young. In addition to academic debates about unemployment, training and the labour market, and increased governmental concerns about 'troublesome' teens, contemporary culture abounds with visual images of new idle youth. Notions such as the 'Generation X' phenomenon in North America, and the 'chemical generation' in the UK raise important questions about whether western capitalist economies can provide young people with interesting and creative work, or even offer enough employment as not to waste the talents of most of the next generation. True, these notions apply to different class and national contexts, lack sociological documentation and indeed, have been used in quite reactionary ways. Yet they offer - alongside various sociological studies - tentative evidence for the formation of alternative cultures and identities which may begin to challenge many of our core assumptions and expectations about the future of 'normal' youth transitions.

The purpose of this chapter is to utilise a combined political economy and cultural studies approach to critically assess some of the conventional definitions, findings and assumptions underlying the employment-idleness debate, explore an emerging literature outlining young people's responses to their current economic situation, and tentatively suggest possible ways of re-conceptualising the issue. For there is a strong social, and indeed moral, argument for providing youth with jobs and an economically secure and stable future; anything else would appear to be tantamount to abandoning the next generation. At the same time, there is much labour market evidence that young people are utilised as a crucial lever in the current restructuring of global capitalism and play a key role as a 'reserve army of labour'. A focus on 'idle youth' can represent tacit support for flexible labour market policies - characterised by low pay, deskilling and essentially 'crap jobs' - and ultimately, a wholesale acceptance of the 'post-Fordist new world order' (Amin, 1994).

To add to this conundrum, there appears to be a growing ideological consensus on the 'problem' of idle youth, which cuts across the political spectrum. The meshing of the liberal philosophy of 'youth *in* trouble' - an ideology which assumes that youthfulness is an age stage requiring help or social assistance - with the more authoritarian stance of 'youth *as* trouble', has resulted in the acceptance of a common set of assumptions revolving around the need for more work discipline, social order and the maintenance of 'normal' generational transitions (Banks et al, 1992; MacDonald, Banks and Hollands, 1993). As Males (1996) cogently argues, when it comes to youth, most adults, organisations and political parties appear surprisingly reactionary. Social democratic welfare-led employment programmes begin to look suspiciously like right wing workfare schemes, while the media unquestioningly link idle youth to problems like crime, drugs and a decline in moral values. So why do our societies appear so fearful of idleness when under- and unemployment are so clearly an endemic part of our economic system? Why do we want youth in particular to be in employment, without any serious evaluation of its quality, meaning or social value?

This chapter seeks to examine more closely the hidden agenda behind these concerns by untangling some of the disparate economic, political and ideological arguments. The first section questions some of the traditional ways of conceptualising idleness, outlines the distinctive labour market position of young people in western capitalist economies,[2] and analyses the consequences of the ideological variants of conventional political economies of youth. The second section seeks to extend the debate and provide an alternative to traditional notions of youth idleness. It assesses the effects delayed and altered transitions in employment and the family household might be having on the 'symbolic work' that young people invest in cultural activity, social movements and various forms of identity politics. While the analysis does not imply an acceptance of the 'end of work' thesis, or an abandonment of the principle of providing interesting and creative jobs for young people, it does imply that there is a pressing need to re-configure debate in light of rapid economic, social and cultural change.

The 'idleness of youth' in political economy

What constitutes a political economy analysis of youth, and what can this offer to the debate about work and idleness? Generally, such an approach seeks to situate and analyse the relationship between a particular age stage (youthfulness), and wider economic and political systems. It is interested in examining young people's position and role in the economy, their relationship with the state, and how these structures work to socially construct and define this age group. I believe it is necessary to further explore the ways in which certain assumptions inherent in political economy generally have created a definition of idleness which has serious limitations, both theoretically and in policy terms. Only then is it be possible to return to youth, so as to put the argument for an alternative economic, political and indeed, more 'cultural' analysis.

All shades of political economy, whatever their ideological inflection, assume the primacy of economic and political processes in structuring the social world. This is the case whether one looks at Marxist, Keynesian, or free-market approaches. Marxism has always insisted that labour is the basis of human creativity and central to the analysis of any society, while New Right perspectives have paradoxically combined an often unquestioning belief in the power of the market, with an authoritarian state. Social democratic approaches, while historically favouring public intervention and welfarism, have been limited by labour market imperatives and economic requirements, despite an insistence on some kind of social contract between workers, state and capital.[3] These varying perspectives share a common landscape, but offer widely different interpretations of economic and political issues.

Political economy creates and links negative concepts like idleness and political apathy, which can then be used to legitimise the 'natural' working of the market and state activity. If work and 'productive' labour undertaken in the market place are primary and highly valued, then being left outside this sector is secondary and negative. However one represents idleness - whether it be with terms like economic marginalisation, social exclusion, or simply unemployment - there is an underlying assumption of absence and loss. *The Oxford Handy Dictionary*, for instance defines idleness in precisely this kind of language: 'lazy, indolent, unoccupied, useless, purposeless'. Economic marginalisation is often linked to political exclusion and it is interesting to note instances in which equally unflattering representations arise in this sphere as well. For instance, Marx talked about the 'lumpen-proletariat' as not only feckless, but as a politically corrupting influence on the working class struggle, while Beveridge specifically tied idleness to ignorance. Similarly, there is a direct connection between early Thatcherite versions of 'dole scroungers' and the more politically threatening character of the 90s underclass debate.

This kind of focus also has implications for comprehending and analysing other spheres and activities lying outside economic and political boundaries. For example, one could point to the way in which the concept of leisure is defined simply as 'freedom from' or the 'absence' of work; or the manner in which domestic labour, gender relations and the household have, for so long, been left out of classical economics. Perhaps most significant, are the mechanical ways in which political economy has often sought to understand and analyse cultural activity, either aesthetically as a set of idealist values, commercially as an adjunct to production, or simply as commodity fetishism. The problem lies in how the relationship between the economic, political and cultural is conceived, and how these different spheres are understood within the wider context of notions like base and superstructure, determinism and hegemony, structure and agency and culture and ideology. I have argued elsewhere (Hollands, 1994b) that there are few attempts to bring together work from different traditions: the work on economic restructuring (Bagguley, 1990), the political economy of signs and space (Lash and Urry, 1994), and post-Fordism (Amin, 1994; Harvey, 1989), as well as some of the current discussions around the economy and the household (see Mingione, 1991; Morris, 1990; Wheelock, 1990), consumption (Featherstone, 1990) and modernity (Giddens, 1990).

Young people play a distinctive role in western capitalist economies in a number of respects, forming a key element in the ideological debate about work and idleness. First, they are used as a 'control valve' on the supply side of the economy. Governments and the private sector can readily use age as a basis for controlling the supply of labour, for example by regulating entry through ROSLA (raising the school leaving age), training and job schemes and expanding further and higher education (Finn, 1987). Additionally, due to the superior malleability of youth labour - young people's experiences and expectations of working life remain to be formed - they also constitute the thin end of the wedge in terms of capital instituting changes in the labour process and redefining desired supply-side characteristics. This is particularly evident in the restructuring of work through the redefinition of occupational skills, the shift towards service sector employment, flexibility, casualisation, low pay and a decrease in workers' rights and protection through collective bargaining. Young people have also been identified as one of the sources of labour market malaise, portrayed as unskilled, unmotivated and lazy - in a word, idle (Hollands, 1990; 1994a). Finally, a whole set of 'moral panics' linking idle youth to issues like crime, violence, sexuality, drugs, youth culture and immorality have been fostered (Hall, 1978; Cohen, 1980; Males, 1996). Not only is idleness bad, in and of itself, in terms of young people not being socialised or 'disciplined' into working life, but it is also conveniently used to explain their involvement in a wide range of other social problems.[4]

The distinctive economic role of youth is indicated in labour market figures, and shows that youth as a social grouping does not easily fit with assumptions about the primacy of work and its impact on structuring everyday life. Despite national differences in modes of calculating 'economic activity' and unemployment rates, there are some remarkable similarities across capitalist economies. For instance, the percentage of 14-24 years olds even participating in the labour market in the European Union is only 50 per cent.[5] A wide range of surveys also demonstrates that in these and other western economies, young people aged 15-24, without exception, have the highest overall unemployment rates of any age group (White and Smith, 1994, p. 105-107).

Despite the depressing nature of these overall statistics, they under estimate the severity of the problem. The grouping together of the age cohort masks the dire economic position held by the least well off members of the younger generation. Class, gender, ethnicity, and national and regional variations, all impact on a young person's economic well-being. In Scotland for instance, only one-third of largely working class school leavers were finding work when they finished education, with nearly 40 per cent relying on government training schemes in place of a job (Central Statistics Office, 1993; 54). In the US, minority groups such as Hispanic and Black youth experience unemployment rates one and a half to twice that of their white counterparts (Males, 1996), while youth unemployment in some Ojibway (aboriginal) communities in northern Ontario, Canada, reaches close to 90 per cent (Minore, 1991). Gender too has an impact on economic position and life-chances. For example, eight-three percent of teenage mothers in America were deemed to have been in poverty, more than double the figure for those without children (Males, 1996).[6]

What of those young people lucky enough to fulfil the economic norm and actually find themselves in employment? What are their prospects, experiences and social position in the labour market and how do these differ from other disadvantaged groups? While the young population itself is diverse, a common pattern is revealed. Young people employed in western capitalist economies are over-represented in low-paid, part-time, service sector jobs, which are likely to be non-unionised. In other words, they have been used to fuel what some social commentators have referred to as the 'MacDonaldisation' of the labour market (Newman and Lennon, 1995).[7] This phenomenon refers not only to the move towards service work, but also reflects declining expectations about wage levels and worker rights, involving a host of new management strategies including 'impression management', 'total quality assessment' and 'just in time' production regimes (Hollands, 1990).

A number of national examples to demonstrate this link will suffice here. In Canada, 77 per cent of 16-19 year olds working were in sales, services, clerical or primary jobs). Academic research also shows that Canadian youth makes up a disproportionate percentage of workers in the low-skilled, low-paid, service sector (Radwanski, 1986; Lowe and Krahn, 1990), and have largely borne the brunt of the introduction of flexible working practices and the decline in real wages (Myles, Picot and Whannel, 1988). In the US there has also been a decline in earnings for young people. For example, employed young Americans under the age of twenty-five earn less today, in real terms, than they did in 1973, while hourly rates of pay have fallen 10 per cent in the last decade (Vogal, 1994). In their study of 200 workers in the fast food industry, Newman and Lennon (1995) found intense competition in this sector, and a developing age hierarchy. Even US college graduates are taking on unskilled work. It has been estimated that almost 30 per cent are working at jobs that do not normally require a degree (Howell, 1994; 88).

Finally, the UK has similarly seen a surge in service sector employment, having experienced a more dramatic decline in manufacturing when compared to other western economies. The impact this has had on young people living in particular regions of the country has been so severe that some commentators spoke in the 1980s of a 'vanishing youth labour market' (Ashton and Maguire, 1983) and 'broken' youth transitions. While in no way compensating for full-time losses in manufacturing, service employment increased by almost 4 million over a twenty year period from 1970, with many of these jobs being unskilled, part-time and filled by women (Maguire, 1991). Working class school leavers increasingly have had to compete with older married women and students in further and higher education, for jobs they would have walked into twenty years ago. A significant number opting for jobs have instead been offered training and work experience on a variety of government schemes (Finn, 1987). Due to their unique position within the capitalist labour market, it is not surprising that the majority of these programs have been specifically aimed at youth[8].

One view might be that the kind of transformations young people are having to cope with in the labour market are simply a reflection of more general changes within capitalism, where other disadvantaged groups such as women, ethnic groups, the disabled and working class people generally, have all suffered a similar economic fate. While this is undoubtedly true, I would maintain that young people play a distinctive role in this transformation. For instance, the degree to which youth as a whole can be excluded from the labour market, their malleability with regard to wage expectations and rights, and the targeting of young people by vocational training programs and the MacDonaldisation of work, are all evidence of their unique position.

Another response is to argue that young people have always been over-represented in low-paid jobs, even in manufacturing and primary industries characterised by trade union organisation. Again, this view is partly correct. Historically, the labour movement colluded in an inequitable apprenticeship system, partly to control the supply of labour and protect the value of craft skills, but also because its own organisation possessed a rigid age hierarchy (Cohen, 1997; Ch8). Yet despite age-discrimination in the labour markets of the past, many young people involved in this type of work were assured of making both an economic transition (including proper rates of pay and full trade union rights) and a social and cultural transition into adulthood, including the transition into marriage and into an independent household. Today, there is little evidence of a comparable social contract. Traditional transitions have been fundamentally altered, not only economically, but socially and culturally as well. There are no economic guarantees now, either of a progression towards a decent wage and security, or even of obtaining a job at all. We are also witnessing a corresponding delay in transitions from the parental household and an extended culture of adolescence or 'post-adolescence' in the leisure and consumption sphere. While youth sociologists are still attempting to assess the implications of what has happened here, what is clear is that many young people's worlds have been turned upside down.

Interpretations of 'idle youth'

The majority of the 'facts' about youth presented here are not in dispute; what is contested are different interpretations of the youth labour problem, its social consequences and the corresponding policy implications raised. In my view there has been a convergence of opinion on the phenomenon of so-called idle youth, both politically as well as economically, in many western countries. This is partly to do with some of the long-standing assumptions made in political economy, but also because certain variants of this tradition have failed to pursue the logic of their own position in order to come to understand the new conditions.

One of the most dominant paradigms influencing the debate about idle youth over the last two decades, has been the New Right perspective, typified by Reaganism and Thatcherism in the 1980s[9]. This hybrid economic and political configuration demonstrates a curious mix of conventional free market economics combined with a conservative and often authoritarian moral value framework. Idleness is largely viewed as an individual and personal quality, although it is acknowledged that unemployment is exacerbated by structural factors like rigid labour markets, a lack of competitiveness, state interference, shifts in the occupational structure and a low skills base. In the specific case of youth, this interpretation has often manifested itself as a public attack on young people's supposed lack of skill, and criticism of their motivation to obtain work. Often, a link is made between high youth unemployment, generous welfare payments and a more general decline in family values, the cultural fabric and community morality.

A typical and high profile example of this approach, which has been applied in both the US and the UK, is Charles Murray's (1990; 1994) castigation of the underclass as a group of 'idle, thieving, bastards' (Bagguley and Mann, 1992). With regard to the young, Murray weaves together a number of popular images of a work shy, crime-ridden, immoral generation. The policy prescriptions of such a perspective fall easily in to place. For example, free market economic policies like deregulating labour markets are combined with social policy measures designed to wean young people off welfare through reducing or stopping payments and tightening up eligibility requirements. Those failing to accept low pay, or temporary work, are branded as lazy, indolent idlers.

While the state withdraws economically, a highly regulatory and indeed authoritarian set of 'law and order' policies are instituted - paradoxically, to police an idle and immoral youth population supposedly 'out of control'. There are numerous examples of these types of government policies ranging from the imposition of teen curfews, crackdowns on juvenile crime including stiffer punishment regimes for young offenders, not to mention attempts to ban or censor various elements of youth culture like explicit record lyrics or 'illegal' raves[10]. Within a New Right political economy, young people provide an instrument for enhancing flexible labour markets, yet at the same time are constructed as idle folk-devils threatening the social order. There have been recurring moral panics around the issue of youth and idleness since the early 1980s (Mungham, 1982; Hollands, 1991).

Centre left and social democratic approaches provide a critique of New Right ideologies, and offer an alternative interpretation of the problem of idle youth. Taking an institutional rather than individualist stance, this approach historically focused in on the inability of capitalism to create full employment, insisting on the need for planning, social investment and welfarism to counteract its negative effects. The centre left was more likely to believe that most young people remain committed to work, challenging assertions about declining skill levels and education standards by pointing towards a lack of investment and planning as plausible explanations for high youth unemployment (Howell, 1994). While accepting the need for markets, this perspective has traditionally seen youth as 'having problems', offering state intervention and investment in education, training and leisure as a remedy.

Yet despite this historical legacy, this perspective increasingly shares common assumptions with the political right. In recent times the centre left has increasingly prioritised the demands of the marketplace over the needs of its citizens, including youth. Evidence for this transformation comes from the explicit support for labour market flexibility from both Blair's New Labour in the UK, and Clinton's Democratic Party in the US. With the exception of Jospin's Socialist government in France, the general thrust of centre left policy has been based on the assumption that a deregulated private sector is the best source of jobs, prosperity and stability. The modern welfare state has become much more fiscally conservative, with cuts in education, and privatisation of much of its training and workfare provision - all policies which disproportionately hit young people.

Social democratic governments have also begun to accept the rhetoric of the right when it comes to various social issues and young people. There is now an almost unquestioning acceptance of the existence of specific youth problems in areas like crime, sexuality, and morality. For example, while the US Clinton administration was inaugurated in 1993 under a 'put the children first' pledge, an analysis of its most recent policies reveals a virulent anti-adolescent stance. Males, in his book *The Scapegoat Generation* analyses a host of examples ranging from distorting facts about teenage pregnancies and the so-called 'war on drugs', to media hype about increases in youth violence; he argues that issues like youth poverty, the decline in educational spending and violence and abuse against young people are all underplayed (Males, 1996). Similarly, in the UK, at the same time as purporting to help youth with their welfare to work programme, New Labour has persistently emphasised a 'get tough on youth crime' stance, while continuing with a range of Tory anti-youth legislation on drug laws, raves and unlawful assembly, as well as state benefit freezes (Collins, 1997b; The Guardian 29.4.97). Proponents of this more liberal approach continue to assume that traditional youth transitions are both desirable and possible under contemporary global western capitalism. A growing convergence between Conservative governments utilising state interventions such as workfare and training or law and order statutes, and socialist parties emphasising individual responsibility and the primacy of the marketplace, helps to confuse any straightforward political analyses of youth policy.

Finally no discussion of the political economy of youth would be complete without a brief mention of Marxist perspectives. In my view, this approach, with its concern to analyse the relationship between a particular socially constructed age stage (youthfulness), an economic mode of production (capitalism), political legitimation (the state), and the social and cultural forms of life this combination engenders, has the potential to offer the most comprehensive analysis of the youth, work and idleness issue. It also acts as a useful critique of the ideological analysis of other forms of political economy, including that of the New Right as well as social democratic perspectives. Marxist perspectives emphasise youth's distinctive economic class position within capitalism. The reproduction of a disciplined and malleable generation of workers through the education and training system, and the use of unemployed young people as part of a 'reserve army of labour'. In addition, Marxism has been most open in its attempt to theorise the cultural aspects of youth, within the wider context of economic and political forces (Hall and Jefferson, 1976; Hebdige, 1979; Willis, 1977).

This is not to suggest that this perspective is without fault. One of the difficulties of a more orthodox Marxist position is its tendency towards a kind of structural and economic determinism. While it provides an analysis of the way in which capital acts upon young workers in particular, it neither articulates young people's own cultural experience nor does it tell us much about their struggles and activities outside the labour market, in the household, family or leisure and consumption spheres (Mizen, 1995 is an example). Capitalism may perpetuate idleness, but Marxism has not adequately recognised the differentiation within the young working class created by state intervention, market position or lifestyle differences. Even the more culturally-based Marxist analyses concerned with youth culture and resistance often end up reproducing orthodox categories of class and mechanical theories of social action. There have been some useful advances, but there remains a need to examine how, and in what ways, modern forms of capital re-organisation and regulation have altered youth transitions, cultures, and identities.

Rethinking work and idleness: symbolic work, altered transitions and generational separation

I have been arguing that while it is imperative to consider young peoples' subordinate economic position, conventional explanations are somewhat unhelpful in extending the debate about youth, work and idleness. There is however, a developing body of literature concerned with outlining recent changes in young people's cultures of work, the effect of delayed transitions out of the family household, political and generational separation, and the formation of alternative youth cultures, which challenges this status quo, as well as providing some insights into the direction the debate might be taken.

While the necessity of material production has always been recognised in political economy, generally as wage labour, the significance of symbolic work has often been lost or down-played in the literature[11]. The importance of the term for the debate about idleness is central. Symbolic work is a crucial, and indeed logically prior element to production, and while all human beings may not be 'productive' (in a restricted economic sense), *all* of them are communicative (Willis *et al*, 1990). In his book *Common Culture* (1990 *et al*) Willis uses the term 'symbolic work' to express the everyday creation of meaning and identity in the social world. He defines this as:

> ...the application of human capacities to and through, on and with symbolic resources and raw materials (collections of signs and symbols- for instance, the language we inherit as well as texts, songs, films, images and artefacts of all kinds) to produce meaning (Willis, *et al.*, 1990;10).

According to Willis, then, symbolic work is as 'necessary' and as fundamental to the production and reproduction of daily life as material sustenance itself.

There is a further way in which symbolic work is critical in the debate about youth and idleness. For young people have not only a unique labour market position, but also a unique cultural position within capitalism. Youth is the social group most likely to be excluded from productive work and material production. This means that the only 'work' left to many is in the symbolic sphere. Yet it is in this socially constructed age stage that people's identities are formed most self-consciously (Willis *et al.,* 1990; 7). The difficulty today, according to Willis is that:

> Many of the traditional resources of, and inherited bases for, social meaning, membership, security and psychic certainty have lost their legitimacy for a good proportion of young people. (Willis *et al.,* 1990; 13)

Meaning and identity for youth is as likely to be developed on and around the products of material production, as it is by engaging in economic labour itself. This has repercussions for other sites and spaces involved in the production of identity. Additionally the political manifestations of symbolic work are also likely to be expressed in different forms, and outside traditional political structures. This is not to argue that paid work and the state have fundamentally diminished in their significance for young people. Only that struggles over the meaning of leisure and culture, unemployment and social movements, and what might be termed 'substitute work' - training, education, the informal economy - have increasingly encroached upon it.

Touraine maintains that there has been a fundamental reorientation in young people's attitudes towards work, when he writes:

> The image of *homo economicus* and the work ethic of periods of major industrialisation (...) which brought about a separation of working and non-working life, must be superseded by efforts to bring occupational activity into line with broader social and cultural norms. Young people are especially eager to see the work experience and relations between hierarchical superiors and subordinates conform to standards prevailing in other areas of social life, and for this reason they often reject rigid forms of organisation in the work-place. (Touraine, 1991; 38)

A concrete example of this phenomenon comes from a study highlighting some of the demands and challenges young people themselves are making at the workplace. Research on young adults in the UK, conducted by the think tank Demos, revealed a number of interesting shifts in their employment culture (Wilkinson, 1995). First, there has been a move away from a belief in old style corporate hierarchy and company loyalty, to an embrace of skill development and transferability as a prerequisite for greater jobs mobility. Second, young people reject the time bravado (overtime) and the make-work cultures of the past, in favour of flexi-time and real-work practices. Third, an increasing number of young workers are opting for either self-employment and contract work, or taking sabbaticals or breaks from employment.

It is not easy to explain why youth - and obviously some young workers more than others - engage in these attempts to alter the culture of work. A synthesis of Touraine's and Willis' arguments might suggest that because young people regularly engage in symbolic work in contexts such as leisure and popular culture, they expect more flexibility, creativity and control than many jobs today currently afford[12]. The process may be led by those young people working in professional occupations who already have a greater degree of control and choice over the nature of their work. Yet the fact is that the great majority of young workers, including many from the middle class, are increasingly apt to be in monotonous low-paid or part-time service jobs. This means that *most* youth are not in a position to modify work practices or have the luxury of choosing leisure time over a higher pay-cheque. Young workers' subordinate position in the labour market overall suggests that any idea of a revolution in the workplace has serious limits.

One difficulty with focusing on careers and full-time employment is that it misses out on that substantial group of youth whose experiences are peripheral to, or exist largely outside the workplace. Young people whose 'career' pattern consists of moving in and out of short-term and part-time jobs, training, education, self-employment, 'fiddly jobs' and long-term unemployment (MacDonald, 1997) raise questions about how youth orients itself and attaches to work. MacDonald and Coffield's (1991) study of youth and the enterprise culture shows a range of responses, with young people embracing the Thatcherite rhetoric of free enterprise and individuality at one end of the scale, and those who plod on, seeing schemes as a substitute job of last resort at the other. My own studies of the Youth Training Scheme or YTS in England (Hollands, 1990) show young people adopting a range of incorporative and oppositional strategies. Some sub-groups of youth aspired to become managers, professionals, even business owners; others simply 'survived' by moving into the 'grey economy', or became politicised through their exploitation as trainees. Paul Willis' study of youth unemployment demonstrates a much wider range of activity levels and creative responses by youth than political economy approaches have traditionally discovered (Willis, 1988; 1990). The empirical evidence then, takes us some distance from the common-sense and stereotypical views of bored unemployed people playing mindless computer games; it shows that youth is a diverse cohort, who actively respond to conditions of substitute work and enforced idleness, rather than submit as hapless victims to structural economic forces (Banks and Ullah, 1998).

The impact economic restructuring has had on young adults' job prospects and incomes also has implications which limit opportunities to move out of the family household.[13] Much of the political economy literature has disregarded the effect delayed movement into employment has had on other transitions - like marriage, or leaving the parental home. Jones' work highlights the emergence of a new intermediate or transitional period, with young adults leaving their family, largely for independence rather than marriage; and then returning to their household of origin for a range of social and financial reasons (Jones, 1995; 25). In her Scottish study, Jones found that as many as 47 per cent of men and 25 per cent of women aged 23 were living in their family of origin (ibid., 63). In the Canadian case, Boyd and Pryor (1989) note an increase in both the age at which young people are still at home, and an increase in the percentage of youth returning to the family household. Similar patterns are also found in the US (Goldschieder and Le Bourdais, 1987).

The implications of such delayed transitions are varied, yet very suggestive. In the first instance, it seems that the family household has become an important site in explaining how young people - and their parents - cope with economic change. Delayed transition may involve conflict or negotiation, according to whether the younger generation are a net drain on household resources, or whether their substitute income provides an important contribution to family incomes (Allatt and Yeandle, 1992). Cuts in family welfare provision make inter-generational relations increasingly significant for livelihoods, but can also render relations more fraught. The resulting stress within the household of origin may lead to young people leaving home. This provides a clear-cut example of how a social problem like youth homelessness, rather than being the fault of idle or immoral youth, may arise from governments off-loading the costs of economic change onto the household.

A second, related question is the reproduction and transformation of gender relations and identities inside the home. Part of this debate concerns distinguishing 'productive' work in the public sphere from unpaid domestic labour undertaken in the private sphere, but a crucial element, often omitted from discussion, concerns the state of generational gender identities in the household. Does the feminisation of the labour market combined with the breakdown of patriarchal ideas of the male 'breadwinner' shift young people's gender identities with respect to work and home? Or do these transformations, in threatening conventional gender identities, simply rebound and lead to a tightening of traditional roles for young people? Studies conducted by Willis (1988), Griffin (1985) and Hollands (1990) show a continuing pattern of traditional gender roles amongst the majority of youth. Thus young women trade domestic labour as payment in kind for being housed in their family of origin, while young men tend to pay for their 'keep' and are not expected to contribute to unpaid household work. More recently however,. there is some evidence of common gender patterns emerging amongst youth, even in areas characterised by traditional male breadwinner industries (Hollands, 1997).

Finally, some researchers have argued that the inability to move out of the family household has created the conditions for an extended or 'post-adolescent' youth phase or identity (e.g. Irwin, 1995). This longer socialisation could deepen parent-young adult relations, but it is equally possible that it may instead fuel generational separation (Moore, 1995). For 'post-adolescence' is not just a delay in moving out of the family home or a postponement of adult values and responsibilities (like marriage), but an extension of youthful behaviours and cultures. Research in an economically depressed region of England, for example, revealed that many young adults experiencing delayed transitions invest much of their identity in peer group socialising rituals like pub-hopping, going to music venues and clubbing. This occurs with not only twenty-somethings, but even with people into their earlier thirties (Hollands, 1995). Paradoxically, the economic imperative which keeps this extended generation in the parental home, also releases resources which do not have to be spent on independent living. This provides a higher disposable income to funnel into leisure and youth cultural activity.

While youthfulness has always been a liminal phase involving separation and difference, one of its functions besides experimentation, has involved the socialisation and preparation of the young for adult roles and responsibilities. A number of commentators, have pointed out some fundamental changes to this pattern. Suzanne

Moore (1995) has recently drawn attention to the contradiction between the pressure western industrial society places on youngsters to grow up faster, particularly in relation to the media and as consumers, and contrasts this with our abject failure to provide young people with even the most basic economic and social infrastructure needed to become fully functioning adults (i.e. decent paying jobs, affordable housing, access to full benefits and citizenship rights). She argues that in the interim, youth have created their own life-world, which very few adults can claim, or even want, to understand. Far from being passive, negative or 'idle', many young people respond to difficult economic circumstances and delayed transitions, by becoming increasingly active in seeking alternative identities in the cultural sphere.

One example of this energised post-adolescent landscape concerns young people's immersion into a variety of cultural styles, conveniently (but perhaps wrongly) labelled rave culture (Newcombe, 1991). Other commentators prefer to use wider terms like the 'chemical' or 'acid-house' generation to describe this (Welsh, 1994; 1996a; 1996b; Champion, 1996). With roots stretching back to gay and Black clubs in 70s America and the importation of Baleric beats brought back by DJs and holiday-makers from Ibiza in the 1980s, the acid house phenomenon peaked in the UK in the so-called 'summer of love' of 1988, and has since mutated into a myriad of dance styles and cultures across Europe and North America (Collins, 1997a). Illegal warehouse parties and outdoor festivals in the UK in the late 1980s brought together working- and middle-class youth, not to mention travellers, ravers and hippies. Commercialisation of the phenomenon, while initially an attempt to control it, served largely to expand and extend its client base to urban dwellers and university students in most major cities. In the UK alone it is currently estimated that up to half a million youngsters attend dance events, parties and festivals each week, and that over one million have tried the dance drug Ecstasy (Redhead, 1993:11). If one adopts a broader definition of the chemical generation, and includes not only the post-rave youth crowd, but also the loose amalgam of attendant cultures like post-punk (hardcore), new ageism/travellers (Goodwin, 1994), grunge (Ferguson, 1994), techno-hippies (Collins, 1993), dolies (politicised young unemployed), squatters, anarchist and ethnic and environmentally influenced youth (Kingston, 1992), the chemical generation grows not only in numbers but in stature and significance.

The expansion and fragmentation of various aspects of this youth phenomenon make it hard to generalise about or assess the wider impact (Thornton, 1995). The idea of a 'counter-culture' as a collective experience or social movement is perhaps too strong a term to describe what is happening here, considering the emphasis on diversity and personal style and taste[14].Yet, the use of broadly shared symbols - like drugs, music, and defiance of the law - and the sheer prevalence and longevity of the phenomenon (now over ten years old), negate the application of any kind of deviancy model or minority sub-cultural analysis. Similarly, it is difficult to square analyses which reduce the various drug cultures and dance styles to simple 'cultures of avoidance' (see Redhead, 1993 for example), with those which proclaim this generational divide as the main movement for social change in the 90s.

Some voices within the movement suggest that rave represents a much larger and more fundamental youth-led cultural revolution, reflecting an alternative 'other society' which can survive outside the confines and limits of western industrial capitalism[15]. It has been suggested, in response to both the criminalisation and commercialisation of the phenomenon, that the best elements of the culture have gone underground and become more political by linking up with movements and issues like environmentalism, bartering and self help, and alternative lifestyle politics. One of the best examples of the political wing of the rave movement is the collective organisation Exodus in England. Exodus has continued to defy the law by organising raves (or as they prefer to call them: 'community dances') for the last five years, but are also involved in channelling money into rebuilding derelict properties for the homeless (The Guardian 15.4.97). Proponents of a movement also cite wider struggles in the UK against repressive legislation: the Entertainments Act 1990 (which involves restrictions to freedom of movement and assembly and the right to party), the Criminal Justice Act (the first act in history to legislate against a particular type of dance), and the most recent anti-clubbing legislation The Public Entertainments Licenses (Drug Misuse) Act passed in 1997 (Collins, 1997a; 1997b).

I would like to offer my own tentative to speculations as to how this cultural phenomenon fits into the debate about youth, work and idleness. Economic marginalisation of youth has been supplemented by state criminalisation of youth activity to fuel a growing generational separation - represented most widely by what has been called the 'chemical generation'. For one of the main sites for the 'convergence' of youth experience is in the economy itself; the proletarianisation of the youth labour market has meant a flattening of economic opportunities for all (even though working class youth still come out worse). Furthermore, state criminalisation of youth, while focused largely on working class housing estates and communities, has been extended to all young people with respect to drug laws, curfews and legislation like the Criminal Justice Act. There has also been an increase in the number of young people who choose not to be idle, but engage in a range of different types of symbolic work, seeking identity in the cultural sphere. Despite the continuing existence of inequalities in the leisure and consumption sphere, there has been a widening democratisation of youth cultural symbols and activities.

There are now widespread concerns that an entire generation may grow up without being either economically or politically socialised. Youth is attacked as 'idle' in the economic sphere, with a parallel vilification of this age group in the political arena, where notions like 'generation X' and the 'apathetic generation' abound. As already suggested, declining possibilities of meaningful work, anti-youth legislation and increased involvement in symbolic work, all have a significant impact on the nature of political action that youth engages in. Interest in traditional political solutions appears to have waned. Instead, youth seems to play a special role within social movements (as defined by Beck, 1992; Melucci, 1988; Offe, 1985; Touraine, 1981). This may be due in part to their exclusion from production, but perhaps also because of their stronger interest in identity-formation in the cultural sphere (Melucci, 1988; Habermas, 1987). If one includes participation in the wider range of youth cultural activity, it could even be argued that the majority in fact are involved in some kind of political act.

Conclusion: a new deal for youth?

In this chapter I have sought to examine some of the contradictions inherent in the youth, employment and idleness debate. While recognising the significance of political economy perspectives in understanding young people's subordinate position, the failure of conventional analyses to comprehend the growing importance of altered transitions and the cultural separation of youth has hampered thinking on this issue. This conclusion seeks to make some general points and suggestions for moving the debate forward, rather than to provide any blueprint of detailed policy solutions.

It is imperative that we begin to broaden our definition of politics and political action, particularly when it comes to a social group like youth, who for all intents and purposes, are largely excluded from political power (see Hollands, 1990; 1991; MacDonald and Coffield, 1991). We have to begin to adopt another language than that of the New Right, and to stop talking about youth in terms of a social problem. The young are a problem largely in as far as they are differentially discriminated against and excluded by the system. Real investment in education and training, equal employment and citizenship rights for young people and an end to the criminalisation of youth and social construction of moral panics about youth, are all within the purview of social democratic projects.

Yet even European social democratic parties appear to be straying from an interventionist role, in favour of the merits of marketplace and a renewed emphasis on responsibility. One needs only look more closely at the British Labour government's welfare to work to see this. Able bodied young people must exercise their responsibility to work by choosing one of four options - work in the private sector, voluntary sector work, training scheme, or work on an environmental task force - in order to claim their right to unemployment benefits. Many commentators have argued that youth have been hypocritically singled out for such treatment:

> The uneveness in attitudes to the young represent a general challenge to Labour, who have made a virtual religion of rights and responsibilities. By asking one group to accept lots of one, without getting much of the other, Labour are exposing a semi-authoritarian streak which should make all of us take notice. They're doing it to kids today; it might be grown-ups tomorrow (Freedland, 1997;15).

The campaign to legalise cannabis has been publicly repudiated by Labour ministers, who seem totally unmoved by the dangers of continued criminalisation of an activity that receives widespread support among young people. Likewise Labour's welfare reform has been accompanied not only by a begrudging unwillingness to repeal a host of Tory anti-youth legislation, but the creation of a range of new moralising around drugs, alcohol and even smoking. There is still no debate around the central contradiction that although a young person of 16 may work and pay taxes, he or she is unable to vote for a further two years.

We clearly need to return to the long-standing debate about what work is, and how it can be re-defined and re-organised in contemporary society to pull out some lessons from the young. Young people's creative attempts to control and redefine work, for example, should be encouraging in-depth investigation by the trade union movement and could serve as the basis for new organising efforts among this under-represented constituency. The conventional wisdom needs to be turned on its head: we need to ask, not whether our youth is good enough for work, but whether work is good enough for them. This could involve a debate around full-time employment; about enhancing rights, remuneration and creativity with respect to part-time jobs; training schemes, education choices and careers involving the movement in and out of work.

For example, the institution of a national social wage for youth, whether in or out of employment, in training or in higher education, could help to eradicate distinctions between working and idle youth, and could form part of an overall redistribution of work strategy, as suggested more generally in Chapter 12. Support for new employment opportunities in the cultural economy (rave culture itself was worth £2 billion annually in the early 90s) could also be considered, as well as exploring some of the new ways of working the 'third sector', such as LETS, self help or co-operatives as highlighted in Chapter 14. There needs to be much more openness, tolerance and support shown towards a variety of alternative youth lifestyles, cultures and ways of life. This may involve governments admitting that the market cannot always provide meaning, or even sufficient work, for many young people.

Young people's faith has to be renewed through active participation and a guarantee of their rights. It is important to begin talking and thinking about young people as participants and creators, rather than as mere 'objects' of social policy. Any shift in language needs to be backed up by real action and commitment. It is not enough to talk about youth responsibilities, without giving rights, and reasons for taking them on. Youth rights should be fundamental, not negotiable. This should include reconstructing policies *with* youth, forged out of their wider experiences of education, the household, and leisure. Finally, it may also mean responding much more favourably to youth cultures, social movements and activities outside the realm of traditional employment and politics.

Most political parties across the western world still appear to cling to functionalist notions of maintaining 'normal' transitions, reproducing the next generation in light of the needs and requirements of a capitalist market society. As Touraine argues:

> ...if those in favour of a youth culture opposed to work and focused on private life are correct, then any policy to combat unemployment amounts to nothing more than a set of measures aimed at reactivating economic life and is bound to meet with resistance from young people. (Touraine, 1991; 25)

The problem is that modern capitalism has shifted traditional transitions to such an extent, that we need to begin to move beyond conventional beliefs (Giddens, 1994), and start to formulate some new responses.

My argument does not involve an unrealistic call for an 'end of work' nor, to paraphrase a famous passage on idleness, to encourage society to 'start a new campaign to induce good young men [and women- my addition] to do nothing' (Russell, 1935). Rather, it is to recognise the effect that our changing political economy is having on the old institutional structures of work, family life, and culture, and to start thinking of alternatives more in tune with the experience of the younger generation. Let us look at ways of harnessing youth's energy, rather than constructing unhelpful representations of idle and apathetic youth. Otherwise, the potential for generational separation will surely grow, so that for many young people mainstream society will continue to be part of the problem, rather than the solution.

Notes

1 I would like to thank both editors, John Vail and Jane Wheelock, for making this a better paper. Also thanks to Vernon Gayle, Helen Carr, Rob MacDonald and Colin Clark for looking at an earlier draft and making constructive suggestions and comments.

2 The paper purposefully focuses on material on youth emanating from the UK, Canada, and the US, to make its argument. See Males (1996) and Loeb (1994) for an assessment of US youth, Griffin (1993) for the US and UK and Cote and Allahar (1994), Tanner (1996) and O'Bireck (1996) for the Canadian context. For a comparative youth study contrasting Canada and the UK see Ashton and Lowe (1991).

3 For youth, although it often meant receiving less pay and benefits at first, the pay-off to the social contract was full rights to both when adulthood was achieved. A discussion of the breaking of this social contract in the UK can be found in Hollands (1990), amongst others (Finn, 1987; Bates, 1984; Hollands, 1991; Mizen, 1995).

4 This also occurs for other social groups who have traditionally held a weak position in the labour market, like the ethnic population and women. However, ethnicity for instance, has been more about disciplining black people (particularly youth), not so much by the labour market, as by the criminalisation of their culture (CCCS Race and Politics Group, 1982). It is interesting that moral panics about single parent mothers, latch-key kids and general debates about the crisis of the family often focus on 'young' women.

5 It is important to note that the category of youth here includes 15-19 year olds, a sub-group most likely to be 'redefined' as trainees and students rather than unemployed. For example, the percentage of 16-19 year olds classed as unemployed dropped from 32.9 per cent in 1983 to 6.8 per cent in 1990, while those gaining jobs stayed relatively constant (White and Smith, 1994; 105).

6 This ties in with disturbing findings about young people and poverty, an issue rarely addressed in the youth literature. The richest country in the world, the US, has the highest percentage of children and adolescents living in families with incomes below poverty guidelines in the industrialised world (Males, 1996).

7 One recent study claims 1 in 15 Americans working today found their first job at MacDonald's (Newman and Lennon, 1995; 66).

8 While many young people in the UK have become disillusioned with what they consider to be 'make-work govvy schemes' which do not lead to real jobs (Coffield et al, 1986; Mizen, 1995), the importance of what has been called the 'new' vocationalism in ideologically re-adjusting young employment, cannot be ignored (Hollands, 1990:65-72; Bates and Reisbrough, 1993; MacDonald and Coffield, 1991).

9 I would include here a shift to the right in Canada, including some of the reactionary policies of the provincial Conservative government in Ontario in education and social security, and the disgraceful antics of the Reform Party, who were publicly debating the issue of bringing back flogging to discipline youth in the winter of 1996. Academic support for this free-market people's perceptions and expectations of work in the service industries and self-analysis of unemployment comes from Friedman and Friedman (1980), Minford and Ashton (1985), and Minford (1991). Critiques of the New Right in the UK and the US can be found in Hall and Jacques (1983); Schram (1991) and CCCS Education Group (1991).

10 About 150 of the 200 largest U.S cities, including Dallas, Miami, San Diego and Washington, have instituted teen curfew laws, though exceptions are made for travelling to school events, work, or church (Ottawa Citizen 15.1.96). The idea of fining parents whose children are out past a certain time, has also been raised in the Green Paper *Preventing Children Offending* in the UK (The Times 5.3.97). The right of assembly in the UK is also threatened by the Entertainments Act (1990) which makes non-commercial raves illegal, while the 1994 Criminal Justice Act legislates against both gatherings and a particular type of music (repetitive beats) (see Collins, 1997a; 1997b).

11 Though Marx of course recognised this, particularly in his early work and in parts of *Capital* (Vol. 1). See H. Braverman (1974), Ch. 1 for a discussion.

12 Young people's quest for more fulfilling work, is evidenced by the figure that nearly 40% of 16-24 year olds leave or switch their jobs every year (GHS, 1987). This is often used to indicate their lack of commitment, but does it rather indicate a rejection of deskilled and routinised work?

13 Italy is often held up as the extreme example of young adults stopping at home (what is referred to as 'mammismo') with one-half of males and 33% of females aged 25-34 still living at home (The Ottawa Citizen, 20.4.96). Youth in former East Block countries (like the former Soviet Union), have also experienced high rates of having to live at home with parents (Riordan, 1989). Despite cultural and politically-created differences here, there is a recognised general trend in young people's delayed movement out of the family household (see Jones, 1995).

14 Social movements exist outside traditional political structures, involve collective forms of action based on a common interest rather than participants sharing a common background and, often generate strong identities. They tend to lie outside of the world of production and work (i.e. student protests), are generally issue-oriented like the peace or ecology movement, and involve strong cultural codes of identification (like new age travellers). There are numerous examples of youth involvement in social movements ranging from support for ecological and green causes, the peace movement, anti-curfew groups, increasing aid to the developing world, human rights, anti-racist organisations, travellers rights and student movements, to name but a few (Evans and Heinz, 1994; Earle et al, 1994; Kovacheva and Wallace, 1994; Loeb, 1994; Gaskin et al, 1996; Males, 1996). For example, in the US, Loeb (1994) examines a number of campus-based movements to do with educational access, divestment in South Africa and struggles to preserve family farms, while Males (1996) documents the San Francisco Youth Uprising Coalition's successful defeat of a city curfew for young people. In the UK youth activists involved in 'Reclaim the Future' have been waging a direct action campaign against waste disposal in addition to supporting and drawing attention to the under-publicised Liverpool Dockers 'unofficial' strike (Pilger, 1996:23). Recent protests against the now opposition Conservatives, like the 'Reclaim the Streets' demonstration, and active dissent against numerous road-building schemes in England, have also brought youth protest to the attention of the media.

15 Terrance McKenna, a spokesperson for the younger generation, suggests this a is culture which can begin to redefine art, socialism, feminism, nature and psychology, while Fraser Clarke, of the collective organisation Evolution, argues there is no other social movement outside rave which has the energy to spread an alternative consciousness (both quoted in Kingston, 1992).

CHAPTER 7

MANAGING THE END OF OCCUPATIONAL LIFE

Geneviève Reday-Mulvey

It is well-known that over the last twenty years, in all industrialised countries, employment has been characterised by an increasingly early exit from the labour market as the end of a career approaches. End-of-career management has essentially taken the form of shortening occupational life and, especially in industry and construction, of exclusion of older workers (Guillemard, 1993). This is one of the most important social paradoxes of our time: while a continuous increase in life expectancy and good health (Morniche, 1996) and a steady extension of schooling for the young have been observed, employment has been entered into later and quitted earlier and, as a consequence, occupational life has shrunk considerably. In some countries such as the Netherlands and France, less than 40 per cent of the active male population aged 55-59 and less than 20 per cent of the 60-64 age-group are now at work, and these labour participation rates are only slightly higher in Germany and the UK (OECD, 1996). In France where the young enter employment especially late and the older worker leaves his or her job especially early, the average citizen now spends much more time outside employment than within it!

The significant trend towards early retirement has been the result of a long-standing consensus among all social actors. For the state, the main purpose of early retirement has been to reduce youth unemployment. For the private sector, it was to modernise the processes of production and to restructure firms without the embarrassment of rising structural redundancies. For the trade unions, early retirement has been a coveted prize in the long struggle to lower the retirement age and so leave workers, who so often started working life young and frequently in strenuous jobs, some years of respite in good health. Faced with the appearance on the labour market of an army of newcomers benefiting from constantly improved levels of training, corporate firms - together with the state and the unions - have prioritised employment to younger workers to the detriment of employees at end of their career. Increasingly early retirement packages have thus been made available on financial terms which, thanks to state aid more often than not in the form of unemployment insurance (e.g. France, Germany) or disability insurance (e.g. Holland), have as a rule been very generous. In some countries where state intervention has been less forthcoming (e.g. UK, USA, Canada), it is frequently the pension funds themselves that have contributed to making early retirement financially viable, on admittedly less favourable terms, while a not insignificant proportion of workers have had to rely on social assistance. Lastly, in most continental European countries, the average citizen has greatly benefited from the early retirement phenomenon.

This chapter is divided into four parts: the first part looks at new constraints (demographic and financial) and developments (employment and life cycle) which might lead to significant changes in the coming years for older workers; gradual retirement is progressively replacing early retirement but, more generally, one can observe a new type of end-of-career management and a later and more flexible age of retirement. The second part describes recent trends of gradual retirement and examines the four models to be found in the OECD countries. The third section provides recent examples of good practice for older workers in France. Section four shows how older workers can participate in activities other than paid employment. Finally the conclusion makes some recommendations for public and company policies and posits a redefinition of 'full' employment which will take account of the needs of those over fifty.

End-of-career management: towards a new consensus

Since the late eighties, the greying of the work force, prospects regarding the future financing of retirement and recognition by the state and enterprise of the high cost of early retirement have forced policy-makers to take a second look at what is happening. Indeed, a new consensus is beginning to emerge about deferring the effective age of retirement and about the need for a new design of end-of-career and of the transition from full career into full retirement (Delsen and Reday-Mulvey, 1996). This non-explicit consensus, which varies considerably from one country to another, is supported by all social partners, and is being driven by demographic changes, financial pressures on the state and employers and changes in occupational structure.

The state is concerned to reduce the cost of retirement because of future demographic prospects and current financial constraints. The proportion of 60 year-olds and over in the European Union is expected to climb from 20 to 27 per cent between 1990 and 2020. The dependency ratio of non-active retirees to active workers is declining sharply and set to fall from one in five in 1990 to a little over one in three by 2020. For public pensions, which are financed on a pay-as-you-go basis, these trends mean either a substantial hiking of contributions rates (and their current very high level in almost all EU states leaves very little room for expansion) or a sharp drop in the replacement rate of pensions or, again, a massive drawing on public funds. But public deficits in most industrialised countries have risen enormously over the last decade and the Maastricht criteria for accession to the single currency require their drastic reduction. States are accordingly left with little alternative to raising the age for pension entitlement and to thoroughly reviewing the terms of the latter's operation.

As early as 1983, the USA passed a law providing for a future rise in the official retirement age from 65 to 67. Most countries have followed suit by increasing either the pension age (Germany, Italy, the UK, Austria, Japan) or the number of contribution years to social security (France) or both. In most countries, conditions for obtaining a full pension have also been made more difficult and pensions are now price-indexed as opposed to wage-indexed. Moreover, several European governments are currently in the process of tightening up the conditions for obtaining early retirement.

The private sector, for its part, concerned to improve the age management of the work force, is slowly becoming wise to the fact that jettisoning older employees is sometimes to incur an irreparable loss of skills and corporate expertise. It is seen as no more than a short-term solution to the problem of an ageing work force. In several countries (e.g. France, Finland), the average age of the working population is currently increasing by almost one year every year. Increasingly, jobs have a high mental content, and scientific studies (Charness, 1985) have shown that mental abilities remain undiminished late in life. It is beginning to be accepted that, in most work functions, experience and reliability in older workers can compensate for certain shortcomings such as their relative slowness to adapt to new ideas and new technology. The private sector is therefore concerned about managing an older work force and a number of tools are beginning to be used in model firms: ergonomics and job design to adapt work functions to older workers, reduction of working time towards the end-of-career, continuing training and promotion until end-of-career. In the UK, for example, some employers are now articulating a 'business case' for employing older workers. This consists of five main components: return on investment, preventing skill shortages, maximising recruitment potential, responding to demographic change, promoting diversity (Walker, 1996).

Moreover, in continental Europe, trade unions in increasing number are becoming aware that the needs of the employee in the service economy are different from those of the worker in manufacturing and that, with entrenched ageing of the work force, continuing training and adjusted work conditions are also issues to be addressed (European Trade Union Institute, 1994).

The desire for a gradual transition also reflects transformation in the wider economy which has modified employment and significantly altered the life cycle. Over the last two decades, the evolution from an industrial to a service economy has produced increasingly flexible work options in terms of time and space (Giarini and Stahel, 1993). Over a third of jobs in a number of countries (Scandinavia, the Netherlands, UK, USA) are now flexible in form: part-time, self-employment, temporary work, etc. In France and Germany - countries where traditionally part-time work was little developed - the same trend can now be observed. It is recognised that full-time jobs are disappearing while forecasts suggest a continuing rise in part-time work and self-employment, even for very qualified work. Legislation also has, of course, had its part to play. In several countries - e.g. France and the Netherlands - legal provision for the equal treatment of part- and full-time workers has now been passed (International Association for the Study of Insurance Economics, 1996 and 1997). These measures concern social benefits, continuing training and promotion. This legislation will serve to make part-time work more attractive to qualified and male employees and, in the community at large, to foster acceptance of part-time as a norm rather than as a second-best, stop-gap or bridge arrangement.

Surveys show that older workers often desire some kind of transition between a full-time career and full retirement (Gaullier, 1993). Indeed, the rigid, linear, three-phase life cycle - youth and training, adult life and full-time work, withdrawal from work to retirement - that has predominated throughout the period of the mature industrial revolution is today gradually being replaced by a cycle which is less certain, less predictable and of necessity more creative (Delsen and Reday-Mulvey, 1996). Among other things it is characterised by more flexible work patterns, more training throughout professional life, periods of unemployment and sabbatical leave, and more active retirement. Indeed new categories of employee nowadays - as well as mothers of young children or young people in training - are concerned to organise their work in new ways, and frequently quite simply to work less. These new categories include workers in the mid-life period who wish to combine regular work with meeting other requirements and workers at end-of-career who wish gradually to move from a full-time working life into healthy retirement. Sometimes these people have had two or three careers (Gaullier, 1992). More often than not, they want to play an active part helping their grandchildren or the community. Voluntary work is one of the unexpected opportunities of earlier or partial retirement and of increasing life expectancy in good health. 'Productive ageing' (Bass, Caro and Chen, 1993) is the term frequently used to describe this process.

Gradual retirement: recent trends

One of the solutions which many countries are adopting in responding to the profound structural shifts just described and in reconciling the often conflicting needs they occasion is to encourage 'gradual retirement', also known as phased, partial or part-time retirement. Gradual retirement provides a transition period between a full-time career and complete rest. The worker, instead of working full-time one day and fully retiring the next, can reduce work hours according to graduated and agreed schedules while drawing part-time pay and in some cases some form of partial pension. Many formulae for workload downsizing exist and the transition periods during which this occurs can run for anything from one to ten years. Approximately five years is the transition period most commonly encountered in the OECD countries. Several EU member states have recently passed legislation facilitating gradual retirement (Denmark, France, Germany, Luxembourg, Spain and Italy) while the three new members (Sweden, Finland and Austria) had already done so. Public policies to stem early retirement have been launched in most countries, but, where not securely articulated into company policies, they have not necessarily produced the expected results.

It should be understood that gradual retirement can be used to reduce working life as well as to extend it. In Sweden, where the retirement age has long been relatively late at 65 years, gradual retirement was originally designed to facilitate a reduction in working life. However, most countries want to use it as a kind of part-time early retirement in place of full early retirement. It is, in fact, my contention that gradual retirement constitutes a flexible extension of work life, and should be promoted as such. Often, at present, a bridge between the official and the effective retirement age, it is, I believe, destined to become the standard mode for extension of working life beyond any notional or reference retirement age.

In 1994 and 1995 Lei Delsen (University of Nijmegen, Holland) and myself were involved in surveys of gradual retirement undertaken by experts in seven OECD countries with the support of the European Commission (Delsen and Reday-Mulvey, 1996). The countries surveyed were Sweden, France, Germany, the UK, Holland, Japan and the USA and the authors focused on company as well as on public policies, and identified examples of best practice. The survey findings revealed four main approaches:

- The Swedish (Nordic) approach: in Sweden, almost one half of workers between 60 and 65 are in gradual retirement on generous financial and professional terms. Availability of part-time jobs, a good partnership between government and employers, and the high replacement rate of partial pensions have ensured success for two decades. However, reforms to the pension system were introduced in June 1994 and will eventually make gradual (partial) retirement less attractive financially. Finland and Denmark are now developing gradual retirement models on similar lines.
- The Japanese approach: a large number of workers work on after the current pension age of 60, frequently up to 65 if not later, mostly part-time, often in a subsidiary firm of their previous employer. The financial and professional conditions they are offered are not as generous as previously, but their income from this work is additional to the pension which for many is still too low (Takayama, 1996). Moreover, Japanese workers value the social 'inclusion' that this type of employment after pension age confers (Shimowada, 1992). A government-led global policy and strong state incentives encourage enterprise to extend working life in a land whose life expectancy in good health is one of the highest in the world. Japan's labour force, it should be added, is aging before those of Europe or America and, it seems, with no loss of productivity.
- The continental approach: this is exemplified by France, Germany and the Netherlands. Public policies to encourage flexibility and phasing have been launched recently, and there are the beginnings of a trend away from early retirement. Part three provides a more detailed account of the situation in France. Following legislation passed in 1996, Germany is currently negotiating a number of new contracts in this direction. Other EU Member States such as Austria, Finland and Denmark have also launched similar policies. In the Netherlands, collective agreements have been passed recently (the Philips Agreement in Spring 1996 is an example) and there is a growing trend away from early towards gradual retirement. A major obstacle to any real progress in this country, however, is that fact that pension funds often remain final-salary based.
- The Anglo-Saxon approach: here no strong public policies exist, but flexibility is common. In the USA downsizing has meant that many employees in their fifties have been losing their jobs. Between the ages of 55 and, hopefully (but all too rarely in practice) 65 when they can draw a pension, they have had to take 'bridge jobs' which

are often part-time, frequently pay less, and almost always provide lower levels of protection than previous employment. And yet, there are several well-known organisations, such as the Travelers (Sheppard, 1996), where working conditions for 'retirees' are excellent. Other examples can be found in banks, insurance companies, town administrations, colleges and supermarkets but the conditions in such cases are not always representative of average conditions. In the UK the idea of gradual retirement has yet to gain the same prominence as in continental Europe. This is partly because early retirement, while significant, has not been so pronounced as in countries such as France and the Netherlands. The other discouragement has been the nature of pensions themselves. Clearly, final salary schemes make it necessary to maximise salary during the last ten years of occupational life. Moreover, Inland Revenue rules effectively prevent people from drawing part of their pension while working part-time. However, this may soon be changed. Research conducted in the UK (Taylor and Walker, 1996) shows that a majority of employers are in favour of some sort of anti-age discrimination legislation since they feel that the current active persuasion policy has not been as effective as was hoped.

Observation of the operation of these four approaches would seem to suggest that in countries where early retirement has been more widespread - the Netherlands, France, Germany, Austria, Finland - those responsible for public policies in collaboration with the social actors are now actively involved in promoting later and more flexible retirement. Legislation postponing the age at which pensions become available, together with less generous public funding of early retirement, unquestionably plays a crucial role. For the time being, however, one is bound to observe that in a number of sectors in several countries there persists the habit of negotiating full early retirement on conditions which, in the eyes of the older worker, make gradual retirement a second best. While company policies remain decisive in this area, we nevertheless strongly believe that only full integration of the latter into a properly thought-out public policy frame will make for sufficiently swift progress in reversing the early-retirement trend.

From early to gradual retirement: the French case

For the time being, France is perhaps the best recent example of a country using gradual retirement to combat early retirement. Since 1987, and increasingly since 1993, there have been a number of laws and measures taken to reverse what had become, over twenty years, a massive swing towards early retirement. First, early retirement has been made more difficult by increasing its cost and the age at which it becomes possible; in particular, a 1993 law pushed up the cost of the public insurance scheme which pays pensions to early retirees, leaving many firms unable to afford it. At the same time financial incentives are being provided for gradual retirement. The government adds a further 25 per cent to the half salaries of workers on half-time, provided the firm fills the vacated time with new employees. The government has also supported continuing training of employees aged 45 and over and exempts companies from paying social costs, such as pension and health insurance costs, for workers between 50 and 60. This is a huge incentive, since the social costs of employment are very high in France. Part-time work is promoted mainly through a 1993 law which provides tax incentives for employing part-timers and gives them the same legal rights as full-timers. Finally the pension reform of 1993 kept the retirement age at 60 but required 40 contribution years instead of 37.5 to qualify for a full pension.

Following recent legislation, many contracts have been concluded by the social partners (enterprise, the government and trade unions) since 1993 to keep employees in the firm until the legal retirement age but, at the same time, to offer them several alternatives for reducing work hours. Such contracts are intended to serve a threefold purpose: to rejuvenate the age-pyramid, stagger exits into retirement and promote part-time work. However, it is not always easy to convince workers who have been used to the idea of quitting the workplace early of the virtues of a flexible extension of working life. By the end of 1995, over 50,000 workers were benefiting from gradual retirement, and another 25,000 entered such schemes in 1996. Full early retirement appears now increasingly confined to exceptional firms or regions. Examples of firms having adopted gradual retirement schemes are: in the manufacturing sector, Rhône-Poulenc, Aérospatiale, Total, Framatome, Hewlett-Packard; in services, Crédit Agricole, UAP, AXA, many hospital and care institutions, many catering companies.

Four examples of firms (visited for survey purposes in 1995) representative of the recent trend can be described here:

- Rhône-Poulenc: part-time early retirement has been growing rapidly since 1987 with positive results. Early in 1995 around 1,000 workers (much more than half the number of employees in the age-group) had chosen gradual retirement. Seventy per cent of the latter were qualified and unqualified blue-collar workers and 10 to 15 per cent professional workers. Between 2,000 and 2,500 workers have been concerned over the three years from 1994 to 1996. The scheme is voluntary and, on the whole, has proved more popular with manual workers than professionals. Gradual retirement, in the eyes of professional workers, is still perceived as a form of part-time work associated with loss of responsibility and social prestige. Workers are over 55 and benefit from this measure during the three years before full retirement. Work flexibility depends on the job to be done. With the possibility of annualising work time, there is a new trend to work 80 per cent of the time the first year, 50 per cent the second year and 20 per cent the third year. Positive effects have been rejuvenation of the age-pyramid and of human resources and greater flexibility in work patterns, and, of course, the opportunities for workers and management afforded by a real transition from work to retirement.
- In 1993 the Crédit Agricole, a very large bank, concluded an interesting gradual retirement agreement with the government which breaks new ground in the banking sector. In 1994/95 more than 600 employees entered the scheme enabling the bank to take on more than 300 new recruits, many of them new apprentices or job-seekers. One of the more interesting features of this scheme they call the 'contract for progress' is that it creates a positive link between gradual retirement on the one hand and training on the other through the active role of partial retirees in training new recruits.

• UAP (Union des Assurances de Paris): in 1994 this company negotiated a very interesting contract covering gradual retirement during the five years before full retirement (which can occur between 60 and 65). Employees of all categories can work half-time for a year with the work load being spread over the year for a salary of 60 per cent, retaining all rights in the firm and social benefits paid as if full-time. Moreover UAP has launched a four-day week for qualified mature employees and professional workers with a view to creating new jobs for qualified younger people seeking employment. The new contract also includes a new work year based on the academic year. The philosophy here is to share employment in a new way since it is believed that further growth will not create enough jobs to reduce significantly the rate of unemployment. In December 1996, this agreement was renewed and its implementation simplified.

• The insurance company AXA releases its workers aged 55 and over (with the requisite number of contribution years and having worked at AXA for fifteen years at least), from regular work and calls on them when they are needed. The idea is to offer this voluntary scheme to employees during the last three or four years before they are entitled to a full pension. The employees receive 65 per cent of their salary, and remain members of the staff. They retain all their welfare benefits and do not have the right to take another job. The company has the option to call them back when the need arises: a sudden increase in the work load, replacement of staff on leave, expertise in a specific area, training or supervision of a new recruit. The employee then works in the same or similar job as before and receives 100 per cent of his salary in proportion to the time he spends back in the company.

In recent years financial incentives provided by the state have been crucial in helping a number of French firms to move from full early retirement to part-time retirement. Firms in all sectors (hospitals, building, manufacturing, services, banking and insurance) have been involved, although few firms as yet have followed UAP's example of implementing a gradual retirement scheme without state subsidies. In our survey, we found that frequently the mind-set of a firm's human resource manager proved a crucial variable for the image that such schemes enjoyed with employees. The most successful firms in this area by far are those that have been running good personnel and age management policies for some years. In such firms gradual retirement has become an established part of the personnel policy package.

1997 saw the conclusion of a number of collective agreements on gradual retirement in the private sector in Germany (Naegele, 1996). Indeed, 1996 legislation provides for incentives which were lacking in previous legislation (Schmähl and Gatter,1994). How successfully the 1997 agreements can be implemented remains to be seen and will undoubtedly prove instructive.

Unpaid work for older workers

Although this chapter deals mainly with paid employment, it is important to provide some account of the current and potential contribution of older workers to community and family life. Traditionally older people were fully involved in family life at home and were useful either in work functions or as minders and carers of children, the sick or the handicapped within the family and neighbourhood. They were also involved in church, cultural or social activities of various kinds. Even if, until very recently, their true importance and value were seldom fully acknowledged, such activities continue very much to be a feature of our modern societies.

More recently, voluntary activities have been developed in every conceivable direction and volunteer and human-service labour force ideas are undergoing conceptual and experimental evaluation. Older people constitute a considerable proportion of volunteers, sometimes a majority. It was shown for example in the USA that 26 per cent of people over 55 were doing some kind of volunteer work (Morris and Caro, 1995). Of these, 29 per cent were helping the sick and disabled, and 38 per cent of those with grand-children were helping as carers on a regular basis. The same study estimates that voluntary work might amount to the equivalent of the work done by 20 million full-time employees. A study across Europe shows that 27 per cent of the population (all ages) volunteer (Murphy, 1995), the proportion of older people at 21 per cent being only marginally less. There are numerous examples of volunteers performing important social tasks for which conventional resources are not available. The effort to reduce hospital costs by using voluntary carers is one example. Implicit in the enormous drive to diminish the cost of hospitalisation is a call for the self-production activities of the family or friends who are expected to take over what within a hospital system is completely monetarised but often, for psychological reasons, less well performed. The same applies to the children of working parents. One either seeks a fully monetarised solution (investment in nurseries) or one mobilises private homes to use their facilities for that purpose (something which is already happening with millions of grandparents), leaving the public authorities to intervene at two levels: verification of the infrastructural adequacy of such 'home' services and the provision of some financial help, encouragement or fiscal incentives for those undertaking such tasks. The total cost of the latter would be much lower than full reliance on the monetarised system. The connections between the monetarised and the non-monetarised economies have today to be better understood and developed, and a number of theoretical initiatives have already incorporated something of this approach (Giarini and Lietdke, 1997). Were it to become the norm for older workers to work part-time, they would, overall, have more time to devote to family, voluntary or semi-monetarised activities of the type described.

Conclusion

While experience in Sweden, Japan and more recently France shows that public policy plays a key part, I would like to mention a few of the company recommendations which need to be integrated into public policies in order to promote work at the end-of-career. I shall also say a few words about the need to redefine 'full' employment.

First, if workers are to remain motivated and productive, continuing training should continue until end-of-career and not terminate at 45 or 50 years. Countries where such company policies exist are in a much stronger position when implementing gradual retirement strategies. In Sweden the extent of training is impressive and there seems to be very little discrimination against older workers. For example, in 1994, 36 per cent of workers aged 55-64 had taken part in training over the previous six months while the average figure for workers overall was 38 per cent (Wadensjö, 1996). In France, especially in bigger companies, the same policy is to be found. In 1992, workers aged 45 and above represented 24 per cent of all workers and 21 per cent of trainees in firms of more than ten employees (Reday-Mulvey in The Geneva Papers, 1994).

The second important variable is pay policy. Seniority-based pay, by raising the wage costs of workers at end-of-career, constitutes a real obstacle to all forms of extension of working life. In several countries, including Japan, there is an observable trend towards reducing the weight of the seniority factor and increasing that of performance. And in France, the insurance industry has shown the way by scrapping its seniority pay system.

Another factor which must be mentioned is pension regulations. It is obvious that final-pay pension schemes will need to be replaced by average-pay schemes (received either throughout a career or during the best 10 or 15 years) in countries like the UK, the Netherlands and the USA where the former are still common. In current French and German schemes for gradual retirement, pension rights are not modified by gradual retirement. In most countries recent legislation postponing the pensionable (for state pensions) age, introducing more flexibility and providing for part-time pensions has clearly been the driving force behind the changes examined in this chapter. The fact that many countries are developing second pillar pensions (occupational and private) is bound to favour gradual retirement, since, once pensions are calculated on a contribution or on average pay and not on final pay basis, many workers will be motivated to increase their pension rights and will not be penalised by part-time work at the end of their career.

Finally, there is a need actively to promote part-time work at end-of-career. The availability of part-time and flexible, but well-protected, employment either inside or outside the main career, is of crucial importance. In some of the companies we visited gradual retirement is seen as an interesting means of promoting skilled part-time work. The advantages of part-time work - it reduces absenteeism and boosts a worker's productivity for example - are now finally starting to be recognised.

Gradual retirement seems to stand at the crossroad of two important issues: the need to extend working life for very sound reasons which have to do with the financing of pensions and the proper management of human resources and skills; and the need to develop well-protected and regular part-time work not only as a transition from full employment to full retirement, but also as a bridge towards a socially proper division of 'full' employment whose redefinition is now long overdue.

Indeed, demographic and financial pressures require that the welfare state define new social and employment policies (Delsen and Reday-Mulvey, 1996). Advances in information technology make it imperative for our societies carefully to re-examine the concept of 'full' employment. While, over the last 25 years, the services sector has unquestionably proved prolific as a creator of jobs, current and foreseeable restructuring in certain branches of the service sector - for example, banks and insurance - is going to result in job losses which will not necessarily be offset by job-creation in other branches, to say nothing of further substantial job losses in the years to come in industry and agriculture (Giarini and Lietdke, 1977). Moreover, in spite of a reduction in the number of young persons entering the labour market, increased productivity and labour substitution by capital will oblige us sooner or later to face the issue of how much work the average citizen will need, will desire, or can expect, to do.

Given the overall volume and new quality of work the service functions offer, new employment policies could be devised around the notions of basic employment. This might mean a shift from 'full-time' employment and exclusion from the labour market of over 30 per cent of potential workers (those receiving social benefits in one form or another: that is the unemployed, early retirees, older people wishing to remain active after the retirement age, young students, mothers with family responsibilities, etc.) to a society where governments and firms are concerned with assuring basic employment for all, that is, part-time work for all citizens of an age and ability to work. This new profile for 'full employment' would be positive for both enterprise (higher productivity, less absenteeism) and the community (less exclusion, more time for community activities) (Reday-Mulvey, 1994). Much less financial support would be needed for the unemployed, the student, the mother, the early retiree and so forth. With such an approach it might be possible to build a society where the average citizen, whether young or old, man or woman, would work at least 1,000 hours per year, more if he or she is able to find extra hours of work, and be integrated socially with free time for other activities, whether economic, social, cultural or artistic. It has actually been calculated that in France the average number of hours worked per year divided by the potentially active population (people from the age of 20 to the age of 65) is around that number. This new full-employment concept is based on the complementarity of equality and efficiency (Delsen, 1995). It constitutes an essential facet of what could be called 'a new welfare deal'.

Social and employment policies, in other words, need to be combined or, at the very least, co-ordinated if we wish in future to promote a society less divided between two extremes: those who work too much and those who are excluded from productive activity of any sort (Chen, 1995).

CHAPTER 8

WORKING OPPORTUNITIES FOR DISABLED PEOPLE

Neil Lunt and Patricia Thornton

Introduction

This chapter explores how the end of full employment and the changing structures of work impact on disabled people. In recent years, the disadvantaged position of disabled people in the labour market has been increasingly recognised, and their experiences of low income, poverty and high unemployment have been well documented. Work has the potential not only to reduce financial disadvantage but also to increase participation in other areas of social life, and so help to combat social exclusion. That enhanced employment opportunities may be a way of reducing benefit dependency has found favour with central government, anxious to reduce social welfare spending and to raise economic productivity. Clearly, disabled people are not a homogenous group and differences in impairment, age, gender and ethnicity may create particular or multiple disadvantages in the job market.

In our chapter, we examine how the changing economic and occupational structure can lead to changes in the employment of disabled people. Non-standard employment is explored in terms of part-time work, very low hours, self-employment, casual jobs, and flexible work patterns. We discuss how these non-standard forms of employment may be uneasy solutions to the problems of low participation. For example, flexible working requires flexibility in other policy areas, notably the structure and delivery of social security benefits. An emerging question is how an in-work 'partial capacity' benefit might supplement the income of disabled people able to do some work but not to earn a full wage. Similarly, flexibility in the provision of community support services, training, transport and housing is required if disabled individuals are to take advantage of new work patterns.

Regardless of the new work opportunities, disabled people still face problems that are deeply and structurally ingrained in society. These include discrimination, assumptions about their reduced productivity, and potentially hostile social and working environments. Such barriers raise questions about the potential of legislation or financial incentives as measures to tackle disadvantage. In the light of such difficulties, we focus on an emerging form of non-standard employment that has particular significance for disabled people - Third sector employment. The United

Kingdom (UK) has seen the growth of an influential disability movement, calling for greater opportunities, participation and control. Organisations of disabled people may act as employers, employing disabled people for the benefit of the disabled community. Such employment challenges traditional assumptions about the rewards of work.

We write from a UK perspective but our discussion also reflects the experience of most western industrialised countries. The issues explored are of relevance to a range of interests, including policy makers and disabled people's organisations.

Disabled people, poverty and participation

Although the post-war years saw a remarkable expansion of welfare state activities, in the UK, as in most western countries, until relatively recently disabled people remained invisible across a range of policy areas, including transport, housing, education, income maintenance and, arguably, employment (Martin and White, 1988; Martin *et al.*, 1989; Berthoud *et al.*, 1993). Public services traditionally were provided in segregated (including residential) settings, contributing to the isolation of disabled people from mainstream social and economic life. Underpinning state activities was a paternalistic and charitable attitude to disabled people as part of the 'deserving poor' (Barnes, 1991) rather than as individuals with either citizens' or consumers' rights.

There is much empirical evidence that disabled people are disadvantaged in terms of employment, income and the incidence of poverty (Martin and White, 1988; Berthoud *et al.*, 1993). According to the Autumn 1996 Labour Force Survey (Office for National Statistics, 1997) fifteen per cent of the working age population in Great Britain has a work-limiting long-term health problem or disability; and at 46 per cent their economic activity rate is just over half of that of the rest of the population, compared to 85 per cent for non-disabled people of working age. Disabled people are much less likely to be in employment: 42 per cent of men and 35 per cent of women are employed, compared with 84 and 73 per cent of men and women with no work-limiting long-term health problem or disability. Unemployment rates among disabled people are more than twice those for non-disabled people at 17 per cent compared with seven per cent; the highest unemployment rates are for people with severe learning difficulties and mental illness, while the lowest are for people with hearing difficulties and diabetes. A similarly unequal employment situation exists across the European Union (European Commission, 1996b) Canada (Roeher Institute, 1993) Australia and the USA (Thornton and Lunt, 1997).

Disability combines with other disadvantages and 'makes a bad situation worse' (Yelin, 1992). The negative relationship between older age and economic activity of disabled people is a universal phenomenon; in the UK, non-disabled males between the ages of 50 and 65 are far more likely to be economically active than their disabled counterparts (Sly *et al.*, 1995). Disabled women also have fewer opportunities on the labour market than disabled men, and USA evidence of higher unemployment among black and Latin-American people with disabilities than among white disabled people (Yelin, 1992) is unlikely to be unique.

Disabled people are more likely to be disadvantaged in terms of pay. Berthoud and colleagues[1] found this was up to £3.50 per hour less than for non-disabled males, although there was no difference between the earnings of disabled and non-disabled women. Thus, disabled people are more likely to find themselves living with low incomes (Berthoud *et al.*, 1993). Disabled and non-disabled people tend to work in a very similar range of jobs, although the former are slightly more likely to be self-employed or in manual occupations. However, disabled people are more likely to be under-employed, doing work for which they are over-qualified, and are often overlooked for promotion (RADAR, 1993).

Work, defined as paid labour, is central to modern life. Work remains the major source of income, and is pivotal to social interaction and self-respect. There is evidence that disabled people wish to work and would do so if adequate and appropriate opportunities were available. In the UK, Prescott-Clarke (1990) found that 22 per cent of 'occupationally handicapped' but economically active men and women 'wanted work', a rate almost twice as high as in the general population.

This last point may appear surprising, perhaps even contradictory. Traditionally it has been assumed that by definition of being 'disabled' members of the group are incapable of work. Such assumptions rest on a misunderstanding of what 'disability' means. The definition of disability rests on an important distinction between ideas of 'impairment' and 'disability' (Oliver, 1990). 'Impairment' can be understood as a functional limitation; for example, a person may have limited hearing, not have the use of their legs, or experience learning difficulties. These impairments are 'neutral' facts. Whether they become a 'disability', a disadvantage for individuals who experience them, is contingent on the economic, social, cultural and political organisation of society. For example, a person with limited hearing has difficulties communicating and is 'disabled' only if we assume that the majority are not proficient in sign-language. It is possible to image a bi-lingual society, where both spoken and sign language are used interchangeably to enable community members to communicate (Christensen and Delgado, 1993). Similarly, wheelchair users may be impaired by limited functioning of the lower limbs or by severe fatigue. But such impairments only become disabilities if the organisation of society makes access difficult for them, through, for example, the design of buildings or the accessibility of transport services. We can conceive of a world physically organised for wheelchair users, where ceiling and door heights are set so low that non-wheelchair users became disadvantaged or 'disabled' (Finkelstein, 1981). According to this perspective, diverse individuals, with different impairments, including physical, sensory, learning and psychiatric impairments, may be disabled in different ways in different circumstances, depending on the barriers they face and the extent to which they are removed.

The barriers presented by employment are amongst the most disabling but, until very recently, the link between employment and disability has not been a priority issue for the disabled people's movement, compared with deinstitutionalisation, personal assistance, transport and housing (Lunt and Thornton, 1994). Governments historically viewed disability as a health and welfare issue, rather than as a labour market concern. In the European tradition, governments promoted a collective responsibility to protect disabled people unable to work, primarily through income protection systems. The increasing costs to the state of long-term sickness and disability benefits, concerns particularly salient in the USA and the Netherlands (Aarts *et al.*, 1996; GAO, 1996; Mashaw *et al.*, 1996), have prompted a new interest in promoting employment opportunities as an alternative to welfare dependency. In the UK, where the number of recipients of the main long term sickness and disability benefit grew by 250 per cent between 1977 and 1995, steps have been taken to increase the financial attractiveness of work by reducing access to and levels of out-of-work benefits and by introducing new incentives to take up work (Thornton *et al.*, 1997). At the same time, the UK has seen increasing criticism by disability income campaigning groups of a benefits system which forces disabled people to declare themselves either 'sick' or 'fit' and which effectively prevents them from taking up work which corresponds to their working capacity (Robbins, 1982; DIG 1996). The notion that disabled people might be capable of some work, though not necessarily a full-time job, accords with the changing structure of the labour market, to which we now turn.

Disabled workers and the new labour market

One major consequence of the restructuring of western industrial economies since the 1970s has been the development of non-standard forms of work in contemporary labour markets. The level of part-time working in the UK is second only to Sweden's and on a par with that in the Netherlands (European Commission, 1996a) and the range of hours worked is among the widest. Most notable are opportunities for very part-time work; in 1990, nearly ten per cent of UK employees worked fewer than 16 hours a week in their main job, nearly twice the European Union average (Coutts and Rowthorn, 1995). The increase in non-standard working among men is mainly attributable to the growth in self-employment which, after rapid expansion during the 1980s, is now stable at 17 per cent of male employment. Overall, the number of people recorded as self-employed in the UK represents about one in eight of all those active in the labour market. Contractual working is replacing permanent job opportunities and in the UK the share of individuals in casual work is around seven per cent of the total (Meadows, 1996). New forms of flexible working include nil-hours contracts, flexi-time and home-based working (including tele-working). In the UK, around 18 per cent of employees usually or occasionally work shifts, and 12 per cent of employees work 'flexitime' (Coutts and Rowthorn, 1995). How far do changes such as these present opportunities for disabled people's participation in the labour market?

Part-time work

It is reasonable to suggest that the expansion of part-time work could enhance opportunities for disabled people. Individuals may prefer part-time hours for a number of household and personal reasons. These include having to devote more time to everyday living tasks such as personal care or child care, or requiring time to attend hospital and rehabilitation appointments. Certain impairments or conditions may cause mental and physical fatigue and be more suited to part-time employment

(Davoud, 1996). However, if disabled people are to benefit from part-time working, jobs obviously must provide adequate income to meet their needs. This will be difficult where jobs offer only limited hours. Combining 'very part-time' opportunities to provide adequate income may be particularly problematic for disabled people. As discussed later, notions of partial capacity are crucial in any discussion of the appropriateness of part-time work.

There is conflicting evidence about disabled people's preferences for full-time or part-time work (Berthoud *et al.*, 1993; Rowlingson and Berthoud, 1996). It is suggested that women are more likely to prefer part-time work (Thomas, 1992) and that disabled men do not perceive part-time employment as a 'real job' (Rowlingson and Berthoud, 1996). Regarding the hours disabled people are able to work, a national survey found that three-quarters of respondents could work a normal full time week, while only seven per cent could not work more than 15 hours (Prescott-Clarke, 1990).

Self-employment

Self-employment offers another pathway to labour market participation. According to the autumn 1996 Labour Force Survey (Office for National Statistics, 1997) disabled people in self-employment constitute 14 per cent of the disabled workforce in the UK, compared to 11 per cent of non-disabled individuals. However, older people are over-represented and there are fewer disabled people who are self-employed aged 16-34 (Floyd, 1995). One explanation may be that individuals in this age group have not acquired the skills, experience, and perhaps capital, necessary for self-employment.

Self-employment has the advantage of offering flexible working patterns which may fit conveniently with other commitments and demands on time. Flexibility and the ability to work around the disability or illness were the main attractions to disabled self-employed people in one study (Thomas, 1992). Home-based self-employment may have particular attractions. As many as 19 per cent of self-employed disabled people say they have to work at home because of their condition (Floyd, 1995). The technological revolution undoubtedly benefits disabled people in professional jobs who may work as easily at home as at a distance. Those who become disabled in later adult life, with established professional experience, are better placed to take advantage of self-employment. However, for long-term disabled people with few qualifications and no employment alternatives, home-based working raises concerns about isolation and deprivation of opportunities for social integration assumed to flow from a shared work-place. Moreover, home-working conditions are unregulated and potentially unsafe.

Self-employed people tend to work longer hours. This is equally true of disabled people who are self-employed. Prescott-Clarke (1990) found that self-employed disabled people worked on average more hours than employed disabled people but a much higher proportion of self-employed disabled people reported that they could not work full hours. Thus, while self-employment offers flexibility in hours worked, the pressures of working on one's own account may limit opportunities for less than full-time work.

Despite the persistent view of self-employed people as affluent and self-sufficient, self-employment embraces the most marginal and insecure forms of work, with wide inequality in income (Eardley and Corden, 1996). As an employment strategy, it is relatively insecure, involving financial risk taking and unpredictable and fluctuating income. It is questionable whether disabled people are prepared to pursue such a route. One study found that few disabled people favoured self-employment, in part because of the risks involved (Thomas, 1992). Limited entitlement to benefits enjoyed by the employed population may be another risk element in self-employment. In addition to exclusion from unemployment benefit and from the earnings-related pension scheme, self-employed people have restricted access to incapacity benefit and are excluded altogether from industrial injury benefit and employment-based schemes for statutory sick pay.

Casual and temporary jobs

The probability of having several jobs in one lifetime has increased. The flexibility required to change jobs may be more problematic for disabled people who may have to organise various support services. Working a series of temporary jobs may pose extra difficulties for disabled persons. If temporary work is too sporadic in nature, there is little possibility to plan wider social supports, such as personal care, transport and childcare arrangements. Income insecurity is particularly problematic for people whose disabilities impose extra costs and who are unlikely to have accumulated savings to draw upon (McLaughlin, 1994).

Finding one job is difficult enough for disabled people, given the practical obstacles and the prevalence of discriminatory attitudes. Securing casual or temporary jobs may require outside help. The UK, as elsewhere, has seen an expansion of specialist placement agencies for disabled people and other groups thought 'hard-to-place' in the labour market. Specialist agencies can offer tailor-made support and links both to employers and to state-supported provision to facilitate access to work. Some temporary work agencies are themselves the employers; thus relieving enterprises of the risks of taking on disabled workers. There may be advantages to disabled people in this new type of opportunity to try out and make a mark in employment (Winkler, 1996).

Changing work patterns may appear to offer considerable opportunities, but only if individuals are able to organise their own patterns of work. The central issue is whether they *do* have such control, or whether the 'casualisation' of labour meets only employer requirements and preferences.

It is difficult to reach general conclusions about whether these labour market trends will be advantageous for disabled people. Clearly, they will have different consequences depending on individual circumstances. However, some groups are likely to be differentially affected by certain trends and we may identify potential 'winners' and 'losers' within the disability community as a whole. Some commentators see opportunities for disabled people in non-standard employment (Oliver, 1995). Self-directed employment, tele-working and flexible working hours may advantage the professional classes (Meadows, 1996). Losers may include individuals with learning difficulties, psychiatric illness, and older workers.

Individuals with learning or psychiatric disabilities have often had services provided through sheltered employment workshops which focused on manufacturing tasks. This type of work is disappearing, with a shift to service and production located outside a workshop environment (Samoy, 1996). Much stress is placed on the development of supported employment initiatives providing real work at market rates of pay within open employment, with (sometimes intensive) levels of 'job coach' support. However, a study by Bass and Drewett (1996) found some individuals working for no pay, and under inadequate - or even dangerous - working conditions. Similarly, individuals who are 'work disabled' and may be in the later years of their working lives may have difficulties taking advantage of new opportunities. Such people are likely to have outmoded skills and may face difficulties in updating skills. There is also evidence that older workers are more disadvantaged in terms of employment, and may experience further discrimination on the basis of age (Sly *et al.* 1995). Clearly for these groups non-standard forms of employment are likely to be uneasy solutions to unemployment and underemployment. The overall shift from industrial to service sector employment, on the other hand, may bring gains to disabled people as whole. The increased visibility of disabled people in service jobs may help change public attitudes to their employability.

Flexible benefits and services

Whether the opportunities resulting from a changing labour market can be utilised depends on access to a flexible social security benefits system. Flexible work patterns - part time work, low hours, casual work - require flexible benefits. Part-time work may be suitable for individuals who do not wish, or are not able, to engage in full-time work. The system of disability benefits, however, is based on self-identification as 'incapable' of work to qualify for higher, longer-term rates of benefit. Some individuals may be disadvantaged if they declare that, under certain circumstances, they could undertake *some* work. This 'incapable'/'capable' distinction forces either/or decisions about attachment to the labour market. In reality there is a continuum of capacity. A flexible benefit system means recognising that individuals may be able to work part-time. Moreover, it should ensure that those who do work part-time or 'very part-time' hours have adequate income to meet their living costs and additional expenses. A flexible benefit would, ideally, also ensure that individuals working a fluctuating number of hours each week receive any additional income necessary to achieve a consistently adequate standard of living.

Temporary work patterns pose substantial difficulties for a system of disability benefits, given likely gaps between short-term contracts. A long wait between pay cheque and benefit receipt creates major problems for household budgeting (Dawes, 1993; McLaughlin, 1994). Such uncertainty may make individuals reluctant to leave the relative 'safety' of a steady stream of benefit income, if there are considerable waits before they can re-qualify for disability benefits. Because disabled people are among the poorest sections of the population, they are unlikely to have savings or other resources they can draw upon in the intervening period (Berthoud *et al.*, 1993). Self-employment raises similar issues. Entrepreneurial activity by its very nature is insecure. Research evidence from the UK suggests many self-employed people have low and often fluctuating incomes (Eardley and Corden, 1996). Thus, there may be times of low revenue and falling business activity when benefits are needed to top-up income. Delay in receiving additional financial support creates budgeting difficulties and may have implications for long-term business viability.

We would argue that there is a pivotal link between labour market activity and the social security system. Whether social security systems act as a bridge or a barrier to employment for disabled people is an issue national policy-makers are increasingly beginning to address (Lunt and Thornton, 1996; Thornton *et al.*, 1997).

A flexible benefits system is a necessary but not sufficient condition for efficient labour market functioning. Further requirements if disabled individuals are to take advantage of flexible labour market conditions include flexible support services such as training provision, transport services, housing opportunities and personal care services.

A labour market that stresses change, adaptability and responsiveness requires a workforce suitably equipped with skills and qualifications. A rapidly changing economy may result in skills quickly becoming outdated, calling for a constant re-skilling and updating in a process of 'life-long learning'. It remains to be seen whether disabled individuals have access to appropriate training that is both flexible and of sufficient quality (Lakey and Simpkins, 1994; Rolfe *et al.*, 1996). Some may require more basic first-order skills, such as numeracy, reading, and even interpersonal skills, before being able to take advantage of more vocational training opportunities (Thomas, 1992).

Disabled people are less likely to be car owners, and more likely to rely on the public transport system (Martin *et al.*, 1989). Such 'transport dependency' raises questions about the accessibility, timing, coverage and affordability of transport services and about the role of the benefit system in providing additional income or grants to cover extra disability-related transport costs. Domestic arrangements, and how they are affected by particular job opportunities, are integral to work decisions. If work decisions require geographical mobility, there must be flexibility in both the rented and public housing sectors. This includes access to appropriately designed and adapted housing (Morris, 1990a). Flexibility in care arrangements and responsiveness to individual requirements is essential; for example, the requirement to start work at nine o'clock cannot be met if care services are available only at midday.

Decisions about labour market participation and whether to take particular jobs are not reducible to purely financial considerations. The choice whether to take a new job, or whether to increase hours, is a holistic decision which includes financial incentives and disincentives, as well as other factors (Dawes, 1993; McLaughlin, 1994; Lunt and Thornton, 1996). The final decision may involve other service support considerations and the views of household members.

Barriers to effective participation

Flexible benefit and service delivery systems for disabled people are important considerations. However, even when these are in place there still remain structural factors and barriers to effective participation.

Discrimination against disabled people is an important factor and may be considered in three forms: direct, indirect and systemic. Direct discrimination in its most obvious form is prejudice, refusing to employ a disabled person, for example, simply because of attitudes to disability. Direct discrimination by employers was evidenced by two research studies which showed that able-bodied people making written applications for certain jobs were one and a half times more likely than disabled applicants to receive positive responses (Graham *et al.*, 1990). Indirect discrimination occurs when a rule or policy that looks fair on the surface impacts unevenly on certain groups. For example, insisting that all applicants for office work hold a driving licence, regardless of the essential function of that job, indirectly discriminates against disabled people as the latter are more likely to have impairments that make holding a licence more difficult or more expensive. Systemic discrimination occurs when practices and policies of an institution or society operate against the interests of a specific group. Thus, societal practices are organised on the basis of a non-disabled person being the norm.

The UK Government has sought to legislate against forms of discrimination, in employment and in the provision of goods, services and facilities, through the 1995 Disability Discrimination Act. These anti-discriminatory measures are likely to be most valuable for specific groups of disabled people, notably those already qualified to compete for the job in question (Thornton and Lunt, 1995). It is too early to evaluate the effectiveness of the Disability Discrimination Act in combatting labour market discrimination. Employment discrimination complaints filed under the Americans with Disabilities Act suggest that anti-discrimination legislation may be more effective in delaying job exit where a health condition starts to affect job performance (over half of the complaints have related to unfair discharge from a job) than in increasing recruitment of disabled people (ten per cent have related to unfair hiring practices).

The second major structural constraint concerns the notion of reduced productivity. How can the labour market and employment policy take account of some disabled people being less productive than their able-bodied counterparts? Segregated employment for disabled people increasingly is considered to be unacceptable and antithetical to notions of integration, and its costs compare unfavourably with supported placements in open employment. Groups previously excluded from mainstream employment, notably people with learning difficulties are now demanding the opportunity for real jobs. But where should the responsibility lie? The UK response, following long-standing practice in several European countries, has been to introduce subsidies to the wages of less productive disabled people entering mainstream employment who would otherwise have been directed to sheltered employment. In this way employers are relieved of the 'burden' of their employment. Thus, while many disabled people aspire to non-discriminatory employment where employers are required to make accommodations to ensure they are able to compete and contribute on equal terms with non-disabled people, wage-subsidised disabled employees' 'problems' are solved through financial intervention on the part of the state. Subsidised employment may offer opportunities for those with reduced productivity but at the cost of limited employment rights.

Third sector employment and disabled people

In several countries, including the UK, new forms of employment for disabled people are beginning to emerge in response to the limited choice between segregated and subsidised employment and the difficulties in accessing mainstream employment. Some of these new forms of employment are promoted by governments and their agencies but more commonly they stem from non-governmental movements, some involving disabled people themselves. The last twenty years have seen the growth of the disability movement, nationally and internationally. Across a number of countries the 'disability movement' has emerged as a major 'new social movement'.

A critical focus of the disability movement has been the attempt to exert control over organisations that purport to act as the voice and representative of disabled people. Consequently, an important shift has occurred away from disability organisations that are run by able-bodied people (organisations 'for' disabled people), to organisations run and controlled by disabled people themselves (organisations 'of' disabled people). Organisations of disabled people are less concerned with fund-raising and instead emphasise direct action, specialist service provision, and pressure group activity. Thus, the disability movement has been concerned to raise consciousness, in the first priority among its own members. Within the grass-roots development of the disability movement, some groups have had a single-issue focus, while others have adopted a wider role bringing a range of disability interests together in 'campaigning coalitions'.

The growing strength and maturity of the disability movement in the UK has led to a rethinking of the traditional approaches to employment and adaptation of a perspective known as the 'Third sector'. In the emerging Third sector disabled people's organisations are frequently acting as employers providing positions and roles that may be paid or unpaid. Examples of Third sector provision includes advice services, counselling services and direct service provision, as well as the arts and specialist media services. The Third sector focuses on forms of self-help and consciousness-raising, and paid work is only one of the available options.

Prominent Third sector activity among disabled people in the UK has been the campaign for anti-discrimination legislation. The campaign activity came under the slogan of Rights Now, an umbrella for a number of disability groups, organisations and other allies, including the trades union movement in the form of the TUC. It involved information, media campaigning, lobbying and demonstration and helped bring about the passage of the 1995 Disability Discrimination Act. The Disability Information Advice Line (DIAL) is a telephone help-line and advice service, offering assistance on disability related matters, provided by volunteers on a regional basis. Groups have also been involved in raising the profile of disability arts and culture, often in reaction to the stereotypical views of advertising and the media (for an excellent account of some of these developments see Hevey, 1992). Further examples include advocacy organisations and user-controlled personal assistance schemes.

There is a crucial distinction between this 'Third sector' growth and work that has traditionally understood as 'voluntary work'. The latter typically is offered by organisations for disabled people, in the tradition of charitable, benevolent activity. Volunteers give their time freely to benefit those they perceive to be disadvantaged compared with themselves. The Third sector, however, provides services for its constituent group, and is organised and controlled by its own disabled members. The 'Third sector' also differs totally from the notion of 'therapeutic' work. The UK social security system allows disabled people to undertake a small amount of work without effects on benefit entitlement. This work must be in some form therapeutic to the individual and the case confirmed by a medical practitioner. Commentators suggest that disabled people perceive therapeutic work as 'patronising' and not the same as 'real' work (DIG, 1996).

Most significantly, the Third sector differs from many traditional notions of work because it is conceived as outside the capitalist system and is akin to co-operative modes of organisation well established in other spheres. Therefore, Third sector employment effectively broadens the idea of what constitutes employment and its production works against market and dominant forms of 'oppressive' social relations, aiming to empower those that come into contact with it. Yet, at the same time, it is insecure. Projects and schemes may be based on grant-aided funding which is insecure in nature and often dependent on political support. Income may be inadequate and continued benefit receipt may be put at risk because of restrictions on 'voluntary work' which may be undertaken.

Conclusion

This chapter has explored how flexible labour market conditions may provide opportunities for *certain* disabled people, but has argued that such an outcome is contingent upon disabled people having access to flexible benefits and support services. Moreover, structural barriers including discriminatory practices require careful attention if disabled people are not to remain disadvantaged in accessing the labour market. Any gains that disabled people make from a changed labour market in any case may be short-lived. If non-standard opportunities, particularly casual and part-time work, are classed as appropriate for disabled people, these are exactly the jobs that will disappear when the economy contracts. Evidence from the USA indicates that '...persons with disabilities have become one of the principle venues for accommodating retrenchment, either from complete to partial employment or from any employment to none' (Yelin and Katz, 1994; 602). Disabled people remain most vulnerable to labour market contraction in non-standard employment just as in standard employment. The growing number of employment alternatives which have developed from disabled people's organisations, where disabled people themselves take control, offer opportunities to those who wish to identify with the disabled people's movement and to join the struggle against oppression. But action on the outside may bring few changes to the mainstream experience of the world of work.

Notes

[1] Using Family Expenditure Survey/Office of Population Consensus and Surveys Models of gross earnings.

CHAPTER 9

REDUCING THE BURDEN OF WORK ON WOMEN?

Rachel Woodward

Introduction

How might women benefit from a redistribution of paid employment and unpaid work? This, in some ways, is an impossible question to address; as many studies of women's experiences within and outside the labour market tell us, the diversity and heterogeneity of these experiences precludes any simple answer. But it is also an extremely pertinent question for many different groups of women, across a range of circumstances. Surely a common experience for most working women is negotiation around the issues associated with combining paid employment with unpaid domestic work.

This chapter is about the negotiation between paid and unpaid work, and as its title suggests, discusses the possibilities for the reduction of the burden of work on women in advanced capitalist economies. It does this in two stages. First, it takes a critical look at the notion of women's double burden, examining some of the evidence for it using both British and international examples, and questions what this double burden might mean within a wider temporal context. Second, the chapter goes on to examine the strategies for the reduction of the double burden deployed by some women in some households. These include the use of waged domestic labour, the adoption of greater responsibility for domestic tasks by men and the potential for change through the adoption of more flexible working practices. The chapter concludes by commenting on the main policy and theoretical issues raised by this discussion.

Women's double burden?

We often speak of the combination of paid and unpaid work as a 'double burden', a 'double day', a 'second shift'. Why? Hochschild with Machung (1989) offer one explanation:

> It was a woman who first proposed to me the metaphor, borrowed from industrial life, of the 'second shift'. She strongly resisted the *idea* that homemaking was a 'shift'. Her family was her life and she didn't want it reduced to a job. But as she put it, 'You're on duty at work. You come home, and you're on duty. Then you go back to work and you're on duty.' After eight hours of adjusting insurance claims, she came home to put on the rice for dinner, care for her children, and wash laundry. Despite herself her home life *felt* like a second shift. That was the real story and that was the real problem. (Hochschild with Machung 1989, pp. 6-7, emphases in original)

It is a burden because a source of enjoyment and pleasure - home and family life - can be hard physical and emotional work, especially when combined with paid employment. Other metaphors abound. Many of us, for example, talk of 'juggling' to describe day-to-day lives revolving around reconciliating the demands of paid and unpaid work. A daily schedule and strategy becomes codified within discourses describing women's work which emphasise the trickiness of combining the two and the skills required to achieve success (and satisfaction) in both. The juggling metaphor is interesting, pointing to the desire to create an illusion of efficient management of the (seemingly) impossible. This of course is not just an issue for women combining paid and unpaid work; as Spencer and Taylor (1994) illustrate, women working full-time within the home also express frustration about coping with competing and conflicting demands. But given long-term trends for increased female labour market participation, this chapter will concentrate on the issues for women bearing the double burden of paid employment and unpaid domestic work.

The end of full employment, at face value at least, signals the possibility for a more equitable division of paid and unpaid work between men and women, as Chapter 4 has argued in some depth. The same processes of economic restructuring that brought the decline of traditional patterns of full male employment, experienced in most advanced capitalist economies in the post-war period, have also brought increased labour market opportunities for women in the 1980s and 1990s. Of course, there is no causal link between the two; it's not that women have been stealing men's jobs. Rather, processes of economic restructuring, operating within a gendered labour market, have resulted in an increase in employment opportunities for women. For example, the 1961 British Census of Population gives an economic activity rate of 47 per cent for women aged between 15 and 69, rising to 71 per cent in 1991 for women in the same age group (Hakim 1993). In turn, the increasing proportion of working women is recognised as a critical factor precipitating broader social and cultural changes. However, there is much debate as to whether this rise in working women has been matched by social and cultural shifts in the organisation of the household, particularly with regard to the redistribution of unpaid work between men and women. Put simply, has women's increased participation in paid work been matched by a decrease in unpaid work - usually taken to mean domestic work, such as housework, childcare and eldercare - or is the double burden still ever-present?

Gershuny *et al* (1994) trace the origins of the study of women's double burden back to a number of studies during the 1970s. They note how studies such as those of

Meissner *et al* (1975) of the time budgets of working Canadian couples, Young and Willmott's (1973) study of time budgets amongst English couples, and Oakley's (1974) study of housework and unpaid domestic labour all provide evidence to support the argument that increasing rates of female participation in paid work have resulted in a dual burden. Married women in employment, it is argued, bear a disproportionate 'double burden' of paid and unpaid work. Following entry into the labour force, the reduction in married women's proportion of household domestic work is insufficient to compensate for their increase in paid work.

Most commentators are wary of attributing the origins of the 'double burden' to any single cause, a reflection of the complexity of this issue. Indeed, most would point to cultural, social and economic factors in combination as marking the origins of the issue. These would include changing labour market structures in advanced capitalist economies, combined with social shifts associated with women's increasing demands for economic independence. Also significant is the fact that the identification of the dual burden is a late 20th century phenomenon. The problem may well be a long-standing issue for women engaged in the labour market (albeit nuanced according to class position). It is the political agenda of so-called Second Wave feminism, demanding economic as well as domestic rights for women that has named the issue as a problem. This is reflected in both academic analyses, with (for example) socialist feminists identifying the centrality of relations between productive and reproductive spheres to analyses of political economy, and in political analyses such as that provided by the Wages for Housework campaign (a campaign established in Britain in the early 1980s which also argued for the value of women's unpaid and hidden domestic labour to be taken into account in assessments of Gross Domestic Product). And of course, the personal is political; Ann Oakley herself has talked of her own experience of domestic labour as a strong influence on her decision to examine housework and unpaid domestic labour.

One method for examining the nature of the double burden for women has been to look at the ways in which entry into the labour force impacts upon the amount of unpaid domestic work undertaken by men and women in households. For example, the 1991 British Social Attitudes Survey, an annual survey of around 3,000 respondents, asked couples which partner was 'mainly responsible for domestic duties' (i. e. housework). Overall, in 75 per cent of cases, the woman was mainly responsible for domestic chores. Where both the man and woman worked full-time, still about two-thirds (67 per cent) of women said they took the main responsibility. Where women worked part-time and men full-time, 83 per cent of respondents said that the woman was mainly responsible for household domestic duties, a figure not far removed from the 89 per cent of full-time homemaker women who were married to a man working full-time and who were not themselves engaged in paid work outside the home (Kiernan, 1992).

These figures raise two points. The first is a blunt one: the broad picture presented here is that women bear greater responsibility for domestic duties than men. This burden takes on a further dimension, as I discuss below, when we include the division of labour over childcare and all the associated work that this involves, within households with children. The second point is that this greater degree of responsibility is not fully explained by women's lower levels of engagement in the waged labour force. There appears to be an uneven relationship between entry into the paid labour force and any reduction in domestic unpaid work. The majority of women working full-time still bore responsibility for most domestic work, and most women working part-time bore almost as much responsibility for domestic work as full-time homemakers.

A distinctive feature of the British labour market over the past thirty years has been the huge expansion of women working part-time. There is much debate as to whether this rise reflects women's free choice, in order to combine paid and unpaid work, or whether it reflects structural changes within the labour market, whereby part-time work becomes the only kind of work available (see, for example, Hakim 1995; Ginn *et al* 1996; Bruegel 1996; Hakim 1996a) and I return to this below. As studies such as that by Spencer and Taylor (1994) demonstrate, a number of factors influence a woman's decision to undertake part-time work, including responsibility for domestic duties. The relationship between levels of paid and unpaid work is thus both uneven and highly complex. In summary, commentaries on this topic often make explicit the connections and (often complex) relationships between paid employment outside the household and unpaid work (usually) within it. They also stress the gendered nature of these relationships.

Who will mind the baby? As with housework, there is overwhelming evidence that women still bear primary responsibility for childcare within the household. As Kim England (1996) argues with reference to North America, despite trends indicating a more equitable division of labour within some households, childcare and responsibility for childcare remain women's work. As with allocations of time for housework, the quantification of time spent on childcare is both difficult and contentious. The figures given below are indicative. First, we can compare the differences between men and women in the amount of childcare they do. For example, a study conducted by Brannen and Moss (1991) of 60 couples where both partners worked full-time after the birth of their first child found that the women spent on average around 25 hours per week in sole charge of the child, compared with their partners' 6 hours per week. Qualitative material from the study cited above by Spencer and Taylor (1994) indicates that most mothers in the study felt that 'it always comes back to the mother'

> It's always been me that's left to make the arrangements. All the jobs I've done, it's always been me. You know, sorted out where they're going to go of a morning, or taxi-ing them around. He'll take them off on a Sunday morning to give me a bit of time, but that's about all (quoted in Spencer and Taylor 1994; 25)

Second, we can compare the experiences of women working for different periods of time outside the home. Figures calculated by Hakim (1996b) on the basis of research reported by Horrell (1994) indicate that full-time homemakers spend 19 hours per week on childcare activities, compared with 7 hours per week for part-time workers and 1 hour per week for those working full-time. The greater a woman's time spent in paid employment, the lower the amount of time she and her partner allocate to childcare. As Horrell points out, this is an obvious reflection of the fact that women working full-time tend, as a group, to have fewer, older children.

The experience of lone parents, the majority of whom are mothers, is also important here. Lone parents in paid employment usually bear responsibility for the vast majority of household domestic chores and for childcare. Spencer and Taylor's study notes how exhaustion is a common problem:

> My main memories of that period are of being permanently tired, never having the energy to do anything other than work, take care of the children, eat and—sometimes if I was lucky—sleep. (quoted in Spencer and Taylor 1994; 27)

As Hakim (1996b) suggests, the decline in childcare as a major activity across women's lives (as fewer women have fewer children) has to some extent been replaced by eldercare and other informal care of sick and disabled relatives, as more of us live longer into frail old age and as policy changes promote the household and community as the locus for that care. On the basis of evidence presented by Hakim from the 1985 and 1990/91 General Household Surveys and 1991 British Household Panel Survey, it appears that, in contrast to domestic work and childcare, men and women are equally likely to care for a sick, disabled or elderly person living with them or in another household. About 4 per cent of both men and women surveyed were likely to spend over 20 hours per week in caring activity. There are only marginal differences between men and women in terms of the caring activities they undertake, particularly amongst older age groups (Brannen *at al* 1994).

There is some evidence for change in these patterns of the domestic division of labour over time; the 1987 British Social Attitudes survey found that in households where both partners worked full-time, 72 per cent of women were mainly responsible for domestic duties, compared with the 67 per cent in 1991, noted above (Kiernan 1992). And as Spencer and Taylor (1994) indicate in their more qualitative analysis of the range of key issues surrounding participation in the labour market for women, a more equal sharing of domestic chores was perceived to be taking place. It is also informative to place Britain within an international context. As Gershuny *et al* (1994) note, the British evidence for a gradual-reduction-but-still-present double burden of work for women fits well within a multinational comparative context as part of a 'regular, indeed rather dramatic, historical trend' (p. 182). There is much evidence to suggest convergence between men and women in terms of time devoted to various types of work. For example, studies of Norwegian data for 1971-80, for the US for 1965-85, and for Finland all indicate that men are doing more unpaid work and less paid work, whilst women are doing less unpaid work and more paid work.

Jonathan Gershuny and his colleagues have also established a multinational longitudinal comparative data file giving information on household time budgets for eight countries — Canada, France, Netherlands, Norway, UK, USA, Hungary and Finland. The data set suggests a regular, steady and substantial growth in men's proportional contribution to unpaid work, from about a quarter in the mid-1960s, to 30 per cent in the 1970s and 40 per cent in the 1980s. This data also suggests that men's proportion of total work is decreasing as women's proportion increases, but although this process of adaptation is underway, 'compensation is not complete, the women's paid work increases faster than the men's substitution of unpaid for paid work' (Gershuny *et al,* 1994; 185). It is worth emphasising that quite marked differences can exist between countries. Vaiou (1996), for example, discussing women's work and everyday life in southern Europe emphasises that caring and domestic labour in southern Europe remain seen as 'women's work'. Duncan, in a discussion of men and women's lives and work in Sweden, highlights how men have become more home-centred, not so much through free choice as through compulsion, forced by the great expansion in two-earner households over the past thirty years (Duncan, 1994 after Acker *et al,* 1992).

The slow but long-standing shift in the domestic division of labour calls for interpretation. Again, it is combinations of factors (economic, political, social, cultural) that explain both the change and its pace. For example, many groups of women have been granted greater levels of economic power, through their engagement with paid employment outside the home. It is possible that this economic power is brought to bear within the household, particular in terms of negotiation over responsibilities for domestic work. But as Jane Wheelock shows in her research into changing divisions of labour in households hit by male unemployment (Wheelock, 1990) the extent of this negotiation is limited. This suggests that cultural and social factors are significant in determining who cleans the carpet and cooks the dinner. Furthermore, any analysis of broad trends such as the changing domestic division of labour must, of necessity, be open to multiple interpretations. For example, much of the increase in female participation in the labour market is accounted for by the high proportion of women who work part-time. However, there is no consensus at all in the literature (and indeed very heated debate) as to whether part-time work is a free choice made by women, an outcome reflecting employer preference, or a solution found by women in response to the demands of combining paid and unpaid domestic work.

We can speculate, of course, that in theory the end of full employment should ease women's double burden over time through a redistribution of work, both paid and unpaid between all those who need it. Gershuny *et al* (1994) address this question by looking at the meaning of the 'double burden' within a wider temporal context. They do this through an analysis of data collected as part of the Social Change and Economic Life Initiative, a major research project conducted between 1985 and 1990 by an interdisciplinary social science team which sought to examine the relationships between labour market change and social change in Britain. Around 6,000 questionnaires and 1,500 interviews were conducted with respondents in six localities, providing a large and complex data set, one analysis of which addressed the 'double burden' thesis. Gershuny *et al* used this survey data plus interview material and information from diaries of weekly activities to explore the changing division of domestic labour within a broader longitudinal context. They argue that domestic practice may change very gradually over an extended period following a woman household members' entry to paid work. There is evidence that this produces increasing equalities in terms of the division of domestic labour over time, but that this change is slow, taking place over generations. They use these findings to argue for a process of 'lagged adaptation'. This they see as a process by which the domestic division of labour 'does indeed, albeit over an extended period, adapt to (or, since these household practices in turn have employment consequences, with) changing employment patterns' (Gershuny *et al* 1994; 152).

A key point about the idea of lagged adaptation is that it emphasises the importance of cultural factors in explanations of changing domestic divisions of labour. Change happens; men do assume greater levels of responsibility for domestic work, but they are slow to do so. Indeed, the Gershuny's evidence showed change over generations, not just in the space of a few years. There is no evidence of immediate changes in the domestic division of labour as a result of women's increased labour market participation. I would argue that this demonstrates how entrenched cultural attitudes towards gender roles can be. The notion of male breadwinner and female homemaker is still highly potent as an ideology of gender roles, even if the reality of increased female employment challenges it. Whilst social expectations of the female homemaker role have changed in the post-war period to include some participation in the labour market (often justified in terms of a 'top-up' wage to achieve higher consumption levels), more radical changes in assumptions about male domestic roles have still to take place. The power of ideologies of masculinity should not be under-estimated. I return to this issue below.

To conclude this first section, the (brief) examination of secondary sources appears to indicate the following: first, that many women in paid employment carry a double burden of work through responsibility for unpaid work within the home. Second, there is some evidence for a slight movement towards equity in the division of domestic labour between men and women. Third, there is no simple relationship between changes in paid and unpaid work; a rise in female participation in the labour market has not been matched with an equal rise in male participation in domestic work. With these three points in mind, I now go on to examine some of the strategies deployed by some women and households for a reduction in this double burden.

Strategies for reducing the double burden

The employment of waged domestic labour

As discussed above, there is some evidence to indicate a gradual movement towards a more equitable division of domestic labour within households where both partners work. This movement is slow, and as Gershuny *et al* imply, parity might only be achieved over a long time scale. One strategy or solution deployed by many households whilst they wait for equality is the employment of waged domestic labour. A study by Nicky Gregson and Michelle Lowe (1993) of the employment of nannies and cleaners in dual-earner households in two labour markets in England (Newcastle upon Tyne in the north east and Reading in the south east) explored the workings and theoretical consequences of this strategy.

Gregson and Lowe estimate that around one third of all dual earner households where both partners worked full-time employ some kind of waged domestic labour. At face value, the strategy is simple. Someone is employed to do the work household members don't have time to do. However, placed within the context of the resurgence of waged domestic labour in the 1980s in Britain, Gregson and Lowe suggest that the rise in the numbers of women working full-time is insufficient as an explanation for the renegotiation of the domestic division of labour that they observe taking place. Certainly, they find evidence that cleaners are employed in order to reduce the burden of domestic work on women working outside the home, and nannies in order to facilitate the return to work for women with children. But nannies and cleaners are not solely employed because women simply don't have the time to do this work. Rather, Gregson and Lowe emphasise the wider socio-economic and cultural context in which this renegotiation of domestic labour is taking place. They suggest that changes in the structure of the labour market, in particular the rise of the so-called service class (i. e. personnel engaged in the production of higher-order services), produce new challenges for traditional arrangements for social reproduction within households. In particular, changing definitions of leisure time, which they see as specific to the service class, work to exclude some forms of domestic labour from this new definition of leisure.

The rise in waged domestic labour reflects not so much a crisis in terms of domestic work being done, so much as a redefinition of what forms of domestic work members of a household are willing to perform. Furthermore, this is 'not simply a potential conflict between doing *either* household cleaning and ironing *or* a more pleasurable something else. *It is also a potential conflict between partners over who is doing what sort of activity and when.*' (Gregson and Lowe, 1993; 95, emphases in original). In short, this is a trend to transfer some forms of household work to non-household members, rather than a growth of sharing domestic work between partners within a household. They note also how couples with a more 'traditional' (i. e. inequitable) division of labour within the household are more likely to employ domestic labour, particularly cleaners. Also, women are still more likely to keep a managerial role through maintaining overall responsibility for ensuring that domestic work gets done; it is generally women who employ other women.

Getting men to take responsibility

The employment of waged domestic labour can remove some of the dual burden of work from the shoulders of some women[1] . Yet as Gregson and Lowe point out, this strategy does not encourage men to take on more responsibility for domestic labour themselves. As Spencer and Taylor (1994) point out in their study of issues for women in terms of their labour market participation, a supportive partner was perceived as essential in enabling women to cope with competing and conflicting demands imposed through combining paid and unpaid work. In practice, however, many women they interviewed stressed that the onus for change lay with women; men would rarely take on further domestic responsibilities of their own accord, but only if pressed or asked:

> Domestically he's a bit sort of slow on the up-take. You know he can pass a sink piled with washing up, sort of five times a day, and when you ask 'Why didn't you do it?' he'll say 'I didn't even know it was

> there'. But he will do it if he's asked, but it's such a pain having to ask all the time. (quoted in Spencer and Taylor, 1994; 24)

The extent to which men do take on extra domestic responsibilities is therefore a pertinent question here.

Jane Wheelock's (1990) study of the domestic division of labour in households hit by male unemployment provides some information on this. Conducted amongst households in Sunderland in the north east of England, the study takes issue with the central question behind this chapter: does the end of full-time male employment provide opportunities for a redistribution of work within the household? The study examined changes in the division of domestic labour in working class households where a previously employed male partner was unemployed and the woman worked full-time or part-time. Using a matrix of household tasks, defined as major and minor, regular and irregular, the study found great variations between households in terms of the redistribution of domestic work.

Two of Wheelock's findings are particularly important here. The first is that - perhaps unsurprisingly - some domestic tasks within households remain highly gendered. When categorisations on the basis of labour time are combined with those of gender, it appears that a significant number of major regular tasks are also strongly gender segregated. Women, though working, still tended to take responsibility for major regular domestic tasks such as washing, ironing and what they termed 'proper' cleaning. Tasks such as vacuuming, cooking and childcare were more likely to be shared between couples. The second point here is that there is some evidence for the adoption of household work strategies which conflict with traditional gender roles. Men's undertaking of housework is directly related to women's employment: the more economic power that a woman has in a household, the more help she is likely to get from a household partner. Men, it appears, are making a pragmatic response to an overall family work situation, a finding supported by Gershuny *et al*'s conclusions outlined above.

Yet we shouldn't get over-enthusiastic about the redistributive consequences for domestic work of women's increased economic power. Wheelock also emphasises the practical basis to this shift; practical circumstances lead to change rather than shifts in abstract attitudes to roles. Two observations follow from this. The first relates to the question as to what happens to the gender division of domestic labour if and when men return to employment. A lack of research on this precludes any definitive statement here, but an implication of Wheelock's findings on the practical basis to shifts in the domestic division of labour is possibly a reversal to more traditional patterns of work. The second point concerns abstract attitudes to gender roles. Ideologies about gender identities underlie the domestic division of labour, and as Wheelock emphasises, these are very slow to change. Attitudes to gender roles are rooted firmly in powerful ideologies about gender identities into which we are socialised from infancy. For this reason, it is difficult to be prescriptive (and optimistic) about how a more equitable division of labour within the household might be achieved within more households, at least in the immediate future. Getting men to take responsibility is a long-term answer, but one that in practice is either difficult to achieve, or achievable only within the context of economic hardship for households through unemployment.

Flexible working arrangements as a strategy

As I noted above, there is much debate about the use of part-time employment by women, particularly as to whether this too is a pragmatic choice in response to an overall family work situation. The issue of part-time work is raised again here because it is part of a wider question about flexible working practices as a strategy or solution to the double burden. One has to be careful when talking about 'flexibility'. There are huge debates as to its theoretical meaning and practical definition, and Chapter 4 examines this in some detail. To clarify, I define the term 'flexible working practices' broadly, to mean working practices that in any way differ from the (now rather out-dated) model of an eight hour 9am to 5pm Monday to Friday working pattern.

The debate about the impact of flexible working patterns on the opportunities for women to engage in the labour market is a complex one. Some see the adoption of such working practices as enabling for groups of people (particularly women), who have hitherto been unable to compete in the labour market, to undertake paid work outside the home. Others view the types of jobs most usually associated with flexible working practices as locking certain groups of employees (particularly women) into new unequal divisions of labour. For example, the previous conservative British government, has presented flexible working arrangements as a facility enabling people (not just women) to engage in paid work:

> Flexible working arrangements are providing increasing opportunities for people to find patterns of work which fit in with their family and domestic circumstances. People are increasingly turning to part-time work and self-employment because it suits them and gives greater control over their working lives. (Employment Department, 1992; 10)

For many women, whilst not a solution to the 'double day', flexible working does at least provide the means to assist, help or ease the fit between the paid and unpaid work (Brannen *et al,* 1994). It may not reduce the burden, but it makes the load a little more bearable. For example, Spencer and Taylor (1994) note how the choice for women they interviewed as to whether to enter the labour market, and their opportunities within it was shaped by their perception of whether flexible working hours and practices were available, which might allow them to continue with their domestic responsibilities.

Evidence from the 1994 British Social Attitudes survey appears to support this. Thomson (1995), drawing on this data, notes the apparent unmet demand for flexible working arrangements that might ease the fit between paid and unpaid work. These include the availability of part-time working, time off to care for sick children, flexible hours, paternity leave, career breaks, job-sharing schemes, the ability to work from home, term-time contracts, workplace nurseries, school holiday care and allowances towards the costs of childcare. Furthermore in questions concerning the unmet demand for flexible working arrangements amongst employees, the survey found that 84 per cent of mothers had access to part-time work, even though they may not use this facility. Thomson (1995) suggests that this indicates a strong propensity among mothers to congregate in occupations where part-time working is at least an option.

Some analysts are critical of the wider trends that this congregation implies. McDowell (1991), for example, argues that the 'taste' many women have for part-time working reflects more accurately the preferences of employers. Furthermore, the expansion of part-time working opportunities for women over the past two decades has created new divisions across employment categories and redefined the status of many workers. She argues that these changes have quite profound consequences for the creation of new gender identities through work. Jobs that can be done part-time often become identified with lower status and lower skill levels.

Mindful of the criticisms of flexible working practices that have been voiced by researchers, employers and (often) union leaders, Hewitt (1993) challenges the idea that flexible working is necessarily negative in terms of its impact on the modes of labour organisation. She argues for employment policy reforms that would enhance the status of those using flexible working practices. For example, the reduced status often associated with part-time working could be ameliorated through the extension of full employment rights to part-time workers. This and other 'sweeping' reforms of employment and social security law to enable greater use of flexible working practices, would, she argues, go some way towards reducing the unequal distribution of paid and unpaid work between men and women in households.

Concluding comments

The first point to make in conclusion is that women's dual burden will be reduced only through a combination of strategies. In this chapter I have discussed market, cultural and policy-led strategies. There are many more, they are not used in isolation, and nor do they remain static over time. Furthermore, some strategies require greater challenges to the *status quo* than others. For example, Hewitt (1993) suggests that legislation on working hours might form part of a strategy for promoting the status of part-time workers. Given the British government's record of resistance to the implementation of limited European Union legislation on working hours, such changes seem a remote possibility. Whilst there may be academic criticism of the strategies used by many women and their wider implications, these strategies, it should be remembered, are pragmatic responses to often difficult situations.

The second point to make is a conceptual one. The gradual redistribution of paid and unpaid work between men and women is taking place within a wider context of webs of social relations which structure social life; this redistribution cannot be seen in isolation from these webs of social relations. Women and men as a group may be moving towards equality in terms of the amount of time they spend on paid and unpaid work, but there is still an issue of the differentials between men and women in terms of pay, employment conditions and the social status this employment confers. The burden of work may be lessened, but inequalities persist in other ways. Furthermore, there is an argument that the (endless) process of restructuring of class and gender relations in turn produces new social divisions between groups of women, often conceptualised as a process of social polarisation. (Humphries and Rubery, 1992). The polarisation thesis can be criticised for the simplification it imposes on changing patterns of social divisions, but it reminds us that vast differences exist between groups of women in terms of their relationships to the labour market and domestic work. Although we can talk about reducing the burden of work on women, we should remember that the burden and reduction affect different groups in profoundly different ways. Even the national childcare strategy proposed by the British Labour government does not avoid the danger of reinforcing polarisation between groups of women as better paid women employ more poorly paid women (and lone parents) to look after their children

Notes

[1] In particular, those women who are well enough paid to be able to employ others.

PART III

BLUEPRINTS FOR ACTION

CHAPTER 10

THE US MODEL: THE WAGES OF INEQUALITY

Jared Bernstein, Lawrence Mishel and John Schmitt

Mass unemployment has become the central economic and social problem facing most European nations in the 1900s. The rise in joblessness is all the more frustrating because it follows a decade of already elevated unemployment rates. Meanwhile, the United States has an unemployment rate in the mid-1990s that is, if anything, slightly lower than rates that prevailed in the 1970s.

The conventional wisdom, best summarized in the Organisation for Economic Cooperation and Development's *Job Study* (OECD, 1994a), suggests that high unemployment in Europe and rising inequality in the United States are related. According to this view, advanced capitalist countries experienced a common shock at the end of the 1970s, one usually described as either a sudden acceleration in the pace of technological progress or as a discrete increase in the openness of world trade. This shock required reductions in the relative wages of 'less-skilled'[1] workers either because new technology was 'biased' against them or because intensified international competition, particularly from low-wage countries, disproportionately affected the less-skilled. Previously successful European labour-market institutions, the thinking goes, could not cope well in the new environment. Generous social insurance systems and related employee and employer taxes, large hiring and firing costs, high minimum wages, strong public and private sector unions, and other institutional features of European labour markets prevented the relative wages of less-skilled workers from falling, resulting in rocketing unemployment. The US labour market, however, is supposed to have dealt much more effectively with the shock. The much freer workings of the market economy allowed the relative wages of less-skilled workers to fall considerably, ensuring much higher rates of job creation, especially for those at the bottom.

This diagnosis has led to a clear prescription: if Europe wants to reduce its unemployment rates, it must move in the direction of more flexible, US-style labour markets. This chapter questions key aspects of both the conventional diagnosis and the corresponding prescription. We argue that US-style wage and income inequality has economic and social implications that are at least as troubling as the high levels of unemployment currently suffered in Europe. Moreover, a dispassionate analysis of US job creation rates inspires little confidence in the ability of the US model to deliver the goods, even after widespread sacrifice.

Many of those urging Europe to adopt or adapt the US model significantly underestimate the scale and the scope of the recent rise in economic inequality in the United States and, at the same time, substantially overestimate the country's relative success in creating stable employment. We begin our analysis with a review of recent trends in wage and income inequality. We then look at the international evidence on job creation rates, including a discussion of recent developments in patterns of employment stability in the United States. We conclude with some thoughts on the transferability of the US model to Europe.

Wage inequality

Wage inequality in the United States has increased dramatically since the end of the 1900s. Among all workers, the ratio of the earnings of those in the 90th percentile (that is, those earning more than 90 per cent of all workers, but less than 10 per cent of all workers) of the hourly wage distribution to the earnings of those in the 10th percentile (those earning more than 10 per cent of all workers and less than 90 per cent of all workers) of the distribution, for example, grew from 3.5 in 1979 to 4.4 in 1995.[2] Figure 1 (panel (a)) demonstrates that wage inequality among male workers increased between 1979 and 1995 primarily because the real wages for low-wage workers and middle-wage workers fell substantially between 1979 and 1995 - 18.2 per cent at the 10th percentile and 14.9 per cent at the 50th percentile. The wages of high-wage workers (those at the 90th percentile) were almost unchanged in real terms over the 16 year period (up 1.0 per cent).[3] The poor performance of real wages even near the top of the wage distribution is particularly striking since labour productivity increased by about 18 per cent over the same period.[4]

For women (see panel (b)), the story is more complicated. As with men, wage inequality grew markedly between 1979 and 1995, but women near the top of the distribution saw strong increases in their real wages (up 21.5 per cent). Women at the median did a little better than holding their own (real wages up 4.0 per cent), though real wages actually fell slightly (1.7 per cent) between 1989 and 1995. Women near the bottom, however, suffered almost as much as their male counterparts between 1979 and 1995, with real wages declining almost 17 per cent over the full period. The rise in the national minimum wage in 1990 and 1991, however, appears to have helped low-wage women to avoid the wage declines that affected better-paid women in the 1990s. In the end, even after almost two decades of relative wage improvements, women's wages still lagged far behind men's wages at comparable slots in the wage distributions. By 1995, for example, the 90th percentile woman worker earned just 77 per cent of the 90th percentile man.

Another feature of recent developments in the US wage structure is the poor *absolute* return to education. The strong rise in the relative return to education, particularly a four-year university degree, has been well-documented (see Blackburn, Bloom and Freeman (1991), for example). Nevertheless, a university degree has provided little protection against stagnating and declining real wages. Table 1 reports the average real hourly wage for male and female workers with a four-year university degree. The real wage for all male graduates grew at an annual average of just 0.04 per cent between 1979 and 1995; for comparable women, real wages increased about

1.2 per cent per year over the same period. Recent graduates (those with one to five years of work experience) fared even worse. Men saw average wages fall, especially in the 1990s. Women saw improvements in the 1980s, but a drastic erosion in the 1990s.

Some economists have argued that data on wage inequality provide an incomplete picture because these data ignore growth in non-wage benefits such as medical insurance and pension plans that have compensated for declining wages. Since 1979, however, average compensation (wages plus benefits) has risen about 0.1 percentage points per year fast that the average wage. Thus, if the median male worker received the average increase in benefits (highly unlikely if benefit growth was as skewed as wage growth), then the decline in total compensation for median workers would have been about 13 per cent between 1979 and 1995 - not remarkably different from the 15 per cent decline for wages alone. Table 2 makes clear, however, that fringe benefits, particularly health care, are unequally distributed across the wage distribution and the distribution has become more unequal since the end of the 1970s. For example, in 1979, 90 per cent of workers in the highest wage quintile had employer-provided health benefits, while only 40 per cent of workers in the lowest wage quintile did so. By 1995, the share of workers in the top quintile with employer provided health benefits had fallen 3 percentage points to 87 per cent, while such coverage for workers in the bottom quintile had fallen 13 percentage points to just 27 per cent.

Income inequality

Since wages are by far the most important source of income for the vast majority of the population, trends for income inequality largely mirror those for wages - widening inequality accompanied by stagnating or declining growth for most US families. Nevertheless, income trends do differ from wage trends because, since the end of the 1970s, families have increased the number of hours worked per year. Taken together, recent change in wage rates and hours have produced stagnating family incomes and a steep rise in relative poverty rates.

Figure 2 summarizes changes in the distribution of family income in the United States over the entire postwar period. Panel (a) shows the average annual growth from 1947 to 1973 in real family income by income quintile. Incomes in this early period grew by roughly equal amounts across all levels of family income, with growth strongest for those at the bottom. This pattern led to a gradual narrowing of income inequality over the period. The bottom panel shows annual growth for the same groups between 1973 and 1995.[5] In this more recent period, growth was very uneven. The bottom two deciles suffered real declines in family income. In the next two deciles, incomes rose slightly. Only the top decile saw modest gains, though these were much smaller than in the earlier period.[6] This new pattern of growth implies a substantial increase in inequality over the period.

Since real wages fell for the median worker between 1979 and 1995, the small increase in real median family income over the 1973-94 period suggests that families worked more hours.[7] The data in Table 3 confirm this. For families in the middle income quintile, for example, between 1979 and 1994, annual hours worked increased 3.7 per cent - 108 hours or almost three additional weeks of full-time employment. Among married-couple families with children, annual hours for those in the middle quintile grew more than 16 per cent over the same period. Families generally supplied these higher levels of hours either by sending more members (typically, married women) to perform paid work or by increasing the number of hours worked by men and women already working outside the home. Between 1979 and 1994, among married-couple families (about three-fourths of all US families), wives' average annual hours increased 255 hours or 37.3 per cent; their husbands' annual hours grew 62 hours or 3.0 per cent over the same period.[8] As the data for different family types in Table 3 indicate, increases in hours were strongest among families in the bottom 60 per cent of the income distribution.

Those men and women who were already performing paid work increased their hours either by putting in more time at their current jobs (switching from part-time to full-time, for example) or by taking second (and even third) jobs. The rise during the 1980s and 1990s in the number of women working more than one job is particularly striking. Between 1979 and 1995, the share of women holding more than one job increased from 3.5 per cent to 6.5 per cent of all employed women.[9] The increase for men (from 5.9 per cent in 1979 to 6.3 per cent in 1995) was much smaller. Among the 6.2 per cent of all workers with multiple jobs in 1995, almost half (45 per cent) reported that they did so for reasons of economic hardship (either to meet regular household expenses or to pay off debts).

Causes and consequences of inequality

Most economists in the United States believe that rapid technological change is the driving force behind the wage and income inequality described in the previous two sections (for two recent examples, see Berman, Machin and Bound (1996) and Autor, Katz and Krueger (1997)). This technological explanation, however, fits uncomfortably with many of the key economic developments of the last two decades. First, the technological advances that are supposed to have produced such upheaval in the wage and income distributions have somehow failed to yield any measurable improvement in US productivity growth rates. Growth in labour productivity since the end of the 1970s, the period when inequality started to climb, has averaged only 1.1 per cent per year, about half its rate in the earlier postwar period (when inequality was on the decline). The productivity figures suggest that popular accounts of the transformative effects of recent technological innovations, especially the personal computer, may exaggerate their real economic impact relative to earlier, (now) less glamorous technological innovations such as main-frame computing, commercial jet travel, the telephone, and others.

Second, the pattern of absolute (as opposed to relative) wage growth appears to contradict the technological explanation. According to the standard story, 'skilled' workers, who have been able to take advantage of new technologies, have benefited from the new economy, while 'less-skilled' workers have been left behind. In relative terms, 'skilled' workers have indeed done better than the 'less-skilled', but the pattern of real wage growth demonstrates that the gap between higher-wage and lower-wage workers has widened because the wages of middle and low earners have fallen while the wages of high earners remained unchanged after adjusting for inflation. The real wages of university-educated men, for example, grew only 0.6 per cent in the 16-year period between 1979 and 1995, with wages for 90th percentile male workers over the same period up just 1.0 per cent after inflation.[10] A closer look at the pattern of wage growth, then, suggests that some force or forces have pulled the rug out from underneath the labour market, leaving the wages of the highest paid workers only where they were two decades earlier. The technology story, which seems to argue that technology has rewarded those with the requisite skills, is ill-equipped to explain this pattern of absolute wage growth.

Third, most of the increase in inequality since the end of the 1970s, is not related to differences in workers' skill levels, the mechanism through which technology is supposed to affect wage inequality. Changes in the financial returns to education and labour-market experience, for example, account for less than half of the increase between 1979 and 1995 in inequality among men and women, separately.[11] The technological explanation, which has so far focused on the link between technology and skills, is therefore unable to explain the lion's share of the increase in inequality.

Technological change has been a central force in the development of the US labour market since before the beginning of this century (particularly by helping to absorb the ever increasing number of college graduate workers) and technology has undoubtedly played a role in determining the current *level* of inequality in the United States (better-educated, more skilled workers tend to work better with all forms of physical capital, especially complex technology). Nevertheless, little evidence exists that a change in the speed or nature of technological innovation during the 1980s and 1990s was responsible for the *change* in the level of inequality over that period. The poor productivity growth rates and the stagnant real wages of high-wage workers raise important questions about the plausibility of explanations of wage inequality based on technology.

How then can we explain growing economic disparities? In our view, the growth in inequality is the outcome of a widespread deterioration in the political and economic bargaining power of US workers. This decline in bargaining power both stems from and is reflected in a series of changes since the late 1970s in US labour and product markets. First, between 1979 and 1996, the share of workers represented by trade unions fell from 24.1 per cent to 14.5 per cent of the private and public sector workforce.[12] Given the well-documented role that unions play in narrowing wage inequality, the decline in union membership rates (as well as in the political influence exercised by unions) contributed significantly to rising wage disparities, especially among the more heavily unionized male labour force.[13] Second, the 30 per cent decline during the 1980s in the real value of the federal minimum wage contributed substantially to the deterioration in the earnings of low-wage workers, particularly women.[14] The increases in the minimum wage in 1990, 1991, 1996 and 1997, arrested the further decline in the value of the minimum wage, but left the minimum wage about 20 per cent below its 1979 purchasing power. Third, the deregulation of domestic product markets, such as airlines, trucking, telecommunications and others also put significant downward pressure on wages, particularly for unionized, male production workers.[15] Fourth, the parallel 'deregulation' of international trade, which was accompanied by a substantial increase in the volume of imported manufacturing goods and declines in the relative prices of imported goods, also reduced the bargaining power of US workers. This 'globalisation' process, which operates through trade volumes, trade prices, international lending, foreign direct investment, international portfolio investment, immigration, and other channels, puts direct pressure on the wages and employment opportunities of US manufacturing workers. Regional labour markets in areas with significant manufacturing presence transmit the impact to workers in industries not directly affected by import competition.[16]

The pattern of economic polarisation implicit in the preceding description of wage and income trends has had profound political and social consequences. While a complete review of the social implications of inequality is beyond the scope of this chapter, rising income inequality and especially the decline in real family incomes for the bottom 40 per cent of families have clearly contributed to a rise in relative poverty rates, increased crime, a disintegration of communities and a national sense of community, and political alienation.[17]

The most obvious social effect of widening inequality is the substantial rise in poverty. Table 4 reports poverty rates for US families by race and ethnic group for the late-1960s, - 1970s and - 1980s, and the mid-1990s. Columns one to three show relative poverty measures, which compare family incomes with that of the median family; the fourth column shows the official US poverty rate, which is based on the inflation-adjusted price of a poverty-level basket of goods.[18] The official poverty measure shows a small decrease in poverty for the population as a whole and for white and black families between 1969 and 1979 (no data are available for Hispanics). Between 1979 and 1995, however, official poverty grew among the entire population (from 11.7 per cent to 13.8 per cent) including whites (9.0 per cent to 11.2 per cent) and Hispanics (21.8 per cent to 30.3 per cent) and fell among blacks (from 31.0 per cent to 29.3 per cent).

The relative poverty measures in the first three columns of Table 4 paint an even bleaker picture. The broadest relative poverty criterion - those families receiving less than one-half the median family income - shows poverty rates well above the official measure: 22.2 per cent of all families in 1995, compared to the 13.8 per cent official rate (19.1 per cent among white families, 11.2 per cent official rate; 40.7 per cent for black families, 29.3 per cent official rate). The data for the stricter definition of relative poverty - those families receiving less than one-fourth of the median income, the poorest of the relative poor - reveal both growth in extreme poverty since the end of the 1960s and the acute relative deprivation of black families. The share of all families earning less than one-fourth of median family earnings increased from 6.7 per cent in 1979 to 8.6 per cent in 1995. White, black and Hispanic families all experienced increases in extreme relative poverty rates over the period and, by 1995, one in five black families received incomes less than one-fourth of those of the median family.

Figure 3 puts the US relative poverty statistics into international perspective. The figure shows the share of children under the age of 18 who live in families with incomes below one-half of the median family income in 17 OECD countries. The United States, with 21.5 per cent of its children living in poverty, has, by far, the highest relative rate of child poverty. The rate in the closest European country

(Ireland) is 12.0 per cent, with all other European nations, including the United Kingdom (9.9 per cent), below 10 per cent, and seven below 5 per cent.

Widening economic inequality may also play an important role in the rise in crime and incarceration rates in the United States. As inequality grew between 1979 and 1995, violent crimes rose 55.2 per cent and arrests for drug violations almost tripled (while the national population grew 16.9 per cent).[19] Freeman (1995) has emphasized the potential links between higher inequality and rising crime rates, noting first that 'the demography of the criminal population closely mirrors that of the groups who have suffered huge losses in real earnings: criminals are young less-educated men' and second that 'surveys of youths in inner cities show that many more perceived crime as being more lucrative than in the past; and their reported reservation wages to legitimate work suggest that 20-30 per cent real pay increases would reduce their criminal participation.' (p.71)

Higher crime has led to even larger increases in incarceration rates. The number of inmates in state and federal prisons per 100,000 people grew 280 per cent between 1980 (139 per 100,000) and 1994 (389 per 100,000),[20] with US rates now six to ten times higher than those in Europe.[21] If US jail and prison population in 1995 (almost 1.6 million) were added to the number of unemployed workers in the same year, the unemployment rate in the US would have been 7.1 per cent instead of 5.6 per cent. Buchele and Christiansen (1997) demonstrate that when the male portion of the US inmate population is treated as long-term unemployed, the long-term unemployment rate in the United State in 1993 was higher than in France and Germany.

Job creation

In the conventional view, the above-documented flexibility in US wages should have lead to higher levels of job creation and lower levels of unemployment in the United States relative to 'inflexible' European economies. US job creation rates, however, have been remarkably lacklustre over the last two decades. Moreover, employment growth has not followed the pattern implicit in the flexibility thesis. Even though wages have fallen throughout much of the wage distribution, employment opportunities did not improve for less-skilled workers in the United States. Casual evidence suggests that job opportunities for the least-skilled workers are at least as good in some European countries as they are in the United States.

Table 5 summarizes employment growth in ten advanced capitalist economies from 1959 to 1995. The employment numbers, taken from the US Bureau of Labor Statistics, measure employment in all countries using the employment concept used in the United States, thus avoiding definitional problems when making comparisons across countries. Panel (b) reports the annual average growth rates in employment over four different time periods, roughly the 1960s, 1970s, 1980s and 1990s. The first striking feature of the table is the historically low level of job creation in the United States in the 1990s - just 1.0 per cent per year between 1989 and 1995, compared to a 1.7 per cent annual rate in the 1980s (already below the average growth rates for the 1960s and 1970s). A second key feature of the table is the range of countries with employment growth rates during the 1980s and 1990s that were at least as good as those of the United States. In the 1980s, Canada (2.0 per cent per year) and Australia (2.4 per cent), solidly outperformed the United States. In the 1990s, Australia (1.1 per cent) and the Netherlands (2.0 per cent) did better than the United States, while Japan (0.9 per cent) did not trail far behind. These 'successful' economies have little in common by way of labour market institutions, but all are less 'flexible' than the United States.[22]

Despite wage flexibility, less-skilled workers bore the brunt of the deceleration of employment growth in the 1980s and 1990s. Table 6 reproduces Current Population Survey data on employment rates by education level, presented by Freeman (1995). The data indicate that between 1980 and 1993 (two years with roughly comparable unemployment rates), the employment-to-population rates of males with less than a high school degree (about 15 per cent of the US male labour force) and of males with a high school degree (about 35 per cent of the male labour force) declined 6 percentage points. This fall was larger in both absolute and relative terms than the 4 percentage point decline in the employment-to-population rate for males with a four-year university degree (about 25 per cent of male employment). Greater wage flexibility for low-wage workers, then, did not improve their labour market outcomes relative to higher paid workers. Nor did greater wage flexibility appear to improve the employment prospects of less-skilled US workers relative to comparable workers in West Germany. Nickell (1996) reports that between 1984 and 1990, West German males over the age of 25 with 'no qualifications' (about 12 per cent of the male working population) had a non-employment rate of 31.6 per cent, while male, high-school dropouts in the same age range in the United States (about 15 per cent of male workers) had an almost identical non-employment rate of 32.5 per cent.

Net job creation rates, even aggregate employment rates, ignore much of the dynamics of job creation. In any given year, the net number of jobs created or destroyed is only a small fraction of the gross number of jobs created and destroyed. In the United States, for example, net job creation has averaged about 1 per cent per year in the 1990s, but each year roughly ten times that number of existing jobs are destroyed. Labour market flexibility - whether through downwardly flexible wages or lower hiring and firing costs or other factors - might have allowed the United States to hasten any adjustment to new economic circumstances by contributing to a higher underlying rate of job 'churning'. Table 7 reproduces data for the United States and ten other advanced capitalist economies from Davis, Haltiwanger and Schuh's (1996) study of job creation and destruction. Job creation, job destruction, and especially job reallocation (job creation plus job destruction) rates for the United States fall in the middle of the range for all countries. 'Inflexible' labour market institutions, then, do not appear to have hampered European economies' ability to reallocate labour.

Job security

Rising job insecurity in the United States is an aspect of recent US economic performance that has been almost entirely absent from discussions in Europe over lessons to be learned from the US 'model'. Recent US data bear out the widespread perception that job insecurity has risen dramatically and underscore the high economic cost of job loss for the typical worker.

Table 8 displays estimates from Farber (1997) on the rate of job loss during four three-year periods: 1981-83, which included the period of highest US unemployment in the postwar; 1989-91, which included the business cycle peak of 1989-90 and the recession of 1990-91; 1991-93, the 'jobless recovery'; and 1993-95, three years of sustained economic growth. Some economists have noted that the rate of job loss has not changed much across these periods. This interpretation, however, ignores variation in the macro-economy over time. For both men and women, the three-year job displacement rate is higher in the most recent period, when unemployment averaged 6.3 per cent, than in any of the earlier periods, which include two recessions with substantially higher unemployment rates. At any given national unemployment rate, then, workers appear much more likely to lose their job in the mid-1990s than in the early 1980s. The data also support the public perception that 'corporate downsizing' (best captured in the 'position abolished' category in the table) grew significantly between the 1980s and the 1990s. For men, the share of workers who lost their job in the previous three years because their position was abolished jumped from 1.4 per cent in 1981-83 to 2.3 per cent in 1993-95; for women, the figure grew from 1.3 per cent to 2.5 per cent. The cost to workers of job loss is substantial. Farber (1997), for example, estimates that the average displaced worker makes 15 per cent less at his or her subsequent job.

Rose (1995) used a different methodology to measure the extent and costs of rising job inequality. Table 9 summarizes his principal findings based on longitudinal data for male workers. Panel (a) shows the share of workers with 'weak', 'medium' and 'strong' attachment to their employers, separately for the decades of the 1970s and the 1980s. Workers with strong employer attachment change employers one or fewer times per decade; those with medium attachment changed employers two or three times in ten years; those with weak attachment, four or more times. The share of workers with strong attachment fell by 15 percentage points between the two decades. At the same time, the share with weak attachment jumped by 12 percentage points. Panel (b) gives an indication of the economic cost of this rising inequality. Workers with strong employer attachment experienced strong growth in annual earnings in both decades: a 24.5 per cent increase over the 1970s, followed by a 29.4 per cent increase over the 1980s. Those with weak employer attachment, however, saw their real wages decline by 3.4 per cent in the 1970s and 13.2 per cent in the 1980s.

Some conclusions

A careful examination of the US model suggests that it has little to offer European economies seeking to combat high unemployment. US-style wage flexibility is not about the bottom 10 per cent or even 25 per cent of the work force accepting stagnant real wages for a short period while relative wages 'adjust' to new economic circumstances, as some advocates of labour market reforms in Europe seem to suggest. Real wages have been stagnant or declining throughout most of the US wage distribution for almost two decades. At the same time, job insecurity and the costs of job loss have increased dramatically. Poverty rates, particularly for blacks and Hispanics, which have been high by European standards for the entire postwar period, have now reached levels that would be politically intolerable in most of Europe.

If a meaningful trade-off exists between inequality and unemployment, then the United States appears to have paid a high price for its employment gains. Job creation rates in the United States have decelerated significantly since the rise of the most extreme forms of *laissez-faire* policies and job growth is not markedly better than in several other countries with more interventionist approaches. Even more disheartening, the US workers who have shown the greatest wage 'flexibility' - those with less formal education - appear to have no better employment prospects than their counterparts in Germany, where workers across the wage distribution have experienced rising real wages throughout the last two decades.

Some argue that European nations can borrow aspects of the US model without giving into its worst excesses. The lacklustre employment performance of the United States, however, suggests that even complete acceptance of US-style deregulation may do little to create new job opportunities for Europe's millions of unemployed. Nothing in the preceding analysis is meant to dismiss the need for decisive action to address mass-joblessness in Europe. From the United States, however, the idea that Europeans are giving serious thought to applying the US model there is a sobering indication of the depth of the continent's economic and political difficulties.

Notes

---

[1] This term, and the term 'unskilled', are usually used in a misleading way. In the United States, the term is frequently applied to those workers without a four-year university degree. Since only about one-fourth of the US labour force has such a degree, this definition implies that about 75 per cent of the workforce is 'less-skilled' or 'unskilled'.

[2] Unless otherwise noted, all US wage figures are derived from the Outgoing Rotation Group of the Current Population Survey and refer to workers 18-64 years old following procedures described in Webster (1996).

[3] We deflate wages using the CPI-U-X1. Recently, a commission of five economists appointed by the Senate Finance Committee (SFC) has criticized the CPI-U (which is identical to the CPI-U-X1 since 1983), alleging that the official deflator overstates inflation relative to a 'true' cost-of-living index by 0.8-1.0 percentage points per year (see Senate Finance Committee, (1996)). Nevertheless, we continue (along with the vast majority of US economists) to employ the CPI. First, none of the discussion of relative wages is in anyway affected by any change in the deflator. Comparisons of the ratio of the 90th to 10th percentile worker in 1979 and 1995, for example, do not rely on the choice of deflator. Second, it appears that the SFC named the commission not primarily because the SFC was concerned with the accuracy of the consumer price index, but rather because the SFC believed that a determination that the CPI overstated inflation could help to reduce the federal government deficit by lowering annual cost-of-living adjustments for Social Security recipients and by slowing down the indexation of tax brackets. Apparently with this goal in mind, the SFC chose to staff the commission with five economists, all of whom had previously stated that the CPI significantly overstated inflation. Other prominent economists, who had argued that the CPI did not overstate inflation or who believed that any overstatement was small, were not included. Baker (1998) has conducted a careful review of the commission's findings and concludes that the commission's evidence is just as supportive of the notion that the CPI understates increases in the cost-of-living. Third, many of the criticisms of the CPI would probably apply to European price indices. Given that real wages have risen steadily across the full European wage distribution, comparable adjustments to European price indices would suggest that real wage growth has been even faster than previously believed, leaving the relative US-European differences unaffected.

[4] Krugman (1997) argues that the CPI commission's conclusions resolve the puzzling gap between growth in average labour productivity and average wage growth. Krugman, however, misses a crucial link. Since labour productivity is measured as output per person-hour, the CPI commission's results require a re-reckoning of productivity. The most important source of mismeasurement (accounting for over half of the commission's estimate of the downward bias in the CPI) was related to improved quality of goods. Essentially, the commission was arguing that prices did not increase as much as thought because the quality of the goods purchased was better than had been measured - consumers were getting more for their money. National output, therefore, was higher than previously believed. Given that the hours worked to produce that output has not been revised, productivity growth must also be higher than previously estimated. Michael Boskin, the head of the CPI commission, estimated informally at the American Economics Association meetings in 1997 that the commission's figures suggests that recent GDP growth was probably 0.6 percentage points higher than earlier calculations. Without any change in the estimate of the hours worked to produce this output, the 0.6 percentage point increase in GDP translates to an identical increase in productivity. This is probably a conservative estimate sine the commission only looked at consumer goods. Commission member Robert Gordon has alleged even more severe problems for investment goods (Gordon, 1990), which would lead to the same conclusion. Thus, even if true, the CPI commission's results do little to close the gap between productivity growth and average real wage growth. In any event, our principal concern is not with the behaviour of the average wage (which is heavily influenced by rapid growth at the very top of the wage distribution), but rather with developments across the bulk of the distribution between the 10th and the 90th percentile. It is still striking that workers at the 90th percentile of the male distribution saw real wage increases (however deflated) that trail significantly behind the average productivity growth rate.

[5] The family income cutoffs for the first four quintiles in 1995 were: first quintile, $19,070; second, $32,985; third, $48,985; and fourth, $72,260. The 95th percentile family in 1995 earned $123,656; the average family, $51,353.

[6] Most of the increases in the top quintile were concentrated at the very top. See Mishel, Bernstein and Schmitt (1996), Table 1.7, p.55.

[7] Families could also have received more non-labour income, but non-labour income represents a small share of total income for the bottom 95 per cent of families and, in any event, changed little in real terms over the period (see Mishel, Bernstein and Schmitt (1996), Table 1.22.

[8] Based on data from the Family Income Data Series (derived principally from the CPS), cited in Mishel, Bernstein and Schmitt (1996), Table 1.23.

[9] Based on Department of Labor data cited in Mishel, Bernstein and Schmitt (1996), Table 4.17.

[10] For detailed descriptions of the overall average wage distribution and wages by education level, see Mishel, Bernstein and Schmitt (1996), table 1,23.

[11] See Mishel, Bernstein and Schmitt (1996), Tables 3.24 and 3.25.

[12] Data from Hirsch and MacPherson (1995), updated with data from the Current Population Survey for 1995 and 1996.

[13] Card (1991), Freeman (1991) and Dinardo, Forin and Lemieux (1994) all attribute at least 20 per cent of the increase during the 1980s in male wage inequality to the decline in unionization rates.

[14] Dinardo, Fortin and Lemieux (1994) conclude that the fall in the real value of the minimum wage can explain 19-25 per cent of the rise in the standard deviation of men's wages over the period 1979-88 and 30-36 per cent of the rise in the standard deviation of women's wages of the same period.

[15] Fortin and Lemieux (1997) find that while deregulation had a 'negligible effect' on overall male and female inequality, it has a 'more sizeable' impact on unionized men (13.3 per cent of the growth in the variance of log wages between 1979 and 1988) and men earning significantly more than the 1979 minimum wage (7.3 per cent).

[16] As former Clinton administration economic advisor Laura D'Andrea Tyson (1997) has noted: 'Economists, politicians and commentators are waging a debate about the globalization explanation of wage inequality. The simple analytical logic of this explanation is compelling - growing import competition and growing immigration from low-skill, low-income countries have made unskilled labor a more abundant factor of production and therefore reduced its relative price. Opinion is shifting toward the view that globalization has had a 'moderate' effect - perhaps accounting for one-fourth to one-fifth of the nearly 20 per cent rise in the wage differential between skilled and unskilled labor - and the estimate of this effect has been creeping up over time'.

[17] For a discussion of the role of wage and income inequality in politics, see Teixeira and Rogers (1996).

[18] The official poverty line in the United State is not a sophisticated measure of poverty. It is based on consumption data gathered in 1955 under the assumption that poor families should spend one-third of their income on food and two thirds of their income on remaining necessities. The original poverty line was then constructed by multiplying the Department of Agriculture's minimum food budgets for different-size families by three. The current poverty level is an inflation-updated measure from this original calculation.

[19] Figures from home page of the Bureau of Justice Statistics, Department of Justice.

[20] Figures from home page of the Bureau of Justice Statistics, Department of Justice.

[21] See Buchele and Christiansen (1997), Table 4 and Freeman (1995).

[22] The persistent 'high' performers, Australia, the United States and Canada (in that order) do all have relatively high population growth rates. This underscores the limited meaningfulness of job creation rates as measures of economic performance. If we were to observe two otherwise identical economies with different rates of population growth, we would expect to observe different rates of employment growth, without believing that this tells us anything about the standard of living of residents of both countries.

Figure 1
Growth in Real Wages by Decile, 1973-95

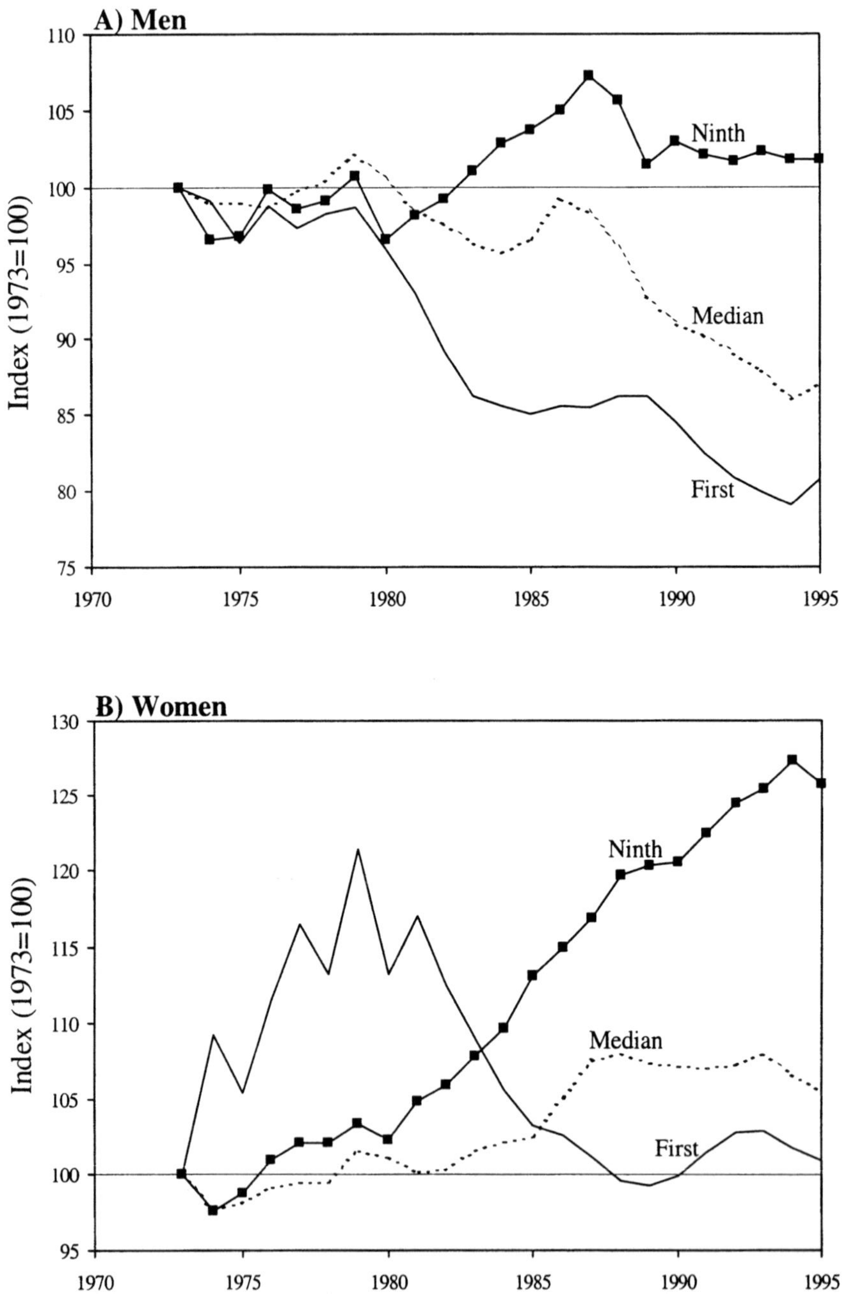

Source: Authors' analysis of Current Population Survey data.

Figure 2
Family Income, Average Annual Change

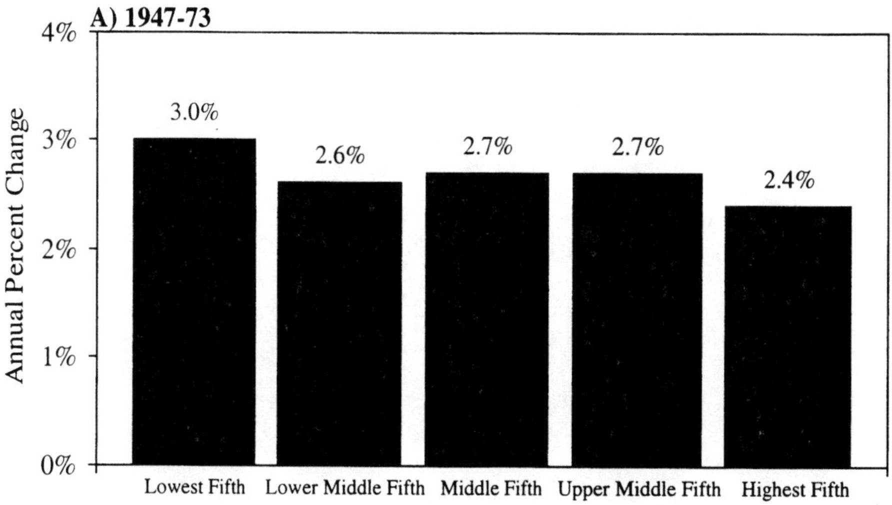

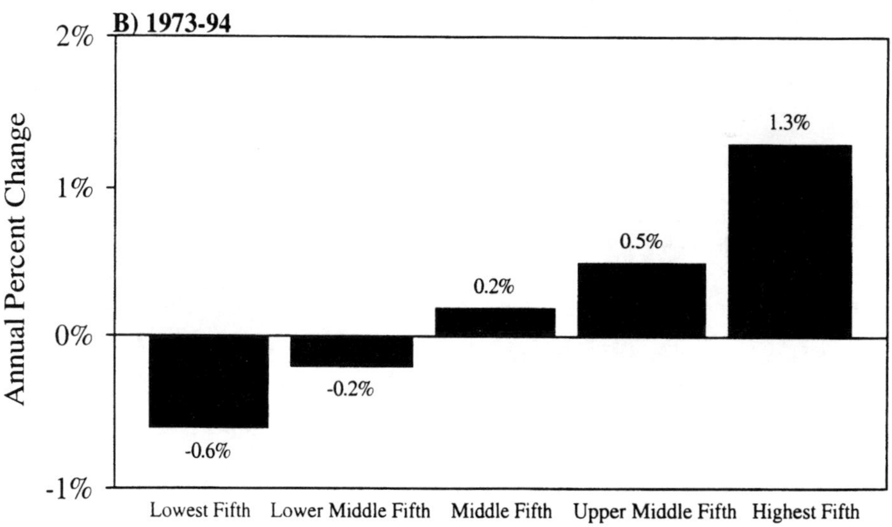

Source: Authors' analysis of Census data.

Figure 3
Relative Poverty Rates* for Children, Mid-1980s to Early-1990s

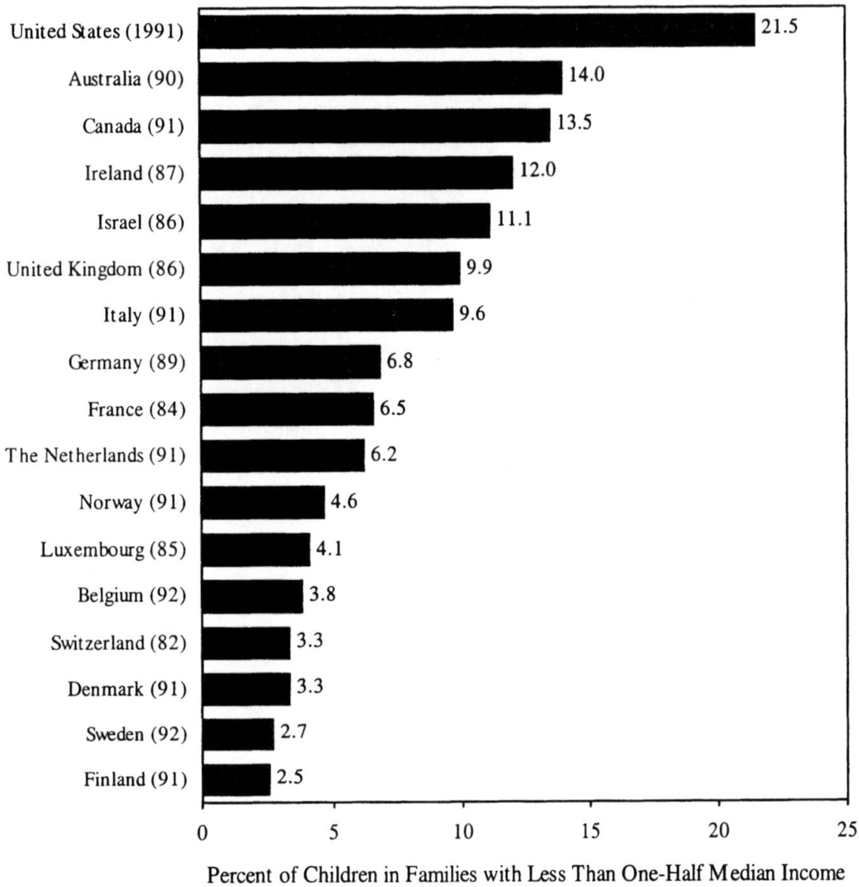

* Income is post-tax and includes near-cash transfers, such as food stamps and housing assistance.

Source: Rainwater and Smeeding (1995).

Table 10.1 Hourly wages for US workers with a four-year college degree, 1979-95 (1995 Dollars)

	1979	1989	1995	Annual Change 1979-1989	1989-95
(a) All College-educated					
Men	$19.43	$19.54	$19.55	0.06%	0.01%
Women	12.42	14.02	14.84	1.29	0.97
(b) College-educated, 1-5 years experience					
Men	$14.04	$13.86	$12.54	-0.13%	-1.59%
Women	11.24	12.51	11.55	1.13	-1.28

Source: Economic Policy Institute (EPI) analysis of Current Population Survey (CPS) Outgoing Rotation Group (ORG) sample.

TABLE 10.2 Rate of private-sector, employer-provided benefit coverage*, 1979-93

Benefit	1979	1988	1993	Change 1979-93
(a) Health				
All	71	69	64	-7
Lowest wage quintile	40	32	27	-13
Second wage quintile	66	62	59	-7
Third wage quintile	79	76	71	-8
Fourth wage quintile	87	83	80	-7
Highest wage quintile	90	90	87	-3
(b) Pension				
All	48	44	45	-3
Lowest wage quintile	18	14	13	-5
Second wage quintile	35	33	34	-1
Third wage quintile	51	45	51	0
Fourth wage quintile	68	59	61	-7
Highest wage quintile	76	69	72	-4

*Private-sector wage and salary workers age 18-64, with at least 20 weekly hours and 26 weeks of work.

Source: EPI analysis of Bureau of Labour Statistics data.

TABLE 10.3 Changes in family hours worked by family type, 1979-94

	Quintile					
	Bottom	Second	Middle	Fourth	Top	Average
(a) All families						
1979	999	2107	2913	3436	4156	2722
1989	1096	2243	3049	3619	4255	2852
1994	1064	2099	3021	3698	4206	2818
Percent change						
1979-89	9.6	6.5	4.6	5.3	2.4	4.8
1989-94	-2.9	-6.4	-0.9	2.2	-1.1	-1.2
(b) Married couples with children						
1979	2186	2943	3232	3700	4288	3270
1989	2395	3268	3609	3918	4294	3497
1994	2296	3344	3762	4051	4292	3549
Percent change						
1979-89	9.5	11.1	11.7	5.9	0.1	6.9
1989-94	-4.1	2.3	4.3	3.4	-0.1	1.5
(c) Unrelated individuals						
1979	649	1387	1822	2034	2170	1612
1989	759	1603	1944	2091	2246	1729
1994	671	1572	1889	2104	2265	1700
Percent change						
1979-89	17.0	15.6	6.7	2.8	3.5	7.2
1989-94	-11.6	-2.0	-2.8	0.6	0.8	-1.7

Source: EPI analysis of March CPS.

TABLE 10.4 Percent of persons with low relative income, 1969-95, by race, adjusted for family size

	Relative income poverty measures			
	Less than 1/4 the Median	1/4 to 1/2 of the Median	Less than 1/2 of the Median	Official Poverty Rate
(a) All				
1969	5.5	12.4	17.9	12.1
1979	6.7	13.3	20.0	11.7
1989	8.3	13.7	22.0	13.1
1995	8.6	13.6	22.2	13.8
(b) Whites				
1969	4.3	10.4	14.7	9.5
1979	5.0	11.7	16.7	9.0
1989	6.3	12.5	18.8	10.2
1995	6.6	12.5	19.1	11.2
(c) Blacks				
1969	15.3	27.3	42.6	32.2
1979	18.8	25.3	44.1	31.0
1989	21.8	22.1	43.9	30.8
1995	20.0	20.7	40.7	29.3
(d) Hispanics*				
1969	n/a	n/a	n/a	n/a
1979	11.6	22.6	34.2	21.8
1989	16.3	23.8	40.1	26.3
1995	18.6	24.6	43.2	30.3

* Hispanics may be of any race. "n/a" indicates data not available.

Source: U.S. Bureau of the Census (1991) and unpublished data.

TABLE 10.5 Civilian employment in ten countries, 1959-95 (approximating U.S. concepts)

	1959	1969	1979	1989	1995
(a) Number of workers (thousands)					
United States	64 630	77 902	98 824	117 342	124 900
Canada	5936	7832	10 761	13 086	13 506
Australia	n/a	5188	6111	7720	8235
Japan	42 430	49 570	54 040	60 500	63 890
France	18 190	19 990	21 390	21 850	22 000
Germany*	25 340	25 790	26 080	27 200	27 720
Italy	20 020	18 940	19 930	20 770	19 970
Netherlands	n/a	n/a	5350	5990	6760
Sweden	3549	3778	4174	4480	4056
United Kingdom	23 220	24 390	24 940	26 350	25 710

	1959-69	1969-79	1979-89	1989-95
(b) Annual growth rate (%)				
United States	1.9	2.4	1.7	1.0
Canada	2.8	3.2	2.0	0.5
Australia	n/a	1.7	2.4	1.1
Japan	1.6	0.9	1.1	0.9
France	0.9	0.7	0.2	0.1
Germany*	0.2	0.1	0.4	0.3
Italy	-0.6	0.5	0.4	-0.7
Netherlands	n/a	n/a	1.1	2.0
Sweden	0.6	1.0	0.7	-1.6
United Kingdom	0.5	0.2	0.6	-0.4

* Data refer to Western Germany only.

Source: Authors' analysis of Bureau of Labour Statistics data.

TABLE 10.6 Employment rates for male workers in the United States, 1980-93

	1980 %	1993 %	Change 1980-93
(a) Men, 25-64 years old			
Less than high school	72	66	-6
High school graduate	87	81	-6
University graduate	92	88	-4
(b) Men, 25-34 years old			
Less than high school	80	74	-6
High school graduate	89	85	-4
University graduate	94	90	-4

Source: Freeman (1995) analysis of March CPS data.

TABLE 10.7 International job creation and job destruction rates*

Country	Period	Coverage	Gross job creation	Gross job destruction	Net job creation	Job reallocation
United States	1973-88	Manufacturing	9.1%	10.2%	-1.1%	19.4%
United States	1976-85	Pennsylvania	13.3	12.5	0.8	25.8
Canada	1979-84	Manufacturing	10.6	10.0	0.6	20.5
Canada	1979-84	Tax-paying firms	11.1	9.6	1.5	20.7
France	1978-84	Private, nonfarm	11.4	12.0	-0.6	23.3
Germany	1978-88	Private	8.3	7.7	0.6	16.0
Sweden	1982-84	All employees	11.4	12.1	-0.8	23.5
Italy	1984-89	Soc. Sec. employees	9.9	10.0	-0.1	19.9
Australia	1984-85	Manufacturing	16.1	13.2	3.9	29.3
New Zealand	1987-92	Private	15.7	19.8	-4.1	35.5
Denmark	1983-89	Private	16.0	13.8	2.2	29.8
Finland	1986-91	Private	10.4	12.0	-1.6	22.4
Norway	1976-86	Manufacturing	7.1	8.4	-1.2	15.5

* Annual averages as percentages of employment.

Source: Davis, Haltiwanger, and Schuh (1996).

TABLE 10.8 Rate of job loss, by gender and reason, 1981-95

	Rate of job loss*				Change	
	1981-83 %	1989-91 %	1991-93 %	1993-95 %	1981-83 to 1991-93	1989-91 to 1993-95
(a) Men						
All reasons	15.2	14.3	14.4	15.8	-0.8	1.5
Plant closing	4.9	4.7	3.8	3.2	-1.1	-1.5
Slack work	6.9	5.5	4.8	4.8	-2.1	-0.7
Position abolished	1.4	1.7	2.3	2.3	0.9	0.6
Other	2.0	2.5	3.4	5.4	1.4	2.9
Unemployment rate	9.1	5.9	7.3	6.3	-1.8	0.4
(b) Women						
All reasons	11.0	10.3	11.0	14.3	0.0	4.0
Plant closing	4.0	4.1	3.3	3.2	-0.7	-0.9
Slack work	3.7	2.9	2.6	2.7	-1.1	-0.2
Position abolished	1.3	1.3	2.2	2.5	0.9	1.2
Other	1.9	1.9	3.0	5.9	1.1	4.0
Unemployment rate	8.8	5.7	6.6	6.0	-2.3	0.3

* Share of labour force that reports having lost a job in the previous three years.

Source: Authors' analysis based on Farber (1997)

TABLE 10.9 Employment stability for men, 1970s versus 1980s

	Employer attachment*		
	Weak	Medium	Strong
(a) Share of workers			
1970s	12%	21%	67%
1980s	24	24	52
Difference	12	3	-15
(b) Growth in annual earnings**			
1970s	-3.4%	16.1%	24.5%
1980s	-13.2	22.7	29.4
Difference	-9.8	6.6	4.9

*Workers with "strong" employer attachment changed employers one or fewer times per decade; those with "medium" attachment changed employers two or three times; "weak" attachment, four or more times

** Growth in real annual earnings between the periods 1967-69 and 1977-79 for the 1970s, and 1977-79 and 1987-89 for the 1980s.

Source: Author's analysis of Rose (1995)

CHAPTER 11

'THE CULT OF TRAINING'; UNEMPLOYMENT AND CAPITALIST EMPLOYMENT POLICY

Gregory Albo

The economic disorder that swept across the advanced capitalist countries with the end of the post-war boom in the mid-1970s signalled an economic turning point at the end of the twentieth century. Real growth rates in the advanced capitalist countries fell from averaging about 4 per cent over the period 1950 to 1973 to less than half from 1973 to 1989, and further still over the course of the subsequent business cycle. The post-war reduction of trade barriers through the GATT process and the growth of trans-nationals, moreover, had steadily synchronised economic cycles and trade interdependencies in the core capitalist countries. The currency convertibility that arrived in 1973 with the end to the Bretton Woods fixed exchange rate system reinforced international economic instability and the constraints imposed by global money and commodity markets on national economies. The intensification of competitive pressures has resulted in a drawn-out and contentious process of restructuring production relations, in terms of both the distributional bargains between workers and owners and the technical conditions of production. Some industries and economies have suffered a stark period of decline, more have stagnated, while just a few sectors (and no countries within this zone) have been ascendant. Workers have universally assumed the burden of the restructuring process, suffering a material loss in their standard of living along with an intensification of work processes.

These two general trends - slower growth of output and increased internationalisation of economic activities - have thus left an indelible mark on the labour market. The International Labour Organisation, in its cautiously optimistic inaugural World Employment Report, observed that over two decades of turbulence and change, no OECD labour market has remained unaffected; labour market performance has deteriorated when compared with the stable environment of growth that prevailed until 1970. And this deterioration has occurred irrespective of differences in labour market regulation (1995; 156). Although there have been distinctive national growth paths and labour market outcomes in the post-boom period - what many have referred to as specific patterns of inadequacy or disaster -

several general features can be noted. First, since the economic clamp-down and oil crisis of the early 1970s, unemployment rates have been increasing remorselessly across the OECD countries. Even in the US where unemployment is an extremely unsatisfactory measure of labour market distress (its wage compression and involuntary part-time work mirror the poor performance elsewhere), across the business cycle average unemployment rates remain above the boom levels. Employment and labour force growth trends, however, have been more steady, although there is mounting evidence of slowdowns in the 1990s. This suggests that with labour productivity growth also declining for much of the period, slower output growth has left a larger reserve of unemployed after each recession that is becoming more intractable over time. Second, the slowdown in industrial output has been even greater than the slowdown in GDP growth. The differential growth in productivity between services and industry has meant, in turn, that employment shares have increased in services but declined in industry. The compositional shift in employment has dislodged wage and skill patterns as industrial employment has typically paid average incomes for acquired skills, while service sector pay and educational requirements vary tremendously. The changes to occupational categories has been characterised as a polarised job market; professional and technical jobs have been increasing their small share of employment, but the largest volume of total employment growth has been in clerical, sales and personal services that have been poorly paid and of minimal skill requirement. Finally, labour market inequality has generally increased; directly for the unemployed and the large number of prime-age males who have dropped out of the labour market; through the shift in employment composition to services for the employed labour force; from higher average educational levels attained relative to pay and job quality in service sector work for new job entrants; and an alarming rise in menial, contingent employment for the unskilled. These common trends of labour market inadequacy have differed between the advanced capitalist countries only in the degree of national disaster and the institutional means by which wage austerity and paid employment has been distributed across the working classes.

These radical changes in the structure of the labour market and industry - and the instability, risk and uncertainty that inevitably follows - have made flexibility in relation to market activities one of the keywords of modern employment policy (Boyer 1988). Such a general, notional concept as flexibility, however, does not lend itself to any ready set of policies to improve the adaptability of economic agents to market turmoil. Indeed, distinct conceptions of flexibility have been a central point of division in contending approaches to capitalist employment and training policies. Flexibility, on the one hand, has been counter-posed to wage and market rigidities, such as trade unions, minimum wages, job controls, standard hours, qualification restrictions, that hinder free market adjustment to altered economic and technical conditions. Reduction of wage costs and realignment of skills is seen as essential to meeting international competition. On the other hand, flexibility is said to arise from innovation and skill capacities so that firm level responses to restructuring, indeed regional and national responses as well, are met by productivity advances and new products rather than wage competition. International competitiveness - and hence the high employment and wages that are seen to follow - is underwritten by a high-skills workforce.

These two opposed conceptions of market flexibility - the pure market adjustment of numerical flexibility versus the process and product adaptability of functional flexibility - have a material foundation in the dualist nature of skills and (un)employment within capitalism, both being individual attributes of a worker and social conditions of production. As the demand for labour is heterogenous, workers acquire and embody diverse skills that are under constant pressure to adapt (in terms of both upgrading some skills and degradation of others) to changing market and technical conditions beyond any individual worker's direct control. This is what the neo-liberal OECD has in mind when it states that

> governments are faced with designing and redesigning a range of polices across the economy and society in order to help foster - or in some cases stop hindering - adaptation to evolving ways of production and trade . . . Businesses, trade unions and workers need to be innovative to develop new products, processes, and ways of working that will create new jobs, and help shape skills to fit with the jobs of the future (1994b; 7).

At another level, however, the competitive capacities of capitalist firms and regions are dependent upon the labour force, or at least portions thereof, having the technical capacities to utilise advanced production technologies. The wider the skills basis, other things being equal, the greater the potential external competitive basis for high-value added production and quality employment. According to social market advocates, training and employment strategies are necessary to avoid

> becoming trapped in a low-skills, low-quality equilibrium with low initial education and poor skills leading to low productivity and a predominantly low-quality market orientation ...of companies... The dynamic challenge is how to develop a vocational education and training system and other mechanisms of quality market re-orientation (Stevens and Walsh 1991; 25-6).

It is difficult, therefore, to disentangle the processes of skill acquisition, the specific object of training policy, from the wider concerns of employment policy with the regulation of unemployment and the labour market. Skills are an integral component of the capacity to labour and thus a critical dimension of the wage bargain between purchasers and sellers of labour-power (Botwinick 1993; 11-3). Indeed, the frequent invocation of training as the key pre-condition to improving employment outcomes - what many have referred to as the 'cult of training' - has become a key element of neo-liberal and social democratic employment strategies in the advanced capitalist countries over the last decade. This essay will situate and critically assess training within these dominant approaches to employment policy, particularly with respect to claims for training policy in the containment of the capitalist tendency to produce surplus labour as part of its competitive processes.

Neo-liberal policy on training and unemployment

The neo-liberal position on unemployment and training policy proceeds from the view that capitalism is an economic system best understood as a process of free individual exchange operating in competitive markets. In a labour market, individual maximising actors voluntarily adjust their labour supply in response to price signals so that the market clears and equilibrium is quickly re-established. The demand for labour itself is a derived demand from the profit maximisation decisions of firms. Under the assumption of perfect competition, firms hire labour until the marginal product is equated with the real wage. As incremental output is a decreasing function of employment, real wages and the level of employment vary inversely. In the labour market individuals compare the current and expected wage rate against the costs of training and their preference for leisure, and, based on this trade-off, voluntarily choose to seek work or not. The structure of individual preferences is 'distorted' by interference in pure market wage-setting. In a flexible price system, labour markets would clear in both the short and long runs. All neo-liberal explanations account for unemployment, therefore, as a consequence of voluntary choice, real wage rates (as a measure of individual productivity), and the obstacles to the flexibility of these variables (Nickell 1990; Cross 1995).

Unemployment results when the real wages being asked are too high and profits are too low to warrant increasing production, leading to fewer job offers, a lower rate of investment and the use of labour-saving techniques. Because of unionisation, or more generally unrealistic expectations about wage offers, wage demands do not adjust downwards until unemployment growth begins to exert its disillusion effect (the famous short run Phillips curve). Attempting to lower real wages through inflation (as Keynesian stimulus does), soon leads to workers' wage expectations adapting to the rise in goods prices, leaving real wages and the aggregate labour supply unchanged. Unemployment remains at its natural, or voluntary, rate of unemployment as demand stimulus does not affect real output and long term 'employment will be back at the level that prevailed before the assumed unanticipated acceleration in aggregate nominal demand' (Friedman 1977; 457; Lucas 1978).

A level of positive unemployment would still, however, represent a *prima facie* case for regulating the market. Unemployment must either be denied or explained away as a result of voluntary decisions that simply produce the statistical artifact that is labelled 'unemployment' (Darby 1976; Romer 1986). The proliferation of neo-liberal refinements to the natural rate of unemployment explanation have, therefore, attempted to demonstrate how the actual existing level of unemployment is a rational outcome producing voluntary unemployment; that is, to explain how a divergence between wages and productivity (represented by workers' skills) causes a 'real wage gap' resulting in unemployment.

The general point of departure for neo-liberals has been to see unemployment as a 'market' phenomenon - simply a temporary transition between equilibria - due to lagged price and wage adjustments. The widely-cited explanation of Bruno and Sachs (1985) of the post-1973 rise in unemployment, for example, contends that the supply side price shocks and the decline in productivity growth lowered the real wage growth rate compatible with full employment. Adjustment did not occur because labour market behaviour has maintained wage growth and hence pushed the unemployment rate up. There are numerous possible reasons for why the market has been 'frustrated' in taking its natural course of adjusting to lower real wages. Many neo-liberals maintain that market forces have been blocked because of institutional rigidities of welfare, skill credentials, trade unions, and minimum wages that prevent individuals from accepting the lower wage rates that would lead to a higher demand for labour. Alternatively, a demographic bulge, due to an influx of the numbers of youth, women, or immigrant workers, may also have led to an autonomous shift in the labour supply, but their lower levels of skills and productivity are incompatible with existing wages, causing temporary unemployment. At the other end, a shift in labour demand from new products or advanced techniques will cause industrial dislocation, and a need for labour reallocation toward higher skills because of the shift in the inter-industry dispersion of employment growth. Efforts to defend declining sectors, old wage bargains and disappearing skills will simply block the transition to the most efficient production techniques. Similarly, if labour has been kept immobile due to 'place' rigidities, such as regionally differentiated unemployment benefits, wage adjustments will lag causing the natural rate to rise. In all these cases, market barriers block short period labour market-clearing; 'purer' markets would resolve much of the adjustment problem (Osberg 1988; Knight 1987).

Neo-liberals also dismiss unemployment as simply a voluntary 'agency' choice that maximises an individual preference between leisure and additional income (with the expectations forming preferences lagging behind harsher market conditions). There are several specific theories to explain the choice. Unemployed individuals have a reservation wage, for example, and simply search for a job until one meets their wage demand or they lower their expectations (Phelps 1972). Inadequate market signalling through asymmetric information flows also might lengthen the search time and the adjustment of individual preference functions. Voluntary quits and labour market turnover that are recorded as unemployment may actually be more an indication of an active market of individuals maximising preferences than unemployment (Feldstein 1976). Alternatively, implicit contracts formed between workers and firms include a wage premium dependent on the probability of layoff (Azariadis 1975). Workers knowingly choose unstable employers, and the combination of contracts and unemployment compensation cause wages that result in unemployment that is expected and accepted. Similarly, unemployment insurance shifts the labour-leisure trade-off toward leisure as unemployment is 'free time' equivalent to leisure (Green and Cousineau 1976). As a portion of leisure-time is compensated by unemployment benefits, some agents maximise their 'utility' by selecting unemployment. Whatever the specific cause the result is the same;

voluntary market decisions leave a positive unemployment rate, yet still at an efficient equilibrium (but one that might not be socially optimal).

Workers' skills enter into all these explanations of unemployment and market adjustment directly or indirectly as wages reflect the contribution to marginal productivity, which is dependant upon individual skills. Skill attributes are a result of individual investment in human capital (including investment in job search, qualifications and so on). Higher wages generally imply higher qualifications, a return to individual investments in human capital (longer periods of unemployment reducing the return to investment in training and thus the over-supply of the qualified). 'This knowledge and skill are in great part the product of investment and, combined with other human investment, predominantly account for the productive superiority of the technically advanced countries' (Schultz 1961; 3). Firms establish their production function in response to relative costs of factor inputs (such as the price of labour and training) with no dynamic variation in technique from a skilled labour supply. In neo-liberal arguments, wage offers - or the lack thereof - are also a register of skills, and the unemployed are always, by definition, deficient in skills relative to their reservation wages (as skills must improve or wages fall). Labour market 'mismatches' involve, therefore, an adjustment of skills and real wages in response to price signals, given the nature of labour market rigidities and individual choices (Bosworth and Wilson 1994). This equilibriating process is the central proposition of neo-liberal employment and training policies; the labour market yields private wage signals (that are also signals of return to investment in skills) that eliminate involuntary unemployment and induce skills formation that is consistent with the social signals (of new technological paradigms, of educational needs, of worthwhile work) for the economy as a whole.

The neo-liberal approach to employment and training policies, therefore, stresses closing the 'real wage gap' by what can be termed measures of market reinforcement (Friedman 1977; Phelps 1992). That is, real wages and skills must be made 'numerically' flexible to be brought in line with productivity and labour demand. One set of measures is straightforward; as government intervention distorts market efficiency and delays adjustment to supply-side shocks, its role should be minimised and stabilised. A stable macro-economic environment of low inflation is central so that capitalists can have more certainty about their investments (with the principle of substitutability of labour and capital making any investment bias to capital-using technological change a transitory phenomenon, unimportant except for determining the composition of growth). Deregulation to eliminate non-market barriers that prevent real wages from falling can then lower the natural unemployment rate. The institutional securities for workers built into the labour market that limited flexibility and compressed wage differentials need to be 'rolled back' and market incentives reinforced. This entails: reducing trade union power; minimising the welfare disincentives to work; improving information flows and labour mobility; leaving investment in training to individual decisions of human capital needs; and eliminating market restraints, such as minimum wages and unemployment insurance, which limit downward wage flexibility.

The other set of policy measures require adjustment to skills formation. It is possible to argue, for example, that skills directly affect the rate of unemployment in that the 'equilibriating' rate of unemployment is kept higher by wages facing less labour supply pressures (Abraham 1991). Semi-skilled industrial workers laid-off are 'mismatched' with high-skilled service sector jobs in computer programming. Improving training markets should lead, in the neo-liberal view, to *pro tanto* positive unemployment results. Transferable skills that raise productivity in any firm, and thus are susceptible to being poached by non-training firms as workers are mobile, could benefit from direct wage subsidies or lower trainee allowances so that all firms would have incentive to hire and train (Becker 1975). Training markets could also be improved by deregulation that restores price signals and incentives to human capital formation; deregulation of education and training monopolies; lowering taxes such as training levies on payroll; encouraging individual savings and decisions with respect to human capital formation; wage subsidies that encourage the basic training and employment of the unskilled who need job entry or to overcome 'job shyness' as with workfare programmes; and even training assistance in job search that realigns wage expectations with the skills of the unemployed (Chapman 1993; Prais 1995).

There are, however, several theoretical objections to neo-liberal training and employment policies. For there to exist a natural rate of unemployment that could be considered a voluntary equilibrium, wage setting must, at least in the long term, act as a flexible price market. If the labour market does not adjust in this way, even neo-liberals concede that 'non-natural' unemployment will exist. In fact, the labour market exhibits various degrees of wage rigidity apart from government interference or unions (whose forms themselves can be dismissed as unwarranted interference in markets only on the basis of ideological prejudice and not by history or reason). Relative wages across occupations and industries are rigid by custom, the heterogeneity of labour, organisational efficiencies, and conceptions of distributive justice ('a fair day's wage') (Thurow 1983; Gordon 1972). These are structural attributes of the labour market that negate the idealist neo-liberal view of purely autonomous self-interested agents. The lack of flexible prices in the real world raises, then, the traditional Keynesian and Marxian arguments that decreasing real wages can trigger perverse consequences from efforts to impose flexibility. That is, quantity adjustments are likely to be as important as price movements so that market-clearing is unlikely to be smooth. Moreover, by taking demand out of the system, rather than increasing employment there may well be a further increase in the jobless unless there is a compensating demand source to maintain realisation conditions. As long as these kinds of wage rigidities exist in the real world, whether in the Keynesian or Marxist senses, the actual and trend rates of unemployment are unlikely to equal the natural rate. The natural rate of unemployment simply serves as a hypothetical assertion, drawn from dubious assumptions, of limited normative value (Cherry 1981; Shulman 1989).

The empirical evidence is not surprisingly quite mixed, despite sustained efforts at neo-liberal employment policies since the early 1980s and the persistent invocation of the North American model of labour market flexibility, that widely reducing labour costs increases employment. And in no case does the evidence support the employment impacts predicted by the wage and market flexibility advocates (Glyn 1995b; Solow 1990). In a thorough assessment of the literature, Bean notes that 'real wage gaps had disappeared in most countries by the mid-1980s' but unemployment remained high (1994; 577). In contrast, the weight of recent studies provides decisive evidence that the inequality and social costs (in the growth in both the inactive and prison populations) of neo-liberal flexibility are quite high and damaging (Freeman 1995; ILO 1995; 157).

Market failures specific to training compound the labour market imbalances caused by the pursuit of wage flexibility. The most widely-cited failure of training markets is convincing theoretically and empirically pervasive. As few skills a worker learns are exclusive to a firm, and all skill development involves costs, it is logical that in competitive markets capitalists attempt to limit their individual expenditures on training. The profit-making incentive for each capitalist agent is in fact to degrade as many jobs as possible and to skill as few workers as is feasible to employ the existing level of technology to maintain a competitive advantage. Firms may well find it to their benefit to 'poach' trained workers away from training firms to reduce their training expenditures even more. If this process occurs systematically some firms may simply cease to train so that markets with poachers and trainers are likely to be unstable and continuously imbalanced. This would reveal itself, as it does in Britain, by persistent skill shortages and bottlenecks alongside pools of low-skilled unemployed for long durations (Senker 1992; Rainbird 1990).

The specific market failures of training can, therefore, compound through time into structural obstacles to adjustment; firms have less incentive to post skilled vacancies as this would increase the returns (wages) to skilled workers; and workers have little incentive to train as the stock of skilled vacancies is low. This reinforcing failure can create a 'low-skills, bad jobs' trap that is systematically linked to national training and education institutions (with different training institutions and historical contexts arguably producing 'high-skill, good jobs', although there are flaws to this contention as we show below) (Snower 1996; 112-3). Education and employment subsidies (as Snower himself proposes) are likely to be insufficient to break the vicious cycle that keeps an economy trapped into minimal skills development. Other labour market failures will probably add to training market deficiencies and the 'low-skills, bad jobs trap' - information asymmetries, innovation externalities, training economies of scale, skill and wage rigidities, differential risk premiums, and so on (Finegold and Soskice 1988).

The distributional obstacles raised by market-driven training structures similarly undermine the general claim that training can serve as a mechanism for the disadvantaged to improve their labour market position. For example, trainees will have to pay for their training either in the form of direct outlays or foregone income. As the period in which these expenditures occur is different from the one in which earnings are made, the training must be financed. Capital markets, however, are unlikely to fill this gap, especially when the link between employment prospects and training is so tenuous or when groups encounter structural societal inequalities as do women, minorities and workers. Skill investments will be less than required and many skills in under-supply, the more the market is relied upon to finance and supply training. But even if some form of state assistance and planning of training expenditures will inevitably have to occur, the efforts to reach those most in need of training, through youth training strategies or special employment training for the long-term unemployed, will tend to be inadequate relative to the problems of the most vulnerable as long as unemployment is conceptualised as an individual problem of skill investments and wage demands. This conceptual point parallels the actual experience; partly because these kinds of programmes have had funding declines as part of neo-liberal retrenchment, and partly because market-based delivery systems have failed so miserably in terms of equity, continuity and skills-upgrading. Indeed, without labour demand for the semi-skilled to provide stable employment, these programmes - and the workfare variants common in North America - have only reinforced the vicious circle of unemployment, low skills and unstable jobs (Skuse 1995; Rubery 1996; Myles, 1996).

Adjustment of the supply and demand of skills and labour through market signals must take place through time and not the abstract equilibrium space of neo-liberal employment policy. The concept of hysteresis has often been invoked to explain the time-dependent path of unemployment. In neo-liberal terms, hysteresis means that a recession creates the conditions for a continuation of high unemployment dependent upon the speed of adjustment of labour market institutions to the supply side shocks which opened a real wage gap. In other words, there will be a period of adjustment before the economy moves to its lower long run equilibrium point. But path-dependent adjustment - the actual historical movement of economies determining outcomes - is susceptible to compounding adjustment problems and indeterminate outcomes. There are, for example, irreducible lags and processes involved in training that can move the market just as easily away as toward a hypothetical equilibrium point. Because training is inherently uncertain, it is hard to estimate what skills will be needed in the future (or in what supply). For production techniques that are only partially known the recovery of training investments may be very risky. Once competitive cost-cutting takes hold, training expenditures become even more uncertain, and the option of poaching from other firms through higher wages is a more reasonable proposition for each firm. For the economy as a whole, however, the 'rational' action by private economic agents can only lengthen the problems of skill adjustment and unemployment. Thus chronic under-supply of skills is likely as long as skills are treated as exclusively 'private' goods and human capital investment decisions. The impact of market adjustment, in such a process of 'cumulative causation' through time, for competitive capacity and unemployment could be quite serious.

If the trajectory of unemployment is history-dependent and institutionally-mediated, as the hysteresis concept implies, it is impossible to sustain the neo-liberal position that unemployment is all voluntary and government policy is impotent. Historical time must be conceptualised as more than an inertial force slowing the tendency of economic processes to move toward some hypothetical equilibrium point of natural unemployment. This point has been acknowledged, at the cost of theoretical consistency, even within the neo-liberal camp; 'What is required is a theory of unemployment in which unemployment, far from returning to a stable equilibrium - or 'natural rate' - over time, is instead strongly dependent on history...to highlight the sensitive dependence of unemployment on current and past events' (Blanchard and Summers 1987; 182). Training and employment policies of market reinforcement to increase functional flexibility are, in the actual movement of economies in a period of instability and restructuring, likely to inflame the capitalist unemployment problem and social inequalities rather than mitigate them.

Social democratic policy on training and unemployment

The neo-liberal position has most often been rejected on the basis of a specific critique of capitalist market failures and its 'simple commodity economy' presumption that buyers and sellers are equal economic agents voluntarily exchanging commodities (McCombie 1985). Social democratic employment policy rejects several claims central to its analysis of market-clearing; that production directly creates demand for consumption goods; that savings leads to demand for investment funds; that the demand for labour varies inversely to the real wage; and that price signals are adequate to generate and adjust skill profiles. However, interpretations vary substantially as to the degree to which employment market failures are systemic to capitalist economies, or whether they arise primarily from short run demand imbalances (Keynesians) or long term supply side transformations (institutionalists).

In the Keynesian view, for example, the capitalist unemployment problem is not located in the labour market *per se*, but in the macro-economic conditions produced by uncoordinated individual actions that determine the utilisation of productive capacity. In opposition to the 'classical school' of Say's law that supply creates its own demand, Keynes argued that 'the volume of employment is not determined by the marginal disutility of labour measured in terms of real wages, except in so far as the supply of labour available at a given real wage sets a maximum level to employment. The propensity to consume and the rate of new investment determine between them the volume of employment, and the volume of employment is uniquely related to a given level of real wages - not the other way around' (Keynes 1936; 30). The analytical and policy problem is to identify and stabilise the factors that determine effective demand, the level of demand actually attained in a monetary economy, and thereby the level of employment.

Although consumption is a relatively stable proportion of income, it does not increase directly as income increases; as income levels rise, savings increase, lowering effective demand unless the demand for investment funds fills the gap. Yet investment is unstable, dependent as it is upon capitalists' *ex ante* expectations of future profits (introducing directly a sense of an economy set in historical time), and, to a lesser extent, on the rate of interest. If balance in the payments position is assumed, all countries logically being unable to run surpluses, the level of employment is determined, therefore, by the level of investment based on short run expectations about the rate of accumulation. A lack of investor confidence, what Keynes termed 'animal spirits', could easily develop from any shift off the full employment equilibrium growth path. Lower interest rates might create more liquidity, for example, but not necessarily increase investment. With effective demand weakened, capitalists would not even realise existing investments, and savings and investment would again become equated *ex post*, but at lower levels of income and employment. Moreover, a decline in real wages would not lead to an increase in employment *pro tanto*, as capital goods embody different capital-labour ratios, and capitalists willingly pay a wage premium to keep skilled workers (reflecting the heterogeneity of labour inputs and the need to recoup training investments). The new short period equilibrium at less that full employment might well extend into indefinite stagnation.

The effect of the 'multiplier' process on expenditures, moreover, is to raise the likelihood of just such an occurrence; disturbances in one of the components of demand, notably investment, are magnified, thereby moving the economy substantially away from the potential level of output. Additionally, investment in this period creates productive capacity in the next but, as Keynesians argue, this does not mean that wage earners will have the income to consume the expanded potential output. This depends upon workers' earnings in other industries, the savings decisions of households, and the payments balance. There is no reason to expect, then, without a regulating force external to the market, that effective demand will be adequate to potential output capacity and that investment will match savings. In other words, against the self-equilibriating neo-liberal view, lack of demand creates a gap with potential supply (as seen by capacity utilisation in the short period). The actual 'equilibrium' can be at a demand level too low to employ the existing labour supply leaving a pool, as Keynes called them, of the 'involuntary unemployed' (Keynes 1936; 6).

The extent of the market instability, and thus the trajectory of growth, employment and skills, is widely disputed (Trevithick 1992; Worswick 1991). In the 'neo-classical synthesis' short-term money wage rigidities mean that it is better to use aggregate demand management than sacrifice output. Moreover, to the extent that money wage expectations incorporate an inflationary component, incomes and labour market policies might assist in managing the trade-off between unemployment and inflation at higher levels of output. In contrast, in the 'Keynesian reappraisal' the volatility of market trading and misinformation mean that a multiple of disequilibria points exist such that labour markets may not easily clear. The possibility of multiple equilibria means that economic growth in the long term may expand at rates of investment and full capacity output levels that may not coincide with full employment. In any case, the 'knife-edge' growth path for full employment will be highly unstable due to investment volatility.

Keynesianism is often equated to government policies that 'fine-tune' capacity utilisation and that manage specific market failures. In the short period situation where unemployment exceeds the full employment level, and unused capacity exists, the central objective is to bolster effective demand. Monetary policy can increase liquidity or lower interest rates to spur purchases of consumer durables and housing, and borrowing for investment. The impact on demand, however, will depend more upon profit expectations than credit availability. In contrast, fiscal policy measures are likely to have a direct impact. Tax cuts encourage consumption; subsidies to business stimulate investment; and government expenditures, financed through deficit spending, can increase consumption or build social infrastructure. Other measures form an integral part of Keynesian employment policies. Currency devaluation, for example, may help switch domestic expenditures and boost exports. Industrial planning and regulation of financial markets will help maintain the 'knife-edge' full employment growth trajectory.

In the institutionalist view, the specific market failures creating involuntary unemployment can also emerge from mismatches between available skills and the 'technical attributes' of the capital stock on the supply-side. The unevenness of economic development and the heterogeneity of the labour stock can show, for example, in a variety of short period adjustment problems. The dualist structure of the economy, divided between a core group of dynamic firms and a backward unstable periphery, as argued by Piore, Doeringer and others, presents a number of structural unemployment problems. Structural unemployment arises from the skill profile of the labour force. Because of institutional blockages in the labour market, for instance barriers caused by race or gender discrimination, segments of the workforce may systematically lack appropriate skills. These marginal workers tend to find employment in the peripheral sector and occupy the lower segment of the labour market, suffering higher rates of unemployment, lower pay and unstable jobs. To the extent their acquisition of skills or mobility is impaired, the average rate of unemployment will tend to be higher, adjustment to new techniques slower and the 'distribution [of unemployment] among various demographic groups' uneven (Piore 1979; 9; Doeringer and Piore 1975). Declining regions and sectors will also suffer a mismatch between existing skills and future employment openings. In these cases, labour market policies could 'improve market efficiency and hence reduce the equilibrium unemployment rate' (Jackman, et al. 1990; 452). If the rigidities preventing market-clearing wages are controlled, demand stimulation to increase job openings is not wasted through wage inflation and skill bottlenecks.

Long run supply-side transformation presents the skills mismatch as a dynamic blockage to adjustment. Involuntary unemployment from technological change arises because 'development is punctuated by periods of unusual structural change to which market economies find it difficult to adapt' (Driver 1987; 4). New production technologies cause a shift in labour demand so that some industries and skills become redundant while others become dynamic growth poles requiring new skills. Although real wage and Keynesian unemployment may occur with structural change, they will not be alleviated either by wage-cutting or conventional demand management. Rather, the potential difficulties of structural adjustment depend on two factors; first, the extent to which 'bunching' of new technologies occurs; and, second, the institutional processes that shape the adjustment of the capital stock and the labour force. Schumpeter, for example, argued that innovation tends to occur in a 'creative gale of destruction' that forms long cycles of growth and transition. The gales of innovation produce investment booms with low unemployment followed by periods of low investment, structural decline and mass unemployment. In Schumpeter's theory of 'disequilibriating' economic growth, 'cyclical unemployment is technological unemployment... periods of prolonged supernormal unemployment, coincide with the periods in which the results of inventions are spreading over the system' (Schumpeter 1939; 515). More recently, Mensch has argued that such a large shift in autonomous investment occurred in the early 1970s, making adjustment of the capital stock and skills crucial to preparing the conditions for a new investment upswing from new technologies and lower unemployment (Mensch 1975). This position is, however, rather one-sided; it leaves the sense that structural crises will inevitably be followed by long booms, and it is quite difficult to correlate diverse national unemployment trajectories to the technical composition of the capital stock or skill attributes of the labour-force.

The detailed study of Freeman, Clarke and Soete (1982) also stresses the unevenness of technological change, although they doubt that such a close correlation exists between periods of investment clusters and those of depressions. In this view, investment in a new technical system initially creates a boom and employment expansion; however, scale economies eventually take over the new technique and investment and employment levels steady. Once this 'mature' stage is reached, the problem is making the leap to a new vintage technology, entailing an institutional transition in production paradigms (technology, organisation, capital stock and skills), without debilitating structural unemployment developing.

For example, the difficult transition between technological systems lies behind the current unemployment crisis that followed the post-war boom. In the boom itself, the older vintage plant was either destroyed in the war or made obsolete by reduced capital values in the 1930s depression; an investment surge at the end of the war, in new industries such as chemicals, electrical goods and autos, produced a long wave of growth and high profits. By the 1960s, however, output was growing by five per cent but industrial employment by less than one per cent. So, by the 1980s, unemployment was higher at any particular level of capacity utilisation. The old technological system was exhausted, Freeman and his colleagues argue, increasing productivity mainly by labour-saving techniques. The wave of new vintage microelectronics technology added to the adjustment problem by raising capital intensity in the most productive sectors. The demand side shocks from oil increases and government restraint meant, therefore, jobless growth, as old vintage industries develop surplus capacity and new ones lack the demand to expand to increase employment (Freeman and Soete 1987; OECD 1985). In contrast to the Keynesian view which offers support for declining industries and protectionism to keep up employment, the institutionalist view argues that delays in the transition to new technologies can make things worse. Competitiveness and payments difficulties are likely to mount, and unemployment will be prone to secular increases. Indeed, a major problem of structural decline may occur, as Britain experienced under Thatcher, if restraint is pursued dogmatically. The unemployment crisis is foremost due, then, to the lag of adjustment of skills and the capital stock on the supply-side, in the context of unstable macro-economic conditions.

The transition between technological paradigms presents, in the institutionalist view, the long period policy problem of establishing the institutions to support a permanent adjustment of the capital stock and skills to a new work regime. (This is often depicted, notably in the work of neo-Schumpeterians and regulationists, as the organisational transition between Fordist economies of scale to post-Fordist economies of scope, as in Freeman and Soete 1987; Piore and Sabel 1984; Boyer 1988). As the structural crisis lies on the supply side, shifting investment out of old industries and techniques to capital stock in new sectors and new technologies is the priority. Keynesian reflation without industrial policies is quite unconvincing. As Freeman, Clark and Soete (1982; 134) warn, the new industries where demand is likely to go might well be at full capacity with skill shortages, causing a burst of inflation. Industrial policies will help alleviate any 'capital shortage' unemployment, but long term employment will emerge only with the expansion of new sectors alongside the growth of demand to absorb new capacity. Worker adjustment policies, such as retraining and mobility assistance will speed the shift to new techniques and production zones, as the substitutability between capital and labour is not instantaneous or neutral (Hudson 1988; 27-35).

Institutionalists like Streeck have therefore argued that skills should be seen as a 'collective good';

> ...moving product ranges "upwards" towards more diversified demands and high quality markets requires not only capital investments in research and development for more diversified products, but also human resource investment in new and higher skills....[But] the fundamental uncertainty for employers of recovering their training expenses...turns skills, from the view of the individual employer, into a collective good. (1989; 90-1)

The specific failures of training markets and hence the differentiated institutionalisation of skills as a collective good leads to commonly observed differences in training regimes. In 'Anglo-American capitalisms' the orientation is toward market-driven training systems with consequently more polarised labour markets and extensive skill shortages; in 'Germanic models' corporatist institutions regulate a highly-developed training complex for high skills as part of industrial adjustment; in 'Scandinavian capitalisms' the state plays a significant role in equalising training opportunities and encouraging labour mobility. Sorge and Warner (1986) contend that national training traditions are in fact linked to capacity for technological adaptation; strong training structures allow workers to be re-deployed, new techniques quickly introduced and competitiveness sustained. Such functional flexibility produces a high skills, high productivity, low unemployment equilibrium, a path that would otherwise be blocked by skill shortages and adjustment lags. The production of skills is therefore a central object of employment policy.

The employment and training policies of market control of both Keynesians and institutionalists recognise, as with Marx, the possibility of unemployment in the temporal disjunctures in a monetary economy between the processes of production, distribution and realisation. Employment policies are seen as operating on the temporal stabilisation of exchange processes and by embedding the institutional context for market relations. Yet even with the instability presented by weak demand conditions that interact with long period technological transformations that add capacity and new techniques, unemployment is posited as a particular, and not a general, failure of capitalist markets. Technical policy adjustments on the demand and supply sides can maintain a stable growth path at low unemployment moving through historical time. Employment and training market failures are always of degree - and not of kind - from the normal operations of capitalist production expanding output and employment opportunities.

The long term structural failure of the capitalist economies to stay on a high employment growth path after 1974 present problems in explaining the spiral of unemployment. It is possible to argue, as Solow (1986; 8) does, that the monetarist shocks from the 1970s on have meant that the capitalist countries have passed through 'a long period of inadequate aggregate demand, with governments unable or unwilling to engage in compensatory fiscal and monetary policy.' This demand constrained environment would also hinder long period adjustment to technological change. This might explain why the base rate of unemployment initially increased, but it is not convincing as to the continual rise in unemployment, at any given level of capacity utilisation, and its resistance to demand stimulation. But as Solow (1986; 11) observes, 'recent [1980s] increases in unemployment have not been accompanied by corresponding reductions in capacity utilisation.' Many Keynesians have thus followed Blinder (1988; 2) into acceptance of neo-liberal arguments on numerical flexibility that 'intransigent trade unions and well-intentioned but unintelligent governments have erected a web of micro-economic barriers to full employment that both make labour more expensive and transform wages from variable into fixed costs.' This view suffers, however, from the same glaring flaw as the natural rate of unemployment theory; the reversal of 'market flexibility' conditions that pushed up unemployment in the 1970s have not brought it down in the 1990s (even in the US recorded unemployment remains higher).

The institutionalist incorporation of supply-side transformations to explain the long term run-up in unemployment also falters. It is hard to draw an association between the sudden onset of the crisis in 1974 with the abrupt exhaustion of old innovations - productivity declines were apparent since the late 1960s - or the introduction of a new technological paradigm. In addition, the supply-side account does not explain why the general rise in unemployment rates has followed particular national patterns of inadequacy and disaster, although all the advanced countries must have faced similar old and new technical systems. National skill and industrial adjustment policies might explain part of the divergence, but not all of it. It is hard to make the case, for example, that Germany's highly-regarded and often invoked technical system or skill policies lag other countries, yet its unemployment rate places it closer to countries like Canada or Italy, neither of which has a strong innovation or training record. On comparative grounds, therefore, it is questionable to see containing unemployment as mainly an issue of supply-side adjustment policies of skills for growth in high value-added sectors.

There is, moreover, the more fundamental problem of treating training policy and skills adjustment like a 'cargo cult' - developing an oversupply of skills as if it will induce a resolution of other economic imbalances. Removing skill blockages in specific industries, for example, will not necessarily produce the conditions to lower unemployment if the problem is a system-wide transition. This will require supportive industrial policies an investment in technology, infrastructure and so on. But even adjusting skills development as a whole *ex ante* to match a new production paradigm *ex post* suggests a smoother process of industrial restructuring than economic history warrants. Indeed, as the advanced capitalist countries have experienced over the last decade, average skill levels might increase but not aggregate employment. If technical change is capital-using, removing either specific or general skill blockages will be insufficient alone to contain unemployment growth. This will depend upon the balance between a decline in the average hours of work, the redistribution of income, the spread of work outside the industrial sector and the overall growth rate achievable (ignoring environmental consequences). This points to a fundamental process of structural transformations and instabilities in market processes that cannot be accommodated by the functional flexibility of workers alone (given a context of adequate effective demand).

Even if we grant the assumptions of the market control case that some amount of involuntary unemployment is related to insufficient demand compounded by skill adjustment problems (views that we have argued are insufficient to account for the unemployment crisis), the sources of effective demand and the maintenance of external balance between competitive states all deploying new technologies in production raises distinct problems. It should be underlined that the hypothesised supply-side transformations between technological paradigms hinges on rapid growth in world markets to absorb the exports of the high value-added industries that training and industrial policies are promoting to reduce unemployment. The internationalisation of economic activity has meant that conditions of realisation are in part determined by 'international' effective demand, that is, the macro-economic strategies of other states. There is, however, neither the institutional capacity at present nor in the foreseeable future to co-ordinate an international reflation. Indeed, international agencies like the International Monetary Fund and the World Bank have favoured deflationary national strategies. Yet even with a different policy orientation, it is not clear how an international reflation is undertaken without at least the pre-conditions of national governments of common inclination, co-operative and not competitive economies, and stronger international, national and local planning capacities than now exist to ensure productive capacity is in place and balances with demand. Without such pre-conditions backed by the legitimacy and capacity to implement coercive sanctions, countries can always gain competitive advantage by 'cheating' by not maintaining demand conditions, engaging in environmental cost externalisation, or by applying non-tariff barriers. It is dubious analytically and politically wreckless, therefore, to posit that export markets will grow to the extent necessary so that the expansion of the high value-added production sector will be large enough to absorb not just the unemployed, but also the loss of jobs in more labour-intensive sectors and from capital-using new technologies.

If the sources of effective demand are uncertain and yet the skills-oriented supply-side policies to increase exports are widely adopted to reduce general unemployment, a compositional fallacy of aggregation immediately has to be confronted. The 'beggar-thy-neighbour' strategy of improving payments balance is impossible for all; some countries must absorb the payments surplus, so all countries facing unemployment cannot adopt it (Robinson 1937; 210-30). This type of competitive strategy is inherently unstable; the trading partners running deficits must respond to improve their own competitive positions by deflation and devaluation (a process that has been unfolding since the mid-80s Plaza and Louvre accords to the Chinese devaluation to the recent competitive devaluations sweeping Asia). As the underlying unemployment remains for the trading partners, a spiral of 'competitive austerity' must ensue. If a country pursues an export-oriented strategy for high employment on a weak competitive base in these deteriorating external conditions (as Canada and Britain have historically done), they stand to lose on several grounds; the national economy further loses its internal coherence and planning capacities to redistribute economic activity and employment; competitive pressures will produce social polarisation as only a few workers are skilled and these are pushed as far as possible by competitive firms to re-coup training investments; and employment growth will have to occur in sectors with high resource rents, low waged and non-tradeable activities as in 'servant-type' services or sectors with high potential cost-externalisation of ecologically-destructive outputs (the real sources of the 'North American jobs machine'). For countries (such as Sweden and Germany) that have a strong competitive capacity built on leading sectors and a high skills foundation, this will intensify efforts to preserve 'good jobs' in a slow-growth, unstable economic climate. To the extent that this 'skills-oriented' employment policy contains a re-distributional component to extend universal access to education and training (as with Germany until recently), it will also come under severe pressure to selectively target reduced training expenditures and limit the access to training and education (Mahnkopf 1992).

The market control argument that training policy could pose as an alternative transition to a more internationalised and technologically advanced economy is theoretically suspect and empirically at odds with actual outcomes. As long as there exist global labour surpluses in an internationalising economic context, the competitive pressures will be toward wages being determined by the supply price of labour whatever the variation in average productivity in national contexts. The most that could be claimed is that countries with institutional structures supportive of employment and training strategies of market control have been 'less inadequate' than others in the transition to the so-called new technological paradigm. Cornwall (1991; 114), for instance, argues that the path-dependence of employment outcomes produces a policy irreversibility that blocks formally realisable goals and allows others. Solow (1990; 59) similarly confesses that the rate of unemployment 'actually observed depends on history.'

The capacity even to maintain alternate market control strategies that are less inadequate is, however, likely to decrease through time in a context of unstable, asymmetrical internationalisation. It has proven difficult even for the leading countries to maintain the share of 'good jobs', never mind increase the overall share through successful export-oriented policies. These will come, in any respect, at the expense of others attempting the same strategy. Streeck (1997; 256) has recently noted with respect to Germany that 'economic globalisation erodes the conditions for such [market-correcting] intervention and, by default but also by design, leaves only de-politicised, privatised and market-driven forms of economic order.' Increased levels of training cannot contain the underlying contradictions producing unemployment; a 'credential inflation' of needing more advanced skills just to get employment in far less demanding jobs in a harsher labour market climate is more likely. Training and employment policies of market control will have a diminishing capacity to contain involuntary unemployment or to compress social inequalities, the general problems that the capitalist unemployment problem continually re-poses.

Capitalism, training and employment policy

The acquisition of appropriate skills by workers is conventionally put forth by government employment departments and business associations as a simple proposition; that individuals improving their skill attributes will better their prospect of being hired in the labour market. This commonplace has a theoretical justification; if individual workers adjust their skills (and relative wage acceptance rates) they will better match labour demand conditions and thereby raise individual and overall social welfare. This reasoning from individual actions to social outcomes is, however, a quite misleading account of the macro-economic conditions that establish labour demand and the micro-economic processes that produce numerous failures in 'training markets'. Even on the narrow terms of improving individual earnings and employment, as even the OECD (1994a) has conceded, training results have often been decidedly indifferent. Neo-liberal employment and training policies of market reinforcement, stressing numerical flexibility leading to hypothesised equilibriating adjustments of the price of labour and skills of workers, are likely to contribute further to the social divisions of modern capitalism. Indeed, the only potential benefit from lowering real wages and reducing the training and non-paid work options such as welfare for workers, increasingly through the coercive form of North American style workfare, is likely to be some easing of recorded rates of unemployment, although at the cost of even more sharply socially polarised societies. This has certainly been the experience of the 'Anglo-American' models of capitalism in adopting market-driven training and employment policies (Gordon 1996; Green 1994; McBride 1992).

The social democratic alternative employment policy linking skill acquisition to long-term structural changes in the technical conditions of production and the market potential for high quality value-added products advances a quite different proposition and path of adjustment; if workers are broadly skilled as a 'collective good' to improve technical attributes, and to directly compensate for the systemic failures of the training market, they will increase external competitive capacities and thereby general employment conditions. This kind of skills-oriented employment policy to improve the functional flexibility of workers via more general transferable skills between workplaces and high-skilled, more team-oriented and less hierarchical practices within workplaces, implies a quite significant reorganisation of general education and skill formation toward the objective of market rationality. The success of the strategy hinges on current unemployment levels being a function of skill shortages or a 'labour demand twist' so that skilled workers are now permanently more demanded than unskilled (Glyn 1995a). This position is unconvincing; general educational and training levels have been increasing alongside increased levels of labour reserves for some time. It is quite unclear, moreover, how such localised supply-side transformations in the labour market will generate adequate national and international effective demand to reduce unemployment imbalances given the problem of co-ordination of competitive states and firms (and, of course, the evidence that most existing unemployment is not Keynesian). This strategy, too, is likely to deepen the social divisions of modern capitalism as competitive labour market pressures orient highly-skilled workers to form 'productivity pacts' with managers of competitive enterprises and peripheral workers are compelled to accept lower wages in marginalised service activities. A social democratic skills-oriented employment policy seeking only to control market failures in training is also likely to increase social inequality. The economic strains breaking apart the German and Swedish models clearly indicate the limitations of this kind of 'progressive competitiveness' employment strategy (Mahnkopf 1992; Albo 1994).

In European policy circles currently, there is much discussion of a 'third way' between these two paths of capitalist employment policy through adopting both measures of labour market flexibility that reinforce market processes and supply side policies that stimulate training expenditures to control market failures. This 'third way' has had political momentum from the recent election of Tony Blair's New Labour government and the bargaining occurring at the European Union level over a European-wide employment expansion. There is little integration, however, of expansionary demand side policies because of the specific Maastricht fiscal convergence criteria and the more general 'prisoner's dilemma' costs for countries choosing expansion in a world of capital mobility. The 'third way' for capitalist employment policy hinges on two premises. There is a premise that a limited market is an external constraint on employment expansion; thus further economic liberalisation through regional trading blocks and global free trade will increase output capacity on the supply side and improved realisation conditions on the demand side. This will, in its turn, lead to increased labour demand and employment. There is also the premise that inflexible labour markets and the lack of skilled workers provide internal constraints to adjustment along the 'globalisation' path of output and employment expansion; thus removing labour market rigidities and disincentives while controlling for specific market failures will allow increased capitalist sector employment to absorb the unemployed and real incomes to rise as productivity improves with output expansion.

There is, however, a great deal of counterfactual argumentation and policy experience to cast serious doubts on these premise and hypothesised economic outcomes. The increased labour market flexibility will add to the growth of involuntary part-time employment, a decline in relative pay, and the expansion of low productivity labour intensive capitalist service sector employment (mainly related to servant-type activity purchased by asset holders or those in high-waged jobs). This is the kind of employment expansion that the US has undergone; distressed labour market circumstances and lack of welfare benefits lead workers to take up all kinds of informal and low paid activities, but low recorded rates of unemployment and productivity increases do not lead to improved wages and incomes for the working classes. This is a labour market outcome Joan Robinson once referred to as 'disguised unemployment', and what Marx had earlier called the 'stagnant reserve army of labour' and the 'pauperised class'. There is little that expanding training incentives or welfare-to-work policies can do to alter this kind of economic outcome in the absence of industrial policies for capitalist sector employment and redistributional policies for the expansion of state sector employment. It is quite difficult, then, to see this strategy as anything but a 'third way' to the same kinds of societal polarisation as the other two discussed strategies. Moreover, to the extent that the current economic conjuncture is already plagued by the deflationary conditions of competitive austerity internationally and deregulation of national labour markets that is placing downward pressure on wages, the 'third way may well compound both problems by attempting to expand the supply side while constricting the demand side. Such a strategy is unlikely to constitute an alternate policy outcome to neo-liberal employment policies; rather 'third way' employment and training policies concede that 'open-economy social democracy', as both a policy strategy and economic outcome, has become incorporated as a subordinate component of the wider dominant processes of neo-liberal economic restructuring and internationalisation.

Thus, there are neither theoretical nor empirical reasons to be optimistic about the prospects of any of these kinds of training policies improving employment outcomes in terms of lower unemployment or social inequality. This conclusion does not deny the importance of developing and equalising training and educational opportunities as a fundamental component of democratic citizenship. It is to insist, however, that more active employment policies that disengage work and incomes from market determination - and thus adopt measures that directly confront the tendency of capitalism to produce surplus labour as Marxists have pointed out - remain fundamental to the achievement of high employment and social equality.

Economists and political scientists would do well to link training policy to a wider set of questions that merit concerted research and policy attention. If technical advances mean hours of work can no longer be what they were, by how much should work-time be cut? If the majority of job growth will no longer be in manufacturing, what kind of egalitarian, collective services should be developed? If high general skills are as important as technical skills, including skills and capacities in democracy and administration, how should equal learning opportunities - including across race and gender divisions - be provided? If economic growth can no longer be the source of increasing employment for reasons of ecology, how do we plan for a re-distributional and quality growth model? If it is no longer acceptable to allow capital mobility and unplanned trade disrupt local communities and employment, what kind of international controls and local planning capacities should be established? These questions have been marginalised in recent discussions of capitalist employment policy by the 'cult of training' as a utopian pursuit of a 'pure market' or as a status-quo 'technical solution' to what are fundamentally social -

hence political - conditions; the structural social inequities and unemployed labour reserves that are produced by the capitalist form of production.

CHAPTER 12

REDISTRIBUTING WORK: THE ROLE OF THE WELFARE STATE

David Purdy

Contemporary social policy has to contend with two profound and stressful transformations. In the labour market, mass unemployment and work flexibilisation have unravelled social cohesion and undermined personal security. In domestic life, the slow demise of the male breadwinner and the partial convergence of gender roles have unhinged the sexual division of labour and underlined the distinction between working and having a job. Many people believe that in order to reduce unemployment and speed up progress towards gender equality without endangering the environment through unrestrained economic growth, society needs to find ways of redistributing paid and unpaid work: between job-rich and job-poor households, between men and women, and between people in different age groups. In this chapter, I discuss what exactly is meant by 'work', why the redistribution of work matters, how this objective might be pursued and what obstacles stand in the way of its achievement.

I begin by reviewing the role of the welfare state in shaping traditional patterns of work and compare the responses of different welfare regimes to the forces which disrupted these patterns from the mid-1970s onwards. In the second section, I argue that work is an essentially contested concept; that different conceptions of work are bound up with competing views about the human good; and that redistribution does not have to be a zero sum game: from some standpoints, society as whole stands to gain, not just the victims of social injustice.

In the next two sections, I consider two alternative strategies for redistributing work. The first involves reducing hours of work in full-time employment so as to create more jobs in the monetised economy and facilitate the redivision of unpaid work in the home. This approach, in my view, is flawed, partly because its proponents tend to overlook its implications for the distribution of income, but mainly because it offers no counterweight to the expansionist dynamic of capitalism and no alternative to contemporary arrangements for childcare.

Similar problems arise in connection with proposals for a Basic Income, financed out of taxation and payable as of right to all citizens of the state concerned. This, it can be argued, would help to bring about a 'soft' form of worksharing without the need for cumbersome and coercive regulations. If people could rely on an unconditionally guaranteed subsistence income, they would be less dependent on the labour market and would have more options in deciding how to use their time and what to do with their lives. Such an accession of personal freedom is greatly to be desired, but we cannot simply assume that Basic Income is feasible: it depends on whether people agree with the idea in principle and are prepared to pay the requisite tax costs.

My general conclusion is that whilst it is essential to speculate about alternative futures, utopian visions should not be confused with political projects. Indeed, it is the failure to make this distinction that has given utopias a bad name. At any given point in time, there are strict limits on the scope for changing the distribution of income and work without provoking counterproductive reactions. Hence, the key task for radicals is to seek out ways of changing the balance of forces and promoting cultural change. To illustrate this point, in the final section, I outline a scheme of 'liberal workfare' designed to challenge prevailing conceptions of work and create the preconditions for moving beyond the workfare state.

The changing worlds of welfare capitalism

One of the most important transformations brought about by the development of capitalism and the rise of the modern state, was the segregation of family and communal life from what came to be known as 'the economy'. Henceforth, a word which had originally meant 'the management of the household', came to refer to that sphere of productive activity which lies outside the household, involving either the production of marketed commodities or the provision of public goods. Every aspect of life was affected. As children were released from work in home, farm and factory, they came to be valued more as repositories of emotion than as economic assets, and childhood itself was reconceptualised as a period for learning and development. At the other end of the life cycle, as the state assumed responsibility for managing the economy and regulating society, the institution of retirement was created: social insurance schemes were extended to provide pensions in old age and, on reaching retirement age, insured workers became entitled, and even obliged, to withdraw from the labour force. For the working population, 'leisure' came to be conceived as 'time off' - the period of the day after 'work' was finished, and the times of the year reserved for holidays - the presumption being that 'workers' are male and remain continuously active in the labour force throughout their working lives, while their womenfolk are content to devote themselves to keeping house and raising children.

Thus, the welfare state played a major role in shaping the way work came to be organised in capitalist social formations - ordering the life cycle, structuring hours of work and institutionalising the sexual division of labour. Yet the idea of deliberately seeking to redesign working arrangements and redistribute social roles - with a view, say, to reducing work-related stress, promoting 'family-friendly' employment, encouraging job-sharing or inducing men to take more responsibility for childcare - is relatively new and remains controversial, particularly in what Esping-Andersen (1990) calls 'liberal' welfare regimes. During the 'golden age' of welfare-capitalism from the end of the Second World War to the mid-1970s, the institutional framework of employment remained broadly settled and to the extent that questions of distribution appeared on the agenda of public policy, the focus was on who gets what, rather than who does what, let alone who decides what. Thereafter, however, the old order was undermined: by de-industrialisation and the growth of the service sector; by the rise of the two-earner family and the diversification of family forms; by chronic job scarcity and pervasive job insecurity; and by the advent of flexible labour markets and the spread of 'atypical' employment. These developments elicited a variety of policy responses. None was successful in forging a new social settlement, but the fact that the attempt was made at all showed that hours of work, forms of employment, the shape of the life-course and the division of labour are subject to challenge and change.

Three main patterns of response can be identified. In the Anglo-American states, where the New Right gained the ascendancy, governments set about deregulating the labour market, commodifying childcare and instituting 'workfare'. The removal or weakening of statutory limits on hours of work enabled employers to diversify patterns of working time and adapt employment practices to the changing tempo of a non-stop society. New working arrangements such as flexitime, annualised hours contracts, 'zero hours' contracts, the compressed working week and weekend working were introduced alongside established arrangements such as part-time work, shiftwork and homeworking, making it easier to reconcile employers' competitive need for greater flexibility with women's gendered need to juggle commitments. There were also small, but significant innovations in family policy. Traditionally, liberal states treated unpaid caregiving as a free service performed for the benefit of society as a whole, neither encouraging mothers to stay at home nor helping them to participate in the labour market. This began to change with the introduction of tax relief or redeemable vouchers to help meet the costs of childcare, together with higher tax thresholds, lower starting rates and targeted tax credits to strengthen labour market incentives. At the same time, in a bid to reduce welfare dependency, uphold the work ethic and force benefit claimants to accept employment on whatever terms they could get, governments introduced more stringent tests to determine whether claimants are actively seeking work, compelling the young and long-term unemployed to participate in job-clubs, training schemes, community projects and the like, on pain of forfeiting their benefit.

In Germany and other conservative welfare states, governments adopted strategies of labour supply management, encouraging mothers to stay at home with their children, inducing older workers to take early retirement and compelling unemployed *Gastarbeiter* to return to their countries of origin. By lowering resistance to redundancies, this approach helped domestic firms to enhance their competitive strength through higher productivity rather than lower wages (Esping-Andersen, 1994). The idea of taking the overall demand for labour as given, while seeking to reduce the supply, also suggested that it might be possible to create more jobs and reduce unemployment by reducing working hours. In both cases, however, the room for manoeuvre was limited. The feasibility of early retirement depends critically on the willingness of employers and jobholders to meet the increased social insurance costs of extended periods of pension entitlement. Likewise, given that employers have their profits to think about and will not accept a policy which significantly raises their unit costs, the scope for creating more jobs by reducing full-time working hours depends critically on the willingness of jobholders to accept a *pro rata* fall in their weekly or monthly money wages.

Rather than trying to reduce the labour force and shorten working hours, the Scandinavian social democratic welfare states sought to preserve full employment with maximum labour force participation through a combination of active labour market policy, public sector expansion and paid parental leave. As the rate of job creation in the private sector fell below the rate of growth of the labour force, jobs were created in the social services to absorb surplus labour and draw women into the labour force. To facilitate this, childcare was partially socialised. Of course, paying some women to look after other women's children did nothing to alter the overall division of labour between men and women. Nevertheless, access to public nurseries made it easier for women to combine paid work with family commitments. So too did generous provision for paid parental leave within the framework of social insurance. All these policies, however, were expensive and posed a dilemma for public finance, particularly in Sweden which, unlike Norway, could not rely on revenues from offshore oil and gas. Borrowing to finance recurrent expenditure was unsustainable, but raising taxes was unpopular, especially at a time when conventional wisdom stressed the need to reduce the burden of taxation in order to sharpen market incentives. In the end, budgetary pressures forced deep cuts in social spending and unemployment rose sharply.

Each of these attempts to recast the relationship between family, market and state had different implications for the various interest groups concerned: employers and employees; jobholders and non-jobholders; taxpayers and claimants; men and women; adults and children. Each was also constrained: the first, by the willingness of the general public to accept the social consequences of the free market revolution; the other two, by the willingness of employers and jobholders to accept higher tax burdens. Given their common commitment to social partnership and consensus politics, conservative and social democratic regimes were better placed to handle conflicts of interest and objective: for the New Right, the very idea of involving private interests in the making of public policy was anathema. Yet even in countries where 'social corporatism' was an accepted feature of politics, access to the bargaining process was generally confined to the big batallions and the range of issues subject to negotiation was limited. An encompassing, united and disciplined trade union movement might conceivably champion the interests of unemployed workers, retirement pensioners, unpaid carers, full-time students, and other 'economically inactive' groups. But the first priority of most trade unions was to defend the interests of their members. Thus, social dialogue continued to be conducted across the fault-line between 'capital' and 'labour', with scant regard for other lines of social division such as gender, generation and race.

Work redistribution and well-being

Before considering whether there might be better ways of tackling the maldistribution of work in contemporary capitalism, it is worth asking what 'work' means and why redistribution matters.

It is generally accepted nowadays that work includes both paid and unpaid activities, though the boundary between them can sometimes be blurred: voluntary workers, for example, may have their expenses paid, may spend their time raising money which is subsequently used to employ them and may, in any case, gain experience and skills that will enhance their future earnings. But where are we to draw the line between work and non-work? How, for example, should we regard unemployed road protesters who chain themselves to trees and squat in underground tunnels while continuing to collect their giros? Are they 'scroungers' living at the taxpayers' expense or front-line conservationists performing an unofficial public service?

In an illuminating discussion, Himmelweit (1995) questions the work/non-work dichotomy. A price has been paid, she argues, for the success of feminism in getting women's domestic activities recognised as work. The assimilation of unpaid work performed in the home to waged work performed outside it meant accepting a reductive definition of work which is by no means universally applicable and which artificially divorces work as a physical activity from the social relations that frame it and the subjective experience it conveys. According to this definition, an activity counts as work to the extent that: (i) it involves the use of time and energy to achieve some extrinsic purpose; (ii) it forms part of a division of labour; and (iii) it is separable from the person who does it. But not even all forms of paid work meet these three criteria. In many jobs, employees put more of themselves into their work than is implied by the idea that it makes no difference who does it. And while the impersonality criterion may apply to domestic chores and the purely physical side of caregiving, it hardly applies to the emotional side of caring work where personal relationships are involved and, for better or worse, the person providing the care is part of the care provided.

A conception of work which includes unpaid domestic labour, but excludes human affectivity, is sadly impoverished, not least because it forecloses debate about what makes the redistribution of work worthwhile. If, for example, it does not matter who looks after children as long as someone does and the job is well done, then the only reason for objecting to the sexual division of labour is that it unfairly disadvantages women. Now, important though it is to resist gender injustice, it is no less important to question prevailing attitudes towards childcare and to explore alternatives to a way of life in which income, power and status depend on paid employment and the requirements of the monetised, male-dominated economy take precedence over unpaid caregiving, personal fulfilment and interpersonal commitment. Certainly, women would benefit if men took more responsibility for childcare; but so, arguably, would everyone else. Children would receive a more balanced upbringing and girls, in particular, would see more of their fathers and thus gain more experience of intimacy with the opposite sex; parents would enjoy more rewarding relations with their children and would have more chance to gain self-understanding and self-acceptance from reliving their own childhood experience; the importance of good childcare would be more fully and widely appreciated; and the raising of confident and well-adjusted children would help to create a more cohesive and adaptable society.

Not that we have to choose between justice and well-being: quite the reverse. According to Rawls (1972), the task of a theory of justice is to formulate principles which apply without distinction to all citizens alike, observing strict neutrality as between alternative conceptions of the human good, about which there is endless room for dispute. But can questions of distribution be separated from questions of value? Can we contemplate alternative distributive arrangements and decide between them without having to adjudicate between rival views about which way of life is best? It depends what is meant by 'way of life'. Rawls is concerned with personal life projects and the just distribution of life chances. Accordingly, he abstracts from the infinite variety of things that people might choose to do with their lives in order to focus on the preconditions for being in a position to think and decide for oneself and hence for becoming a moral agent capable of choosing among alternative courses of action. Having grouped these 'primary goods', as he calls them, into four general categories - rights and liberties, opportunities and powers, income and wealth, and the social bases of self-respect - he proceeds to discuss how they would be allocated among the citizens of an ideally just society.

But what about the life we share with others as members of society - our collective way of life? One can easily visualise alternatives to the way we live now, involving radical changes in our metabolism with nature, our social institutions and our cultural norms, just as one can speculate about alternative distributive arrangements. But one cannot conduct these exercises independently of each other. Consider the sexual division of labour and imagine what it would be like to live and work in a world where gender division, as distinct from sexual difference, had ceased to be a feature of society. Doubtless, different people will have different ideas about what such a world might look like and how it would function, as well as different views about how or whether it could ever be achieved. But it is hardly possible to contemplate the prospect at all without realising how profoundly its ways of living and working would differ from our own and without, therefore, recognising the far-reaching institutional and cultural changes that would be required to make it possible. And what is true of gender applies equally to other deep-seated and long-lasting sources of social division such as property ownership, ethnic identity and genetic endowment.

Of course, if we want to understand and evaluate social arrangements, we have to use some analytical scheme: it is impossible to deal with everything at once. But having conceptually divided society into parts, we should not forget that these parts interlock and cohere. In studying welfare-capitalism, for example, it has become conventional to distinguish between economic production and social reproduction. This usage does no great harm as long as it is understood that the processes referred to are interdependent and need to be considered together. Thus, families and voluntary associations perform economic functions - servicing people's needs, developing their capacities and creating social assets - just as business firms and public agencies are social institutions - shaping people's attitudes, influencing their behaviour, and transforming social life. 'The economy' is not something apart from society, but a part of society, on a par with 'the polity' and 'the culture'. Economy, polity and culture form an interrelated complex - a social formation - and when people produce goods, raise children, wage conflicts, make rules, form relationships and exchange ideas, their combined activities serve to reproduce their forms and ways of life, conserving some aspects and changing others, as the case may be.

Which of these activities count as 'work'? To this question there can be no value-free or timeless answer. 'Work' is an essentially contested concept and our conceptions of it are inevitably selective, focusing on those of its forms or aspects that best encapsulate our basic values and beliefs. Thus, work may be viewed as a burden, to be compensated, at the margin, by the utility of the extra consumption it makes possible. Alternatively, it can be seen as an essential human activity, at once a source of personal gratification, and the means by which human societies transform their conditions of existence. Perspectives on work also vary from one culture or era to another. According to the Protestant work ethic, for example, work was a God-given duty. As Sayers (1986) notes, this idea was double-edged. During the English Civil War, the Puritans invoked it to attack the landed aristocracy as an idle and parasitic ruling class. Later, as the nascent bourgeoisie gained economic and political power, the doctrine lost its revolutionary edge and the emphasis on work as a social duty came to outweigh its potency as a source of political rights.

Provided one rejects the false antithesis between economy and society, the concept of social reproduction can accommodate any conception of work. Activities are socially reproductive to the extent that they serve to keep society going and enable it, in some sense, to flourish. It makes no difference where these activities take place, what kinds of output they produce or what kinds of social relationship they involve. People will, of course, disagree about what is meant by 'flourishing' and which activities contribute to it. In this sense, substituting the algebra of social reproduction for the arithmetic of work solves nothing. But it does change the terms of debate in a potentially fruitful manner. Arguments about what counts as work cannot ultimately be settled unless those involved can be persuaded to agree about which way of life is best. In pluralistic societies, comprehensive agreement on this matter is unlikely. But it may be possible to achieve a partial, overlapping consensus to which people would be prepared to subscribe in their common capacity as citizens. This idea is explored later.

Reduced working time

For the past twenty years, most advanced capitalist states have been plagued by mass unemployment. At the same time, despite the virtual disappearance of the exclusive male breadwinner, women continue to bear disproportionate responsibility for unpaid domestic work. Here, one might suppose, are two problems with a common solution. Reducing hours of work in full-time employment would simultaneously help to create more jobs in the formal economy and facilitate a redistribution of unpaid caring work in the home.

However, although patterns of working time vary considerably from one age or culture to another, it does not follow that they are easy to change. Advocates of shorter hours of work sometimes overlook the implications for income. Wage earners are normally reluctant to accept shorter working hours without a compensating increase in hourly rates of pay. Low paid workers simply cannot afford to reduce their hours of work, especially if they have family dependants. Higher paid workers may well prefer extra consumption to more free time, especially if they have no responsibility for unpaid caring work. And even in two-earner families, men typically remain the primary breadwinners and may be loath to surrender the status and power this gives them, especially if they have few other sources of self-esteem. Employers, for their part, will not want to pay the same money wages for fewer hours unless there is an offsetting increase in labour productivity. But if increased productivity enables the existing workforce to produce the same output in a shorter time, there will be no reason to take on extra labour.

Incumbent jobholders might be induced to trade lower earnings for shorter hours as part of a co-ordinated policy for the economy as whole. But even then, there is no guarantee that employers will create new jobs: the general uncertainty surrounding a policy for which there are few, if any, precedents might well give them pause, especially in view of the adjustment costs and additional social security charges they would incur in adding to their payrolls. A particular source of anxiety would be the impact of cuts in money wages on consumer spending. Business confidence is a crucial determinant of economic outcomes and if the fear of recession is not to become a self-fulfilling prophecy, government would need to reassure employers that aggregate demand would be maintained.

An alternative might be to hold weekly or monthly money wages contant when working hours are reduced, while allowing prices to rise so as to offset the implied increase in unit costs and preserve employers' profit margins. Real wages would fall, of course, but again government could offset any anticipated fall in consumer spending by increasing public expenditure or lowering taxes, always providing this can be done without causing alarm in financial markets and driving up interest rates. The danger is that what was intended as a strictly limited rise in prices designed to obviate the need for cuts in money wages, might precipitate a wage-price spiral, with workers putting pressure on employers to raise their money wages, and employers seeking to protect their profits through further increases in prices. Thus, in one way or another, attempts to redistribute paid work are bound to impinge on the distribution of income - between capital and labour, between different groups of workers, between those with jobs and those without, and between men and women. We may think it desirable that paid and unpaid work should be more equitably shared, but this will only happen to the extent that privileged groups are willing to acquiesce. The alternative is fruitless social strife.

It might be objected that this prognosis is too gloomy and that distributive conflict could be avoided if the productivity growth which is a normal concomitant of capitalist development were applied to lowering hours of work rather than raising per capita income. For even if jobs remained scarce and jobholding remained a privilege, time would still be 'released' for other activities, including unpaid caring work. This is, indeed, a theoretical possibility, but powerful forces militate against it. Suppose that changes in technology, better methods of management, improvements in human capital or enhanced levels of work effort make it possible to produce a given output in less time. In principle, society now has various options: it can expand output and hold hours of work constant; it can maintain output and reduce hours of work; or it can opt for some combination of increased output and reduced working time. According to neo-classical economics, which of these 'options' society 'chooses' depends on how much workers value consumption and free time, respectively, at the margin.

Unfortunately, the same competitive imperative that continually impels capitalist firms to seek out ways of raising productivity, also inhibits them from agreeing to reduced working time. As productivity grows, firms do not, as a rule, take the opportunity to shorten hours of work. Instead, they seek to expand output, either in their existing product range and sales outlets or by developing new products and opening up new markets. And firms do this not because those who run them are irrational or malevolent, but because if they do not, they will eventually lose ground to their rivals. Thus, the theoretical 'choice' between alternative uses of productivity growth is biased towards output expansion. Conceivably, this bias could be countered if the demand for shorter working hours were sufficiently strong. But except for certain minority groups - overworked women, early retirers and cultural dissidents - most people show no great desire to work less and spend less. On the contrary, the restless expansionism of capitalism continually generates new wants and disturbs old habits, inducing people to buy into a way of life based on boundless economic growth.

Contemporary childcare arrangements are also a barrier to change. For many women, childcare leads to social isolation, unrelieved by diversity, and tends to be regretted as an interruption of working life, not welcomed as an opportunity to gain new experience. It thus becomes a burden to be endured, not a satisfying and worthwhile occupation in its own right. Not surprisingly, this negative view of childcare affects men too, discouraging fathers from taking responsibility for their offspring and distorting the balance of their lives. Indeed, the whole pattern of social reproduction is thoroughly lopsided. When fathers are absent and mothers are stressed, the net result is a parenting deficit which is no good for anyone.

Paid parental leave would help to correct this imbalance, provided the period of entitlement is long, the scale of support is generous and parents are given incentives to make equal use of their joint entitlement. But these are exacting requirements. Employers chafe at having to find replacements for staff on leave and are reluctant to hold posts open for long periods of time. Nor is it easy to design a scheme which is at once generous in scale, favourable to women and acceptable to taxpayers. Following the Scandinavian example, the scope of social insurance could be extended to include earnings-related parental benefits subject, perhaps, to a minimum floor and a maximum ceiling. But would people with regular, full-time jobs be prepared to accept the vertical redistribution of income and the dilution of the contributory principle implied by extending full insurance cover to those in low paid, part-time or intermittent employment? More generally, would people who may never derive any personal benefit from the system be willing to bear the cost? The answer to both questions will depend on the context, but it is more likely to be affirmative in circumstances where recurrent or periodic negotiation over distributive arrangements is an accepted feature of public life and where the tax-transfer system is designed to highlight the rights and obligations that people share as citizens rather than the sectional conflicts that divide them. With this in mind, it is instructive to approach the problem of redistribution from the other side of the work-income nexus and to consider the case for some form of Citizens' Income.

Citizens' income[1]

The basic aim of Citizens' Income (CI) is to loosen the link between income and employment. Existing social transfer systems - contributory social insurance, means-tested social assistance, selective categorical benefits and implicit tax expenditures - would be phased out or scaled down in favour of a recurrent cash transfer, financed out of taxation and payable on a lifelong basis to every legal resident of the state concerned, each in his or her own individual right, with no means test and no work requirement.

Thus defined, the concept of Citizens' Income has no necessary connection with any conception of subsistence - absolute, relative or otherwise: in principle, the scale at which CI is paid could lie anywhere between zero and the highest sustainable level. This said, most proponents of CI look forward to the day when it can safely be paid on a scale which would make it possible to eliminate all other kinds of social transfer without plunging anyone into poverty. It is convenient to reserve the term 'Basic Income' (BI) for a system that meets this requirement.

Basic Income represents a critical benchmark. If people could be sure that whatever happens, their subsistence needs will be met, and if this assurance were vouchsafed on the same terms to all citizens without regard for divisive distinctions based on previous employment history, current employment status and willingness to seek paid employment, individuals would gain greater freedom in deciding how to spend their time and what to do with their lives. Released from constant anxiety about job insecurity and family commitments, people would find it easier to adopt flexible lifestyles, moving in and out of the labour market as their needs and circumstances changed. They would also be free to take up financially unrewarding, but intrinsically gratifying activities in the non-market or semi-commercial sectors of the economy. Women, in particular, would enjoy greater financial independence and, it can be argued - though this is a moot point - would be better placed to insist that their partners accept their fair share of responsibility for unpaid work in the home.

These are enticing prospects. They are also problematic, for they would only materialise if people were prepared to pay the correlative costs: the taxes required to finance Basic Income and the psychic costs of knowing - or believing - that some of their fellow-citizens were free-riding by living on their Basic Income without doing any work. If people were unwilling or unable to pay these costs, either BI would never be introduced in the first place, or if it were somehow to be installed despite popular misgiving, the resulting economic damage and political discontent would almost certainly lead to its early demise.

Now it is not difficult to imagine the citizens of some democratic state deciding that the prospective benefits of BI outweigh its prospective costs and proceeding to introduce it, whether all at once or little by little. But from the vantage point of welfare-capitalism - and what other vantage point is there? - they cannot be sure that what they expect to happen *ex ante* will be what actually happens *ex post.* And because they cannot be sure that BI will work, neither can we whose imaginations they inhabit. Why should this be so?

One reason is that there are many variants of Citizens' Income and it is quite impossible to assess the consequences of paying it at the Basic Income standard unless we know how it is to be financed, what the tax structure will be, how the tax-transfer system will be co-ordinated with other branches of economic and social policy, and so on. These may be 'operational' details, but they can hardly be dismissed as 'mere technicalities'. Moreover, even when the abstract idea of Citizens' Income has been translated into a working model, a second complication arises. There are, to date, no examples of societies which provide all their members with a guaranteed subsistence income without imposing some reciprocal work obligation. It is, therefore, impossible to predict with any degree of confidence how people would respond to the options and costs associated with BI - as employees, as parents, as citizens or as bearers of any of the manifold social identities that shape the pattern of social behaviour, from gender, class and race to kinship, generation and lifestyle. Conversely, unless we can predict how Basic Income will affect the pattern of economic activity and the social division of labour, it is impossible to say with any degree of precision what these options and costs will be. Thus, to add to the problem of institutional indeterminacy and the lack of historical precedents, there is a problem of interdependence between micro-social responses and macro-social outcomes.

In a purely formal sense, resolving this latter problem is relatively straightforward. [See Purdy (forthcoming) Chapter 10]. But if social behaviour is subject to cultural change, mathematical models can, at best, indicate the relevant range of possibilities. The way people respond to Basic Income will depend on who they are and what they care about, and whilst identities and values can be taken as given when we are dealing with incremental policy adjustments within a tried and tested framework, it is unwise to maintain this assumption when the framework itself is being reshaped. As people experience and reflect on their new regime, they may well begin to think in new ways about themselves, their relations with others and the world in which they live.

In the face of all these imponderables, we can only speculate about the dynamics of a Basic Income society. Before the advent of universal suffrage, exactly the same could have been said about the dynamics of parliamentary democracy. Speculation need not be unbridled, however: indeed, controlled thought-experiments can be valuable tools of moral and intellectual inquiry. Nevertheless, a social vision is not a political project and distributive radicals who have nothing to say about the politics of social change are unlikely to make much impact on the course of public policy.

As long as most people continue to labour under the influence of the Protestant work ethic, remain strongly attached to the view that transfer entitlements should be conditional on work contributions, take a narrow view of what is to count as work and display a marked aversion to taxation, the prospects for Citizens' Income are distinctly unpromising. On the other hand, in the long run, even the most entrenched social attitudes may change, particularly if the conditions in which they first took root are fast disappearing. In the meantime, the problem is to bridge the gap between long-range vision and time-bound politics.

Liberal workfare

Since it is difficult to generalise about the politics of cultural change, a specific illustration must suffice. In liberal welfare states, as we saw earlier, the broad principle of 'workfare' is now widely accepted. But this still leaves several important issues unresolved. What is workfare for? What kinds of work should it involve? How much should be spent on it? And how should it be organised?

Workfare schemes may be variously designed to uphold the work ethic and strengthen moral fibre, to prevent benefit fraud and reduce the claimant count, to combat social exclusion and promote social cohesion, to improve the human capital of the long-term unemployed and increase their lifetime earnings, to enforce social discipline and reassure taxpayers that public funds are being put to good use. Not all these aims are mutually compatible. There is, for example, an obvious tension between using workfare as an instrument of social control and using it to enhance personal autonomy. How this tension is resolved depends on what claimants are required to do in order to fulfil their side of the workfare contract. And this, in turn, depends on which activities are thought to qualify as work.

If one takes an expansive view of social reproduction, the work that makes the world go round includes unpaid caregiving, voluntary service and non-vocational learning, as well as waged employment, self-employment, job training and job search. Why then, one might reasonably ask, should activities of the former kind not count for workfare purposes? Why the fixation on the labour market? Would it not be better, both for jobless citizens themselves and for society as a whole, especially at times of chronic job scarcity, to recognise the role of unpaid work and to extend the scope of workfare accordingly?

Believing that most unemployment is 'voluntary' and being doctrinally opposed to 'big government', the free market right favours low budget workfare, restrictive in scope and stigmatising in effect. Keen on putting welfare to work, but reluctant to campaign for higher taxes, the communitarian centre-left is only slightly less niggardly, only slightly more liberal and equally obsessed with the labour market. A third alternative, less coercive than the former, less conservative than the latter and more imaginative and inspiring than either is to acknowledge frankly that for the foreseeable future, the demand for conventional jobs at socially acceptable wage rates is likely to continue to exceed the supply by a wide margin. In these conditions, purely job-centred workfare is not enough: what is needed are opportunities for work outside the labour market, so that jobless citizens can contribute to the common good in a variety of ways, according to their circumstances, capacities and wishes.

But this cannot be done without resources. What is required is a three-way compact between taxpayers, claimants and government. Taxpayers have to be persuaded that money spent on extending opportunities for socially useful work, paid or unpaid, is money well spent. Able-bodied claimants, for their part, must accept an obligation to contribute to society's work, broadly understood. And government must act as broker and facilitator, mobilising funds, commissioning projects and galvanising civic initiative.

A start could be made by converting the existing Employment Service into a 'Social Opportunity Service' (SOS). This would provide advice and assistance for all jobless claimants, whether officially unemployed or not, offering access not only to job placement and training programmes, but also to sheltered employment, remedial education, co-operative childcare, voluntary service, subsistence farming and Local Exchange and Trading Schemes (LETS). The SOS would not organise projects itself. Rather, its offices in each locality would solicit proposals from associated groups of citizens and non-profit making organisations, and would act as a clearing house both for conventional job vacancies and for unwaged 'quasi-jobs'. Projects would have to be vetted and monitored to ensure they were properly managed, gave good value for money, and posed no threat to existing jobs, whether in the public or private sectors, while still encouraging social innovation and responding to public demand.

Anyone participating in an approved project would qualify for a 'Jobless Person's Allowance' at an hourly rate sufficient to provide 'full-timers' with a 'subsistence' income, exclusive of housing costs. In effect, the allowance would be equivalent to a national minimum wage and employers would have to pay whatever premium over and above this baseline was necessary to elicit an adequate supply of suitably qualified and motivated labour. Means-tested housing benefits would need to be retained for households which would otherwise fall below the poverty line, while means-tested income supplements for families with low paid breadwinners could be abolished or reduced depending on what happened to other family benefits.

Besides enabling jobless claimants to lead more productive and fulfilling lives, liberal workfare would help to allay the fears of jobholders about becoming unemployed. It would also create space for resisting the invasive spread of commodification and nurturing more eco-friendly and socially cohesive ways of living and working. In these conditions, people might become less averse to taxation. Indeed, as they got used to the distinction between working and having a job, and grew to appreciate the value of a thriving civic life, they might be persuaded to move beyond the workfare state to a regime in which every citizen is entitled to a Basic Income with no state-imposed work requirement whatsoever.

Notes

---

[1] Van Parijs (1992) and Purdy (1994) review recent European debate about proposals for some form of Citizens' Income. Van Parijs (1995) seeks to put the idea on a firm ethical foundation. Purdy (forthcoming) discusses its feasibility.

CHAPTER 13

WORKING TIME IN EUROPE: CURRENT TRENDS

Giuseppe Fajertag

Introduction

This paper examines current working time developments in Germany, the Netherlands, France and Sweden, the main focus being on similarities and differences in trade union bargaining strategies concerning reduction of working time (RWT) in a period characterised by slow economic growth and unprecedented levels of unemployment. The choice of countries is mainly intended to identify specific patterns that are common to other national situations in Europe.

In recent years, European unions have been negotiating reductions and reorganisations of working time in the framework of more general economic strategies mainly aimed at safeguarding existing jobs and stimulating work sharing. The results of national strategies of RWT through either collective bargaining or national framework agreements or legislation in terms of employment protection/creation are generally disappointing. The Swedish/Scandinavian approach (and the Dutch experience for some aspects) based on high co-operation and trust among the social partners and providing for an extremely high level of individual negotiated working time flexibility over the life cycle can represent an interesting and valid model of reference for a new European approach to working time policy.

A diversity of working time arrangements

As a result of the changes that have taken place in the last two decades, it is almost impossible to keep track of the great diversity of working time arrangements that now exists in Europe. This diversity reflects the fact that pressure for change has arisen for a variety of very different reasons.

It is apparent that in all industrialised countries both employers and employees, albeit for different reasons, welcome more flexible working times, though not necessarily the same kinds. At the same time, policy makers in different countries have reacted to this change in very different ways, with the result that a wide variety of national working time arrangements has emerged. Employers' reasons for seeking more working time flexibility can be summarised (Bosch 1996) under three major headings:

- the attempt to replace expensive working time arrangements by cheaper ones (not necessarily by introducing innovative working time patterns, but rather by making existing working time structures cheaper by, e.g. not paying overtime or night-work bonuses or employing part-time workers)
- increasing operating hours (reduction of unit capital costs, faster amortisation of fixed capital)
- annualised working hours (working time fluctuations during the year become a replacement for stock holding and workers become a sort of buffer in the production system).

On the workers' side, there is a growing divergence in working time preferences and this is due to a number of factors, such as:

- increasing female participation on the labour market,
- need to combine education and work,
- diversification of lifestyles (smaller families, etc.),
- rejection of night and weekend work particularly by core workers.

As a result, 'flexitime' arrangements are becoming more and more widespread and popular among workers.

The declining transparency of working time implies the decline in opportunities for monitoring by both public authorities (e.g. factory inspectors) and employee representatives (e.g. works councils). This seems to lead to a more or less marked shift in the balance of power in favour of employers who, alone, have the global overview of hours actually worked. This trend has been further reinforced in the last few years by: firstly exceptionally high, and rising, unemployment rates in almost all European countries, and secondly, the economic constraint linked to an extremely moderate, and sometimes negative, wage growth.

In several European countries, the issues of flexibilisation, reorganisation and reduction of working time represent an important element of recent collective bargaining rounds. The unions have been conducting negotiations in this area mainly with the aim of safeguarding existing jobs, and to stimulate work-sharing. There has been a generalised preference for decentralised negotiations, usually taking place at the sectoral or company levels, focusing on a more flexible approach (annualisation, more recourse to part-time and other atypical contracts, reduced recourse to overtime, job sharing, etc.) in the use of working time. A 'defensive' approach is the one currently prevailing in Europe, even if signs of a more 'offensive', pro-active, job-creating strategy are emerging, as the recently introduced legislation in France seems to indicate.

Recent developments in legal, negotiated and actual working hours in Europe

Table 1, taken from the last ETUI report on collective bargaining in Europe (Fajertag 1997), provides a summary overview of working hours as determined by legal provisions and collective agreements. We can see that statutory working hours are predominantly fixed at 40, and that a 48-hour working week is still allowed in some countries. Positive exceptions are constituted by Denmark (39 hours since the end of 1986) and France (39 hours since 1982). The situation is more difficult to assess in terms of average working hours as determined by collective agreements. For most countries you can see that figures vary between 36 and 40 with an average that can be roughly estimated at 38-38.5 hours per week. Table 2, based on data from Eurostat's Labour Force Surveys (Eurostat 1996a, 1996b, 1997), indicates that average hours usually worked per week by full-time employees did not register any substantial change between 1994 and 1996, with a European average of 40.3 hours (41.1 for male workers and 38.9 for female workers). Belgium, Italy, Denmark and Finland are below the 39-hours ceiling; Germany, France, Netherlands, and Luxembourg are below 40 hours per week; while all the other countries are at or above the 40-hour ceiling, with the UK at the top of the league with an average of nearly 44 hours and 45.7 hours for male workers.

In effect, at least until the appointment of the new Labour government, the debate on working time in the UK did not develop as in other European countries. There has been no real discussion in the UK around the role of reduced working time as a way of minimising redundancies during recession and spreading employment opportunities more widely at a time of growth. Reducing working time has not been a particular priority for British trade unions either in recent years. At the same time, the UK is one of the European countries with the highest levels of working time flexibility. Apart from part-time work (the total number of part-time workers between 1984 and 1994 rose from 4.8 million to nearly 6 million), around 2 million employees or 9 per cent of the UK workforce are now covered by annualised hours arrangements (Coats, 1996a). In contrast with the situation existing in other countries (e.g. Netherlands), part-time employment in the UK evolved without an explicit government policy concerned with either re-organising working time or re-distributing employment (Fagan, Plantenga and Rubery, 1995). It is not surprising therefore if, in such an unregulated context, British workers now have the longest average working week in the European Union. In addition, average working time in the UK has increased over the last decade at a time when average working time in all the other EU member states has been falling.

Figures on hours usually worked should be considered in relation to the situation illustrated in Figure 1 referring to the year 1995, which provides a breakdown of the previous averages for the manufacturing industry and the services sector. It clearly indicates how articulated and differentiated the situation is not only from country to country but also inside each European country.

Part-time work over the last few years has registered a sharp increase in most European countries. Part-time employment represents (see Figure 2) 38 per cent of total employment in the Netherlands, around 25 per cent in Sweden and the UK, and around 15 per cent in Germany and France. Even in the case of part-time, work hours usually worked per week (around 20 as a European average) (see Table 3) did not register relevant changes between 1994 and 1996 at the national level. There are however marked differences by country and by sex in terms of hours usually worked by part-timers ranging from a maximum of 24-25 hours per week in Greece, Italy and Sweden to a minimum of around 18 for the UK and Spain.

These figures clearly show how difficult it is to assess quantitative developments and trends in working hours at the European, national, sectoral and gender levels in particular when the traditional notion of 'hours of work per week' is taken as measure.

Reductions of working hours through collective bargaining: the German and Dutch experience

In both Germany and the Netherlands, reductions in working hours have played a significant role in employment policy in recent years. The German and Dutch trade unions, more than those in other European countries, have backed reductions in working hours as a means of preventing unemployment from getting out of control. In Germany, in particular, the 35-hour week with no reductions in pay was finally introduced in the printing sector in April 1995 and in the metalworking industry in October 1995, fully respecting the schedule agreed in the sectoral agreements of 1990 (Rosdücher J., Seifert H., 1996). However, while progress towards the achievement of the 35-hour week was still being made in these industries, the average number of agreed working hours for industry as a whole remained unchanged in 1996.

Developments in the area of working time have come to a standstill in real terms with regard to the number of agreed weekly working hours. The average working week provided for in collective agreements amounted to 37.4 hours at the end of 1996. At the same date, around a quarter (22.5 per cent) of German employees had an agreed working week of 35 hours, while almost 3 per cent were working 36 (or 36.5) hours a week and almost one third of the workforce between 37 and 38 hours per week. A quarter of employees still have a 38.5-hour working week and a further 15.5 per cent work 39 hours a week. The 40-hour mark still applies for 3 per cent of the workforce. Provisions regarding reductions in working time applied to around 2.9 million employees at the end of 1996 in the form of an average of 2.0 days off (Bispinck, 1996).

During 1996, negotiations focused on working time reductions and flexibility in an attempt mainly to preserve employment levels. Several sectoral agreements included provisions such as time off in lieu for overtime worked (chemicals, steel, engineering, banking), temporary reductions in working time accompanied by pay cuts (engineering, paper manufacturing, printing, banks, insurance) and flexible working time arrangements, part-time work for older workers (chemicals, rubber, banking).

As an example we can refer to the agreement reached in the textiles industry in May-June 1996 which provides for pay increases of 1.5 per cent, but allows for a great deal of flexibility at company level on their payment and on working time arrangements. The normal working week of 37 hours may be extended by up to eight hours a week without payment of overtime supplements as long as the weekly average is 37 hours over a period of one year. This may be extended to 18 months in exceptional circumstances. Total working time may not exceed 48 hours a week and 9.5 hours a day. Where overtime compensation is payable, it will be granted as time off in lieu wherever possible. At the company level, it is possible to negotiate agreements to reduce or increase the working week by 6.75 per cent with corresponding pay reductions or increases, during which time no compulsory redundancies are allowed. While Saturdays are already included in the calculation of normal working time, Sunday working is permitted in some circumstances to ensure international competitiveness.

A new type of shorter working time agreements (work-sharing schemes) developed in Germany during the 1994-95 economic recession: in order to avoid a dramatic increase in unemployment levels, additional reductions of working time were negotiated in return for job security. The car-maker Volkswagen pioneered the campaign in 1994 by introducing a 4-day week, or a 28.8 hour week. This agreement was followed by a second one in September 1995 representing a compromise on the issue of Saturday working (up to 12 Saturdays a year may be worked and the Saturday premium rate is reduced from 50 per cent to 30 per cent) and allowing for flexible working time up to a maximum of 38.8 hours a week and eight hours a day from Mondays to Fridays, with an average of 28.8 hours a week.

The VW agreement and other comparable agreements in the coal mining industry, the chemical industry, etc., can be defined as 'temporary reductions of working hours for saving jobs' (Rosdücher J. and Seifert H., 1996). They are in fact usually characterised by:

a) A time limit. The agreements expire without subsequent effects if they are not replaced by a new agreement. In other words, temporary reductions do not lead to a new standard working time;

b) Wider scope. They do not represent gradual linear reductions in agreed standard working hours but offer immediate reductions of between 6 and 20 per cent or up to 8 hours per week;

c) Loss of pay. None of the new arrangements has been made without loss of pay in proportion to the shortening of working hours.

In the Netherlands, after being absent for some years, the reduction of working time again formed part of the claims of a number of unions in 1995 and 1996 (Van den Toren, 1996). For most employees agreed working hours had already been fixed at 38 hours per week (on average) during the 1980s. By contrast with the earlier period of general working time reductions (between 1982 and 1987), in the mid-nineties the unions did not lay down any collective goals for working time. Even if most agreements are linking the introduction of an average 36-hour week to flexible working hours, each sector and undertaking judged what is possible and how to introduce it in its own case. Cuts in weekly working hours have mainly been brought back on the agenda by a number of successful agreements combining flexibility and shorter working hours, often coupled with a four-day working week. Flexibility means in most of these cases that workers can also work in the evenings and/or on Saturdays. The negotiators refer in this case to 'win-win combinations'.

At the end of 1996 it was estimated that 32 per cent of collective agreements and 38 per cent of employees had, or would get, a 36-hour working week. Some of these agreements have included such a working week since the end of the 1980s, while others are based on changes agreed in 1995 or 1996. Particularly in the latter category, there is scope for details to be agreed at company level. The collective agreements for banking staff and national government employees refer to variants such as four nine-hour days, a day off once every two weeks, weekly timetables and annual timetables (in the form of scheduled days off). The agreement in the educational sector also creates the opportunity to save up scheduled days off over a longer period, for example in order to take a sabbatical. At the end of 1996 the average working week was 37.9 hours. Based on changes agreed in 1996 it can be predicted that this will fall in 1997 or 1998 to an average of 37.3 hours per week. In a number of sectors where there are wide variations in the supply of work or seasonal fluctuations, provisions are agreed on working longer hours at busy periods and shorter hours or time off during slack periods, or times of no work.

Part-time work in the Netherlands is seen as an important instrument for increasing the employment prospects of women in the labour market and also for achieving a redistribution of paid and unpaid work between men and women. Since the General Agreement (*Stichtingsakkoord*) in 1982, part-time work is strongly stimulated by government, management and the unions through agreements, recommendations and advice about policies. Between 1988 and 1994 the number of part-timers has increased by around 32 per cent while full-time employment levels did not register any significant change. Over the same period, as a consequence of the strong growth of part-time jobs, the female participation rate has sharply risen from 35 per cent to 42 per cent. During 1994 and 1995 an ever-growing number of collective agreements included the right to work part time. In most cases, the collective agreement stipulates that the worker's request to work part time should in principle be honoured, unless there are important reasons involving the company's interest which preclude such action. In a survey conducted in May 1995, it appeared that in 223 of the 400 collective agreements investigated, applying to 80 per cent of the workers covered by these collective agreements, provisions on part-time work were included.

During the period up to 1985 the reduction of agreed weekly working hours from 40 to 38 mainly led to a safeguard of employment levels, but hardly any new jobs were created. From 1995 onwards, when a reduction of average weekly working hours from 38 to 36 hours has been introduced in various collective agreements, some cautious signals of a positive effect on employment have been registered.

Reductions of working hours through centralised framework negotiations or legislation: the French case

Since 1995, working time and its relationship with employment have been at the top of the bargaining agenda in France, at central, sectoral and especially company level. Central employers' organisations and trade union confederations signed an agreement on the reorganisation and reduction of working time in October 1995, aimed at encouraging sectoral bargaining on the subject. This accord provided for sectoral talks on working time to open by 31 January 1996, with an assessment of progress to be drawn up at central level in June. Thereafter, new central talks would be held to conclude a more concrete agreement, which would apply to those sectors which had failed to agree their own provisions. However, apart from a few quite controversial agreements, it appears that the sectoral bargaining which was meant to implement the October 1995 inter-sectoral agreement has not been a great success (Dufour, 1996).

In order to stimulate the signature of more proactive or 'offensive' employment agreements, a new law (*Loi de Robien*) urging working time cuts and providing financial incentives for employers to reduce their employees' collective working time was adopted in June 1996. The new legislation extends a number of experimental provisions on reducing employers' social security contributions in return for hours cuts, which had already been set out in the so called 'five-year employment law' of December 1993.

The new incentives apply to companies or establishments where a new collective working time schedule is introduced, accompanied by a reduction of at least 10 per cent in normal working hours. The new schedule must be based on a company or establishment collective agreement, or the application of a sectoral agreement. The incentive takes the form of a reduction in employers' social security contributions for the employees covered by the agreement. The details are as follows:

- following the signature of a specific sectoral or company level agreement, the employer, in order to obtain reductions in social security contributions, has to sign a contract with the government specifying the reduction and reorganisation of working time he is envisaging to introduce in his company/sector;
- cut in normal hours of at least 10 per cent must be accompanied by new recruitment increasing the workforce by a similar proportion: in this case, the reduction in contributions amounts to 40 per cent in the first year and 30 per cent in the six following years;
- f the hours reduction, and the consequent recruitment, amount to 15 per cent or more, the reduction in employers' contributions can be increased to 50 per cent in the first year and 40 per cent in the six following years;
- the employer concerned has up to one year to carry out the necessary recruitment. Thereafter, the employer must maintain the new employment levels for at least two years, in order to carry on claiming the reductions;
- unlike the five-year employment law, the new legislation does not require that the new working time arrangements be accompanied by a reduction in pay, leaving this up to the social partners to negotiate.

The reductions arising from the new scheme may be added to those resulting from other existing schemes. The legislation also allows for a 'defensive' use of the new scheme, in order to prevent redundancies rather than create new jobs. Similar social security contribution reductions may be claimed by companies which sign an agreement aimed at avoiding planned redundancies through hours cuts.

The new law met with immediate success on both the employers' and the unions' side, even if some of the French trade unions (FO and CGT in particular) and some major employers' organisations expressed (divergent) reservations and doubts on the employment results and on the costs of the new legislation (Freyssinet 1997; Aznar 1997). According to recent estimates by the Ministry of Labour, by the end of November 1997, 1,442 company-level agreements had already been signed, of which 1,030 were 'offensive' and 412 'defensive'. They provide a reduction of working time for a total 153,943 employees. A great majority of the agreements (86.5 per cent) have adopted a 10 per cent reduction in working hours. The costs to the state of subsidising a job created by the *'Loi Robien'* stands at an annual average figure of between FF 52000 and FF 65000.

Following the general elections in Spring 1997, the new government led by the Socialist leader, Lionel Jospin, has put reduction of working time on top of its political agenda. By the end of the year the Government presented a 'guidelines and incentives' bill (*'Loi d'orientation et d'incitation sur la réduction du temps de travail'*) whose adoption by the Parliament is foreseen during the first months of 1998. The new draft legislation, also known as *'Loi Aubry'* from the name of the new Minister of Labour and Social Affairs, couples a revised version of the *'Loi Robien'* with the objective of reducing the statutory working week from 39 to 35 hours by the year 2000.

The Swedish/Scandinavian approach: individual negotiated flexibility over the life cycle

While working time has been a key component of Swedish welfare policy, governments and social partners have consistently refused to consider an across-the-board reduction of working time as an effective means of combating unemployment.

Recent bargaining trends are quite contradictory. On the one hand, in 1995, the union of metalworkers put forward the claim for shorter working hours. The demand was for a reduction of 100 hours per year to be achieved by the year 2000. The result of the three-year agreement was a reduction of 12 minutes per week in 1995 and a further 12 minutes in 1997 (24 minutes per week is equivalent to 19.6 hours a year). The working time reductions may be implemented either on a daily basis or as shorter Fridays or as extra holidays. On the other hand, in the 1995 collective bargaining round, the union of health services accepted a trade-off between higher pay increases and higher retirement age, thus increasing the total amount of lifetime working hours.

Since the mid-1970s, however, the most relevant feature of Swedish working time policy has been the creation of conditions for greater flexibility in individual working time over the life cycle while preserving firm competitiveness. Such a policy could not succeed without a broad and active co-operation between the social partners. Not only is working time policy a major component of family policy, with some of the most highly developed and flexible parental leave entitlements in Europe, it is also seen as a means to promote equal gender opportunities. Hence, the ability to modulate individual working time over the life cycle has without doubt contributed to the marked rise in female labour force participation (Anxo, 1995).

The fact that Swedish working time regulation is characterised by large possibilities to adapt working time patterns to prevalent and actual production constraints guarantees a certain flexibility but does not *per se* guarantee good transition possibilities during the life cycle. Such a smooth transition is allowed by the combination of institutional and societal aspects and the decentralisation of the decision making process concerning working time.

Part-time work is a crucial component of Swedish working time policy. Part-time work accounts for a high proportion of female employment (according to 1995 figures, 46 per cent of the female labour force worked part-time and almost 90 per cent of part-time workers are women). The incidence of involuntary part-time is low and the possibility of shifting from part-time to full time work seems not to present major difficulties. Actually, part-time work in Sweden constitutes, along with the various forms of leave of absence (parental leave, training/study leave) a means to regulate and combine household activities and professional life and promote a more equal gender division of labour.

The parental leave scheme which was introduced in 1974 also contributed to increased female participation on the labour market. Parental leave (15 months with full subsequent job security) offers considerable scope for flexibility due to the fact that part of the leave can be taken over a longer period by working a shorter week with wage compensation. A further element of individual flexibility is provided by the legislation on training/study leave. Legislation is exceptionally liberal in allowing all workers with at least six months' service to follow training of their choice, with no restriction on either the type or length of training which may be in a field totally unconnected with the worker's job. Leave can be taken either hourly (several hours a week combined with normal work) or taken in a block (Anxo and Lundstöm, 1996).

Since 1976 pension may also be taken on a part-time basis (*Delpension*). The recipients may reduce working time up to 10 hours per week. Weekly working hours must range between 17 and 35 hours. The replacement rate is 55 per cent of gross income (which due to the strong progressiveness of the Swedish tax system means a considerably higher replacement rate). About 20 per cent of wage earners between 61 and 64 years are covered by this scheme.

All these labour market measures were developed in Sweden (and in the other Scandinavian countries) mainly in the first half of the 1970s, the years of full employment (Schmid, 1995b). The dramatic rise of unemployment rates registered in Sweden and Finland in particular during the 1990s (and much earlier in Denmark, has contributed to a generalised re-orientation of the existing systems of paid leave (parental, educational, sabbatical) and part-time work as components of active labour market policies aimed to promote and stimulate job-sharing (e.g. the 'Job Alternation Act' in Finland, the 'Job Rotation Model' in Denmark, the various examples of temporary job-sharing in Sweden).

Conclusions

Legal and agreed working hours in most European countries have not registered substantial changes in recent years although by some important sectoral agreements in Germany present an exception.

Unions may generally not be opposed to a negotiated approach to flexible and innovative working time arrangements. But the fact that negotiations are taking place at the plant level implies a difficulty on their side over a full assessment and monitoring of developments, results and the practical implementation of general guidelines agreed at the national and (or) sectoral levels. The relevant differences between 'agreed hours' and 'usually worked hours' which existing in almost all European countries, are a clear indicator of this difficulty.

The resulting declining transparency of working time arrangements has led to a more or less marked shift in the balance of power in favour of employers who, alone, have a global overview of hours actually worked. This trend has been further aggravated during the 1990s by unprecedented constraint linked to an extremely moderate, and sometimes negative, wage growth. As a consequence, it is difficulty to assess the relevance to employment policy of these reductions of working hours. Flexibilisation of working hours has in fact generally been associated with job protection rather than job creation. In order to produce satisfactory results for all parties, working time flexibility should be negotiated ensuring the equality and mutual trust of the social partners at all levels and with the active involvement of governments (e.g. legislation in France, the employment pact in Italy, social partnership, social pacts).

The impact on employees' working conditions and quality of life is even more difficult to appraise. Reductions in working time have often been made possible only in return for concessions in flexible working hours (uneven distribution of working times within certain periods and, so that employers can match fluctuations in demand, increased recourse to shift, night and weekend work). Shorter working times have induced additional increases in productivity with the result that work has intensified even further.

Freely chosen part-time work can be considered as an important element of employment and working time strategies, as is the case in Sweden and the Netherlands. Also in other countries (France, Belgium) considerable progress has been made by introducing legislation or regulations to reduce the risk of part-time work being associated with discrimination against women, low incomes and social segregation.

Finally, the Swedish experience of combining working time flexibility at the company level with individual negotiated flexibility over the life cycle of employees (part-time, parental leave, education/training leave, part-time early retirement) represents an interesting example of a possible new European model, based on lifetime working hours, capable at the same time reducing unemployment by work-sharing and reconciling working and private and family life.

Figure 13.1 Hours usually worked per week, EU countries 1995, full-time employees by sector

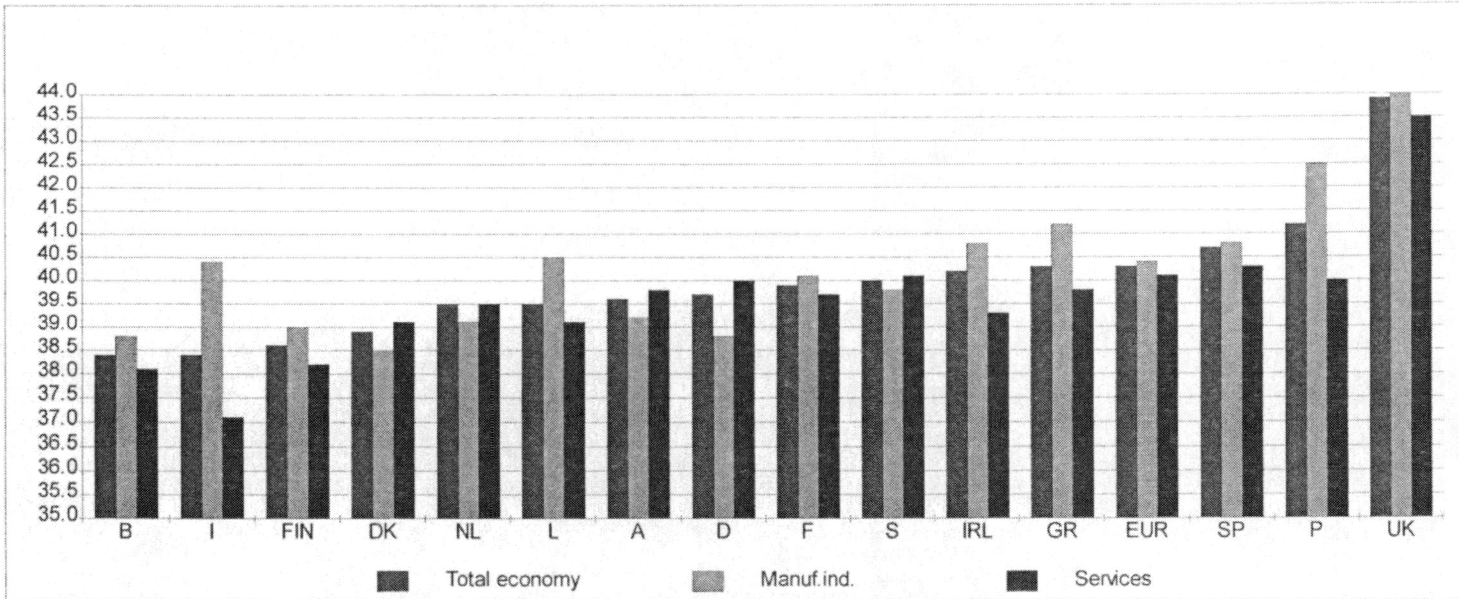

Source: Eurostat, Labour Force Survey, Results 1995

Figure 13.2 Part-time work in the EU, 1996, per cent of total employment

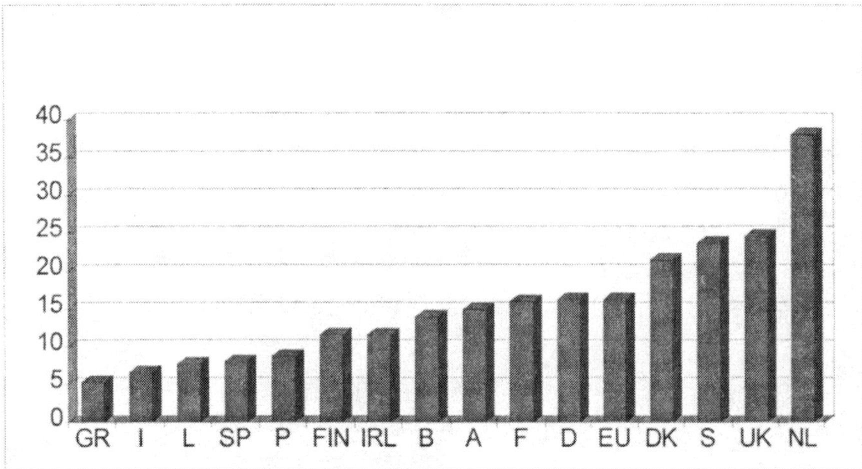

Source: Eurostat, Labour Force Survey 1996

Table 13.1: Working hours in Europe as determined by law and/or agreement

Country	Situation by the end of 1996	
	Legal	*Agreement*
Austria	40	38.5 (av.)
Belgium	40	36 - 38
Denmark	39	37
Finland	40	35 - 38
France	39	35 - 39
Germany (New Länder)	40	37-40
Germany (West)	40	37.4 (av.)
Greece	48	37.5 - 40
Ireland	48	39
Italy	48	36 - 40
Luxembourg	40	36 - 40
Netherlands	45	37.9 (av.)
Norway	40	37.5
Portugal	40	35 - 40
Spain	40	37 - 40
Sweden	40	35 - 40 (38.3 av.)
United Kingdom	n/a	35 - 40

Table 13.2: Average hours usually worked per week EU countries (total economy)
Employees working full-time

Country	1994			1995			1996		
	All	*Male*	*Female*	*All*	*Male*	*Female*	*All*	*Male*	*Female*
Europe	40.3	41.1	38.9	40.3	41.1	38.9	40.3	41.1	38.9
Belgium	38.2	38.8	36.9	38.4	38.9	37.3	38.3	38.8	37.1
Denmark	39.1	39.8	38.0	38.9	39.6	37.9	38.7	39.4	37.6
West Germany	39.7	39.9	39.2	39.7	39.9	39.1	na	na	na
Greece	40.5	41.4	39.0	40.3	41.3	38.8	40.4	41.4	38.9
Spain	40.5	41.0	39.5	40.7	41.1	39.6	40.6	41.0	39.6
France	39.9	40.6	38.7	39.9	40.6	38.7	39.8	40.5	38.8
Ireland	40.0	41.5	37.8	40.2	41.7	37.8	40.4	42.0	38.0
Italy	38.5	39.7	36.3	38.4	39.7	36.2	38.6	39.8	36.4
Luxembourg	39.8	40.6	37.9	39.5	40.6	37.2	39.5	40.4	37.7
Netherlands	39.4	39.6	39.1	39.5	39.6	39.1	39.4	39.5	39.0
Austria	na	na	na	39.6	40.0	39.0	40.0	40.2	39.8
Portugal	41.2	42.7	39.3	41.2	42.8	39.2	41.2	42.7	39.9
Finland	na	na	na	38.6	39.2	37.9	38.7	39.4	38.0
Sweden	na	na	na	40.0	40.1	39.8	40.0	40.1	39.9
United Kingdom	43.6	45.4	40.5	43.9	45.7	40.5	43.9	45.7	40.6

Table 13.3: Average hours usually worked per week EU countries (total economy)
Employees working part-time

Country	1994			1995			1996		
	All	*Male*	*Female*	*All*	*Male*	*Female*	*All*	*Male*	*Female*
Europe	19.6	19.5	19.7	19.9	19.4	20.0	19.9	19.5	20.0
Belgium	21.0	21.1	20.9	21.5	21.7	21.4	21.5	21.5	21.5
Denmark	19.4	14.2	21.2	19.2	13.3	21.2	19.1	13.5	21.2
West Germany	20.1	18.9	20.2	19.5	18.1	19.7	na	na	na
Greece	23.3	25.6	21.5	23.5	25.9	21.9	25.2	28.6	22.5
Spain	18.0	19.6	17.5	17.8	19.1	17.5	18.0	19.4	17.6
France	22.4	22.5	22.4	22.6	22.6	22.6	22.7	22.5	22.7
Ireland	18.8	20.5	18.3	18.8	20.4	18.3	19.0	20.4	18.5
Italy	24.7	30.1	23.0	24.5	30.5	22.5	24.5	29.8	22.6
Luxembourg	20.3	26.7	19.7	20.0	28.6	19.2	20.8	30.9	19.6
Netherlands	18.1	18.6	17.9	18.4	18.7	18.3	18.7	19.3	18.5
Austria	na	na	na	23.3	21.5	23.5	22.1	22.3	22.0
Portugal	21.6	26.3	20.2	22.4	29.1	20.7	23.0	32.3	20.9
Finland	na	na	na	22.0	21.6	22.1	20.7	19.0	21.3
Sweden	na	na	na	23.6	19.6	24.4	23.9	18.7	24.9
United Kingdom	17.6	16	17.9	17.8	16.1	18.1	17.8	16.3	18.0

CHAPTER 14

SOCIAL LABOUR AND DEMOCRATIC CAPITAL: THE MARGINS OR THE MAINSTREAM?

Hilary Wainwright and Paul Gosling

Introduction.

Suddenly, everyone is taking an interest in the 'third sector,' the social economy, the not-for-profit sector. The IMF looks to it for shock absorption as the tremors of its structural adjustment programmes rip through the social fabrics of North and South; neo-liberal governments use it to provide the services in which the 'for profit' sector has little interest and for which the state itself claims to have insufficient resources; Conservatives and Christian Democrats give an astringent sort of support to workers co-operatives on the grounds that through them workers will learn the real costs of running a company and moderate their wage demands as a consequence. Social democratic governments seeking to protect their citizens - and their own political position - against deregulated international markets see it as an ally in achieving social cohesion; and greens and libertarian socialists see it as a space for at best, feasible utopias and at the minimum, a dignified strategy for collective survival.

These are not merely conflicting beliefs. The relative strength of the interests and organisations behind each of them will itself influence the shape, the character and the relative importance of different components of this third sector. In Britain, under the Conservatives for instance, the voluntary, unpaid sector grew enormously as the government dismantled the welfare state, and the voluntary sector took over the functions that offered no gain for the private sector. On the other hand, in Denmark where social democratic municipalities have considerable power and resources, the third sector gains positive support from the state and is a significant source of paid employment. And in parts of Ireland, European funding has stimulated coalitions of local authorities, trade unions, voluntary organisations and local businesses to create a variety of community owned enterprises.

The term 'third sector' then is misleading in so far as it implies an integrated sub-economy, with clear distinguishing characteristics. In reality this 'sector' is made up of a huge variety of unconnected economic organisations driven by different, sometimes contradictory, goals and values. They have in common the fact that they are economic activities which are not driven primarily by the private market and yet are not a part of the state; it is thus, using the most primitive kind of description, that they represent some kind of 'third' sector. Does the activity to which this residual, almost negative, description refers amount to anything historically or potentially significant? Does it have any special importance at a time when both the state and the rampant market are in trouble as far as providing people with useful and dignified jobs is concerned (and indeed the creation of democratic conditions for lasting social stability)? What is its potential - recognising that whether there is or could be a coherent 'it' is itself open to question?

Our focus in this essay will be not-for-profit, non-state economic activity in Britain, though in analysing its potential we will be drawing on international experiences. We will pay most attention to those aspects of this sector which are directly concerned with saving or creating jobs or helping the unemployed find work. Discussion of employment issues, however, will lead into consideration of what infrastructural support is necessary: finance, training and common marketing services for example. In fact, how far third sector employment is viable depends, we will argue, on its internal integration and its support from local, national and/or continental political institutions. We will argue that common infrastructure and direct trading connections, along with political support - from finance, to constraints on (or the break up of) the power of multinational concentrations of wealth - are a condition for social enterprises to thrive and create fulfilling employment.

We are not morally or socially neutral in our approach and will consider the different experiences of the third sector in terms of their capacity or potential capacity to provide useful, fulfilling employment. The terms 'useful' and 'fulfilling' are not mere milk and honey adjectives; they are intended to link the character of work to the needs it is meeting, to the democracy of its organisation, to the well-being of the community in which it is located and to the personal development of the workers who carry it out. Our assessment of the third sector depends on its record and potential for the quality of work rather than simply the numbers of jobs saved or created. This leads to wider questions: what could be the distinctive importance in present economic circumstances of the 'third sector' for providing useful, fulfilling jobs for all those who are able to be economically active? What could be its purchase on the wider economy? And what conditions would be necessary for the third sector to achieve real influence or power over both market and state? We aim to answer these questions through a brief survey of what exists and compare the present context of the third sector with its first and classic emergence, with Owenism and the co-operative experiment in Lanarkshire in the early-nineteenth century.

The third sector in practice and theory

First and perhaps most enduring as an alternative source of employment are co-operatives: both enterprises that have started as co-ops and those where co-ops have been created out of the resources - or from the ashes - of a conventional company. A government funded study in 1993 estimated that there are 1,200 worker co-ops in the UK employing over 11,000 people. Their combined turnover was 300 million. A small and somewhat beleaguered component of the 'third sector' are worker management buy outs organised on the basis of Employee Share Ownership

(ESOPS); these should be distinguished from co-ops in that they do not necessarily aspire to co-operative forms of management. The third component of the 'third sector' is what is known as the charitable or voluntary sector. Much of this sector, however, has become a source of paid employment, drawing an increasingly large percentage of its income - now over 28 per cent - from the state. Consequently, the term 'voluntary' tell us very little, beyond the existence of a voluntary board or management committee.

In one respect the voluntary sector, should not be too sharply distinguished from the co-operative sector. Co-operatives are voluntary associations of labour in the sense that they driven in part by voluntary commitment. On the other hand, most voluntary and charitable organisations were not formed with employment directly in mind; it is only in recent years, as the Conservative government has turned local government from a service provider into a service sub-contractor, that the voluntary sector has become a major employer, especially in the care for the elderly, the mentally sick or handicapped. Over the past fifteen years or so, as central government has steadily eroded their funding, city and district councils in Britain have had to sub-contract 85 per cent of social service provision.

Then there are community enterprises which sometimes begin as a voluntary organisation to meet a community need but become a community co-operative or enterprise as a way of meeting one of most communities' fundamental needs: employment for young people. These are commonly described as a 'community enterprise' where their purposes are social rather than private profit, where it is socially rather than privately owned and where its directors include representatives of other non-profit organisations who have an interest in the company.

A further component of the third sector is one which combines both co-operatives and voluntary organisations: projects or enterprises driven by a social cause or the needs and aspirations of a particular social group and concerned to mobilise labour and finance to meet that need or further that cause. Among the most successful are projects initiated by and for women, environmental initiatives, or enterprises organised by and for an ethnic community or by and for disabled people - a kind of collective self-help. These flourished under Labour local authorities committed both to economic regeneration and to the strengthening of social movements. The experience of organising these kinds of businesses gave many people a glimpse of the satisfaction of earning a livelihood, however meagre, while at the same time pursuing a purpose about which they really care. The motivation and with it the drive to find the necessary resources, has survived cutbacks in local authority funding. In the 1990s, where the project is not self-funding, the animators of such enterprises put together portfolios of funding from the national lottery or in some areas, from the European Commission, sympathetic foundations, trade unions, the local authority and schemes of national government.

Another part of the third sector which depends on such portfolios of funding are organisations responding specifically to the needs of the unemployed by creating an 'intermediate labour market.' The experience so far, pioneered by the Wise Group (see below) based in Glasgow, involves employing significant numbers of the unemployed (the Wise Group takes on 400 a year in Glasgow) as trainees for one year and pays a wage to carry out a range of socially useful work - environmental and housing work, childcare and community transport would be examples. The intention is to enable these unemployed people to be better equipped to get a long term job when they leave. It is funded partly from public funds, local, national and European, and partly from the revenue from its activities.

Finally, Local Exchange Trading Schemes are a means of mobilising the human resources of skill and time within a community to meet many of the day to day needs of that community. They do so on the basis of a barter system, oiled by their own local currency. There are over 400 LETS schemes in Britain, with probably over 20,000 individual members. They provide many of their members with part-time work in exchange for services or commodities they would otherwise have to buy on the market. The work carried out under LETS is not officially recognised as work, except occasionally by zealous benefit officials who consider that it disqualifies claimants from full unemployment benefit. Ironic given that an impetus for LETS has been the inadequacy of benefits.

How are we to interpret the wider significance of these diverse attempts at employment and enterprise driven by social survival and social justice? The social economy has always been motivated by a variety of different ideologies. Almost by definition it is a sphere of social experimentation, where alternative visions of political economy are given practical form, for better or for worse. Some collapse like Heath Robinson contraptions would, if anyone tried to build them; others provide a living illustration of alternative options. With the collapse of the Soviet model, the limits of the central state as itself a manager - as distinct from source of support - for economic enterprise, and now the social dislocations of the unregulated market, 'the third sector' has become a veritable ideological adventure playground for those seeking to find alternatives to command economies and unregulated markets. Libertarian socialism, co-operativism, communitarianism and new variants of social democracy all test their muscles on economic forms that are independent of, but yet in various, sometimes hidden ways, affected by both the character of the market or state within which they exist.

The extent and eclectic character of interest in a 'third sector' is an indication of a degree of crisis or at least lack of confidence in both of the historically predominant economic agencies, state and private corporation. It is an indication of the scale and scope of the profound economic and social transformations that are now emerging. The direction of these transformations is unknown; what is clear is that the institutions of both state and of the market are going through radical change. Moreover, there is little sign that the dominant changes are meeting the needs of the people; if anything, they are exacerbating economic inequalities and insecurities. The growth of the third sector is a sign of initiatives coming from beyond the conventional economic circuits, in ingenious popular responses to unmet needs - and gaining some, albeit ambiguous, reactions from governments and private corporations. These social economic initiatives are practical rather than ideological because, in most cases, they are rooted amongst people whose livelihood depends on the success of these 'experiments'. They are the creation of people who cannot afford to wait for a change of government, the rebuilding of the labour movement, the rethinking of socialism; people who demand a remedy now and who are prepared to work on one of their own and draw on whatever support they can get. The almost invariably local and fragmented character of such survival driven initiatives does however pose a problem: of how their innovative approach to employment can influence national and international politics - a necessary condition of long term survival.

Are these necessity-driven innovations doomed to exist like lichen in the crevices of big business? Or are there other changes in motion which could produce a different landscape, closer to their egalitarian, socially responsible values? To answer this question it is useful to draw on our historical imagination and make a comparison with the first, short-lived, emergence of the social, co-operative economy: Robert Owen's Lanarkshire Mills, in the early nineteenth century. This was a time when the private market was establishing itself for the first time, subordinating almost every area of society to its logic. This first microcosm of the social economy was going against the tide, the tide of the private market, and was soon followed by the regulatory state. We will consider how far widespread experience in recent years of the flaws of both market and state mean that modern day Owenites have a greater chance of rooting their initiatives in wider social changes than those original visionaries whose experiment occurred before either capitalist market or social democratic state had been tried and tested.

The focus in such a comparison will be the implications for the particular form and growth of the third sector in the late 20th century when the private market is once more rampant but in conditions in which people have witnessed the limits of this market in satisfying the wants of the majority. Not only this but people know from experience that democratic social institutions can in principle control and frame the market, even if the best most sustainable forms these institutions of social and ecological justice should take has yet not been arrived at - especially in the face of the global reach of private corporations. In the process of developing such institutions we have had the historical experience of testing and finding both the importance and the limits of a particular form of social control over the market: the nation state. This historical memory is bound to influence the choices people now believe to be theirs; it also provides the tools and the stimulus to innovation. Finally, we cannot expect a pristine third sector; innovation will often involve turning the old and the familiar to new purposes in new combinations and contexts.

The importance of these issues becomes clear on reflecting on the fate of the Owenite movement which had all the strengths which are manifest, in a more scattered way, in to-day's third sector (see Polanyi 1946). It was eminently practical. It did not seek to resist the new machinery but rather to make it the servant of human need and aspiration through the principle of co-operation or 'union.' For a short time, Owenism brought together almost a million workers and artisans in its loose federation of trade unions and co-operatives. The assumption was that by providing for one another's needs, via a co-operative 'Labour Exchange,' artisans could emancipate themselves from the ups and downs of the market. New Lanark, the town and mills organised on Owenite principles contained precedents for most of what we now are now familiar with as part of the third sector: co-operatives, consumer and producer; its own currency based on labour; voluntary associations and a financial infrastructure.

The key to its viability, albeit short-lived, in an increasingly hostile environment, was that it accepted the introduction of machinery and recognised the increase in productivity which this made possible. Owen insisted that this could be exploited on a social, co-operative basis, for the benefit of all. Moreover, this social productivity could be enhanced if full recognition was made of the conditions under which labour could be more productive. That, argued Owen, involved organising production in ways that took full account of human needs and hence enabled society to modify the market. At that time however, the commercial factory system built around the new machinery and utilising the existing market activity was turning everything into commodities to be bought and sold at a price. It was not simply factory products that it was commodifying but also labour, land and money, none of which were themselves strictly 'products.' Labour is a central part of human life, interdependent on other aspects of human life, land is part of nature, and money should simply be a means of exchange. Once they artificially became commodities in this way, their allocation was driven by the market, mediating between competing private enterprises. And as a result, both workers' social and personal lives and the environment became subordinated to the economy.

The scope for economic survival outside this all-encompassing market was progressively squeezed. A micro-economy such as New Lanark, organised on an entirely different relationship between the market and society - a relationship whereby the market was a mechanism directed by institutions of social co-operation - was not totally self-sufficient. It needed to trade. But there were no economies organised on similar lines with which to trade. The wider market place was based on prices that took into account the costs only of each factory, buying labour, land and raw materials at the cheapest price. New Lanark's economic calculations took into account the social costs of production and the social benefits of labour performed under physically and psychologically convivial conditions. As a micro-economy it would compete well if there were similarly integrated social micro-economies in the wider market, but on an individual enterprise basis, the prices of its enterprises would be high as labour and land were highly valued and consequently expensive. As an economy it was doomed, once the capitalist market had spread.

What lasted, however, was resistance to the commodification of labour: Owenism was one of the many origins of the trade union movement. What was lost was social institutions that directed and regulated the market from within production and distribution themselves, making market exchanges a part of a social economy rather than the driving force of an economy which had sucked society into its motor, like a squashed fly. As the self-regulated market became established, economy and state, economics and politics, became increasingly separate. The state, as the main focal point of popular struggle, became seen as the chief instrument with which to regulate the market.

Forms of production that refused to treat labour and land as commodities have continued on the margins of the market economy. Without some political protection, however, labour in such enterprises ends up in practice being treated as a commodity, whatever the principles of those involved, through the market pressures of the wider economy. The question now is whether as the limits of both state and unregulated market have become apparent in practice as well as theory, the principles of co-operative economics become relevant again, in some combination - not envisaged by Owen - with democratic political institutions and a socially framed market? To answer this question, it is necessary to pay close attention to the detail of the third sector in Britain and how it has changed as the wider economic and political environment has been transformed.

The third sector in Britain: some exemplary cases.

Over one and a half million people are directly involved in the third sector in Britain. What is striking is the social range of people: experienced trade unionists, young unemployed, alternative life-stylers, residents of old style working class estates, who have chosen to build some kind of co-operative economic organisation as a means of gaining a livelihood.

Co-operatives

Let us consider each component of the third sector in Britain. First, co-operatives, starting with worker co-operatives. In the past ten years several thousands of jobs have been saved as a result of workers taking the initiative to form a co-op. On average co-ops survive longer than conventional small businesses. They offer greater than average job security, they have greater flexibility to avoid redundancy through redeployment, voluntary short-time working or occasionally wage cuts. They also tend to pay higher average wages than conventional business and avoid fat cat salaries.

Co-operatives usually have been rebel companies, rejecting the goal of individual profit and the managerial prerogatives that tend to go with it. How the function of management is carried out varies but there are common principles: namely, accountability of management back to the workers or, in the case of a community co-operative, to some wider social grouping, and common control over profits - and responsibility for losses.

In Britain, the history of these constructive rebellions are closely associated with wider historical ebbs and flows, including of other institutions of economic rebellion and reform, especially the trade unions and the Labour Party. In the early days of the organisation of labour, much faith was placed in the co-operative movement, and not merely as a pragmatic means of achieving improved conditions and some modicum of economic control but as the foundations of a new social order. Utopian hopes frequently diverted energies from pragmatic strategies for survival in the market, and as the combination of a somewhat patchy record of success with the growth of the trade unions as an admittedly more defensive yet more reliable means of economic betterment, co-operatives waned as a labour movement strategy.

In the 1970s for an exceptional and ultimately tragic moment, co-operative initiatives, trade union organisation and Labour government converged. The national level was most dramatic and most flawed: the trade union initiated co-ops - Meriden, Scottish Daily News and KME - were supported by Tony Benn's Department of Industry as both a means to save what many believed were viable jobs and to implement manifesto commitments to industrial democracy. Within government, however, there was no expertise about how co-operatives might be helped and very little commitment. They were treated almost as a joke, a hobby of Tony Benn's. Their eventual failure became a self-fulfilling prophecy by Tony Benn's enemies in the civil service and the Cabinet alike. The government fatally constrained material support for the newly formed co-operatives - in the process pushing co-operatives off the national agenda of employment and industrial policy just at a time when both the European Commission and local government saw them has having especial employment potential.

In the early and mid-eighties, powerful metropolitan and city councils saw co-ops as central to strategies to defend and recreate jobs against the tide of de-industrialisation coming from multi-national companies, aided by the free-market policies of national government. Innovative Labour local authorities gave co-operatives extensive support, mainly through a network of Co-operative Development Agencies, with the wary but generally helpful approach of major trade unions such as the Transport and General Workers Union. The 80s saw over 500 new co-operatives being formed. The decimation of local government weakened the support system for this new generation of co-ops and especially the possibility of a strategic and well-resourced approach to building the basis of a co-operative economy. The experience of Co-operative Development Agencies and sympathetic local authorities, however, has left a positive legacy, most notably a body of people experienced in running both co-ops themselves and a much enhanced infrastructure of support.

Two more recent success stories - which have drawn on this legacy - point to some of the economic, organisational and cultural conditions of success. They are entirely different in their origins: the first, the case of Tower Colliery, arose out of trade union resistance to privatisation; the second, a wholefood wholesale company, SUMA, was founded as a co-operative by counter-cultural enthusiasts with a practical bent.

Tower Colliery, one of the largest employers in the Cynon Valley, South Wales, was officially closed by British Coal in April 1994. Several private companies were interested in re-opening it but all wanted lower wages and longer hours. The National Union of Mineworkers at Tower has a radical tradition, sustained by the surrounding community - the fate of the pit was seen a community matter not just a union matter. The miners and the union knew that the anthracite coal had a strong demand, and many years of extraction left in it. With strong community support and after a long campaign to press British Coal to reverse its decision to close, the NUM lodge decided on a workers buy out.

Lodge union officials approached the Welsh TUC's Wales Co-operative Centre, an advice agency, to help miners bid for their own colliery. Tower Employee Buy-Out, TEBO, was formed, and recruited experienced mining managers to write a business plan and raise finance in the government's sell-off of the colliery. All the members of the bid team, including the brought-in managers, had to pledge £8,000 - which most found from their British Coal redundancy money - which, after a considerable struggle, trying several different banks, raised a £2m bank loan for start-up capital and 239 miners produced £1,930,000 from redundancy payments. The pit was re-opened on 2nd January 1995 to the tune of the Red Flag sung by 2,000 supporters as the miners walked through the colliery gates. By April 1997 it had a record profit of £4.3 million on a turnover of £22m. Within months they had taken on 30 further miners and are now (Spring 1998) taking on more. They all earn a flat rate of £400 a week compared with £210 at other privatised mines. Absenteeism has been cut from 18 per cent to 0.03 per cent

Its structure and funding have been carefully thought through. It is still run as a co-operative with a strong commitment to keep it that way. Because it is too large for a direct democracy or a collective management structure to operate the co-operative is run by a six member board, three of whom are employed as industry experts, one as a non-executive chair, and two worker directors elected by the workforce as a whole. As the business clears debt finance from the banks, the workforce representation on the board will double. It has learnt a historical lesson as far as how to ensure longevity. Large industrial co-operatives are not new in Britain - as the Owenite experience testifies - but most of these closed by the 1920s, as the majority of members became retired workers and were able to make what might be today termed a 'windfall profit' by selling the assets of businesses they were no longer intimately involved in. To prevent a repetition of this, Tower requires workers who cease employment in the co-op to sell their shareholding to the Employee Benefit Trust.

Success depended on markets, available finance and commitment and determination, community engendered as well as workplace. Their success could be applied to many other mines although another miners' takeover failed at Monkseaton in Scotland, mainly because of structural limitations to the pit itself. The NUM at Tower are not parochial: they believe that their experience could be the basis of a new kind of public ownership based on both co-operative workplaces and common marketing. 'We are not capitalists. We are putting socialist principles into practice' said one of the workplace leaders.

Another critical ingredient which enabled such a large workers' takeover to succeed was the pre-establishment, ten years before, of a cooperative advice agency that was founded by the trade unions, and which had strong trade union support. While there is a network of co-operative agencies across Britain (and in other parts of the world) they have for the most part been set up by local authorities, and have seldom had such close links with trade unions.

However, collective commitment and real democratic involvement of the whole workforce may not be a sufficient condition of success. In several towns, under pressure from the Conservative government's de-regulation of the buses, local authorities encouraged management-led takeovers based on Employee Share Ownership Schemes ('ESOPS') as alternatives to selling out to one of the private companies which were dividing up the country's bus systems between them. The trade unions have supported these schemes on a similar basis, assuming they would be in their members' interests. However these experiments have generally been short-lived. Stage Coach in particular, seeking a monopoly on private bus routes, have made the management very attractive financial offers to sell the company. The workers too have been offered a financial reward for their shares and in the absence of a positive commitment to the co-operative or industrial democracy principle, workers have accepted the deal.

Another success story is Suma, the whole food co-operative founded in 1977. With a turnover of £8.5m and 60 full-time staff on a good, and equal, wage with a high level of training, this is one of the most successful of those companies which started out as co-operatives. Here again commitment is an important factor: commitment not only to the co-operative principle but also to wholefood and a strong belief that they are supplying healthy products to the public while much of mass produced food sold in the conventional commercial sector is in the long run unhealthy. They have a 'mission statement' which sums up both the worker and the consumer side of this commitment: to 'provide a high quality of service to customers and a rewarding working environment for the members, within a sustainable, ethical, co-operative business structure; to strive to provide a healthier lifestyle by supplying ethical eco-friendly vegetarian products.'

In their twenty odd years they have evolved, by conscious trial and error, an effective and democratic management structure. Judging from their own account of the process, this has not been painless. This account is of value in itself both for other would-be co-operators and also for anyone sceptical or curious of how efficiency of service and egalitarianism in production can be combined. Initially the co-operative management was by weekly General Meetings - for which they closed trade down for the afternoon - and by spontaneous, on the spot decision. Markets were easy and self-sacrificing commitment high, sustained by the alternative sub-culture in Leeds in which they all lived as well as worked. At one point the co-op provided a hot lunch because everyone worked so late that all they could do when they got home was sleep. As competition intensified, profits fell and their Leeds warehouse became impossibly small, they made both a physical move, to a large mill building near Halifax (and out of the supportive sub-culture of their origins) and a management move, away from weekly General Meetings to a delegated management system. Called the Hub and the Doughnut it involved sector meetings and decisions and then delegates to the Hub to make corporate decisions. This went through various crises, with a drop off in involvement and a certain cumbersome inefficiency of decision making. Finally, after great team effort at survival in the face of financial and natural (the warehouse was flooded) disasters they now have quarterly general meetings and an elected management committee to take strategic decisions and implement them through company officers, personnel, finance, information and operations. These officers return to their 'day job' in between these management tasks, just as everyone in the company rotates jobs and becomes multi-skilled.

In a variety of ways - multi-skilling, lack of hierarchy, high training levels - SUMA, like many third sector enterprises, has been carrying out many of the management practices that gurus of management theory rave about but which conventional companies often find very difficult to put into practice. Their management methods, both made easy by and also reinforcing of strong team bonds, is no doubt one secret of their success. Another factor explaining Suma's success is close links between the company, primarily a wholesaler, and a large number of retail outlets - most of whom share a similar approach to food and many are themselves co-operatives.

Health/whole food is one of the few examples in Britain of an economic sector in which co-ops have an organised presence. Such an organised network of co-operatives has obvious benefits in terms of sharing of information and understanding, achieving favourable trading relations and economies of size. On the continent, most notably Italy and France, such linkages are positively encouraged, both by law and by provision of shared facilities for a co-operative network (e.g. marketing, financial or research facilities). This has real benefits for employment. In Italy, where a law was passed to enable workers to participate in the share capital of the company and set up production and employment co-ops through a financing company created specifically by the co-operatives federation 19,162 jobs have been created between 1985 and 1996.

Voluntary sector

The second major expansion of the third sector is coming from the expansion of the voluntary sector. In the neo-liberal 80s and early 90s this commonly occurred as a consequence of the withdrawal of the state; more rarely, for example with innovative Labour local authorities, it was the result of an expansion and simultaneous transformation of public provision through grant aiding democratic voluntary organisations. It might be useful here to distinguish between the 'functional third sector' and the 'transformative third sector.' The former simply providing what used to be a public service on a cheaper reduced basis outside of direct public control and the latter involving an expansion of public provision pioneered by voluntary campaigning groups negotiating a new and accountable relation to elected state bodies.

The heyday of radical municipal government in London, Sheffield and to a lesser extent other cities gave us a glimpse of the latter and the role that the voluntary sector might play within it. In London, for example, the 1982 Greater London Council achieved a unique expansion of public provision, and public intervention, mainly through funding and working with (in to-day's purposefully vague jargon, a 'partnership') the voluntary sector. In the case of childcare, the Womens Committee of the GLC along with the Employment Committee (childcare was seen as a source of employment as well as a community service) drew up a childcare strategy, in consultation with voluntary groups and experts of various kinds - practical and theoretical. This became the basis on which the grants division of these two committees funded and supported over 350 organisations involved with childcare provisions, campaigns or research to carry out and further develop the strategy. The aim was to improve as well as to expand childcare provision in London and most of all to enable parents to have more control over the management of that provision. Democratisation was also the aim underpinning a similar partnership with local groups defending their inner city community against City based land speculators or government imposed development agencies who would prefer to see the area developed for offices or infrastructure to suit the needs of the City - luxury flats, an inner city airport for example. Coin Street in Waterloo, Canary Wharf and the Royal Docks, site of the City Airport, are classic examples. The case of Coin Street is, relative to the difficult times into which it was born, a third sector/local state success story. Here the GLC bought the land and transferred it to a trust made up of local people, Coin Street Community Builders, representing different community groups.

This trust has been responsible for overseeing the development of an attractive and thriving inner city residential and working community.

The drive behind most of the expansion of the voluntary sector, however, is quite different from either these radical initiatives which have transformed the way public resources are administered and public services delivered, or the predominant drive behind the co-operative sector - at least it is very much more ambiguous. Whereas the drive behind the co-operative sector comes usually from a positive, collective rebellion against the kind of jobs available in the private sector or the difficulty, sometimes impossibility of finding jobs at all, in state or private sector; the drive behind the recent expansion of the voluntary sector has quite explicitly been to provide services more cheaply and to trim down local government. In theory, jobs are protected by the EU's Acquired Rights Directive but there are many loopholes so that in practice, after the first year or so of privatisation, trade union bargaining power is typically weak. On the other hand there is a growing demand for socially purposeful voluntary work, especially from young people facing a dead end job market and at the same time a growing number of experienced people setting up voluntary projects in response to social problems abandoned by the state.

A lot of charities have become sub-contractors of the state. Contribution to charity income by central and local government rose by 56 per cent between 1991 and 1994/5. From a position where state or local authority funding of charities was under 10 per cent, the state now provides 28 per cent of revenue in payment for services which local government, under pressure from national government, has contracted out. The most notable examples of contracting out to the voluntary sector are care of old people or of the mentally ill or the physically handicapped. In the health service the purchaser/provider split gave real impetus to contracting by charities. But many have ended up subsidising services because of inexperience in bidding. According to a survey carried out by the National Council of Voluntary Organisations, at least two in three service providing organisations report that they have had to top up contracts from their own resources. This has changed the role of such voluntary organisations, in ways they regret or about which they feel ambiguous. Three quarters of the organisations surveyed believed that 'we are increasingly becoming more like a business.' Take the Hull and East Yorkshire branch of Mind: this has grown in 12 years from 8 to 60 staff with three quarters of its income coming from NHS service agreements. The drawback is that Mind, a campaigning organisation on issues of mental health, is in danger of losing its independence, a fear strongly felt by many of the beneficiaries of this ambiguous boost.

Community enterprises

The third component of the social sector, linking co-op and voluntary in the form of community enterprises provides many cases of collective initiative, living counter-evidence to the Thatcherist myth that the spirit of enterprise arises only from private property and the free market.

For the last 15 years, Glasgow has been at the heart of Britain's community business movement. It offers a vision for how communities can re-build their social and economic environments, earning more income for their communities while providing the services their own communities need. The GLC's idea of 'popular planning' has had its reflection in the day-to-day lives of many Glasgow estates.

The Allander Group, based on the Possil estate, north of Glasgow, provides local employment while meeting the demands of the community. It employs 120 people across its four divisions, and is now the largest non-state employer in the area. These divisions cover security, cleaning, painting and decorating, and landscaping, with dramatic results for the material and cultural life of the estate, reducing crime and improving morale. It has a turnover in excess of £1m, and is profitable - with profit going back into the community, and to generate further business opportunities.

Typically, a community business will be set up by people within the community who recognise local needs - these may be for improved security, nursery care or a café. A committee of community activists will be established, which may also include a local councillor, to run a company to provide the services and take responsibility for employing people. Training may be conducted internally, or be assisted by the local authority or Training and Enterprise Council. Profits made by the company must, under the rules of the constitution, be ploughed back into the local community, often by creating new associated companies. The main company will normally be a company limited by guarantee, membership of which is open to any local person.

Community businesses such as Allander have been extremely successful, though others have not succeeded. Like any group with a voluntary management committee, a community business must attract the right balance of skills amongst its employees and its management, which can be difficult on the deprived estates where they are most needed. Equally important, outside advisors and trainers must balance providing expert support while allowing local people to run their own business, providing the services they most want. It can be a difficult balancing act.

The fourth component of the third sector, which may be quite specific to the times that we live in - high unemployment, widespread unmet social need - is hybrid organisations in the 'intermediate labour market', the labour market that provides useful and rewarding work for the unemployed but not necessarily long term jobs. As already mentioned, the most well known example in Britain is Wise Group. It is a registered charity which describes its purpose as 'to beat unemployment. We work with people to help them into jobs'. It provides 400 unemployed people with a one year contract on a £118 a week wage working for the Wise Group of companies, Heatwise, Landwise and Treewise who all work in close partnership with community groups, local authorities and other public authorities and private companies. It secures 25,000 homes, insulates 100,000, improves the environment of 5,000 and plants 750,000 trees. Its funding consists of 25 per cent from Glasgow District Council which buys its services, 25 per cent from the European social fund, 25 per cent from urban aid and energy conservation projects, 25 per cent from sales. It provides training programmes and work experience in horticulture, environmental improvement and education, childcare, catering, building and business administration.

This part of the social economy could well expand as a result of the government's Welfare to Work programme, but there are plenty of big 'ifs' involved in such a prediction. Properly done, that is, with good training and meeting social needs, it is in the short run and for the individual project decidedly expensive - though in the long run and for the economy as whole it is a very useful investment. The Wise Group gains much of its funding from Europe as do similar projects in other parts of the country. There are few signs that the British government is willing to provide the kind of funding that would enable the Wise model or something like it to spread. The government, searching for options which will minimise its costs, has encouraged major private companies in the employment agency business such as Reed International to run Welfare to Work schemes in many areas. The government is divided on exactly how to run Welfare to Work but given the attraction partnerships with private business appear to have for the Prime Minister, it is unlikely that a well funded third sector option will be favoured.

Finally there are Local Exchange Trading Schemes. LETS has taken off most successfully in Australia where national and state governments have been very favourable towards LETS. The schemes there might also have been favoured by a pre-existing tradition of barter between companies; but this is not a feature of commercial life in Britain. Some Labour-controlled local authorities have, however, been keen to encourage LETS schemes. But national governments both Conservative and Labour have not been interested and the Inland Revenue has been positively hostile.

Several connected principles lie behind LETS providing a system of exchange notes that operate as a local currency to facilitate barter trade. Because the currency is only accepted locally it ensures that the income earned within the scheme can only be spent within the same community. Further, barter trade is based on the promise of supplying other goods or services in kind. This means that purchases are made when required. Usury is effectively by-passed. Some LETS schemes also operate the principle of equal wages, so that the local currency is earned according to the number of hours a task has taken, rather than being based on the amount of sterling that would have been earned in the outside economy.

It is often in smaller towns, especially in the south west where there remains a stronger community culture, that LETS schemes have taken off, not in the larger cities. Schemes that are large can be difficult to administer, and volunteers run out of spare time and willingness to keep the schemes going. LETS schemes that operate within clearly defined local neighbourhoods, rather than across giant cities, would probably have a greater prospect of success. An alternative, which the national promotional body LETSLINK is investigating, is for them to operate on the basis of a community of interest, which may be among people with learning disabilities, or in a single parents' club.

LETS can be a genuine bridge from unemployment into paid employment, giving participants new skills and greater self-confidence. It would be logical for LETS schemes to run alongside credit unions, especially those credit unions operated by housing associations or local authorities to improve the financial circumstances of tenants. But LETS in the UK can only make a real impact if the tax and benefits problems can be overcome. At present it is not really possible to conclude whether they have been successful or unsuccessful. In some areas they are very active, yet in others they are weak.

What future for the social economy?

The experience so far in Britain illustrates at least a potential for the third sector as a source of useful and fulfilling employment, a democratic means of distributing work. At its best, it has unique advantages on its side: the motivation, practical know-how and vested interest in self-organisation, problem solving and self-discipline of its participants and a local rootedness that enables it to deploy local labour to meet local needs - or international needs and markets identified through local know-how and determined imagination.

Tower Colliery and SUMA, viable co-operative enterprises based in very different social constituencies, both illustrate that management genuinely based on principles of democracy - both in terms of accountability and creative development - and of co-operation between equals, can be economically efficient. Indeed they are able to draw on sources of efficiency unavailable to a management that is accountable to private or undemocratic institutional shareholders. Hence efficient management does not depend on private ownership. Nor on the other hand is social responsibility the prerogative of the state. The work of the Wise group and the growing number of similar organisations subsidised to match unemployed human capacities to unmet social needs, shows that useful work is there to be done. 'Unemployment' in other words is an artifact of the unregulated private market not an indicator of social redundancy. Community enterprises like the Allander Group, and the numerous enterprises or forms of self-employment initiated by and for women, disabled people, ethnic minorities and through LETS schemes point both to 'markets' whose needs and aspirations are not acknowledged, unprompted, by either existing market or state, and to people with the know-how to respond.

Some of these needs cannot be met viably by an individual enterprise; like childcare or community development they are viable looked at from the point of view of a city or town as a whole. Hence provision for such needs requires public resources. But as the experience of the GLC illustrated such resources are sometimes best managed, within a framework of standards and objectives laid down and negotiated by an elected political authority, by democratic civic organisations. In these ways, 'third sector' organisations illustrate on the one hand ways of socialising the market, most notably the labour market, and on the other hand ways of democratising the administration of public resources.

At a time when market led and profit driven economics has proved inadequate in matching resources with needs, and the state has proved to have insufficient knowledge for either understanding the full diversity of people's needs or for grasping the opportunities to meet them, the third sector holds the moral high ground. But the lesson of the first social economy, Owen's Lanarkshire Mills, born as the market swept all before it, shows that the moral high ground even when combined with pragmatic efficiency is not sufficient for lasting success. On the low ground, there must be powerful material trends or possibilities with which the social economy can combine. The third sector is not going to grow until like an amoeba, it reaches such a point that quantitative growth leads to qualitative change and the social economy becomes the dominant economic form.

Third sector forms of enterprise organisation are perfectly viable but for them to be the norm would require a radical transformation in the wider economic environment, the character of which we can only sketch. First it would require a transformation in the allocation of investment capital. There are two immediate steps, already well debated and developed as feasible measures. The first would be the democratisation of pension funds which represent literally billions of investment funds, now deployed by fund managers concerned only about maximising the rate of return. Future pensioners too have an interest in the rate of return but they also have an interest in the jobs and economic and social well being of the locality and country in which they live and of future generations. Greater employee control of this prime source of institutional finance would enable this balance to be consciously debated, hence bringing social priorities into investment decisions (Minns, 1996). Such a degree of social control over the capital markets would require legislation as well as pressure from trade unions and social movements representing the would-be pensioners, if it were to have any effect.

A further measure to socialise investment finance would be through the tax system to redistribute a significant proportion of corporate profits to public regional investment boards with the brief to invest in co-operative and other third sector enterprises on the basis of criteria combining social and commercial efficiency.

The other front on which political action is needed to enable society to dominate the economy - and hence the social economy to thrive, rather than *vice versa* is labour: protecting the humanity of labour from the pressures to turn it into a commodity. As we have seen, the most socially efficient third sector enterprises achieve this at the micro level but unless their markets are particularly buoyant, it is very difficult to sustain this in a wider economic environment in which labour is reduced to the level of a commodity. Trade unions have provided some resistance to this relentless market pressure but in many Western countries, especially the US and the UK, they are defeated and on the defensive. Two fundamental measures are under extensive debate to add to trade union defence of the social needs of labour: the reduction of working hours and the right to a basic or 'citizens' income and hence some autonomy from the labour market. (See Chapter 12) Were these measures to be achieved, they would mark a significant move beyond the Beveridge Welfare state and traditional employment protection legislation. Whereas both the latter assume wage labour as the defining, determining condition of the economically active, a significant reduction of working hours - in theory possible due to the high productivity achievable with the new technologies - and the right to a basic income whether the citizen is in waged employment or not, recognise the human aspirations of labour and its daily and generational reproduction.

Of course the achievement of anything like a social economy is likely to be uneven, with regions or sectors organised on social priorities having to compete in a conventional profit-maximising environment. Such social economies whether local, regional or national will be more viable if there are institutions of co-ordination and mutual support. Again this is something with which many localities and regions have experimented: in the Basque country, the highly successful Mondragon co-ops are supported and kept in equilibrium through a highly developed bank; in the Moderna region of Northern Italy, textile entrepreneurs have pooled resources on joint market research; shared design facilities and combined marketing. The latter companies are not strictly 'third sector' though many are small companies with strong unions and egalitarian ethos. The importance of Mondragon bank and the Moderna example of co-operation in the textile industry - funded partly by the regional government and partly by the entrepreneurs themselves - is that they illustrate the potential for regional co-ordination to provide, on a co-operative 'horizontal' basis, the 'co-ordination' and central services provided by multinational corporations for their different branches through centralised control.

There is nothing inevitable about the prospect of conditions for economic relations dominated by social need falling into place to marginalise economic forces driven by profit. The unfettered global market is proving unstable (Elliot and Atkinson, 1998) but the trajectory of the unstable 1930s bears a salutary warning against facile assumptions that a rickety capitalism gives way to democratic alternatives.

An important force driving modestly towards social solutions in Europe at any rate, is a population with high expectations and assumptions about their social and economic rights. After all they or their parents began to savour them, even depend on them after the Second War. In Britain, the most respected surveys show that Thatcherite, neo-liberal values had never spread to the extent that had been deduced from the new right's electoral success. In France, Germany and Italy the repercussions of market de-regulation have been met with such determined industrial militancy that right wing governments have either fallen (France) or adapted for fear of falling (Germany). No such sustained social democratic experience had shaped people's consciousness in the 1930s.

The unfettered global market place could stabilise, however, through new global economic institutions: this is the logic of the World Trade Organisation, the continental and cross-continental free trade agreements. This would represent a 'Great Transformation' of the kind that overwhelmed the social economy of New Lanark, only on a global level. A potentially decisive difference however is that the momentum of market forces that almost sucked Owenism into its motor occurred before democracy, or at least before universal suffrage, had enabled people to make choices about the wider economic environment. Participants and supporters of the twentieth century social economy have conceptions of democracy shaped by over seventy years of the vote, however blunt an instrument this may have proved to be. Some would argue that this counts for little now that multinational corporations overshadow nation states in many ways. Against this it is important to remember - a growing number of citizens certainly do - that the bodies that agree to de-regulate, that erect new global architecture - are made up of elected governments. The first phases of de-regulation were completed with all the discretion that was intended. But from the late 1980s and the massive and nearly successful campaign against the North American Free Trade Agreement, multinationals no longer have governments to themselves.

The most recent deregulatory measure, the Multilateral Investment Agreement, was withdrawn as a result of governments having to respond to popular pressures. This agreement would have made illegal any national restriction or constraint on multinational investment. The success, however short term, of the pressure against this particular deregulation indicates that the growth we have described of third sector initiatives in localities is paralleled by an increasing awareness of the need for global political pressure if such local initiatives are to thrive. Certainly, like the early nineteenth century we are going through a historic period of transformation. But the third sector does not have to retreat to its own world; it has economic and political allies - weak and battered though some of them may be - in the dominant economy as well as modest international economic linkages of its own. Transformation usually involves conflict and the outcome of the prolonged struggle between unfettered market forces and an emerging social economy is an open one.

CHAPTER 15

THE FEASIBLE UTOPIA OF A REDISTRIBUTION OF WORK: RADICAL ALTERNATIVES FOR FULL EMPLOYMENT

John Vail

Introduction

One of the most important tasks in building popular support for a transformative project is to present a compelling vision of the good life that may be within our reach. It is critical for us to begin to free ourselves from the paralysis of the imagination that has afflicted the left for decades. The last three chapters in Part III have presented an appealing vision of the potential of a redistribution of work: full employment, a breakdown of gender barriers, a revitalised and democratised polity, an improved quality of life, a series of new services linked in a responsive and democratic system.

But it is also incumbent, as Eric Olin Wright cautions, to demonstrate that our utopias are indeed 'real': what this entails in practice is a careful appreciation of the obstacles the left may face in implementing our programme (Wright, 1995). If our vision is to become reality, people need to be persuaded that our utopian vision can be realised in practice; that the inevitable obstacles and predicaments which will arise can be solved; that we can actually get to the promised land in our lifetimes. 'Probable impossibilities', as Aristotle argued, 'are to be preferred to improbable possibilities'.

This chapter is devoted to exploring the feasibility of a redistribution of work. It is divided into three parts. The first explores the conditions under which radical reform may be possible under capitalism and the extent to which a project for a redistribution of work is able to meet them. In the second part, I examine the numerous economic, political and ideological obstacles which these barriers face. Finally, I conclude with an investigation of how these barriers could be overcome and whether a redistribution of work can become a successful transformative project.

When is radical reform possible under capitalism?

The question of the possibility of reform under capitalism has long been a central debating point, and minefield of contention, within the left (Bronner, 1990). It has always been incumbent on social reformers to have some notion of the conditions under which reform in democratic capitalist societies is possible. Joel Rogers and Wolfgang Streeck have enunciated a concise formula that I find persuasive. 'The democratic left makes progress under capitalism', they argue, 'when it improves the material well-being of workers, solves a problem for capitalists that capitalists cannot solve for themselves, and in doing both wins sufficient political cachet to contest political monopoly on articulating the "general interest" (Rogers and Streeck, 1994: 130). The last successful Left project for reform, they argue, was Keynesian social democracy: it achieved success by providing the foundations for full employment and mass consumption that substantially raised the livelihoods of the working class; by solving the dilemma of demand (capitalists have an incentive to raise profitability by cutting costs - labour costs in particular - which can have a detrimental effect on overall demand and hence economic growth) that is endemic to capitalism; and by transforming the particular worker interest in redistribution into a societal interest.

It is universally accepted on the Left that this model is fatally compromised and that a new model for an egalitarian political economy is urgently required, of which there is no shortage of rival claims. Rogers and Streeck themselves argue for an 'egalitarian productivism' that concentrates on supply side measures; Robert Pollin has highlighted the importance of reforming the financial system and establishing democratic control over investment (Pollin, 1995), policies which have important echoes in the arguments for a stakeholder capitalism so prominent among the British left (Hutton, 1995; Kelly, Kelly, and Gamble, 1997); others make the case for a European Keynesianism which would promote a continental expansion of employment and a system of social transfers (Michie and Grieve Smith, 1994). There is not sufficient space in which to develop a sustained critique about the limits of these models, but in any case I believe that a positive argument on behalf of a political project is always far more convincing than the most damning indictment of a competing alternative. To that end, I argue below that a redistribution of work not only meets the conditions which Rogers and Streeck have laid out above, but that it alone of the other alternatives, has the potential not just to meet the conditions for an egalitarian political economy but at the same time to lead to a radical transformation of gender relations, the public sphere and the world of work itself.

Improving material well-being

As discussed in the introduction of the collection, a redistribution of work has the unparalleled ability to solve the structural crisis of unemployment that is gripping Europe. As Greg Albo and John Schmitt and his colleagues describe in Part III, neither the neo-liberal policies of flexibility nor social democratic policies of training and skills development are capable of solving the jobs crisis. But a redistribution of work is also especially adaptable, in ways that progressive policies of the supply side cannot match, to the spatial character of unemployment in modern capitalism (Massey and Meegan, 1982). It has long been recognised that job loss is often heavily concentrated in areas of high social depression and poverty; in these depressed local economies, it is almost impossible for workers to price themselves into a job given that there are so few private sector employers who have jobs on offer. As a consequence, the job subsidies, skills upgrading and various welfare to work programmes of the centre left are doomed to failure in these marginalised areas; they have little effect in providing actual opportunities for work and their punitive approach to the unemployed (who are forced to take 'work' or risk losing their benefits) is not only morally repugnant but utterly counterproductive for it destroys work incentives and the good will which these programmes need to succeed. A third sector approach, on the other hand, can be specially adapted to meet the crisis of a local labour market and the unmet needs of the community; it can provide economic security and provide a release from the exploitative environment of low wage employment; and it can generate much greater legitimacy and support.

A redistribution of work does more than just provide jobs: it has the unique feature of being able to transform the very nature of the jobs themselves. Basic income, in particular, can be seen as part of the long tradition on the left - which has seemingly dropped out of its vocabulary in recent years - of a concern for how work could be reorganised in a more humane and less alienating fashion.[1] Because of the added income (even a subsistence level would provide advantages), workers would find it more affordable to refuse the most exploitative and alienating dead end jobs (Standing, 1992; Offe, 1992) It would provide the foundation for a democratic flexibility, premised not on compulsory insecurity imposed by employers, but rather on the ability of workers to enhance their personal autonomy. Basic income would give idealistic young people the chance to take on challenging projects of social activism, such as campaigning activity or joining social movements, which could never realistically hope to offer a decent wage.

Individuals would realise a tremendous expansion in their possibilities for personal autonomy. A redistribution of work, by freeing up time and providing a modicum of economic security, would give people the ability to choose between a much richer range of life chances and opportunities. While personal autonomy is often viewed narrowly as a form of individualism, it can be seen more broadly as a collective resource that can justify the development of institutional practices, such as a redistribution of work, that expand all individual's capacity for self empowerment. This transformation of self determination into a feature of democratic equality is essential to a construction of an egalitarian political economy.

Solving a problem for capitalists (and the state)

The issue of winning support from capital for left reforms could be seen as simply a matter of strategy: charting the potential lines of attack in order to strengthen ones own defences or designing efficacious counter measures. However, Rogers and Streeck want to make a stronger claim, namely that social reform is impossible unless sections of capital can be convinced to support it because it offers them some discrete advantage (see also Swenson, 1997). The question of how to engender this support is not so easy, especially when the appropriate solution chosen will often be based on profound ideological assumptions. As an example, should reform programmes be designed in such a way as to maximise employer support; or should the state construct institutional incentives that lead to modified behaviour; or should employers be compelled to comply by virtue of mobilisational activity that raises the cost of non-compliance (although this may unintentionally damage economic growth)?

The first issue is to identify what the left considers to be the primary problem facing capitalists in today's global economic environment. The consensus in this regard is that there are two major constraints: stagnating demand in the advanced societies which has led to a structural imbalance of overproduction and under-utilised capacity; and the need for sustained innovation and productivity because of the fierce product market competition arising from globalisation (Glyn, 1995a; Albo Chapter 11). In the first instance, a redistribution of work, by increasing total employment levels, would have an immediate positive impact on the overall level and stability of demand. It would also contribute to the second dilemma as well: workers who had the benefit of a basic grant, or the knowledge that there was a substantial pool of quality jobs outside their own workplace, would be far more receptive to the 'flexibility' which employers need to ensure their competitiveness (Standing, 1992; Offe, 1992; Purdy, Chapter 12). Workers would be less resistant to changes in workplace organisation or the introduction of new technology, and more inclined to contribute to productivity improvements, when their legitimate fears of losing their jobs as a result of such changes could be reasonably allayed. The collective goods of trust, co-operation and co-ordination, which are essential characteristics of this new environment, would be immeasurably improved as well: both employers and workers would have the freedom to negotiate contested issues in a more positive and relaxed atmosphere when the risk of job loss was not quite so prominent.

A redistribution of work could help in the development of a dynamic economy in other ways as well. Workers would have a much greater opportunity to interrupt their careers for further education or enhanced training which would certainly enhance the overall skills level of the workforce. It could also stimulate entrepreneurial activity: a basic income could provide just the incentive for unemployed or underemployed workers to invest in self employment. This impact would be especially felt in deprived inner city areas where any revitalisation of shopping districts or service provision would be quite welcome. Finally, a redistribution of work could have important ecological effects. Any transformation of the capitalist economy from the dominant productivist model to a more sustainable system would undoubtedly involve a series of short term costs that would have to be borne by the working population; these sacrifices may be more easily contemplated when workers are assured of an independent income and have access to wider employment opportunities (Offe, 1995).

Despite these advantages for capital, there can be no question that the inducements which a redistribution of work could offer would not be enough to dampen employer opposition in its entirety: the state would have to find ways of constraining the actions of capital to ensure their continued co-operation (this is discussed in further detail below). What this implies, argues Leo Panitch, is that the left must 'seek the transformation of the material and ideological capacities of states so that they can serve to realise popular, egalitarian and democratic goals and purposes' (Panitch, 1996: 109). A redistribution of work could play a vital role in this democratisation of the state. One of the least attractive, yet most widely pervasive features of modern political life, is the democratic deficit of participation, the withdrawal of many citizens from active political and civic life. This is undoubtedly affected by the time paradox of modern employment: that time poor/income rich individuals are chained to the world of work with little time to participate in social affairs while those who are time rich/income poor have plenty of involuntary free time on their hands but are beaten down by the grinding weight of poverty. Reducing work hours could be an important step in revitalising public life and opening the way for a democratic renewal.

A redistribution of work is also essential to revitalising civil society. Third sector associations constitute a tremendous reservoir of valuable experience and knowledge that arises from their close links to the community. This social knowledge serves as an incubator of new ideas and programmes, and the development of social entrepreneurial skills, as well as the fostering of collective self confidence and self reliance. It also provides an implicit critique of what constitutes 'expert' knowledge that enables associations to be proactive in postulating their own conceptions of needs and allows them to be receptive, if not accountable, to wider interests (Wainwright, 1994). Finally, a successful redistribution of work would greatly enhance the legitimacy of the state itself: it would provide social reformers with a large constituency of potential allies who would be more inclined to support further government initiatives that sought to extend the reach of popular control of the economy.

Constructing a new general interest

And yet it is one thing to win concessions from capital for a programme of reforms; it is quite another to wrest material, political and ideological power away from capital itself. A redistribution of work has the potential to begin constructing a new framework of material relations of power: working time reductions implicitly embrace the principle of establishing democratic control over the workplace which could be extended to much wider areas of the economy; basic income has the power to weaken the coercive force of market commodification by uncoupling income from work; third sector employment puts forward a social logic of development that directly challenges the individualist logic of the market. In short, the most important, and far reaching, aspect of a redistribution of work may be its ability to establish the material foundations of society along non-capitalist criteria even while it is satisfying the very criteria for a successful capitalist economy.

In a period where the unparalleled commodification and marketisation of society continues to ravage the very society it rests upon, there is no doubt that a reform that promises social protection against the market by reducing the reach of capitalism itself has the potential to attract support across the entire population. This social protection function, which was so persuasively argued for by the economic historian Karl Polanyi in his work *The Great Transformation* (Polanyi, 1946), may very well constitute the new general interest of the next generation of the left and a redistribution of work will be a vital force in this new double movement.

The feasibility of a redistribution of work

A redistribution of work may offer convincing solutions to the paradox of democratic reform but it is certain to encounter serious obstacles before it can become a reality. In this section, I have chosen to focus my account of the feasibility of a redistribution of work on four key constraints: redistributive conflicts, macro-economic barriers, political/institutional obstacles, and ideological constraints. The discussion to follow is largely conceptual: although empirical examples are used, they are largely intended to highlight the analytical issues involved, not to serve as a comprehensive overview.

Redistributive conflicts

All redistributive programmes, including a redistribution of work opportunities, inevitably generate a series of conflicts rooted in structures of power (class, gender and other social divisions), material interests and competing preferences for social change. Egalitarian policies by their very nature imply a shifting of resources from one group to another and as such pose a series of collective action problems that need to be resolved by solidaristic co-operation within and between groups. This necessitates a high degree of social solidarity and collective discipline in order for a redistribution of work to succeed.

Working time: Distributional conflicts are perhaps most intense in relation to the question of working time which poses these potential divisions in their starkest outline. Three arenas of conflict regarding working time can be highlighted: between employers and workers; between different groups of workers; and between men and women. Proposals for changes in working time, particularly reductions in the work week, have the potential to create severe employer unrest. Employers could face higher adjustment costs (extra training expenses, larger social security payments) in adding new workers which might lower profit margins or damage competitiveness especially if their competitors did not face similar pressures to reduce hours. Despite evidence that these costs will depend upon the specific competitive position of their firms - those who faced greater turbulence in their product markets or were under pressure to make radical design changes, were more inclined to overestimate the costs of work time reductions - many employers take it for granted that reductions in working time present a great risk to the competitive health of their firm (Richardson and Rubin, 1993).

Employers therefore have a permanent incentive to neutralise the extra costs of reductions in work hours by making them contingent upon concessions on flexible work practices, a policy that is likely to spark conflict with employees across a broad front. This was precisely the Pandora's box that was opened with the onset of campaigns for a collective reduction of working hours by European unions in the 1980s. Trade union movements in Germany, Great Britain, France and the Netherlands were able to win small changes in weekly hours (usually down to 39 hours) but were forced to make huge concessions in work practices in return (Hinrichs, *et. al.,* 1991; Bastian 1994). In the 'drive for flexibility', unions gave firms the discretion to alter workplace arrangements on a host of issues as best fitted their market conditions. The unions' campaigns in essence completely backfired: the net employment effect of the hours reductions was marginal; changes in workplace practices tilted the balance of power even more precipitously to the employers' side and opened up a series of new areas where unions were forced to compromise; and ultimately, the original impetus of using reductions in working time to increase employment disappeared from the bargaining agenda entirely (Hinrichs, et al, 1991; Bastian 1994).

The question of what is acceptable on the bargaining table highlights the larger political problem which capital has with working time reform. Notwithstanding their desire to manipulate the work time issue to their favour, employers are generally reluctant to agree to any significant expansion of the bargaining arena. More importantly, their willingness to negotiate over work hours is an implicit recognition of the failure of the market to provide sufficient employment which can damage employers' ability to resist further challenges to their managerial prerogatives (Purdy, chapter 12). This analysis recalls the famous point which Michael Kalecki raised about employers' lack of commitment to full employment: capital's 'class instinct', he warned, would lead them to reject any movement toward full employment which was likely to undermine their unchallenged primacy over economic decision making or which gave workers the self assurance to mount wider challenges to the economic system (Kalecki, (1943) 1990).

Conflicts over working time may be equally contentious between workers. On the one hand, this is likely to arise because of a growing asymmetry of preferences towards changes in working time. The increasing differentiation of the working class in terms of work place situations, life experiences, hours worked, incomes, and the like, has generated a wide variety of preferences toward working time policies, in terms of both the policy chosen (reduction in work hours versus caring leaves; reduction in overtime versus early retirement) and the groups who should benefit most from them. This has created a fundamental representational crisis for labour movements (Hyman, 1992; Regini, 1992): how is it possible to take into account this extraordinary diversity of preferences in order to arrive at a common strategy or uniform standards? Karl Hinrichs argues that this dilemma means that any collective strategy on working time will be increasingly divisive and problematic: 'one can no longer think of a single and collectively agreed upon formula to change working hours that has top priority with every employee and that would be preferred to all alternative changes, including the opportunity of a rise in income' (Hinrichs, 1991; 42). This fragmentation of interests gives employers greater opportunity to utilise divide and conquer strategies that can provoke increased competition among workers.

Conflicts are also likely because of an asymmetry of costs involved in working time reductions (Bastian, 1994; Purdy, Chapter 12; Hinrichs, 1991). This is particularly acute between the employed (work rich) and the unemployed (work poor): a reduction in work hours that leads to an expansion of employment opportunities would obviously most benefit the unemployed but the costs in obtaining the policy (both in terms of income forgone, as well as those incurred as a result of the mobilisation needed to obtain it) would be borne primarily by the employed. What is required therefore is a class solidarity whereby individual workers are prepared to sacrifice their own individual preferences for the benefit of all potential workers: workers in full time employment would forego overtime, endorse early retirements and leaves, and continue to press for recruitment gains in their firm negotiations. This class solidarity and consciousness, as has long been recognised in the literature on labour movements, can never be assumed to be automatic but rather is the product of long struggles and historical legacies as well as favourable conjunctures that are highly contingent. Co-operative solutions to this collective action dilemma are also much more difficult in the current era with the resurgence of company (even plant) based unionism which privileges individualist rewards and loyalty to the firm rather than egalitarian demands (Hyman, 1992). A demand for shorter working hours therefore suffers from what Claus Offe and Karl Heinze call a 'motivation gap': 'although it might be best for everybody if it could happen, it is by no means in the perceived interest of the individual to demand it, or to support those who are demanding it' (Offe and Heinze, 1993; 218).

The final distributional conflict over working time concerns the division of interest between men and women. On the one hand, this could be construed in similar terms as above. Women and men would be seen to have divergent preferences for the appropriate version of working time policy: women may prefer longer holidays or more flexible starting and ending times while men prefer a four day week or early retirement. What these preferences are premised on however is not a collective action dilemma but rather disagreements rooted in fundamental aspects of gender power experienced both materially and ideologically. As Irene Bruegel and her collaborators note in their contribution, working time has always been a 'marker for masculinity and femininity'. The male breadwinner ethos that sustained post war full employment was predicated on men's privileged position in terms of income provision to the household and the long hours this may have entailed were equally valuable in allowing them to opt out of domestic life. Given the inequality that still persists within the realm of household work, there may be every reason to believe that men will consume their extra time in leisure pursuits rather than in greater participation in domestic responsibilities unless given strong incentives to change their behaviour.

Basic income: A programme of basic income faces similar distributive problems as those presented above. In the first place, basic income will require a higher share of national income being devoted to the most disadvantaged citizens (those without paid work or income generating assets) who would be presented with a wider range of options and alternatives of what to do with their lives. Other individuals already in paid employment may derive similar benefits from self realisation but this added freedom comes at a price. Because the overall social product is likely to remain roughly the same, this shift in societal resources and opportunities will have to be paid for in terms of lower incomes for the most advantaged. Workers in strong bargaining positions therefore will have an incentive to use their advantageous position to increase their own wages to make up the difference. This could lead firms to try and improve their technological efficiency so as to lower their total wage bill, which may have the effect of increasing job loss and thereby nullifying any gains that may have accrued from increased working hours. 'In addition to social solidarity', writes Andrew Glyn, 'the labour movement has to show strong collective discipline if employment spreading is to be successful' (Glyn, 1992; 133).

The fundamental issue is how to persuade these groups that such a trade-off is in their interest, always a difficult prospect at the best of times, and one that typically requires an institutional solution to the collective action problem (see below). With basic income, this dilemma is worsened by a complementary ideological barrier. Many of those in paid employment will resent the 'right to idleness' which a basic income provides - typically expressed at the unfairness of having their hard work exploited by free riders - and as a consequence will be inclined to keep the value of the basic income grant at a penurious level. Employers face a contradictory preference set *vis à vis* basic income that dovetails with these issues. On the one hand, they may value the positive contribution that basic income makes to labour market flexibility; on the other, such a grant represents a 'political' interference with the 'free labour market' and as such gives workers more bargaining power against low paying employers. Employers therefore may also support the grant being kept as low as possible to give the coercive force of the market more compulsory effect.

Another potential source of conflict is the possibility that basic income could lead to 'a deeper and more firmly cemented division of society into the camp of those to whom labour is 'permitted' and those who are excluded, and 'maintained' by a 'basic income' (Offe, 1996; 212). Those who relied primarily on the grant for their source of living could very well be stigmatised by their refusal to undertake paid work. This new exclusionary divide is particularly worrying for the gender inequalities that it could perpetuate. While a basic income could provide a minimum income for men, it may very well serve as a maximum income for women: those who are limited in their job choices due to caring responsibilities may need to rely exclusively on these funds in order to make ends meet.

Third sector: Third sector redistribution would appear at first glance to replicate the traditional divisions previously highlighted. Well paid public sector workers would demand that the wages of the new third sector hires be set high enough to eliminate the danger that these workers could be used as a cheap alternative; on the other hand, low wage workers in the private sector would be angered by the special treatment if third sector pay was substantially higher than their own wage levels. All work rich households would worry that an increase in their tax burden would be needed to pay for the greater prospect of employment for the work poor. Yet as will be discussed in greater detail below, there are good reasons to assume that any tax rise will have only a moderate impact and more importantly, there is considerable evidence that most taxpayers are willing to trade-off small increases in taxes for better access to a range of public services (Page and Shapiro, 1992).

This calculation would be true for employers as well. For a modest increase in taxes, they would derive a substantial increase in the amount of collective goods on offer that would directly benefit their own firm: cleaner environment, improved infrastructure, wider education and health services. Objections are likely to arise from the small business sector which may fear that government financed service delivery could begin to compete with their own services. A local housing association that sought funding to train its own contracting crew for use in rehabilitating older buildings or building new ones would undoubtedly come into conflict with private contract firms. Pressure from the private sector could be intense to restrict the scope of projects which may have equally serious consequences for the efficacy of output by the social economy (Offe and Heinze, 1993).

Third sector conflicts are likely to develop on other grounds as well. First, choices by the state regarding the appropriate mix of services to be offered by third sector organisations are bound to provoke debate because of the differential benefits (in terms of service delivery, not employment prospects) that may accrue. As an example, a combination supported by young parents that emphasised child care facilities, nursery schools, and improvements in education could be counterposed against a selection of community care, housing and hospices that would appeal to elderly groups. An effort to build generational solidarity would be needed to minimise these divisions and other potential conflicts that may be precipitated by other social divisions.

The question of who benefits from better service delivery implies a similar conundrum of who should get the jobs. A policy of spreading employment opportunities across the population does not automatically contain a guiding principle of how to allocate these opportunities among all the groups that need them. Different third sector organisations may have closer links to one constituency than another and can be expected to direct their job openings to these groups. Co-ordination by the state and third sector groups will be necessary to ensure that principles of fairness and equality are being observed (discussed below) and mechanisms will be needed to alleviate destructive competition among the unemployed.[2] Competition may extend to the associations in the social economy themselves. The race of each to garner the 'spoils' of employment contracts - and the concomitant gains in power and prestige for the organisation - could seriously jeopardise the co-operative ethos that these organisations were founded upon.

Macro-economic issues

Working time: The main economic barrier to a reduction in working time is the oft remarked dilemma of whether the policy will actually lead to significant job creation (Hinrichs, 1991; Purdy, Chapter 12; Bastian, 1994). The key to the paradox is the nature of productivity gains that may accrue from innovation in capitalism. Purdy has argued that each society has three distinct options when it comes to distributing the benefits of improvements in productivity: it can expand output and hold the total work hours steady; it can maintain output and reduce the hours of work; or it can choose some combination of the first two choices. What road is taken will depend on the organisation and interests of capital, the state of the external economic environment, political institutions and above all, on the balance of power among social forces. However, Purdy in Chapter 12 argues that there is a built-in structural bias to capitalism which compels firms to use productivity improvements to expand production and seek out new markets rather than to reduce working time; unless they act in this manner, their profitability will decline as other competitors move in to fill the void they have inadvertently created. This is even more pressing in today's highly competitive environment. Firms would be opposed to any programme of work reductions that is imposed unilaterally by a national government for fear that they will lose their competitive edge to foreign competitors who face no such constraints on their action. This in turn will create tremendous pressure on political leaders to abandon working time proposals for fear that disinvestment and capital flight will damage the country's overall economic health and their own electability.

Even if society opts for the redistributive goal, there may still be no easy way to ensure that job creation is forthcoming. A firm that reduces its working hours still has an abiding interest in ensuring that their wage bill does not exceed their productivity gains; they will also be looking to add extra labour only in so far as their adjustment costs are minimised. What is very likely to occur is that firms will increase work intensity and if output remains broadly the same even with a decline in hours, they have no real incentive to jeopardise this productivity improvement by hiring new labour. New workers may make sense if the firm intends to expand production but even then there is a continual drive for management to get as much out of their existing workers as possible. The conclusion many writers have come to is that a reduction in work time will only have a limited impact on job creation as a result of this calculus (Bastian, 1994; Hinrichs, 1991; Wells, Chapter 2).

Another obstacle concerns the impact of a redistribution of working time on the labour market. It is maybe extremely difficult to ensure that any job creation gains from working time reductions will be extended across the entire population. It is obvious that a policy of working time reductions is prejudiced in favour of rapidly expanding and labour intensive sectors at the expense of declining or capital intensive sectors. Some jobs where people are already working long hours (health workers, managers, truck drivers, academics) are not the type of jobs that provide easy access into the field for the unemployed and they are also the sort of jobs where long hours go hand in hand with greater personal autonomy and fulfilment. Sabbaticals are similarly limited to high professional groups and are typically self funded by the voluntary acceptance of a heavier workload by other employees. The social differentiation of the workforce means that the effect of job creation will vary substantially in terms of its costs and benefits and it may very well be that it is the least qualified and least skilled who bear the brunt of the hours reductions.

Basic income: The primary economic concern regarding basic income is also one of its primary strengths, namely its impact on labour market flexibility. The debate is whether basic income would give workers the ability to stay away from low paying, exploitative jobs, in which case employers could conceivably face a shortage of willing workers; they therefore might have to pay higher wages for their workers which may put them at a competitive disadvantage to other low wage firms, in which case many would be driven out of business. This potential scenario may be outweighed by a societal interest in higher productivity in which case low wage firms would be compelled by a basic income to adapt new innovative practices that would make up for their higher wage bill.

A related concern is whether workers would opt out of the labour market altogether because of the increased security of the grant: this is the famous 'surfer' scenario, which Van Parijs highlighted, that individuals who chose to use their grant to opt out of productive contributions to the economy (i.e. went surfing) could be accused of free riding on others' hard earned work (Van Parijs, 1995). The fear is that as more and more people chose this option, work incentives for the rest of the population who continued in paid employment would be irrevocably damaged. This is also referred to as recreating a new Speenhamland, after the legislation in late 18th century England which set up a framework of poor houses to redress rural poverty which horribly backfired, creating even greater destitution and destroying labour productivity (Polanyi, 1946). It is hard to estimate what the potential impact on work incentives may be, although a partial withdrawal from the labour market in a period of mass unemployment, could hardly be considered a catastrophic outcome. In any case, there is perhaps good reason to think that the overall impact of this free riding will be negligible: assuming that the grant was set near or slightly above the subsistence level, people would still need to work in order to obtain a higher income as well as the other rewards of work such as higher social status, creativity and socialisation.

The final obstacles revolve around the financing of a basic income. There is no question that a greater tax yield will be required to maintain a basic income welfare system. Even if there may be a number of creative financing initiatives which governments could enact (see below for a discussion), the presumption is that marginal tax rates would have to rise. The higher tax yield (which would be balanced against the savings garnered from eliminating the high costs of administering a bureaucratic system of social transfers) could begin to exert a downward pressure against the national product although the Scandinavian experience is evidence that this fear may be overstated. In any case, a basic income does have a built in financial discipline given that the scope for upgrading the size of the grant is constrained by the amount of taxable income it can obtain, which is surely limited. The increase in workers' bargaining power noted above raises fears of a squeeze on profits and the establishment of an inflationary spiral although the role of institutional constraints such as incomes policies may alleviate this concern as well.

Third sector: The scale of job creation of a third sector stimulus is likely to be quite substantial but it may have effects on the labour market that pose problems. There is some likelihood of a substitution effect on local labour markets; in other words, that workers in private sector firms may be pushed out of a job because third sector organisations are better able to compete than local low wage employers. This may not be too critical if the combination of reduced working hours and employment in the social economy allow for the ready deployment of these workers. What may be a more significant problem is whether third sector employment can attract sufficient numbers of people from outside the formal labour market, such as the long term unemployed, underground workers, caregivers, and other socially disadvantaged. Again, this may not be too serious an obstacle given the likelihood of third sector associations having first hand, practical knowledge of their local labour needs, although it does pose thorny institutional issues which are treated in the next section.

The main macro-economic problem for the third section option concerns its impact on the state budget. The cost of subsidising high quality, long lasting jobs in the third sector is estimated to be anywhere from £10,000 to £15,000 per job created, which is considerably higher than the normal costs of training programmes (Wainwright and Gosling, Chapter 14). This would of course be balanced against the substantial benefits of added infrastructural improvements and new social services and the savings from individuals no longer collecting unemployment benefits and paying taxes. The programme may very well pay for itself after 3 to 5 years (Berry, et al, 1995) but in the long run a system of such extensive subsidies is economically unsustainable. Limits on the amount of time new hires could spend in subsidised employment would have to be established and workers encouraged to move into the regular labour market.

Political-institutional issues

The shape, progress and outcomes of social reforms are profoundly shaped by the institutional environment within which social change takes place. Institutions determine the resources, incentives, and interests of social actors and structure how they respond to change in their environment. My focus is on government institutions and the organisations of civil society that are implicated in a policy of work redistribution. I will especially focus my attention on the following issues: institutional capacity, institutional learning, and state-civil society relations.

Working time: A rethinking of work time elicits a number of institutional concerns. Most writers endorsing a proposal for reduced working hours have been careful to insist that such a programme would need to be voluntarily negotiated between employers and workers, at both the sectoral and firm level, and not imposed unilaterally from above by political fiat whether at the national or transnational level. This is partly a recognition of the multiplicity of time preferences of workers as well as an expectation, given the tremendous diversity of labour market institutions between states, that a European reduction of work time would be too diffuse an instrument to utilise for effective job creation.[3] Social negotiation however presumes that there is sufficient institutional capacity to facilitate such bargaining as well as the expectation that both parties possess the required good will to enter into a bargaining relationship (or else can be constrained in exercising their right to exit from such negotiations).

The structural disincentives which mitigate against such employer interest have been discussed earlier and here I merely highlight the importance of an 'institutional deficit' to the equation. In recent decades, collective bargaining institutions across both Europe and North America have been transformed by a growing decentralisation which has reduced both the scope and the efficacy of peak level bargaining (Katz, 1993). Employers are no longer willing to commit themselves to centralised bargaining negotiations which limit their flexibility to exploit local labour market conditions to their benefit. As a result, many employer associations have simply abandoned any pretence of interest in social negotiation. In Great Britain, to take one extreme, there is no longer even a single sector that still conducts industry wide bargaining. This institutional shortfall, where it exists, would have to be remedied if a negotiated solution to working hours was to be effective. This logic is valid as well in the case of incomes policies: the collective discipline that is required to redress the impact of distributional conflict would not be forthcoming unless there was sufficient institutional capacity and political will to call upon, circumstances which have become increasingly rare in contemporary Europe (Grieve Smith, 1997).

If working time requires increased institutional capacity, it also makes a restructuring of existing state capacity imperative. This is particularly true in regards to the profound way in which public institutions and services, indeed social life in general, revolves around the organisation of working time. Office hours, transport and communication timetables, opening hours of health, educational and welfare offices, and leisure services typically reflect the prerogatives of traditional patterns of work rather than a concern for greater time flexibility (Hewitt, 1993). Attempts at reorganising the state in this way are bound to encounter opposition from entrenched social interests and recalcitrant state bureaucrats, and require a process of institutional learning and adjustment which is likely to prove challenging for many local governments. However, there has been a slow shifting of the terrain across Europe in recent years. In Italy, the *Tempi della Citta* initiative has given municipal governments the freedom to reorganise social services in a more flexible way and in Great Britain, initiatives for a 24 hour city in cities such as Leeds and Manchester have made important inroads into this mentality (ETUI, 1994).

Basic income: Basic income presents a rather different set of institutional constraints. Institutional capacity is not a key requirement: most experts assume that basic income would be a simpler and more sensible administrative system to operate and that there would be a net gain in efficiency as a result of the streamlining and wholesale elimination of much of the welfare state apparatus (Goodin, 1992). Institutions matter for basic income, first with regard to the restructuring of relations between the state and civil society. The decisions about basic income which are most likely to precipitate redistributive conflicts –the form and level of taxation needed to finance the programme, the level of grant, the requirements for eligibility - would all need to be conducted with the fullest public debate and commitment to democratic consultation (Purdy, Chapter 12).

Secondly, the implementation of basic income must address how the programme could be institutionally entrenched over time. This has long been a concern of social reformers: to ensure that their programmes are given sufficient institutional grounding so as to prevent the gains of reform being held political hostage by future governments. The success of the Swedish social democrats in erecting state institutions that were impervious to change is exemplary in this regard (Pontusson,

1992). Because basic income would have to be gradually introduced over time to facilitate the institutional learning required to measure its distributive impact and effectiveness, there will be a constant danger that the programme could serve as an attractive target (in terms of transfer levels or eligibility requirements) for tax-cutting politicians.

Adapting to institutional diversity is also a problem for basic income, especially when proposals to implement basic income at the European level are considered. Within the single political entity of Europe, there are many distinct social policy regimes, each of which has institutionalised unique labour market and welfare transfer policies, and as such, would have radically different impacts on how a basic income programme would be implemented. As Phillipe Van Parijs writes, this policy would also face: 'powerful obstacles that stem from a widespread distrust of highly centralised institutions, from a lack of identification and hence of spontaneous solidarity between residents of the various areas, and from the difficulty of generating a common public debate across national and linguistic boundaries about the extent and shape of the solidarity you advocate' (Van Parijs, 1996; 66). However, he goes on to argue that these circumstances are precisely the reason why the only way to develop a common welfare policy for the EU would be to endorse a European basic income. It would be the only transfer system that is simple and uncontroversial enough to win broad support and yet at the same time could be granted directly to individuals rather than indirectly by block grants to governments thereby avoiding the sticky barrier of administrative complexity and the constraint of the widespread ideology which views state action as illegitimate and inefficient.

Third sector: The primary impact of institutional factors on the redistribution of work rests with our third mechanism, the third sector. It is clear that a job creation programme predicated on a third sector approach would have to radically reorganise the nature of state employment institutions. The amount of planning and co-ordination that would be required at a local level - to determine community needs, local employment shortages, worker skills - would be impossible if addressed at the central level by large, bureaucratic and hierarchical agencies. In Chapter 12, David Purdy recommends that local employment centres should be completely transformed from their narrow province as transmission belts for central decision making into democratic outposts of information and innovation that would see them converted into 'social opportunity services'. These institutions would act as local labour market clearing houses, formulating local labour plans, co-ordinating training and educational opportunities, and accumulating and disseminating vital labour market information to employers and citizens, which would enable firms and employees to evaluate the terms and conditions of job offers. They would be responsible as well for setting common standards of pay, working hours, work conditions, and forms of employment that could act as the basis of democratic job evaluation across the entire spectrum of the social economy. In this regard, the state could play an important egalitarian role, guaranteeing not only equal pay for equal work and a fair wage, but also ensuring that any system of evaluation incorporated feminist concerns for an equal treatment of skill that did not automatically privilege brawn over dexterity.

Building state capacity at this level is likely to engender sharp conflicts of interest within state institutions and among state elites. In the first place, third sector job creation would constitute a critical shift in the economic growth priorities of local governments (and national governments as well). The standard package of tax breaks and subsidies to stimulate firm relocation alongside highly visible urban development projects such as malls and sports complexes - typically blessed with laudatory press coverage for their 'impressive' job figures - are completely reliant on market forces for their impact and as such have little directive or targeting potential. For a social economy approach to job creation to succeed, the state would have to embrace a 'developmentalist' perspective, with the local state encompassing an active policy of intervention and regulation of the labour market.

The balance of power within local government would certainly change as a result of this reordering of priorities; managers within the losing agencies, together with elected officials who may have profited (either directly or indirectly) from the old regime, can be expected to resist this restructuring. Many state bureaucrats will resent the loss of control that inevitably results from a shifting of responsibilities to the third sector. This may be especially true when the state already has an adversarial relationship with an association which is now being delegated new tasks. Many managers will be reluctant to provide third sector groups with an employment role, for fear that this will enhance their ability and opportunity to protest. Indeed, there will be many in government who will shrink from the premise of even an indirect relationship with the social economy, if it entails the development of an active and informed citizenry, who may be ready to hold local officials and managers to account for actions that go beyond the issue of employment. Finally, the social entrepreneurial skills that would be needed to operate such an ambitious programme may not necessarily exist in every local government; this is especially true in countries like Great Britain where these capacities have been systematically eroded by the relentless accumulation of powers by the central state (King and Stoker, 1996).

Third sector job creation will have far reaching effects on relations between the state and civil society. The existence of associations in civil society and the resources and capacities these groups possess is a function of the opportunities and incentives that are produced by the political system and structures of social power (Cohen and Rogers, 1995). The very people who would benefit most from collective organisations are often those who have the least access to the expertise and resources necessary for group formation. The state can therefore play an important 'crafting' role in encouraging the self-organisation of the social economy, although this role would certainly be circumscribed by the democratic norms and traditions (or lack thereof) of the political culture in which this local government was embedded.[4] The local state would be responsible for determining the proper mix of services which it wanted to provide for each locality and this would necessitate choosing the appropriate third sector groups to operate the services. Here, the critical issue would be determining what criteria to utilise in choosing between groups. Joshua Cohen and Joel Rogers have suggested that secondary associations can be evaluated according to certain qualitative aspects of groups that foster egalitarian and deliberative norms (Cohen and Rogers, 1995 pp 48-50), yet this assumes a level of state neutrality which may not be valid and an equally questionable capacity for making normative comparisons where issues of principle may be involved.[5]

Although the government would want to rely on third sector organisations precisely because of their flexibility and accountability, the state would still have to ensure that these organisations were limited in the discretion they were able to exercise.[6] Local governments would be required to establish a system of monitoring, evaluation and enforcement of third sector organisations. This would go beyond simply establishing performance standards to measure efficiency (numbers of workers placed, trained, etc.) to include holding them accountable to common standards of equity and justice. The state would need to ensure: that leaders of these non profit organisations did not use the programmes as a vehicle for self-enrichment; that workers were not placed in exploitative work environments; that the jobs allocated did not replicate the worst aspects of misguided government placement schemes. Enforcement could follow traditional mechanisms of contract compliance but a far more effective method would be to encourage an open atmosphere and maximise adverse publicity for the worst violators.

Likewise, although third sector groups may possess a unique ability to embrace an internal culture of caring and reciprocity, there is no guarantee that they will automatically deliver services that are equitable and accessible to everyone. The state would need to ensure that organisations were inclusive in their behaviour: that they chose an appropriate mix of disadvantaged groups to participate and did not discriminate in job placements by defining their appropriate constituency along narrow lines or by attaching any kind of unjust conditions to participation (Taylor, 1996). Of course this is a classic Catch-22 dilemma: these tasks could only be initiated by a strong state that had a high degree of authority and autonomy yet such a state would have no incentive to pursue a third sector approach in the first place (Offe, 1996).

There is no question that civil society organisations would themselves be transformed by participation in job creation initiatives and their relations to the wider community would also have to be reformed to promote maximum accountability. Activists in the voluntary sector would be the first to acknowledge, and it has been well observed in the academic literature, that involvement with the state can be extremely disruptive. Being held accountable to state authorities can impose immense burdens on organisations with shoestring budgets and little managerial expertise. This is true in terms of both the sheer administrative costs of time and energy that prevent other important work from being accomplished, to the tensions that arise between participation in a government scheme and wider organisational interests. Contractual obligations to the government can begin to squeeze the life force out of an organisation: a change from looser, friendlier modes of conduct to more professional styles of organisation; the weakening, or even the abandonment of the original animating spirit of the association; the reversal of a critical, more adversarial, outlook on political actors.

Ideological barriers

Transformative projects require a vision that can offer an outline of the good society to come and an idea of how to get there. In both cases, social reform inevitably comes up against the dominant ideologies of a society that are limiting or supportive of the new project. On the one hand, a redistribution of work espouses core values - autonomy, community, liberty, equality - that are broadly supported by the public in Europe and North America and by the dominant political ideologies as well (Page and Shapiro, 1992). Yet it equally faces a large hurdle because it challenges dominant notions of what constitutes work, what is a fair income, what is an appropriate balance of leisure and work, and what is the proper scope and role of state action. All projects for social reform face the same dilemma elaborated by David Purdy in his contribution: 'how do we persuade people with different conceptions of the good life, different interests, and different versions of a just society, that redistribution will be the basis for a new settlement'.

Working time: The dominant culture of consumption, the continual generation of new needs and desires which characterises capitalist societies, is a permanent barrier to any redistribution of working time. For all the talk that we are entering a post materialist era and press reports highlighting a trend towards 'voluntary simplicity' and 'downshifting', there is no evidence that workers are any more inclined to attribute greater value to leisure than they did in the past, or are prepared to work fewer hours (with less pay), or are prepared to reduce their addiction to 'consumer sovereignty'. Indeed, surveys in Europe and North America indicate that the cycle of work and spend is as hegemonic as ever before (Schor, 1992; Hinrichs 1991).

This is not entirely surprising given the structural forces that underpin this consumptionist ethos. In the first place, the income generated by the long hours of paid work is a necessary precondition for a decent quality of life. As Claus Offe writes:

> ...in our work-oriented society the dominant institutions in fact reserve the things that make life worth living (freedom, independence, security, recognition, self esteem) for those people who prove themselves in economic life as earners. Those who fail (by being unemployed) to fulfil the norm or decide not to adhere to it (for instance, mothers, or 'mere housewives', or house husbands) need pretty good justifications if they want to avoid appearing to be losers to themselves and others (Offe, 1995; 80)

Workers faced with profound job insecurity have every incentive to accept as much overtime as they can possibly manage given they may not have a job to go to tomorrow (Wheelock, forthcoming).

The imperative in capitalism towards continual growth also underlies the priority of consumption. Growth plays a central political, economic and ideological role in most advanced societies and indeed, there are strong vested interests that continually reaffirm this core value. Firms depend upon continual expansion to guarantee their profits; workers depend upon the prosperity of their firm to ensure their quality of life; the state depends upon a healthy economy in order to finance itself and care for those out of work; politicians depend upon the promise of future growth to underwrite their electoral success (Przeworski, 1985). As Greg Albo argues, the internationalisation of economic life has made this expansionist bias even more pronounced with the fight for national competitive advantage a mantra for politicians of all ideologies (Albo, 1994). A redistribution of work therefore needs not only to change the hearts and minds of the populace, it has to provide a convincing alternative model of economic development that can serve as a guidepost to a new society.

Basic income: The first ideological constraint on basic income concerns the dominant conception of 'idleness' in advanced societies. There are a number of interlocking images which join together to fuel the dominant ideology. The first of these is a persistent belief that because human nature is intrinsically driven by a desire to work, idleness is both a personal and public evil. 'The first condition of human happiness', wrote Beveridge, the architect of the British welfare state, 'is the opportunity for useful service'. Indeed, when he was cataloguing the 'Five Giants' that plagued society, Beveridge did not hesitate to claim that the greatest evil of all was idleness. This sentiment has received considerable support in religious doctrine: the 'Protestant ethic', which Weber wrote so incisively about, was predicated on the belief that idleness was the 'devil's workshop' and that work was a morally superior existence which needed to be continually asserted in everyday life. The idea that time was too precious a commodity to be squandered was based on the belief that life needed to be filled with measurable attainments in order to receive the affirmation of religious blessings.

Contemporary debates on the underclass or unruly youth are riven with such assumptions: even the most progressive writers in the literature are quick to judge the idle for their personal failures (Wilson, 1997). What is largely assumed is the familiar sentiments of work as a character building institution and idleness as a generator of immorality: idleness is said to be detrimental to individual self esteem and contributes to exclusion from social interaction and the community. Of course the class prejudices of these views could not be more striking: there is very little moral outrage in public life about the idleness of the very wealthy yet we are all free to express our distaste with the harmful idleness of youth, ethnic minorities, welfare scroungers, *ad nauseam*. The work ethic is also intimately intertwined with masculinity: the male breadwinner identity that dominated the Fordist era is part of the story here, but there was also the abiding male fixation on the virtues of old fashioned hard work and self discipline which were seen as the panacea for any problem (emotional, material or otherwise) that arose.

The equally pejorative side of the work ethic is the precept of reciprocal obligation. There is a deeply intuitive belief in many advanced societies that able bodied individuals who voluntarily choose to opt out of paid work can not, and should not, rightfully make a claim on society's resources (Doyal and Gough, 1991). This translates into a fear that people who live off a basic income without making any positive productive contribution would 'free ride' off, and thereby exploit, the hard work of the vast majority (Van Parijs, 1995).This ethic of social justice as a norm of reciprocity is rooted in the historical development of many welfare states. The English Poor Laws as an example denied welfare provision to any able bodied person who refused to work. Scandinavian welfare states are premised on a firm belief in a 'work society' where the obligation to work is deeply ingrained in institutional practices and personal conduct. The work ethic has also been exacerbated by contemporary labour markets in some nations. American workers on the secondary labour market have been forced to resort to working longer and longer hours, in more than one job, just to keep their incomes at a minimal level. This hard struggle, against terrible odds, has reinforced a belief in the Horatio Alger virtues of hard work, self reliance and responsibility, all of which are deeply entrenched in the American political culture in the first place. The 'undeserving poor', not to mention the 'undeserving idle', are people who remain outside this value system and thus have not earned the right to state support. This is undoubtedly one of the reasons why welfare to work programmes in both the United States and Great Britain have received such widespread support.

Basic income, by virtue of its very name, conjures up yet another ideological dilemma, namely defining what precisely constitutes a basic grant. This is not simply the technical problem of establishing the proper balance or rate of taxes, or of settling thorny issues of residence requirements, or of finding the best way to weight regional variations in the cost of living. What matters most to this question is the way in which each society develops socially and politically validated conceptions of what constitutes a proper level of funding. Welfare states, argues Claus Offe, always embody:

> a widely shared set of assumptions concerning some operationally appropriate notion of social justice which specifies the social and substantive limits up to which security enhancing public arrangements are necessary, and who is to carry the burden of such provision...The only politics which are likely to become effective are those which 'make sense' (i.e. are widely accepted as 'plausible', 'tolerable' or sufficiently 'meaningful' in the context and by the criteria established by those considerations. (Offe, 1992; 64)

To arrive at a grant that has social approval requires reformers to ensure that their choices are consonant with prevailing social norms of justice, institutional practices and the everyday assumptions of ordinary people – no mean task to be sure and one that would challenge the strategic capacity of even the most broad based movement.

Third sector: Third sector proposals face two main ideological obstacles. The first of these reflects the ideological hegemony of neo-liberalism in the past two decades: namely the propagation of the belief that the market is dynamic, efficient, modern, a realm of free choice and true equality; while the state is bureaucratic, hierarchical, backward and a site of compulsion and unfreedom. Because of the continuing sway of this ideology, the active role of the state in generating third sector employment will undoubtedly encounter significant questioning about what the proper scope of state action should be as well as scepticism about whether the state can expect to efficiently direct economic activity without recourse to the market.

Only a few nations have actually tried to co-ordinate the amount of labour as envisioned in a third sector employment policy without recourse to the private labour market. Sweden's active labour market policy, in its demarketisation phase, placed a high percentage of workers in sheltered state employment (Glyn, 1992). Yet traditional public sector employment in this regard could be said to start with several advantages over a third sector approach: it faces much lower monitoring costs and avoids the high transaction costs associated with the democratic decision making that is a hallmark of a third sector approach. Similarly, public works initiatives, such as the New Deal programmes of the 1930s, were able to marshal huge numbers of workers into employment but they were temporary, one off models that looked to expansion of the market to integrate workers back into permanent employment. Even if one accepts that state intervention into the market can generate positive benefits, it may seem less compelling to believe that this massive scale of co-ordination and planning of job creation can possibly succeed, in terms of either efficiency or fairness, without recourse to market allocation (Elson, 1988).

The other ideological constraint on social economy employment regards the prevailing notions of what constitutes meaningful work. The dominant ideology of the work ethic may have severe consequences for those who seek to remain idle but it also leads to a circumscribed view of what actually constitutes work. The entrenched denigration of unpaid work has been discussed earlier, but there is also a refusal to see other socially productive activities as worthwhile 'work'. Much of what we exclude from a definition of work actually provides valuable services to society and offers the people who perform them intrinsic satisfaction. This ideological blinder also extends to the suspicion that any government sponsored work by definition is bound to be worthless, dead end jobs that contribute nothing whatsoever to the social good. As Robert Hollands discusses in his contribution, the failures of so many government schemes to provide anything more than make-work employment has been a potent source of this dissatisfaction. Even when the work is seen as valuable, or even 'empowering', there is a strong presumption that it should be undertaken by voluntary activity rather than state sponsored, paid employment. This hegemony of voluntarism, particularly in the United States and Great Britain, can have a crippling effect on efforts to expand the public sphere in innovative ways.

Finally, to conclude this section, there is an ideological impasse which all three proposals for a redistribution of work will be required to surmount. This is the uncertainty that pervades all transformative projects: uncertainty that the proposals are feasible, that they will accomplish what they set out to do, and that they will make things better not worse. All projects that propose massive rather than incremental transformations to political, economic and social systems by their very nature create effects that are difficult to estimate and this is no less true for a redistribution of work. Proposals for working time as an example are utterly dependent upon actions by other social actors that are impossible to predict. Even if workers manage to overcome their collective action problems and commit themselves to a solidaristic programme, there is no guarantee that their sacrifice will necessarily pay off. Employers, as we have seen earlier, may respond to the increased productivity created as a result of reduced working hours to expand output rather than to increase employment opportunities.

Given this 'credibility gap' (Hinrichs, 1991), workers have every incentive to emphasise individual self interest and forego co-operation with their fellow workers. It is very easy for employers to translate this unease into a self fulfilling prophecy by providing workers with a range of incentives to follow their particularistic interests. Proposals for a basic income suffer from a similar dilemma. As David Purdy notes, there are so many variables that need to be assessed in order for it to work properly - the size of the grant, the level of tax established to pay for it, how it will effect worker motivations, its impact on economic growth or labour market flexibility - that it is impossible to predict what kind of consequences basic income will generate. Since there are no historical precedents of industrial societies that have ever implemented such a policy, the benefits of institutional learning which other social reforms can rely on are also entirely absent.

A leap into the unknown is what is seemingly required yet this presumes a faith in the future, indeed of progress itself, which has been greatly eroded in the current period (Giddens, 1994; Lasch, 1991). The high cult of TINA ('there is no alternative') infects the body politic of all advanced societies: be it arguments on behalf of globalisation, privatisation, or communitarianism, we face a relentless barrage of conventional wisdom whose sole purpose is to convince us that meaningful change is a chimera. This is not to say alternatives do not exist but rather that clarity of vision must come face to face with the deep seated belief that change is impossible. With the implosion of left ideologies in the aftermath of the collapse of 'actually existing socialism', there are fewer guideposts of certainty which people can rely on. A belief in change also comes up against a pessimism of the spirit that reflects experiences of what Ralph Miliband called a 'century of cruelty': given the relentless horrors of the 20th century, it is not that surprising that so many have concluded that the Enlightenment belief in the perfectibility of humankind and the inevitable progress of humanity was mere wishful thinking (Miliband, 1994). To establish a redistribution of work, it will be incumbent on us to find ways of cultivating a belief that change is not just necessary but feasible as well. Yet this remains a formidable project: as Raymond Williams so perceptively argued: 'The last recess of the division of labour is the recess within ourselves, where what we want and what we believe we can do seems impossibly divided' (Williams, 1989).

Conclusion: can we get there?

We appear to have come full circle. The optimistic by-products that were to result from a realistic accounting of the feasibility of our project for changes, have now been revealed as a series of seemingly insurmountable barriers. Is a redistribution of work truly feasible or is this yet another of the doomed projects of the left which are bound to suffer the consequences of the perversity of unintended effects? Of course history, to paraphrase Marx, is not based on infallible blueprints: if we were to insist that the only changes that were possible were those whose effects could be entirely predictable, there would be no historical movement whatsoever. As so many of our contributors have urged, we must continue to insist that transformations are within our grasp and reiterate a belief in the necessity of change. 'The art of the possible' wrote E.P. Thompson, 'can only be restrained from engrossing the whole universe if the impossible can find ways of breaking back into politics again and again'. In the remainder of this chapter, I would like to examine how these barriers could be overcome, although given the space limitations, not every single obstacle identified can be treated at equal length. I will highlight the way in which the three policies for a redistribution of work can have mutually reinforcing benefits; how the state can redress some of these shortcomings; and how the vision of a redistribution of work can form the basis for a political coalition that may in turn help bring it to fruition.

It may be helpful to offer a brief recapitulation of the areas discussed in the previous section where appropriate action would be required across the four fronts: distributional conflict, macro-economic obstacles, institutional problems and ideological barriers. These are summarised below and will be referred to throughout the following discussion:

Level of action required:

a) Distributional
1. achieve a high degree of social solidarity: shift from individual to collective preferences.
2. need for a high degree of collective discipline
3. convince men to utilise free time for domestic work
4. enhance social capacity to deal with redistributive conflict
5. overcome employer opposition
6. prevent social divisions from being exacerbated

b) Macro-economic
1. productivity gains put into job creation
2. benefits of job growth extended to all sectors of workforce
3. ensure labour market discipline does not collapse
4. ensure third sector workers find way into regular labour market
5. find adequate financing for all programmes

c) Institutional
1. institutionally entrench reforms
2. establish institutions for social negotiation
3. create capacity for social learning
4. restructure institutional capacity
5. adopt developmental perspective
6. enhance density and capacity of social economy
7. ensure inclusive behaviour of associations
8. develop social entrepreneurs

d) Ideological
1. address uncertainty: create belief in change
2. overcome male breadwinner identity
3. create belief in state efficacy
4. overcome negative image of idleness, free riding

The synergy solution

One of the familiar pitfalls of progressives is their insistence that successive social reforms have the potential to build upon each other into a virtuous circle. This brand of progressive rhetoric was named the 'synergy illusion' by Albert Hirschman who warned that the belief that all advances were mutually reinforcing obscured the necessary recognition that some methods of struggling for reform made it more difficult to fight for others (Hirschman, 1992)[7]. 'In the political division of labour no one can hope to do everything at once' writes Anne Phillips, 'but if the choices we make block out other issues, it does not help to just say that everything is interconnected' (Phillips 1997:150). Nevertheless, reformers need to continually emphasise the potential for strategic choice: we need to evaluate not only the conflicts and tensions that may arise in our programmes but we should explore with a clear mind the potential that some dilemmas can be solved by virtue of a dynamic of reform. When elements of a comprehensive reform like a redistribution of work can create mutually reinforcing benefits, then a 'synergy solution' may be on offer.

Basic income has the unique potential to help resolve many of the distributional conflicts discussed above (a1, a2). Class solidarity and collective discipline can not be based upon mere exhortation or wishful thinking but has to be constructed materially and organisationally. Basic income in this regard has been described by Van Parijs and Purdy as a 'soft strategy for job sharing': even a small grant could provide the economic security that makes it more feasible for workers to consider cutting back their hours or working part time. 'The key to the interlocking barriers that stand in the way of a strategy of reduced hours', concludes Purdy, 'is basic income'. The increase in social services provided to all citizens by third sector employment, which would constitute an important increase in the social wage, could also ease the anxieties that many workers have about a loss of income if they accepted a drop in work hours. By providing more opportunities that make the exercise of free time more valuable and satisfying, third sector employment could begin to create the conditions for the class solidarity needed to get reduced working time off the ground.[8] Similarly, if access to work was more evenly distributed as a result of an egalitarian time policy, and a third sector provided more opportunities for meaningful work, the danger of a new social divide emerging between those in paid work and those living solely off their basic income grants (a6) could be substantially minimised.

With the extra security provided by basic income, workers would be less inclined to put up defensive resistance to workplace changes where a democratic flexibility was at stake. This could help convince many employers that the gains in flexibility outweighed the potential threat to profitability associated with a reduction in working hours (a5) (b1). Indeed, the benefits that basic income provided to labour market flexibility - by ending the unemployment trap, by divorcing the link between paid work and income, by giving people the security to take on new jobs even at a lower wage than they might desire - should convince many sceptical policy makers of the possible benefits. The indirect benefits for employers of third sector employment - infrastructural improvements, wider range of services, social cohesion - could also help overcome firms' objections.

Working time proposals have the potential to address key institutional obstacles. Most of the problems listed in b) above have at their core two main issues: one, the absence of a culture of democratic participation and second, the lack of sufficient time to develop such a culture (c2, c6, c8). An extra day a week and a few hours each day in free time that could result from a cut in working hours (not to mention other innovations in working time) could provide the foundation for a cure to the democratic deficit. Although free time is not an absolute guarantee that change will be forthcoming, it is certainly a necessary condition for a shift towards a democratic culture. Basic income is also a way of providing the extra incentive of curing the institutional and democratic deficit highlighted above, and by changing the way in which benefits are distributed, could help develop the very values that are needed to sustain the programme itself.

Similarly, the greater the jobs effect a programme of working hours enjoyed, the easier it would be to demonstrate that everyone who wanted a job at a decent wage had the potential to get one. This realisation could make the right to idleness espoused by basic income less objectionable and undermine any incentive for people to automatically assume that 'scrounging' or 'free riding' was a social bad (d1). Likewise, the more people were encouraged to see the positive benefits of non-traditional 'socially productive' work, the easier it may be to break down the ideological barriers regarding social reproduction (d2, a3). The more men took jobs in an expanded non profit caring sector, the greater the likelihood that they would embrace a more egalitarian stance towards domestic work in their own home. Finally, the more jobs which became available that were satisfying and provided a decent income, the less those who held them would be deemed more deserving than those who remained idle: people in paid work would be seen simply as those who valued the attributes (materially and socially) of paid work more than others. Idleness would no longer be construed as an issue of personal failure (of laziness or immorality) but rather as one of people exercising their autonomy in different ways (Van Parijs, 1995).

Harnessing the role of the state

The state's ability to act strategically to redress some of these dilemmas would also be critical. Employer opposition to working hours reductions (a5), as an example, could be somewhat mollified by defraying the higher costs through temporary subsidies for new hires or a corresponding reduction in payroll contributions for each new employee taken on (both of these have been included in the policy package of the Jospin government reforms for a 35 hour work week). But it is also critical to look at what Peter Swenson calls 'strategic anticipation', namely the 'strategic behaviour of experienced political agents who anticipate capitalist's reactionary as well as progressive potential' in order to ensure the successful passage of reform initiatives (Swenson, 1997; 70). This brokering role could encompass a wide range of policies to generate cross class support for working time reductions (and the principle of social negotiation more broadly) (a4, c3): identifying corporations who have distinct material interests in favour of the programme to act as standard bearers; encouraging these firms to speak out on behalf of the reforms or to institute pilot programmes at a firm level that demonstrate the viability of the programmes; designing policies in such a way that they engender support from the business community; mobilising popular support for these policies and using this as moral persuasion to entice more recalcitrant firms to agree to negotiations. The economic summit meeting, *'L'Evenement'*, which the Jospin government held in the fall of 1997 with French employer associations and trade unions, was an excellent example of this sort of tactical acumen.

Yet there is no doubt that a redistribution of work, like most radical reforms, would generate a bedrock of capitalist opposition which no amount of tactical manoeuvring could possibly ameliorate. As Rogers and Streeck convincingly argue, 'while all firms may eventually be willing to live under a demanding social order of production, and many may even come to support it ...all this will as a general matter occur only after that regime has become a social fact' (Rogers and Streeck, 1994; 137). Positive inducements may be useful but no state could afford to ignore the need for a framework of constraints that prevented capitalists from defecting from the work redistribution regime. In this instance, many of the suggestions highlighted by other left political economists would play an important role, such as controls over capital mobility; democratic control over pension funds; and the establishment of new international institutions of economic governance (Crotty and Epstein, 1996; Pollin, 1995; Michie and Grieve Smith, 1995).

Worker opposition to reduced hours could be assuaged by offering state services (such as library fees, leisure activities, education) free of charge or by granting free access to facilities (transport and the like) that were lightly utilised during the day. More importantly, individual workers could be given the right to design their own work time policy by choosing the particular hours, days or weeks in which their hours would be cut. This would certainly be a much more popular, and effective, policy than a uniform, nationally mandated reduction in working hours of an hour (or half hour) a day. It would also be seen quite clearly as an alternative to the employer mandated time reductions that are premised solely on the needs of the firm rather than the lives of their workers. Finally, the state could impose statutory limits on working hours or tax excessive hours at prohibitively higher rates in order to change the incentives workers have for overtime work.

The state could play an important role in ensuring that work time reductions and a basic income had a major impact in transforming gender relations (a3; d2). As noted earlier, no one could be sure how men would choose to allocate their extra free time or energies if they enjoyed less hours and a basic grant; much would depend on how the state provided incentives for these choices to be made in the proper direction. Universal day care provision would certainly be required to help overcome the deeply embedded structural inequality of household work. Parental leave could be organised in such a way that a certain percentage (perhaps a third to half) of the time in which individuals are able to obtain the maximum available funding, could be reserved for fathers.

There is no question that all governments would need to find innovative means to finance a redistribution of work. Most of the literature on basic income, as an example, assumes that the programme would be paid out of a higher rate of personal income taxes which could range anywhere from 50 per cent to 85 per cent (Purdy, 1988; Van Parijs, 1995) or through elimination of certain kinds of tax relief for corporations and wealthy individuals, both of which are believed to be politically unsustainable in today's tax averse climate. But there is nothing inherent in basic income itself that requires reliance on any specific source of funding (Barry, 1996). Basic income could be financed by taxes on capital gains or estates and inheritances; it could be financed by taxes on short term stock market or exchange transactions (akin to a Tobin tax); it could be financed by an increase in VAT; or by a series of green taxes on ecologically damaging production (although these would have a lower yield over time as the taxes produced their desired effect). As Brian Barry has persuasively argued, the more imaginative and creative governments could be in their financing schemes, the more likely they will encounter success in getting people to agree to pay for them (d3).

Much of the uncertainty that faces third sector employment creation could be alleviated by a joint consultation process between local governments and third sector groups: there is no reason why both sides could not conduct a preliminary social audit in advance of a full scale nationally funded effort to identify the unmet needs of the locality, the range of groups who could play a meaningful role, who was in most need of the jobs, and the estimated costs of running such a project. It is precisely this kind of 'art of the practical' which can serve as a stimulus to other groups and help overcome the inherited bias of policy makers against democratic development (c5). Progressives should never underestimate the selling power of practical accomplishments: the impact of even a single national success story of work redistribution would undoubtedly generate tremendous popular support for a European level expansion (c4).

Building a political coalition for a redistribution of work

Finally, it is incumbent to realise that a redistribution of work will require a sustained, concerted campaign to advance this transformative vision. Robert Cox has argued that the:

> critical awareness of potentiality for change...concentrates on the possibilities of launching a social movement rather than on what that movement might achieve...In the minds of those who opt for change, the solution will most likely be seen as lying not so much in the enactment of a specific policy programme as in the building of new means of collective action informed by a new understanding of society and polity. (Cox, 1987; 393-94)

The left has long dreamed of finding an appropriate vehicle that could link the disparate forces of the left together yet have often overestimated the potential of this or that social agent or programme to deliver the goods. In recent years, postmodernists have argued that this search for the mythical Holy Grail is fundamentally misguided because fragmentation of interests and identities is our contemporary fate. I believe a politics of work redistribution which seeks to reconceive the very nature of work, if not time itself, has the potential to act as the glue for a new progressive political coalition.

In the first place, a redistribution of work has the distinct advantage of being able to articulate a common political project which can appeal to the material and social interests of an extremely heterogeneous constituency: the unemployed and poor on social assistance; workers who desire a richer life and greater autonomy; women who would like to have better prospects for employment and to be released from their burden of household work and caring responsibilities; trade unionists who would like to improve the conditions of work and economic security of their members; green activists who would like to establish a sustainable economy. It is also unique in its ability to address the concerns of nearly all the key social movements on the left today: the labour movement, green movements, democratic and human rights movements and feminism. (Peace movements would be the sole exception). This does not imply that a broad oppositional movement can be simply conjured up out of thin air but rather that a redistribution of work offers a multitude of common interests that can serve as important starting points for joint agreement and action.

One of Gramsci's most enduring insights was that the nature of a movement's identity and habits of struggle can be transformed from their engagement with other groups (Gramsci, 1990). The early success of the Italian Communist party, he argued, lay in its ability to construct meaningful alliances with other social forces on the left such as trade unions, co-operatives, and anti-Mafia groups (and this was precisely what separated this earlier period from the Togliatti era onwards). These were not purely tactical but rather involved a fundamental transformation of consciousness of all actors involved: the give and take of the struggle of a single movement implied a continual willingness to sacrifice narrow group concerns for the aims of the collective, as well as a recognition that each group's demands could only be achieved if they took into account the needs of their counterparts as well. In some sense the virtuous circle ('synergy solution') which a redistribution of work involves means that these trade-offs may be easier to manage in our putative coalition.

There are also compelling reasons to believe that this same fusion of self interest and collective goals may be increasingly possible in today's insecure world (Vail, Wheelock and Hill, forthcoming). The relentless neo-liberal restructuring of the advanced economies; the precarious conditions of employment that plague the working and middle classes alike; the pervasive destruction of our natural environment; the transformation of family life and personal identities: each of these changes has generated a profound uncertainty which may paradoxically offer an opportunity for the left. The desire for protection against the ravages of the market has created a sort of embattled solidarity, a feeling that everyone is being equally afflicted by this pervasive insecurity. A redistribution of work may very well turn out to be the programme for an 'enlightened selfishness' of a new left majority.

Notes

I would like to thank Jane Wheelock for her helpful suggestions and comments on this chapter.

[1] The lack of attention on the left to the question of work humanisation can be illustrated by reference to Ralph Miliband's last published work, *Socialism for a Sceptical Age*. In chapter 1, 'The Case Against Capitalism', Miliband provides a marvellous indictment of the various ills of the capitalist economic system yet makes only a passing reference to the dehumanising and deeply alienating aspects of the capitalist labour process. The traditional concern for the labour process, and of reorganising work in such a way as to make it a liberating experience, has been overridden by attention paid to the equally important structural inadequacies of capitalism as a global system.

[2] The only way this sort of internecine competition is kept at bay on the labour market is through the influence of collective organisations like trade unions and work councils. There may be an important role for trade unions to play in this regard in a redistribution of work. There is no reason why the newly employed in the third sector should not enjoy the protection of trade union representation: to ensure fair treatment, decent working conditions, to facilitate information gathering, to aid in the sort of consensus building that could eliminate the worst excesses of competition.

[3] The European case is instructive in this regard. The labour market there is extremely heterogeneous in terms of different cultures of work time, the use of part time work, the nature of industrial relations systems, the level and composition of unemployment. To take only a single example, Southern European nations (Spain, Portugal, Greece, Italy) have a much lower share of part time work than their northern European counterparts in Netherlands, Great Britain, Denmark or Sweden. Likewise, the countries that would require the largest reductions in working time are also those with the lowest GDP figures in the EU. The introduction of a European wide directive on working time would encounter tremendous obstacles as a result of this institutional diversity.

[4] States have the capacity to: eliminate formal obstacles to group formation; provide affirmative action for underrepresented groups; promote greater equality in the distribution of resources that are necessary for organisations; and give groups special judicial standing. (Cohen and Rogers, 1995). They are certainly aware of the problems which a democratic deficit at the state level would pose for this crafting role and address these concerns in their concluding chapter. For a view that challenges the feasibility of this 'crafting' role and which emphasises the spontaneous, bottom-up development of associations, see the article by Paul Hirst in the same collection. For an illuminating case study of how a local government can take an activist role in this regard, see MacIntosh and Wainwright, 1987.

[5] Cohen and Rogers suggest the following evaluative criteria for secondary associations: democracy and accountability within the organisations, decentralisation of authority, group encompassingness, and co-operative relations with other social groups. Yet as Iris Young argues, these criteria may not be entirely successful in choosing between groups, be it for the purpose of administrative regulation or job creation. She uses the example of Christian fundamentalist organisations in the United States, who are among the most internally democratic, decentralised, encompassing and co-operative groups in the country, (not to mention possessing a high level of organisation and administrative competence), yet we may still object to them being chosen to run a child care programme on the grounds that they may be fundamentally hostile to (if not repressive of) categories of difference (sexual preference, race, etc.) that violate their religious identity (Young, in Cohen and Rogers 1995). Likewise, neutrality is notoriously difficult for many local governments to achieve: the web of nepotism, special interests, petty corruption and 'one hand washes the other' mentality that pervades local government might make choosing the appropriate agencies a veritable minefield. The widest possible system of transparency regarding what criteria are used, rights of appeal and similar democratic criteria would need to be rigorously applied.

[6] As has been well documented in the literature, discretion in the field of social welfare has generated: wide inequalities in awards, high regional variations, and an unacceptable level of discrimination of claimants based on race, lifestyle and gender. The recognition of the virtues of local flexibility need to go hand in hand with an understanding of how bias and prejudice can flourish alongside discretion .

[7] Hirschman uses the three stages of citizenship developed by T.H. Marshall to illustrate when reforms are indeed contradictory. This is what he calls the 'getting stuck' syndrome, where the first step in a sequence makes achieving a later step even harder. Nations which firmly entrenched the second stage of citizenship (the achievement of widespread political suffrage and civil liberties), which promoted liberal values based on individual rights and responsibilities, may have had a harder time moving forward to the third stage of citizenship (creation of social rights and economic security) where a collective ethos was more highly valued (Hirschman, 1992).

[8] Claus Offe and Karl Heinze have highlighted the special role of LETS in this regard. Workers may be willing to bear a potential decline of income from reduced hours if it was possible to satisfy some of the needs previously met by paid income by way of moneyless exchange. The hours lost would no longer be seen as wasted but rather could be used to exchange productive services outside the money economy. LETS would foster a better understanding of the local economy and could therefore serve as a bridge back to the regular labour market (Offe and Heinze 1994).

BIBLIOGRAPHY

Aarts, L., Burkhauser, R. and de Jong, P. (1996) *Curing the Dutch Disease*, Aldershot: Avebury.

Abraham, K. (1991) 'Mismatch and labour mobility', In F. Padoa-Scioppa (ed) *Mismatch and Labour Mobility*, Cambridge: Cambridge University Press.

Albo, G. (1994) 'Competitive austerity and the impasse of capitalist employment policy', In R. Miliband and L. Panitch (eds) *Socialist Register 1994: Between Globalism and Nationalism*, London: Merlin.

Albo, G. (1997) 'A world market of opportunities? Capitalist obstacles and left economic policy', *Socialist Register 1997*, London: Merlin.

Allatt, P. and Yeandle, S. (1992) *Youth Unemployment and the Family*, London: Routledge.

Amin, A. (ed) (1994) *Post-Fordism*, Oxford: Basil Blackwell.

Anderson, M., Bechhofer, F. and Gershuny, J. (eds) (1994) *The Social and Political Economy of the Household*, Oxford: Oxford University Press.

Anxo, D. (1994) 'Working time policy in Sweden', *A Time for Working and Time for Living*, London: ETUI-LRD.

Anxo, D. and Lundström, S. (1996) *Company Policies with Regard to the Reduction of Working Time in Sweden*: Interim Report for the Dublin Foundation, mimeo, November 1996.

Appelbaum, E. (1992) 'Structural change and growth of part-time and temporary employment', In V. L. du Rivage (ed) *New Policies for the Part-Time and Contingent Workforce*, Armonk, NY: M.E. Sharpe.

Appelbaum, E. (1995) 'New work systems in the new world order', In L. Mishel and J. Schmitt (eds) *Beware the U.S. Model: Jobs and Wages in a Deregulated Economy*, Washington, DC: Economic Policy Institute.

Appelbaum, E. and Batt, R. (1994) *The New American Workplace: Transforming Work Systems in the United States*, Ithaca: ILR Press.

Ashton, D. and Lowe, G. (eds) (1991) *Making Their Way: Education, Training and the Labour Market in Canada and Britain*, Milton Keynes: Open University Press.

Ashton, D. and Maguire, M. (1983) *The Vanishing Youth Labour Market*, London: Youthaid Occasional Paper No. 3.

Aslaksen, I. and Koren, C. (1996) 'Unpaid household work and the distribution of extended income: the Norwegian experience', *Feminist Economics*, 2 (3): 65-80.

Aslanbeigui, N., Pressman, S. and Summerfield, G. (eds) (1994) *Women in the Age of Economic Transformation: Gender Impact of Reforms in Post-Socialist and Developing Countries*, London: Routledge.

Atkinson, A. B. (1997) 'Bringing income distribution in from the cold', *Economic Journal*, 107 (March): 297-321.

Autor, D., Katz, L. and Krueger, A. (1997) *Computing Inequality: Have Computers Changed The Labor Market?*: Industrial Relations Section, Princeton University, Working Paper No. 377.

Azariadis, C. (1975) 'Implicit contracts and underemployment equilibria', *Journal of Political Economy*, 83 (6): 1183-1202.

Aznar, G. (1997) 'Réduction du temps de travail: la loi Robien', *Futuribles* (Février).

Babson, S. (ed) (1995) *Lean Work: Empowerment and Exploitation in the Global Auto Industry*, Detroit: Wayne State University Press.

Bagguley, P. (1990) *Restructuring: Place, Class and Gender*, London: Sage.

Bagguley, P. and Mann, K. (1992) 'Idle, thieving, bastards: scholarly representations of the underclass', *Work, Employment and Society*, 6 (1): 113-126.

Baily, M. N., Burtless, G. and Litan, R. E. (1993) *Growth with Equity: Economic Policy Making for the Next Century*, Washington, DC: The Brookings Institute.

Baines, S. and Wheelock, J. (Forthcoming, 1998) 'Reinventing traditional solutions: job creation, gender and the micro-business household', *Work, Employment and Society* .

Baker, D. (Forthcoming) 'Does the CPI overstate inflation? An analysis of the Boskin Commission's Report', In D. Baker (ed) *Getting Prices Right: The Debate over the Accuracy of the Consumer Price Index*, Armonk, New York: M.E. Sharpe.

Bakker, I. (ed) (1994) *The Strategic Silence: Gender and Economic Policy*, London: Zed Books.

Bakker, I. (ed) (1996) *Rethinking Restructuring*, Toronto: University of Toronto Press.

Banks, M., Bates, I., Breakwell, G., Bynner, J., Emler, N., Jamieson, L. and Roberts, K. (eds) (1992) *Careers and Identities*, Milton Keynes: Open University Press.

Banks, M. and Ullah, P. (1988) *Youth Unemployment in the 1980s*, Bechenham: Croon Helm.

Barmby, T. (1994) 'Household labor supply: some notes on estimating a model with Pareto optimal outcomes', *Journal of Human Resources*, 29 (3): 932-40.

Barmby, T. (1996) 'Computation of Nash-bargained models of household labour supply', *Bulletin of Economic Research*, 48 (2): 161-165.

Barnes, C. (1991) *Disabled People in Britain and Discrimination: A Case for Anti-Discriminatory Legislation.*, London: Hurst and Co/University of Calgary Press.

Barro, R. J. (1988) 'The persistence of unemployment', *American Economic Review*, 78 (2): 32-37.

Barry, B. (1996) 'Real freedom and basic income', *Journal of Political Philosophy*, 4 (3): 242-276.

Bass, M. and Drewett, R. (1996) *Supported Employment for People With Learning Difficulties*, Bristol: The Policy Press.

Bass, S. A., Caro, F. G. and Chen, Y.-P. (eds) (1993) *Achieving a Productive Aging Society*, Westport: Auburn House.

Bastian, J. (1994) *A Matter of Time*, Aldershot: Avebury.

Bates, I. (1984) *Schooling For The Dole*, Basingstoke: Macmillan.

Bates, I. and Riesborough, G. (1993) *Youth and Inequality*, Milton Keynes: Open University Press.

Bean, C. (1994) 'European unemployment: a survey', *Journal of Economic Literature*, 32 (2): 573-619.

Beatson, M. (1995) *Labour Market Flexibility*: Research Series No.48, Department of Employment, Sheffield.

Beck, U. (1992) *Risk Society*, London: Sage.

Becker, G. (1975) *Human Capital*, New York: Columbia University Press.

Becker, G. S. (1991) *A Treatise on the Family*, Harvard: Harvard University Press.

Beechey, V. and Perkins, T. (1987) *A Matter of Hours: Women, Part-time Work and the Labour Market*, Minneapolis: University of Minnesota Press.

Benería, L. (1992) 'Accounting for women's work: the progress of two decades', *World Development*, 20 (11): 1527-60.

Berman, E., Bound, J. and Griliches, Z. (1994) 'Changes in the demand for skilled labor within US manufacturing industries', *Quarterly Journal of Economics*, 109 : 367-98.

Berman, E., Machin, S. and Bound, J. (1996) *Implications of Skill-biased Technological Change: International Evidence*: Mimeo.

Berry, R., Kitson, M. and Michie, J. (1995) *The First Million Jobs: Towards Full Employment*, London: Full Employment Forum.

Berthoud, R., Lakey, J. and McKay, S. (1993) *Economic Problems of Disabled People*, London: Policy Studies Institute.

Bispinck, R. (1996) 'Germany', In G. Fajertag (ed) *Collective Bargaining in Western Europe 1995-1996*, Brussels: ETUI.

Blackburn, M., Bloom, D. and Freeman, R. (1991) 'The declining economic position of less-skilled American males', In G. Braless (ed) *A Future of Lousy Jobs?*, Washington, DC: The Brookings Institution.

Blanchard, O. and Summers, L. (1987) 'Beyond the natural rate hypothesis', *American Economic Review*, 78 (2): 182-99.

Blanchard, O. J. and Summers, L. (1990) 'Beyond the natural rate hypothesis', In L. H. Summers (ed) *Understanding Unemployment*, Massachusetts: MIT Press.

Blanchard, O. J. and Summers, L. H. (1987) 'Fiscal increasing returns, hysteresis, real wages and unemployment', *European Economic Review*, 31 : 543-66.

Blank, R. M. (1994) *Social Protection versus Economic Flexibility: Is There a Trade- off?*, Chicago: University of Chicago Press.

Blinder, A. (1988) 'The challenge of high unemployment', *American Economic Review*, 78 (2): 1-15.

Block, F. (1996) *The Vampire State*, New York: New Press.

Boris, E. (1994) *Home to Work: Motherhood and the Politics of Industrial Homework in the United States*, Cambridge: Cambridge University Press.

Bosch, G. (1996) *OECD, External Relations Division, Labour/Management Programme, Working Hours, Final Report on the Meeting*, Paris: OCDE/GD(96)140, OECD.

Bosworth, D. and Wilson, R. (1994) 'The demand for skilled labour', In R. Layard, K. Mayhew and G. Owen (eds) *Britain's Training Deficit*, Aldershot: Avebury.

Botwinick, H. (1993) *Persistent Inequalities: Wage Disparity Under Capitalist Competition*, Princeton: Princeton University Press.

Boulding, K. (1966) 'The economics of the coming Spaceship Earth', In H. Jarret (ed) *Environmental Quality in a Growing Economy*, Baltimore: John Hopkins UP.

Boyd, M. and Pryor, E. (1989) 'The cluttered nest: the living arrangements of young Canadians', *Canadian Journal of Sociology*, 14 (4): 461-477.

Boyer, R. (1988) *The Search for Labour Market Flexibility*, Oxford: Clarendon.

Boyer, R. (1997) 'Why does employment differ in the course of time and across nations? An institutional answer in the light of the 'regulation' theory', *Metroeconomica*, 48 (1): 1-35.

Brannen, J., Mészáros, G., Moss, P. and Poland, G. (1994) *Employment and Family Life: A Review of Research in the UK (1980-1994)*: Employment Department Research Series No. 41.

Brannen, J. and Moss, P. (1991) *Managing Mothers: Dual earner households after maternity leave*, London: Macmillan.

Braverman, H. (1974) *Labour and Monopoly Capital*, New York: Monthly Review Press.

Brodsky, M. M. (1994) 'Labor market flexibility: a changing international perspective', *Monthly Labor Review*, 117 (November): 53-60.

Bronner, S. E. (1990) *Socialism Unbound*, London: Routledge.

Bruegel, I. (1989) 'Sex and race in the labour market', *Feminist Review*, 32 (Summer): 49-68.

Bruegel, I. (1996) 'Whose myths are they anyway?: a comment', *British Journal of Sociology*, 47 (1): 175-177.

Bruegel, I. and Perrons, D. (1995) 'Where do the costs of unequal treatment for women fall? An analysis of the incidence of the costs of unequal pay and sex discrimination in the UK', *Gender, Work and Organization*, 2 (3): 110-121.

Bruegel, I. and Perrons, D. (1997) 'Deregulation and women's employment: the diverse experiences of women in Britain', *Feminist Economics*, 3 (3): 139-161.

Bruno, M. and Sachs, J. (1985) *The Economics of Worldwide Stagflation*, Cambridge: Harvard University Press.

Buchele, R. and Christiansen, J. (1997) *Do Employment and Income Security Cause Unemployment? A Comparative Study of the U.S. and the E-4*: Unpublished.

Bureau of the Census. (1991) *Studies in the Distribution of Income: 1964 to 1989*, Washington, DC: P-60 Series, No. 177, U.S. Government Printing Office.

Burrows, R. (1991) *Deciphering the Enterprise Culture*, London: Routledge.

Burrows, R. and Loader, B. (eds) (1994) *Towards a Post-Fordist Welfare State?*, London: Routledge.

Butcher, S. and Hart, D. (1995) 'An analysis of working-time, 1979-94', *Employment Gazette* (May): 211-222.

Calmfors, L. and Driffill, J. (1988) 'Centralisation of wage bargaining and macroeconomic performance', *Economic Policy* (6): 13-61.

Calmfors, L. and Forslund, A. (1991) 'Real wage determination and labour market policies: the Swedish experience', *Economic Journal*, 101 : 1130-48.

Campbell, B. (1976) 'Whose full employment?', *Red Rag*, 5 .

Card, D. (1991) *The Effect of Unions on the Distribution of Wages: Redistribution or Relabelling?*: Industrial Relations Section, Princeton University, Working Paper No. 287.

CCCS Education Group. (1991) *Education Limited: Schooling and Training and the New Right Since 1979*, London: Unwin Hyman.

CCCS Race and Politics Group. (1982) *The Empire Strikes Back: Race and Racism in 70s Britain*, London: Hutchinson.

Central Statistics Office. (1993) *Social Trends 23*, London: HMSO.

Champion, S. (1996) *Disco Biscuits*, London: Sceptre.

Chapman, P. (1993) *The Economics of Training*, London: Harvester.

Charness, N. (1985) *Studies in Human Performance*, New York: John Wiley and Sons.

Chen, Y.-P. (1995) *Partial pensions for partial retirements: need for coordinating social security policy with employment policy*, Paper presented at the Mini-White house Conference on Aging, Baltimore, national Council of Senior Citizens, 23-25 February.

Cherry, R. (1981) 'What is so natural about the natural rate of unemployment?', *Journal of Economic Issues*, 15 (3): 729-43.

Chiappori, P.-A. (1992) 'Collective labour supply and welfare', *Journal of Political Economy*, 100 (3): 437-67.

Christensen, K. M. and Delgado, G. L. (1993) *Multi-Cultural Issues in Deafness*, London: Longman.

Christopherson, S. (1991) 'Trading time for consumption: the failure of working hours reduction in the U.S.', In K. Hinrichs, W. Roche and C. Sirianni (eds) *Working Time In Transition: The Political Economy of Working Hours in Industrial Nations*, Philadelphia: Temple University Press.

Ciancanelli, P. and Berch, B. (1987) 'Gender and the GNP', In B. B. Hess and M. M. Ferree (eds) *Analyzing Gender: A Handbook of Social Science Research*, Newbury Park: Sage Publications.

Cloud, K. and Garrett, N. (1996) 'A modest proposal for inclusion of women's household human capital production in analysis of structural transformation', *Feminist Economics*, 2 (3): 93-119.

Coates, D. (1996b) 'Labour governments: old constraints and new parameters', *New Left Review*, 219 (Sept/Oct).

Coates, D. (1996a) 'United Kingdom', In G. Fajertag (ed) *Collective Bargaining in Western Europe 1995-1996*, Brussels: ETUI.

Coffield, F., Borrill, C. and Marshall, S. (1986) *Growing Up at the Margins*, Milton Keynes: Open University Press.

Cohen, J. and Rogers, J. (1995) *Associations and Democracy*, London: Verso.

Cohen, P. (1997) *Rethinking the Youth Question*, London: Macmillan.

Cohen, S. (1980) *Folk Devils and Moral Panics*, Oxford: Martin Robertson.

Coleman, M. T. and Pencavel, J. (1993) 'Changes in work hours of male employees, 1940-1988', *Industrial and Labor Relations Review*, 46 (2): 262-283.

Collins, M. (1993) 'Turn on, tune in, and sort it out', *The Observer Life*, December 5th .

Collins, M. (1997a) *Altered State: The Story of Ecstasy Culture and Acid House*, London: Serpent's Tail.

Collins, M. (1997b) 'We fought the law and the law won', *The Big Issue* (April 7-13, No. 227).

Cornwall, J. (1991) 'Prospects for unemployment in the 1990s with hysteresis', In J. Cornwall (ed) *The Capitalist Economies*, Aldershot: Edward Elgar.

Cote, J. and Allahar, A. (eds) (1994) *Generation on Hold: Coming of Age in the Late 20th Century*, Toronto: Stoddart.

Coutts, K. and Rowthorn, R. (1995) *Employment in the United Kingdom: Trends and prospects*, Working Paper Series 3, ESRC Centre for Business Research: University of Cambridge.

Cox, R. (1987) *Production, Power and World Order*, New York: Columbia.

Cross, G. (1993) *Time and Money. The Making of Consumer Culture*, London: Routledge.

Cross, R. (ed) (1995) *The Natural Rate of Unemployment*, Cambridge: Cambridge University Press.

Crotty, J. and Epstein, G. (1996) 'In defence of capital controls', In L. Panitch (ed). *Socialist Register 1996: Are There Alternatives?*, London: Merlin Press.

Curry, J. (1992) 'The flexibility fetish: a review essay on flexible specialization', *Capital and Class* (50): 99-125.

D'Andrea Tyson, L. (1997) 'Inequality amid prosperity', *Washington Post* (July 8).

Daly, H. E. and Cobb, J. B. (1994) *For the Common Good: Redirecting the Economy Towards Community, the Environment, and a Sustainable Future*, Boston: Beacon Press.

Darby, M. (1976) 'Three-and-a-half million U.S. employees have been mislaid: or, an explanation of unemployment, 1934-1941', *Journal of Political Economy*, 84 (1): 1-15.

Darity, W. J. (1989) 'What's left of the economic theory of discrimination?', In S. Shulman and W. J. Darity (eds) *The Question of Discrimination: Racial Inequality in the Labor Market*, Middletown, CT: Wesleyan University Press.

Davidoff, L. (1995) *Worlds Between: Historical Perspectives on Gender and Class*, London: Routledge.

Davis, S. J., Haltiwanger, J. C. and Schuh, S. (1996) *Job Creation and Destruction*, Cambridge, Massachusetts: MIT Press.

Davoud, N. (1996) *Welfare to Work: Disability Perspective*, London: Report from the London North CEPD Incapacity Benefit Working Group, London: North London Committee for the Employment of People with Disabilities.

Dawes, L. (1993) *Long-Term Unemployment and Labour Market Flexibility*, Leicester: University of Leicester: Centre for Labour Market Studies.

Delsen, L. (1995) *Atypical Employment: An International Perspective*, Groningen: Wolters-Noordhoff.

Delsen, L. and Reday-Mulvey, G. (eds) (1996) *Gradual Retirement in the OECD Countries*, Aldershot: Dartmouth.

Dex, S., Gustafsson, S., Smith, N. and Callan, T. (1995) 'Cross-national comparisons of the labour force participation of women married to unemployed men', *Oxford Economic Papers*, 47 : 611-635.

Dinardo, J., Fortin, N. and Lemieux, T. (1994) *Labor Market Institutions and the Distribution of Wages, 1973-1992: A Semiparametric Approach*: Unpublished.

Disablement Income Group (DIG). (1996) *Barriers and bridges: benefit barriers preventing disabled people from moving into work and some policy options for overcoming them*, Paper prepared for Joseph Rowntree Foundation Seminar, 12 November 1996.

Dobson, A. (1995) *Green Political Thought*, London/New York: Routledge.

Doeringer, P. and Piore, M. (1975) 'Unemployment and the dual labor market', *The Public Interest*, 38 : 67-79.

Doyal, L. and Gough, I. (1991) *A Theory of Needs*, Basingstoke: Macmillan.

Driver, C. (1987) *Towards Full Employment: A Policy Appraisal*, London: Routledge and Kegan Paul.

Dufour, C. (1996) 'France', In G. Fajertag (ed) *Collective Bargaining in Western Europe 1995-1996*, Brussels: ETUI.

Duncan, S. (1994) 'Women's and men's lives and work in Sweden: A review of J. Acker, A. Baude, U. Böjrnberg, E. Dahlström, G. Forsberg, L. Gonäs, H. Holter and

A Nilsson (1992) Kvinnors och Mäns Liv och Arbete', *Gender, Place and Culture*, 1 (2): 261-268.

Eardley, T. and Corden, A. (1996) *Low Income Self-Employment: Work Benefits and Living Standards*, Aldershot: Avebury.

Eatwell, J. (1996) 'Unemployment on a world scale', In J. Eatwell (ed) *Global Unemployment: Loss of Jobs in the '90s*, Armonk, NY: M.E. Sharpe.

Ehrenberg, R. G. and Schumann, P. L. (1982) *Longer Hours and More Jobs?*, Ithaca: ILR Press.

Ekins, P. and Max-Neef, M. (eds) (1992) *Real-life Economics: Understanding Wealth Creation*, London: Routledge.

Elliott, L. and Atkinson, D. (1998) *The Age of Insecurity*, London: Verso.

Elson, D. (1988) 'Market socialism or socialisation of the market', *New Left Review*, 172 (Nov/Dec): 3-44.

Employment Department. (1992) *People, Jobs and Opportunity*, Cm 1810, HMSO: London.

England, K. (1996) 'Mothers, wives, workers', In K. England (ed) *Who Will Mind the Baby? Geographies of Child Care and Working Mothers*, Routledge: London.

EPI - Employment Policy Institute. (1996a) *Employment Audit*, Issue 2, Autumn.

EPI - Employment Policy Institute. (1996b) *Employment Audit*, Issue 1, Summer.

EPI - Employment Policy Institute. (1997) *Employment Audit*, Issue 3, Summer.

Esping-Andersen, G. (1990) *The Three Worlds of Welfare Capitalism*, Cambridge: Polity.

Esping-Andersen, G. (1994) 'Welfare states and the economy', In N. Smelser and R. Swedborg (eds) *A Handbook of Economic Sociology*, Princeton, NJ: Princeton University Press.

European Commission. (1993) *Growth, Competitiveness, Employment: The Challenges and Ways Forward into the 21st Century*, Brussels: EC.

European Commission. (1996a) *Employment in Europe 1996*, Luxembourg: Office for Official Publications of the European Community.

European Commission. (1996b) *Wider Employment Opportunities for People with Disabilities*, Employment-Horizon Special Report.

European Metalworkers' Federation (EMF). (1996) *Collective bargaining in a Europe without frontiers*, Report presented to the 2nd EMF Collective Bargaining Conference, Brussels, 24-25 October.

European Trade Union Institute. (1994) *A Time for Working, a Time for Living*, Brussels: European Trade Union Institute.

Eurostat. (1996a) *Labour Force Survey, Principal Results 1996*, Luxembourg.

Eurostat. (1996b) *Labour Force Survey, Results 1994*, Luxembourg.

Eurostat. (1997) *Labour Force Survey, Principal Results 1996*, Luxembourg.

Evans, K. and Heinz, W. (1994) *Youth, Identity and Transition*, London: Anglo-German Foundation.

Fagan, C., Plantenga, J. and Rubery, J. (1995) 'Part-time work and inequality, lessons from the Netherlands and the UK', *A Time for Working and a Time for Living*, London: ETUI-LRD.

Fajertag, G. (ed) (1997) *Collective bargaining in Western Europe 1996-1997*, Brussles: ETUI.

Farber, H. S. (1997) *The Changing Face of Job Loss in the United States, 1981-95*: Industrial Relations Section, Princeton University.

Featherstone, M. (ed) (1990) *Global Culture: Nationalism, Globalisation and Modernity*, London: Sage.

Feldstein, M. (1976) 'Temporary layoffs in the theory of unemployment', *Journal of Political Economy*, 84 (5): 937-57.

Ferguson, S. (1994) 'Kurt Cobain: the comfort of being sad', *Utne Reader* (64).

Finegold, D. and Soskice, D. (1988) 'The failure of British training: analysis and prescription', *Oxford Review of Economic Policy*, 4 (3): 21-53.

Finkelstein, V. (1981) 'To deny or not to deny disability', In A. Brechin, P. Liddiard and J. Swain (eds) *Handicap in a Social Work: A Reader*, Sevenoaks: Hodder and Stoughton.

Finn, D. (1987) *Training Without Jobs*, London: Macmillan.

Floyd, M. (1995) 'Self-employment and disabled people in the United Kingdom', *International Journal of Practical Approaches to Disability* (2): 9-14.

Folbre, N. (1991) 'The unproductive housewife: her evolution in nineteenth-century economic thought', *Signs: Journal of Women in Culture and Society*, 16 (3): 463-484.

Folbre, N. (1994) *Who Pays for the Kids? Gender and the Structures of Constraint*, London: Routledge.

Folbre, N. (1995) '"Holding hands at midnight": the paradox of caring labor', *Feminist Economics*, 1 (1): 73-92.

Folbre, N. and Wagman, B. (1993) 'Counting housework: new estimates of real product in the United States, 1800-1860', *Journal of Economic History*, 53 (2): 275-288.

Foreman-Peck, J. (1985) 'Seed corn or chaff? New firm formation and the performance of the interwar economy', *Economic History Review*, 38 (3): 402-22.

Fortin, N. M. and Lemieux, T. (1997) 'Institutional change and rising wage inequality: is there a linkage?', *Journal of Economic Perspectives*, 11 (2): 75-96.

Frader, L. L. (1996) 'Engendering work and wages: the French labor movement and the family wage', In L. L. Frader and S. O. Rose (eds) *Gender and Class in Modern Europe*, Ithaca: Cornell University Press.

Freedland, J. (1997) 'Age of consent goes up in smoke', *The Guardian*, July 15 .

Freeman, C., Clark, J. and Soete, L. (1982) *Unemployment and Technical Innovation*, London: Frances Pinter.

Freeman, C. and Soete, L. (1987) *Technical Change and Full Employment*, Oxford: Blackwell.

Freeman, C. and Soete, L. (1994) *Work for All or Mass Unemployment?*, London: Pinter Publishers.

Freeman, R. (1991) *How Much has De-unionization Contributed to the Rise in Male Earnings Inequality?*, Cambridge, Massachusetts: National Bureau of Economic Research, Working Paper No. 3826.

Freeman, R. (1995) 'The limits of wage flexibility to curing unemployment', *Oxford Review of Economic Policy*, 11 (1): 63-72.

Freyssinet, J. (1997) 'La loi "Robien": rupture qualitative ou aubaine éphémère?', *La Revue de l'IRES* (23).

Friedman, M. (1968) 'The role of monetary policy', *American Economic Review*, 58 (1): 1-17.

Friedman, M. (1977) 'Inflation and unemployment', *Journal of Political Economy*, 85 (3): 451-72.

Friedman, M. and Friedman, R. (1980) *Free to Choose*, New York: Harcourt, Brace and Jovanovich.

Gardiner, J. (1997) *Gender, Care and Economics*, London: Macmillan.

Gaskin, K., Vlaeminke, M. and Fenton, N. (1996) *Young People's Attitudes to the Voluntary Sector*, London: Commission on the Future of the Voluntary Sector, NCVO.

Gaullier, X. (1992) *The Changing Ages of Man*, The Geneva Papers on Risk and Insurance, Studies on the Four Pillars, no 62, Geneva: International Association for the Study of Insurance Economics.

Gaullier, X. (1993) *Salariés âgés: Conditions de Travail et Transition vers la Retraite*, Rapport sur la France pour le Bureau International du Travail, Paris: Laboratoire de Sociologie de Changement des Institutions (CNRS).

Gelder, U. (1998) *Childminding: does it work for women*, Paper presented at the Social Policy Association Conference, University of Lincoln.

Gelder, U. and Wheelock, J. (1998) *Does the other woman mean business? The economic experience of childminders*, Paper presented at the Gender, Work and Organisation Conference, Jan., UMIST.

General Accounting Office (GAO). (1996) *Program Redesign Necessary to Encourage Return to Work*, Report to Chairman, Special Committee on Ageing, U.S. Senate: United States General Audit Office.

Geroski, P. (1992) 'Price dynamics in UK manufacturing : a micro-economic view', *Economica*, 59: 403-19.

Geroski, P. and Hall, S. (1995) 'Price and quantity responses to demand and supply shocks', *Oxford Bulletin of Economics and Statistics*, 57: 185-204.

Gershuny, J. (1978) *After Industrial Society. The Emerging Self-Service Economy*, London: Macmillan.

Gershuny, J., Godwin, M. and Jones, S. (1994) 'The domestic labour revolution: A process of lagged adaptation', In M. Anderson, F. Bechhofer and J. Gershuny (eds) *The Social and Political Economy of the Household*, Oxford: Oxford University Press.

Giarini, O. and Lietdke, P. (1997) *The Employment Dilemma - The Future of Work*, Report for the Club of Rome, Geneva: International Association for the Study of Insurance Economics.

Giarini, O. and Stahel, W. (1993) *Limits to Certainty*, Dordrecht: Kluwer.

Giddens, A. (1990) *The Consequences of Modernity*, Cambridge: Polity.

Giddens, A. (1991) *Modernity and Self-Identity: Self and Society in the Late Modern Age*, Cambridge, Oxford: Polity Press.

Giddens, A. (1994) *Beyond Left and Right*, Cambridge: Polity.

Gill, S. (1998) 'European governance and new constitutionalism: economic and monetary union and alternatives to disciplinary neo-liberalism in Europe', *New Political Economy*, 3 (1): 5-26.

Ginn, J., Arber, A., Brannen, J., Dale, A., Dex, S., Elias, P., Moss, P., Pahl, J., Roberts, D. and Rubery, J. (1996) 'Feminist fallacies: a reply to Hakim on women's employment', *British Journal of Sociology*, 47 (1).

Glenn, E. N. (1996) 'From servitude to service work: historical continuities in the racial division of paid reproductive labor', In C. L. Macdonald and C. Sirianni (eds) *Working in the Service Society*, Philadelphia: Temple University Press.

Glyn, A. (1992) 'Corporatism, patterns of employment and access to consumption', In J. Pekkarinen, M. B. Pohjola and B. Rowthorn (eds) *Social Corporatism: A Superior Economic System*, Oxford: Clarendon Press.

Glyn, A. (1995a) 'Social democracy and full employment', *New Left Review* 211, May/June 1995: 33-55.

Glyn, A. (1995b) 'Unemployment and inequality', *Oxford Review of Economic Policy*, 11 (1): 1-25.

Glyn, A. and Rowthorn, B. (1990) 'The diversity of unemployment experience since 1973', In S. Marglin and J. Schor (eds) *The Golden Age of Capitalism*, Oxford: Clarendon.

Godfrey, M. (1986) *Global Unemployment: The New Challenge to Economic Theory*, Brighton: Wheatsheaf.

Golden, L. (1996) 'The economics of worktime length, adjustment, and flexibility', *Review of Social Economy*, LIV (1): 1-45.

Goldschieder, F. and Le Bourdais, C. (1987) 'Nest-leaving patterns and the transition to marriage for young men and women', *Journal of Marriage and the Family*, 49: 507-516.

Goodin, R. (1992) 'Toward a minimally presumptuous social welfare policy', In P. Van Parijs (ed) *Arguing for a Basic Income*, London: Verso.

Goodwin, J. (1994) 'A dark new age', *The Guardian Weekend*, May 7th .

Gordon, D. (1972) *Theories of Poverty and Underemployment*, Lexington: Lexington Books.

Gordon, D. M. (1987) 'Six-percent unemployment ain't natural: demystifying the idea of a rising natural rate of unemployment', *Social Research*, 54 (2): 223-246.

Gordon, D. M. (1996) *Fat and Mean: The Corporate Squeeze of Working Americans and the Myth of Managerial "Downsizing"*, New York: The Free Press.

Gordon, R. (1990) *The Measurement of Durable Goods Prices*, Chicago: University of Chicago Press.

Gorman, W. M. (1976) 'Tricks with utility functions', In M. Artis and R. Nobay (eds) *Essays in Economic Analysis*, Cambridge: CUP.

Gottschalk, P. (1997) 'Inequality, income growth and mobility: the basic facts', *Journal of Economic Perspectives*, 11 (2): 21-40.

Graham, P., Jordan, A. and Lamb, B. (1990) *An Equal Chance? Or No Chance? A Study of Discrimination Against Disabled People in the Labour Market*, London: The Spastics Society.

Gramsi, A. (1990) *Selections from Political Writing; 1921-27*, Minneapolis: University of Minnesota Press.

Green, C. and Cousineau, J. (1976) *Unemployment in Canada: The Impact of Insurance*, Ottawa: Economic Council of Canada.

Green, F. (1994) 'Training: inequality and inefficiency', In A. Glyn and D. Miliband (eds) *Paying for Inequality: The Economic Cost of Social Justice*, London: Rivers Oram.

Gregg, P. (1994) 'Share and share alike', *New Economy*, 1 (1): 13-19.

Gregg, P. and Wadsworth, J. (1995) 'Gender, households and access to employment', In J. Humphries and J. Rubery (eds) *The Economics of Equal Opportunities*, Manchester: Equal Opportunities Commission.

Gregson, N. and Lowe, M. (1993) *Servicing the Middle Classes: Class, Gender and Waged Domestic Labour in Contemporary Britain*, London: Routledge.

Grieve Smith, J. (1997) *Full Employment: A Pledge Betrayed*, Basingstoke: Macmillan.

Griffin, C. (1985) *Typical Girls*, London: Routledge.

Griffin, C. (1993) *Representations of Youth*, Cambridge: Polity.

Grubb, D., Jackman, R. and Layard, R. (1982) 'Causes of the current stagflation', *Review of Economic Studies*, 49 (707-30).

Guha, R. and Martinez-Alier, J. (1997) *Varieties of Environmentalism. Essays North and South*, London: Earthscan.

Guillemard, A.-M. (1993) *Travailleurs Vieillissants et Marché du Travail*, Travail et Emploi, no 57, Paris: Ministère du Travail.

Habermas, J. (1987) *The Theory of Communicative Action, Vol 2*, Cambridge: Polity.

Hahn, F. H. and Solow, R. M. (1996) *A Critical Essay on Modern Macro-Economic Theory*, Oxford: Basil Blackwell.

Hakim, C. (1993) 'The myth of rising female employment', *Work, Employment & Society*, 7 (1): 97-120.

Hakim, C. (1995) 'Five feminist myths about women's employment', *British Journal of Sociology*, 46 (3): 429-455.

Hakim, C. (1996a) *Key Issues in Women's Work: Female Heterogeneity and the Polarisation of Women's Employment*, London: Athlone Press.

Hakim, C. (1996b) 'The sexual division of labour and women's heterogeneity', *British Journal of Sociology*, 47 (1): 178-188.

Hall, R. E. (1988) 'Fluctuations in equilibrium unemployment', *American Economic Review*, 78 (2): 269-275.

Hall, S. (1978) *Policing the Crisis*, London: Macmillan.

Hall, S. and Jacques, M. (1983) *The Politics of Thatcherism*, London: Lawrence and Wishart.

Hall, S. and Jefferson, T. (eds) (1976) *Resistance Through Rituals*, London: Hutchinson.

Harrison, B. (1994) *Lean and Mean: The Changing Landscape of Corporate Power in the Age of Flexibility*, New York: Basic Books.

Hart, R. A. (1987) *Working Time and Employment*, Boston: Allen and Unwin.

Harvey, D. (1989) *The Condition of Postmodernity*, Oxford: Basil Blackwell.

Haskey, J. (1996) 'Population review: (6) families and households in Great Britain', *Population Trends* (85, Autumn): 7-24.

Hebdige, D. (1979) *Subculture*, London: Methuen.

Hevey, D. (1992) *The Creatures that Time Forgot: Photography and disability imagery*, London: Routledge.

Hewitt, P. (1993) *About Time: The Revolution in Work and Family Life*, London: IPPR/Rivers Oram Press.

Heylen, F. (1992) 'Long-term unemployment in the OECD countries', *Tijdschrift voor Economie en Management*, 37: 53-83.

Himmelweit, S. (1995) 'The discovery of unpaid work: the social consequences of the expansion of work', *Feminist Economics*, 1 (2): 1-19.

Hinrichs, K. (1991) 'Working time development in West Germany: departure to a new stage', In K. Hinrichs, W. Roche and C. Sirianni (eds) *Working Time in Transition*, Philadelphia: Temple.

Hinrichs, K., Roche, W. and Sirianni, C. (eds) (1991) *Working Time in Transition*, Philadelphia: Temple.

Hirsch, B. and MacPherson, D. (1995) *Union Membership and Earnings Data Book 1994: Compilations from the Current Population Survey*, Washington, DC: Bureau of National Affairs.

Hirschman, A. O. (1992) *The Rhetoric of Reaction*, Cambridge, Mass.: Belknap Press.

Hochschild, A. and Machung, A. (1989) *The Second Shift: Working Parents and the Revolution at Home*, London: Piatkus.

Holland, S. (1997) 'The feasibility of full employment', *European Labour Forum*, (Summer): 5-23.

Hollands, R. G. (1990) *The Long Transition: Class, Culture and Youth Training*, London: Macmillan.

Hollands, R. G. (1991) 'Losing the generation game revisited: youth, politics and vocationalism ', *Youth and Policy* (33): 38-41.

Hollands, R. G. (1994a) 'Back to the future? Preparing young adults for the post-industrial Wearside economy', In P. Garrahan and P. Stewart (eds) *Urban Change and Renewal: The Paradox of Place*, Aldershot: Avebury.

Hollands, R. G. (1994b) *Geordie youth cultures and the city*, A Paper presented at the conference City Cultures, Lifestyles and Consumption Practices, University of Coimbra, Coimbra, Portugal, July 14-17.

Hollands, R. G. (1995) *Friday Night, Saturday Night: Youth Cultural Identification in the Post-Industrial City*, Newcastle: Newcastle University.

Hollands, R. G. (1997) 'From shipyards to nightclubs: restructuring young adult's employment, household and consumption identities in the North-East of England', *The Berkeley Journal of Sociology*, 41: 41-66.

Horrell, S. (1994) 'Household time allocation and women's labour force participation', In M. Anderson, F. Bechhofer and J. Gershuny (eds) *The Social and Political Economy of the Household*, Oxford: Oxford University Press.

Horrell, S. and Humphries, J. (1995) 'Women's labour force participation and the transition to the male-breadwinner family, 1790-1865', *Economic History Review*, 48 (1): 89-117.

Horrell, S. and Rubery, J. (1991) 'Gender and working time: an analysis of employers' working-time policies', *Cambridge Journal of Economics*, 15 (4): 373-391.

Howell, C. (1992) 'The dilemmas of post-Fordism: socialists, flexibility, and labor market deregulation in France', *Politics & Society*, 20 (March): 71-99.

Howell, D. (1994) 'The skills myth', *The American Prospect* (18, Summer).

Hudson, J. (1988) *Unemployment After Keynes*, New York: St. Martin's Press.

Humphries, J. and Rubery, J. (1992) 'The legacy for women's employment: integration, differentiation and polarisation', In J. Michie (ed) *The Economic Legacy 1979-1992*, London: Academic Press.

Hutton, J., Hutton, S., Pinch, T. and Shiell, A. (1991) *Dependency to Enterprise*, London: Routledge.

Hutton, W. (1995) *The State We're In*, London: Jonathan Cape.

Hyman, R. (1992) 'Trade unions and the disaggregation of the working class', In M. Regini (ed) *The Future of Labour Movements*, London: Sage.

ILO. (1995) *World Employment Report 1995*, Geneva: ILO.

Ironmonger, D. (1996) 'Counting outputs, capital inputs and caring labor: estimating gross household product', *Feminist Economics*, 2 (3): 37-64.

Irwin, S. (1995) *Rights of Passage: Social Change and the Transition from Youth to Adulthood.*, London: UCL Press.

Jackman, R., Layard, R. and Nickell, S. (1996) *Combatting Unemployment: Is Flexibility Enough?*, London: Discussion Paper No.293, Centre for Economic Performance, London School of Economics.

Jackman, R., Layard, R. and Savouri, S. (1991) 'Mismatch: a framework for thought', In F. Padioa Schioppa (ed) *Mismatch and Labour Mobility*, Cambridge: CUP.

Jackman, R., Pissarides, C. and Savouri, S. (1990) 'Labour market policies and unemployment in the OECD', *Economic Policy*, 11 : 449-490.

Jackman, R. and Roper, S. (1987) 'Structural unemployment', *Oxford Bulletin of Economics and Statistics*, 49 (1): 9-36.

Jahoda, M. (1982) *Employment and Unemployment: A Social Psychological Analysis*, Cambridge: Cambridge University Press.

Jones, G. (1995) *Leaving Home*, Buckingham: Open University Press.

Jones, T. (1993) *Britain's Ethnic Minorities: an anlysis of the Labour Force Survey*, London: Policy Studies Institute.

Kalecki, M. (1990: Originally published 1943) 'Political aspects of full employment', In J. Osiatynski (ed) *Collected Works of Michael Kalecki Vol 1*, Oxford: Oxford University Press.

Katz, H. (1993) 'The decentralization of collective bargaining: a literature review and comparative analysis', *Industrial and Labor Relations Review*, 47 (1): 3-22.

Kelly, D., Kelly, G. and Gamble, A. (1997) *Stakeholder Capitalism*, London: MacMillan.

Keynes, J. M. (1936) *The General Theory of Employment, Interest and Money*, London: Macmillan.

Kiernan, K. (1992) 'Men and women at work and at home', In R. Jowell (ed) *British Social Attitudes: the 9th report*, Aldershot: Dartmouth Publishing.

Killick, T. (1995) 'Relevance, meaning and determinants of flexibility', In T. Killick (ed) *The Flexible Economy*, London: Routledge.

Killingsworth, M. R. (1983) *Labor Supply*, Cambridge: CUP.

King, D. and Stoker, G. (1996) *Rethinking Local Democracy*, Basingstoke: Macmillan.

Kingston, S. (1992) 'From anarchy to shamanarchy in the UK', *The Crack* (November).

Knight, K. (1987) *Unemployment: An Economic Analysis*, London: Croom-Helm.

Korten, D. C. (1995) *When Corporations Rule the World*, West Harford: Kumarian Press.

Kovacheva, S. and Wallace, C. (1994) 'Why do youth revolt', *Youth and Policy* (44): 7-20.

Krashevski, R. S. (1988) 'What is so natural about high unemployment?', *American Economic Review*, 78 (2): 289-293.

Krugman, P. R. (1997) 'New math, same story', *The New York Times Magazine* (January 5): 32-33.

Kuttner, R. (1997) *Everything for Sale: The Virtues and Limits of Markets*: Twentieth Century Fund.

Lakey, J. and Simpkins, R. (1994) *Employment Rehabilitation for Disabled People: Identifying the Issues*, London: Policy Studies Institute.

Larson, T. and Ong, P. (1994) 'Imbalance in part-time employment', *Journal of Economic Issues*, 28 (1): 187-196.

Lasch, C. (1991) *The True and Only Heaven*, London: Norton.

Lash, S. and Urry, J. (1994) *Economies of Signs and Spaces*, London: Sage.

Layard, R. (1996) 'False fears about EMU', *Financial Times* (December).

Layard, R., Nickell, S. and Jackman, R. (1994) *The Unemployment Crisis*, Oxford: OUP.

Layard, R., Nickell, S. and Jackman, R. (1991) *Unemployment: Macro-Economic Performance and the Labour Market*, Oxford: OUP.

Leete, L. and Schor, J. (1994) 'Assessing the time-squeeze hypothesis: hours worked in the United States, 1969-89', *Industrial Relations*, 33 (1): 25-43.

Levine, A. (1995) 'Fairness to idleness: is there a right not to work?', *Economics and Philosophy*, 11: 255-274.

Lindbeck, A. and Snower, D. (1988) *The Insider-Outsider Theory of Employment and Unemployment*, Boston: MIT Press.

Linder, S. B. (1970) *The Harried Leisure Class*, New York: Columbia University Press.

Lipietz, A. (1992) *Towards a New Economic Order: Postfordism, Ecology and Democracy*, Cambridge: Polity.

Lipietz, A. (1995) *Green Hopes: The Future of Political Ecology*, London: Polity.

Lipietz, A. (1997) 'Job sharing: why and how', *European Labour Forum*, (Summer): 45-46.

Loeb, P. (1994) *Generation at the Crossroads: Apathy and Action on the American Campus*, New Brunswick, NJ: Rutgers University Press.

Lovins, A. B., Lovins, L. and Weizsäcker, v. E. U. (1995) *Faktor Vier*, München: Droemer Knaur.

Lowe, G. and Krahn, H. (1990) *Young Workers in the Service Economy*, Ottawa: Economic Council of Canada, Working Paper No 14.

Lucas, R. (1978) 'Unemployment policy', *American Economic Review*, 68 (2): 353-7.

Lundberg, S. (1985) 'The added worker effect', *Journal of Labour Economics*, 31 (1): 11-37.

Lunt, N. and Thornton, P. (1994) 'Disability and employment: towards an understanding of discourse and policy', *Disability & Society*, 9 (2): 223-238.

Lunt, N. and Thornton, P. (1996) *Disabled people, work and benefits: review of the research literature*, Paper prepared for a Joseph Rowntree Foundation Seminar, November 1996, Social Policy Research Unit Working Paper, York: Social Policy Research Unit, University of York.

MacDonald, M. (1995) 'Feminist economics: from theory to research', *The Canadian Journal of Economics*, 28 (1): 159-175.

MacDonald, R. (1997) 'Informal work, survival strategies and the idea of the underclass', In R. Brown (ed) *The Changing Shape of Work*, London: Macmillan.

MacDonald, R., Banks, S. and Hollands, R. (1993) 'Youth and policy in the 1990s', *Youth and Policy* (40): 1-9.

MacDonald, R. and Coffield, F. (1991) *Risky Business?: Youth and the Enterprise Culture*, London: Falmer.

Machin, S. (1996) 'Changes in the relative demand for skills', In A. L. Booth and D. J. Snower (eds) *Acquiring Skills*, Cambridge: CUP.

Maguire, M. (1991) 'British Labour Market Trends', In D. Ashton and G. Lowe (eds) *Making Their Way: Education, Training and the Labour Market in Canada and Britain*, Milton Keynes: Open University Press.

Mahnkopf, B. (1992) 'The skill-oriented strategies of German trade unions: their impact on efficiency and equality objectives', *British Journal of Industrial Relations*, 30 (1): 61-81.

Maier, F. (1994) 'Institutional regimes of part-time working', In G. Schmid (ed) *Labor Market Institutions in Europe: A Socioeconomic Evaluation of Performance*, Armonk, NY: M.E. Sharpe.

Males, M. (1996) *The Scapegoat Generation: America's War on Adolescents*, Monroe, ME: Courage Press.

Maloney, T. (1990) 'Unobserved variables and the elusive added worker effect', *Economica*, 58 : 173-87.

Manacorda, M. and Petrongolo, B. (1996) *Skill Mismatch and Unemployment in OECD Countries*, London: Discussion Paper No. 307, Centre for Economic Performance, London School of Economics.

Marchand, O. (1993) 'An international comparison of working times', *Futures*, 25 (5): 502-510.

Martin, J. and White, A. (1988) *The Financial Circumstances of Disabled Adults Living in Private Households*, London: HMSO.

Martin, J., White, A. and Meltzer, H. (1989) *Disabled Adults: Services, Transport and Employment*, London: HMSO.

Mashaw, J., Reno, V., Burkhauser, R. and Berkowitz, M. (1996) *Disability, Work and Cash Benefits*, Michigan: W. E. Upjohn Institute for Employment Research.

Mason, C. (1991) 'Spatial variations in enterprise: the geography of new firm formation', In J. Curran and R. A. Blackburn (eds) *Deciphering the Enterprise Culture*, London: Routledge.

Massey, D. and Meegan, R. (1982) *The Anatomy of Job Loss*, London: Methuen.

McBride, S. (1992) *Not Working: State, Unemployment and Neo-Conservatism in Canada*, Toronto: University of Toronto Press.

McCombie, J. (1985-86) 'Why cutting real wages will not necessarily reduce unemployment', *Journal of Post Keynesian Economics*, 8 (2): 233-48.

McDowell, L. (1991) 'Life without father and Ford: The new gender order of post-Fordism', *Transactions of the British Institute of Geographers*, 16: 400-419.

McElroy, M. B. (1990) 'The empirical content of Nash-bargained household behaviour', *Journal of Human Resources*, 25 (4): 559-83.

McLaughlin, E. (1994) *Flexibility in Work and Benefits,*, Commission on Social Justice Issue Paper 11, London: IPPR.

Meadows, P. (1996) *The Future of Work: Contributions to the Debate*, Social Policy Summary 7, York: Joseph Rowntree Foundation.

Meissner, M., Humphries, E. W., Meis, S. M. and Scheu, W. J. (1975) 'No exit for wives: sexual division of labour and the cumulation of household demands.', *Canadian Review of Sociology and Anthropology*, 12 (4): 424-439; reprinted in R. Pahl (1990) (ed) *On Work*, Blackwell: Oxford.

Melucci, A. (1988) *Nomads of the Present: Social Movements and Individual Needs in Contemporary Society*, London: Radius.

Mensch, G. (1975) *Stalemate in Technology: Innovations Overcome the Depression*, New York: Ballinger.

Michie, J. and Grieve Smith, J. (eds) (1994) *Unemployment in Europe*, London: Academic Press.

Michie, J. and Wilkinson, F. (1992) 'Inflation policy and the restructuring of labour markets', In J. Michie (ed) *The Economic Legacy 1979-1992*, London: Academic Press.

Miliband, R. (1994) *Socialism in a Sceptical Age*, Cambridge: Polity.

Minford, P. (1991) *The Supply Side Revolution in Britain*, Aldershot: Elgar and Institute of Economic Affairs.

Minford, P. and Ashton, P. (1985) *Unemployment: Cause and Cure*, Oxford: Basil Blackwell.

Mingione, E. (1991) *Fragmented Societies: A Sociology of Economic Life Beyond the Market Paradigm*, Oxford: Basil Blackwell.

Minns, R. (1996) 'The social ownership of capital', *New Left Review* (219, Sept/Oct): 42-61.

Minore, B. (1991) 'Looking in, looking out: coping with adolescent suicide in the Cree and Ojibway communities in Northern Ontario', *The Canadian Journal of Native Studies*, XI (1): 1-24.

Mishel, L., Bernstein, J. and Schmitt, J. (1996) *The State of Working America 1996-97.*, Armonk, New York: M.E. Sharpe.

Mishel, L. and Schmitt, J. (eds) (1995) *Beware the U.S. Model: Jobs and Wages in a Deregulated Economy*, Washington, DC: Economic Policy Institute.

Mizen, P. (1995) *The State, Young People and Youth Training*, London: Mansell.

Moore, S. (1995) 'Stressed out on life', *The Guardian*, June 1st .

Morniche, P. (1996) 'Vie et santé progressent de concert', *Risques, Les Cahiers de l'Assurance* (26): 21-22.

Morris, J. (1990a) *Our Homes, Our Rights: Housing, Independent Living and Physically Disabled People*, London: Shelter.

Morris, L. (1990b) *The Workings of the Household*, Oxford: Polity.

Morris, R. and Caro, F. G. (1995) *Using Retirees to Address Social Ills*, Washington: Ageing International.

Mungham, G. (1982) 'Workless youth as a moral panic', In T. Rees and P. Atkinson (eds) *Youth Unemployment and State Intervention*, London: Routledge.

Murphy, F. (1995) *Older Volunteers, A Worldwide Phenomenon*, Washington: Ageing International.

Murray, C. (1990) *The Emerging British Underclass*, London: Institute for Economic Affairs.

Murray, C. (1994) *Underclass: The Crisis Deepens*, London: Institute for Economic Affairs.

Myles, J. (1996) 'When markets fail: social welfare in Canada and the U.S.', In G. Esping-Anderson (ed) *Welfare States in Transition: National Adaptations in Global Economies*, London: Sage.

Myles, J., Picot, G. and Whannel, T. (1988) *Wages and Jobs in the 1980s: Changing Youth Wages and the Declining Middle*, Ottawa: Statistics Canada Research paper Series, No. 17.

Naegele, G. (1996) *New Trends in Gradual Retirement in Germany*, The Geneva Papers on Risk Insurance, Studies on the Four Pillars, no 81, Geneva: International Association for the Study of Insurance Economics.

Negrey, C. (1993) *Gender, Time and Reduced Work*, Albany: SUNY Press.

Nelson, J. A. (1995) 'Feminism and economics', *Journal of Economic Perspectives*, 9 (2): 131-148.

Newcombe, R. (1991) *Raving and Dance Drugs*, Liverpool: Rave Research Bureau.

Newman, K. and Lennon, C. (1995) 'The job ghetto', *The American Prospect* (22, Summer): 66-67.

Newman, P. (1997) *Environmental Ethics and Cities. A Perspective Based on Gilberg White, Fritz Schumacher and Jane Jacobs*, Melbourne: Environmental Justice.

Nickell, S. (1990) 'Unemployment: a survey', *Economic Journal*, 100: 391-439.

Nickell, S. (1995) *The Collapse in Demand for the Unskilled: What can be Done?*: Institute of Economics and Statistics, University of Oxford.

Nickell, S. and Bell, B. (1995) 'The collapse in the demand for the unskilled and unemployment across the OECD', *Oxford Review of Economic Policy*, 11: 40-62.

O'Bireck, G. (ed) (1996) *Not a Kid Anymore: Canadian Youth, Crime and Subcultures*, Toronto: Nelson.

O'Connor, J. (1996) 'The second contradiction of capitalism', In T. Benton (ed) *The Greening of Marxism*, New York/London: The Guilford Press.

O'Hara, P. A. (1995) 'Household labor, the family, and macroeconomic instability in the United States: 1940s-1990s', *Review of Social Economy*, 53 (1): 89-120.

Oakley, A. (1974) *The Sociology of Housework*, London: Martin Robertson.

OECD. (1985) *Employment Growth and Structural Change*, Paris: OECD.

OECD. (1989) *OECD Employment Outlook: July 1989*, Paris: OECD.

OECD. (1990) *OECD Employment Outlook: July 1990*, Paris: OECD.

OECD. (1994a) *The OECD Jobs Study: Evidence and Explanations*, Paris: OECD.

OECD. (1994b) *The OECD Jobs Study: Facts, Analysis, Strategies*, Paris: OECD.

OECD. (1996) *Employment Outlook*, Paris: OECD.

OECD. (1997) *OECD Employment Outlook*, Paris: Organisation for Economic Co-operation and Development.

Offe, C. (1985) *Disorganised Capitalism*, Cambridge: Polity.

Offe, C. (1992) 'A non-productivist design for social policies', In P. Van Parijs (ed) *Arguing for a Basic Income*, London: Verso.

Offe, C. (1995) 'Full employment: asking the wrong question', *Dissent* (Winter).

Offe, C. (1996) *Modernity and the State,* Cambridge: Polity.

Offe, C. and Heinze, K. (1993) *Beyond Employment*, Philadelphia: Temple.

Office for National Statistics. (1997) 'Labour market participation among people with long-term health problems/disabilities', *Labour Force Survey Key Facts* (March).

Office for National Statistics. (1997) *Labour Market Trends*, March.

Oliver, M. (1990) *Politics of Disablement*, Basingstoke: Macmillan.

Oliver, M. (1995) 'Disability, empowerment and the inclusive society', In G. Zarb (ed) *Removing Disability Barriers*, London: Policy Studies Institute.

Osberg, L. (1988) 'The disappearance of involuntary unemployment', *Journal of Economic Issues*, 22 (3): 707-27.

Oulton, N. (1995) 'Supply side reform and UK Economic growth: What Happened to the Miracle?', *National Institute Economic Review* (154): 53-70.

Page, B. and Shapiro, R. (1992) *The Rational Public: 50 Years of Trends in American Policy Preferences*, Chicago: University of Chicago Press.

Panitch, L. (1996) 'Rethinking the role of the state', In J. Mittelman (ed) *Globalization: Critical Reflections*, Denver: Lynne Rienner Publishers.

Phelps, E. (1972) *Inflation Policy and Unemployment Theory*, New York: Norton.

Phelps, E. (1992) 'A review of unemployment, macroeconomic performance and the labour market', *Journal of Economic Literature*, 30 (3): 1476-90.

Phelps, E. S. (1968) 'Money wage dynamics and labour market equilibrium', *Journal of Political Economy*, 76 : 678-711.

Phillips, A. (1997) 'From inequality to difference: a severe case of displacement', *New Left Review*, 224 (July/Aug): 143-153.

Picchio, A. (1992) *Social Reproduction: The Political Economy of the Labour Market*, Cambridge: Cambridge University Press.

Piore, M. (1979) 'Unemployment and inflation', In M. Piore (ed) *Unemployment and Inflation*, New York: M.E. Sharpe.

Piore, M. and Sabel, C. (1984) *The Second Industrial Divide*, Oxford: Basil Blackwell.

Polanyi, K. (1946) *The Great Transformation*, London: Victor Gallancz.

Pollin, R. (1995) 'Financial structures and egalitarian economic policy', *New Left Review*, 214: 26-61.

Pollert, A. (ed) (1991) *Farewell to Flexibility?*, Oxford: Basil Blackwell.

Pontusson, J. (1994) *The Limits of Social Democracy*, Ithaca, N.Y.: Cornell.

Prais, S. J. (1995) *Productivity, Education and Training*, Cambridge: Cambridge University Press.

Prescott-Clarke, P. (1990) *Employment and Handicap*, London: Social and Community Planning Research.

Przeworski, A. (1985) *Capitalism and Social Democracy*, Cambridge: Cambridge University Press.

Purdy, D. (1988) *Social Power and the Labour Market: A Radical Approach to Labour Economics*, London: Macmillan.

Purdy, D. (1994) 'Citizenship, basic income and the state', *New Left Review*, 208 (Nov/Dec): 30-48.

Purdy, D. (forthcoming) *Income, Work and Citizenship: An Enquiry*, London: Verso.

Putnam, R. (1995) 'Bowling alone: America's declining social capital', *Journal of Democracy*, VI: 65-78.

RADAR. (1993) *Disability and Discrimination in Employment*, London: RADAR.

Radwanski, G. (1986) *Ontario Study of the Service Sector: Background Papers*, Toronto: Ministry of Treasury and Economics.

Rainbird, H. (1990) *Training Matters: Union Perspectives on Industrial Restructuring and Training*, Oxford: Basil Blackwell.

Rainwater, L. and Smeeding, T. M. (1995) *Doing Poorly: The Real Income of American Children in Comparative Perspective*: Working Paper No. 127, Maxwell School of Citizenship and Public Affairs, Syracuse University.

Rawls, J. (1972) *A Theory of Justice*, Oxford: Oxford University Press.

Rebitzer, J. B. and Taylor, L. J. (1991) *Do Labor Markets Provide Enough Short Hour Jobs? An Analysis of Work Hours and Work Incentives*: National Bureau of Economic Research, Working Paper 3883.

Reday-Mulvey, G. (1994) *Continuing Training until End-of-Career*, The Geneva Papers on Risk and Insurance, Studies on the Four Pillars, no 73, Geneva: International Association for the Study of Insurance Economics.

Redhead, S. (1993) *Rave Off: Politics and Deviance in Contemporary Youth Culture*, Aldershot: Avebury.

Regini, M. (1992) (ed) *The Future of Labour Movements*, London: Sage.

Richardson, R. and Rubin, M. (1993) *The Shorter Working-Week Campaign in Engineering: A Pyrrhic Defeat?*, Seminar paper: Centre for Economic Performance, LSE.

Richardson, R. and Rubin, M. (1995) 'The shorter working week in engineering: surrender without sacrifice?', In D. Metcalf and S. Milner (eds) *Perspectives on Industrial Disputes*, London: Routledge.

Rifkin, J. (1995) *The End of Work: The Decline of the Global Labor Force and the Dawn of the Post-Market Era.*, New York: G.P. Putnam's Sons.

Riordan, J. (ed) (1989) *Soviet Youth Culture*, London: Macmillan.

Ritchie, J. (1991) 'Enterprise cultures: a frame analysis', In J. Curran and R. A. Blackburn (eds) *Deciphering the Enterprise Culture*, London: Routledge.

Robbins, D. (1982) *The Chance to Work: Improving Employment Prospects for Disabled People*, London: DIG.

Robertson, J. (1985) *Future Work: Jobs, Self-Employment and Leisure After the Industrial Age*, Aldershot: Gower.

Robinson, J. (1937) *Essays in the Theory of Employment*, London: Macmillan.

Robinson, P. (1996) 'Skill shortages and full employment: How serious a constraint?', In J. Michie and J. Grieve Smith (eds) *Creating Industrial Capacity: Towards Full Employment*, Oxford: OUP.

Robson, M. (1989) 'Unemployment and real wages in Britain, 1967-1983', *Oxford Economic Papers*, 41 : 789-801.

Roediger, D. R. (1991) *The Wages of Whiteness: Race and the Making of the American Working Class*, London: Verso.

Roeher Institute. (1993) *On Target? Canada's Employment-related Programs for Persons with Disabilities*, North York, Ontario: Roeher Institute.

Rogers, J. and Streeck, W. (1994) 'Productive solidarities: economic strategy and left politics', In D. Miliband (ed) *Reinventing the Left*, Cambridge: Polity.

Rolfe, H., Bryson, A. and Metcalf, H. (1996) *The Effectiveness of TECs in Achieving Jobs and Qualifications for Disadvantaged Groups*, DfEE Research Studies RS4, London: HMSO.

Romer, C. (1986) 'Is the stabilization of the post-war economy a figment of the data?', *American Economic Review*, 76 (3): 314-34.

Rosdücher, J. and Seifert, H. (1996) *The Reduction of Working Hours and Employment*, Brussels: ETUI.

Rose, S. J. (1995) *Declining Job Security and the Professionalization of Opportunity*, Washington, D.C.: Research Report No. 95-04, National Commission for Employment Policy.

Rose, S. O. (1992) *Limited Livelihoods: Gender and Class in Nineteenth-Century England*, Berkeley: University of California Press.

Rosenberg, S. (1993) 'More work for some, less work for others', *Futures*, 25 (5): 551-559.

Rowlingson, K. and Berthoud, R. (1996) *Disability, Benefits and Employment: Evaluation of the Disability Working Allowance*, Social Security Research Report No 59, London: The Stationery Office.

Rowthorn, R. E. (1995) 'Capital formation and unemployment', *Oxford Review of Economic Policy*, 11 (1).

Rowthorn, R. E. (1996) 'Unemployment, wage bargaining and capital-labour substitution', Cambridge: mimeo.

Rowthorn, R. E. (1977) 'Conflict, inflation and money', *Cambridge Journal of Economics* (1).

Rubery, J. (1988) *Women and Recession*, London: Routledge and Kegan Paul.

Rubery, J. (1996) 'The labour market outlook and the outlook for labour market analysis', In R. Crompton, D. Gallie and K. Purcell (eds) *Changing Forms of Employment: Organisations, Skills and Gender*, London: Routledge.

Russell, B. (1935) *In Praise of Idleness and Other Essays*, London: George Allen and Unwin Ltd.

Rustin, M. (1994) 'Social membership in a privatised society', *Renewal* .

Samoy, E. (1996) *(Re-) integration of people with disabilities in view of developments in the labour market*, Paper prepared for an Expert Meeting, Rehabilitation of Partially Disabled Workers in the Workforce in Various European Countries: Decisive Factors Seen from an International Perspective: University of Utrecht.

Sanne, C. (1995) *Arbetets Tid*, Stockholm: Carlssons.

Sayers, S. (1986) 'The need to work: a perspective from philosophy', *Radical Philosophy*, 46 (Summer): 17-26.

Schmähl, W. and Gatter, J. (1994) 'Options for extending the working period and flexibilising the transition to retirement in the German insurance industry - the current situation and assessment for the future', *The Geneva Papers on Risk and Insurance*, 19 (73): 433-471.

Schmid, G. (1995a) 'Is full employment still possible? Transitional labour markets as a new strategy of labour market policy', *Economic and Industrial Democracy*, 16 (3): 429-456.

Schmid, H. (1995b) *Labour market policies, work time reductions and welfare strategies in Scandinavia*, Paper presented to the conference Reparto del Tiempo de Trabajo, Bilbao, October 25-26.

Schmitter, P. and Streeck, W. (1991) 'From national corporatism to transnational pluralism: organised interests in the single European market', *Politics and Society* (2).

Schor, J. (1992) *The Overworked American: The Unexpected Decline of Leisure*, New York: Basic Books.

Schram, S. (1991) 'Welfare spending and poverty: cutting back produces more poverty not less', *American Journal of Economics and Sociology*, 50 (2).

Schultz, T. (1961) 'Investment in human capital', *American Economic Review*, 51 (1): 1-17.

Schumpeter, J. (1939) *Business Cycles: A Theoretical, Historical and Statistical Analysis of the Capitalist Process, Vol.2*, New York: McGraw-Hill.

Scott, J. W. (1988) *Gender and the Politics of History*, New York: Columbia University Press.

Seiz, J. (1995) 'Bargaining models, feminism, and institutionalism', *Journal of Economic Issues*, 29 (2): 609-618.

Senate Finance Committee. (1996) *Toward a More Accurate Measure of the Cost of Living*, Washington, D.C.: Final Report to the Senate Finance Committee from the Advisory Commission to Study the Consumer Price Index, United States Senate.

Senker, P. (1992) *Industrial Training in a Cold Climate*, Aldershot: Avebury.

Sheppard, H. (1996) 'Gradual retirement in the USA - micro issues', In L. Delsen and G. Reday-Mulvey (eds) *Gradual Retirement in the OECD Countries*, Aldershot: Darmouth.

Shimowada. (1992) 'Aging and the Four Pillars in Japan', *The Geneva Papers on Risk and Insurance*, 17 (62): 40-80.

Shulman, S. (1989) 'The natural rate of unemployment: concept and critique', *Journal of Post Keynesian Economics*, 11 (4): 509-21.

Shulman, S. (1991) 'Why is the black unemployment rate always twice as high as the white unemployment rate', In R. R. Cornwall and P. V. Wunnava (eds) *In New Approaches to Economic and Social Analyses of Discrimination*, New York: Praeger.

Singh, A. (1995) 'Institutional requirements for full employment in advanced economies', *International Labour Review*, 134 (4-5): 471-495.

Skinner, C. (1995) 'Urban labor markets and young black men: a literature review', *Journal of Economic Issues*, 29 (1): 47-65.

Skuse, F. (1995) 'Thatcherism and unemployment in the UK', In P. Arestis and M. Marshall (eds) *The Political Economy of Full Employment*, Aldershot: Edward Elgar.

Sly, F., Duxbury, R. and Tillsley, C. (1995) 'Disability and the labour market', *Labour Market Trends* (December): 439-459.

Snower, D. (1996) 'The low-skill, bad job trap', In A. Booth and D. Snower (eds) *Acquiring Skills: Market Failures, Their Symptoms and Policy Responses*, Cambridge: Cambridge University Press.

Solow, R. (1986) 'The unemployment of nations', *Business Economics*, 21 (1): 5-12.

Solow, R. (1990) *The Labour Market as a Social Institution*, Oxford: Basil Blackwell.

Soper, K. (1996) 'Greening Prometheus. Marxism and ecology', In T. Benton (ed) *The Greening of Marxism*, New York/London: The Guildford Press.

Sorge, A. and Warner, M. (1986) *Comparative Factory Organization*, London: Gower.

Spencer, L. and Taylor, S. (1994) *Participation and Progress in the Labour Market: Key Issues for Women*: Employment Department Research Series No. 35.

Standing, G. (1991) 'Structural adjustment and labour market policies: towards social adjustment? ', In G. Standing and V. Tokman (eds) *Towards Social Adjustment: Labour Market Issues in Structural Adjustment*, Geneva: International Labour Office.

Standing, G. (1992) 'The need for a new social consensus', In P. Van Parijs (ed) *Arguing for a Basic Income*, London: Verso.

Statistics Canada. (1994) *Youth in Canada*, Ottawa: Statistics Canada.

Steindl, J. (1945) *Small and Big Business: Economic Problems of the Size of Firms*, Oxford: Basil Blackwell.

Stevens, J. and Walsh, T. (1991) 'Training and competitiveness', In J. Stevens and R. Mackay (eds) *Training and Competitiveness*, London: National Economic Development Office.

Stewart, M. B. and Swaffield, J. K. (1997) 'Constraints on the desired hours of work of British men', *Economic Journal*, 107 (March): 520-535.

Stiglitz, J. (1996) *Marshall Lecture*, Cambridge.

Streeck, W. (1989) 'Skills and the limits of neoliberalism', *Work, Employment and Society*, 3 (1): 89-104.

Streeck, W. (1997) 'German capitalism: does it exist? Can it survive?', *New Political Economy*, 2 (2): 237-56.

Summers, L. and Blanchard, O. (1986) 'Hysteresis and the European unemployment problem', In S. Fischer (ed) *NBER Macroeconomics Annual 1986*, Massachusetts: MIT Press.

Summers, L. and Clark, K. M. (1979) 'Labour market dynamics and unemployment: a re-consideration', *Brookings Papers on Economic Activity* (1): 13-60.

Swenson, P. (1997) 'Arranged alliance: business and market security in the new deals', *Politics and Society*, 25 (1): 66-116.

Takayama, N. (1996) 'Gradual retirement in Japan - macro issues', In L. Delsen and G. Reday-Mulvey (eds) *Gradual Retirement in the OECD Countries*, Aldershot: Darmouth.

Tanner. (1996) *Teenage Troubles*, Toronto: Nelson.

Taylor, M. (1996) 'Between public and private: accountability in voluntary organisations', *Policy and Politics* (1): 57-72.

Taylor, P. and Walker, A. (1996) 'Gradual retirement in United Kingdom', In L. Delsen and G. Reday-Mulvey (eds) *Gradual Retirement in the OECD Countries*, Aldershot: Dartmouth.

Teixeira, R. and Rogers, J. (1996) *Volatile Voters: Declining Living Standards and Non-college-educated Whites*, Washington D.C.: Economic Policy Institute Working Paper No. 116, Economic Policy Institute.

Thomas, A. (1992) *Working With a Disability: Barriers and Facilitators*, London: SCPR.

Thomas, D. (1990) 'Intra-household resource allocation: an inferential approach', *Journal of Human Resources*, 25 (4): 635-664.

Thomson, K. (1995) 'Working mothers: choice or circumstance?', In R. Jowell (ed) *British Social Attitudes: the 12th report*, Aldershot: Dartmouth Publishing.

Thornton, P. and Lunt, N. (1995) *Employment for Disabled People: Social Obligation or Individual Responsibility?*, Social Policy Report Number 2, York: Social Policy Research Unit.

Thornton, P. and Lunt, N. (1997) *Employment Policies for Disabled People in Eighteen Countries: A Review*, York: Social Policy Research Unit.

Thornton, P., Sainsbury, R. and Barnes, H. (1997) *Helping Disabled People to Work: A Cross-national Review of Social Security and Employment Policies*, Social Security Advisory Committee Research Paper No 8, London: The Stationery Office.

Thornton, S. (1995) *Club Cultures: Music, Media and Subcultural Capital*, Oxford: Blackwell.

Thurow, L. (1983) *Dangerous Currents*, New York: Random House.

Thurow, L. (1992) *Head to Head: The Coming Economic Battle among Japan, Europe and America*, New York: William Morrow.

Tilly, C. (1996) *Half a Job: Bad and Good Part-Time Jobs in a Changing Labor Market*, Philadelphia: Temple University Press.

Toffler, A. (1980) *The Third Wave*, London: Collins.

Topel, R. H. (1997) 'Factor proportions and relative wages: the supply-side determinants of wage inequality', *Journal of Economic Perspectives*, 11 (2): 55-74.

Touraine, A. (1981) *The Voice and the Eye: An Analysis of Social Movements*, Cambridge: Cambridge University Press.

Touraine, A. (1991) 'A world that has lost it's future', In UNESCO (ed) *Facing the Future: Young People and Unemployment Around the World*, Hyderabad: Orient Longman.

Trevithick, J. (1992) *Involuntary Unemployment: Macroeconomics from a Keynesian Perspective*, London: Harvester Press.

Turner, R. K., Pearce, D. and Bateman, I. (1994) *Environmental Economics. An Elementary Introduction*, New York: Harvester/Wheatsheaf.

UN (1991) *The World's Women 1970-1990: Trends and Statistics*, New York: United Nations.

Vail, J., Wheelock, J. and Hill, M. (eds) (Forthcoming) *Insecure Times: Insecurity in Modern Society*, London: Routledge.

Vaiou, D. (1996) 'Women's work and everyday life in southern Europe in the context of European integration', In M.-D. García-Ramon and J. Monk (eds) *Women of the European Union: The Politics of Work and Daily Life*, London: Routledge.

Van den Toren, J. P. (1996) 'Netherlands', In G. Fajertag (ed) *Collective Bargaining in Western Europe 1995-1996*, Brussels: ETUI.

Van Parijs, P. (ed) (1992) *Arguing for a Basic Income*, London: Verso.

Van Parijs, P. (1995) *Real Freedom for All: What (if anything) Justifies Capitalism?*, Oxford: Oxford University Press.

Van Parijs, P. (1996) 'The two dilemmas of basic income', *Political Quarterly* .

Vogal, J. (1996) 'Throw away the key: juvenile offenders', *Utne Reader* (64): 56-57.

Wadensjö, E. (1996) 'Gradual retirement in Sweden', In L. Delsen and G. Reday-Mulvey (eds) *Gradual Retirement in the OECD Countries*, Aldershot: Dartmouth.

Wagman, B. and Folbre, N. (1988) 'The feminization of inequality: some new patterns', *Challenge* (November/December): 56-59.

Wainwright, H. (1994) *Arguing for a New Left*, London: Routledge.

Walker, A. (1996) *The future of retirement in Europe*, Paper presented to the Geneva Association's International Seminar, The Elder in the Year 2000, Turin.

Walter, T. (1989) *Basic Income: Freedom from Poverty, Freedom from Work*, New York: M Boyars.

Waring, M. (1988) *If Women Counted: A New Feminist Economics*, San Francisco: Harper Collins.

Watson, G. (1992) 'Hours of work in Great Britain and Europe', *Employment Gazette* (November): 539-557.

Webster, D. E. (1996) 'Wage analysis computations', In B. Mishel et al. (eds) *The State of Working America 1996-97*, Armonk, New York: M.E. Sharpe.

Welsh, I. (1993) *Trainspotting*, London: Minerva.

Welsh, I. (1994) *The Acid House*, London: Vinatge.

Welsh, I. (1996a) '"Drugs and the theatre darling", introduction to the playscripts', *Trainspotting & Headstate*, London, Minerva .

Welsh, I. (1996b) *Ecstasy*, London: Johnathon Cape.

Wheelock, J. (1990) *Husbands at Home: The Domestic Economy in a Post-Industrial Society*, London: Routledge.

Wheelock, J. (1992) 'The household in the whole economy', In P. Ekins and M. Max-Neef (eds) *Real-life Economics: Understanding Wealth Creation*, London: Routledge.

Wheelock, J. (Forthcoming) 'Insecurity in employment', In J. Vail, J. Wheelock and M. Hill (eds) *Insecure Times: Insecurity in Modern Society*, London: Routledge.

Wheelock, J. and Baines, S. (1998) 'Creating your own job: the behaviour of micro-business households in the risk society', In J. Mitchie and A. Reati (eds) *Employment, Technology and Economic Needs*, Aldershot: Edward Elgar.

Wheelock, J. and McCarthy, P. (1997) 'Employed mothers and their families in Britain', In J. Frankel (ed) *Families of Employed Mothers: An International Perspective*, New York: Garland.

Wheelock, J. and Mariussen, Å. (eds) (1997) *Households, Work and Economic Chamge: A Comparative Institutional Perspective*, Boston MA: Kluwer Academic Publishers.

Wheelock, J. and Oughton, E. (1996) 'The household as a focus for research', *Journal of Economic Issues*, 30 (1): 143-159.

White, L. J. (1967) 'The historical roots of our environmental crisis', *Science*, 155 .

White, M. and Ghobadian, A. (1984) *Shorter Working Hours in Practice*, London: Policy Studies Institute.

White, M. and Smith, D. (1994) 'The causes of persistently high unemployment', In A. Petersen and J. Mortimer (eds) *Youth Unemployment and Society*, Cambridge: Cambridge University Press.

Wilkinson, H. (1995) *Generation X and the New Work Ethic*, London: Demos.

Williams, F. (1994) 'Social relations, welfare and the post-Fordism debate', In R. Burrows and B. Loader (eds) *Towards a Post-Fordist State?*, London: Routledge.

Williams, R. (1989) *Resources of Hope*, London: Verso.

Willis, P. (1977) *Learning to Labour*, Westmead: Saxon House.

Willis, P. (1988) *The Youth Review*, Aldershot: Avebury.

Willis, P., Jones, S., Canaan, J. and Hurd, G. (1990) *Common Culture*, Milton Keynes: Open University Press.

Wilson, F. D., Tienda, M. and Wu, L. (1995) 'Race and unemployment: labor market experiences of black and white men, 1968-1988', *Work and Occupations*, 22 (3): 245-270.

Wilson, W. J. (1987) *The Truly Disadvantaged*, Chicago: University of Chicago Press.

Winkler, A. (1996) *Integration of persons with disabilities into the labour market and state intervention*, Paper prepared for an Expert Meeting, Rehabilitation of Partially Disabled Workers in the Workforce in Various European Countries: Decisive Factors Seen from an International Perspective: University of Utrecht.

Wood, A. (1994) *North-South Trade, Employment and Inequality: Changing Fortunes in a Skill Driven World*, Oxford: Clarendon Press.

Woody, B. (1989) 'Black women in the emerging services economy', *Sex Roles*, 21 (1/2): 45-67.

Worswick, G. D. N. (1991) *Unemployment: A Problem of Policy*, Cambridge: Cambridge University Press.

Wright, E. O. (1995) 'Preface', In J. Cohen and J. Rogers *Associations and Democracy*, London: Verso.

Yelin, E. (1992) *Disability and the Displaced Worker*, New Brunswick: Rutgers University Press.

Yelin, E. and Katz, P. (1994) 'Making work more central to disability policy', *Millbank Quarterly*, 72 (4): 593-619.

Young, M. and Willmott, P. (1973) *The Symmetrical Family: A Study of Work and Leisure in the London Region*, London: Routledge and Kegan Paul.

INDEX

A
accumulation 81, 89
Australia 76, 79, 132, 164, 169
autonomy 73, 87, 132, 206, 214, 248, 255, 277

B
bargaining, collective *see* collective bargaining
bargaining power 24-7, 29, 33-4, 59, 77, 161, 188, 220, 259
basic income 2, 13-15, 114, 205-6, 214-5, 250, 255-7, 260-1, 263-4, 266-7, 271-2, 277-9
benefit system 16, 24-5, 29, 36-7, 55, 58, 131, 134, 136-8, 159, 187, 217
Beveridge, W. 101, 271
Blair, T. 2, 106
breadwinner, male 7, 17, 69, 71, 73-4, 79-80, 110, 149, 205, 211, 260, 276
Bretton Woods 32, 183

C
Canada 103, 109, 116, 120, 132, 145, 147, 163-4, 169, 197
capital, human *see* human capital
caring crisis 3, 7, 9-10, 14, 78-80, 147, 213
childcare 9-10, 144, 146-7, 207-10, 213, 245, 262
citizen's income *see* basic income
collective bargaining 29, 34-5, 39, 55-6, 59, 220, 222-8, 258-9, 261, 265-6
commodification
    labour 4-5, 8, 79-80, 240
community enterprises 237, 246-8
competition/competitiveness 183-5, 195, 198-9, 256, 263, 271
consumption 27, 35, 73, 86, 88, 90, 213, 270
co-operatives 236-7, 241-5, 249
crime 30, 105-6, 163

D
deflation 12, 26, 198
demand 24-7, 35, 53, 65, 73, 186, 191-3, 196, 198, 254, 256
demarketisation 17, 253
democracy 2, 96, 245, 249, 257, 266-8, 277, 279, 282
deregulation 2, 4, 9-10, 37, 76, 81, 105, 188-9, 207, 243
discrimination, labour market 71, 74-5, 104, 131-3, 137, 139, 194
disability 132-3
disabled people 4-5, 18, 131-42, 246, 249
division of labour, gender *see* gender
double burden 14, 79, 143-9, 152

downsizing 9, 123, 165

E
economic activity rates *see* labour market participation
economic
 growth 29, 32, 35-8, 87-9, 183, 202, 213, 251, 256, 263, 270-1
 shocks 7, 23-7, 29, 33-4, 52, 58, 65, 157, 187, 191, 197
employment
 female 5, 10, 14, 16, 30-1, 34-6, 65, 69, 76, 82, 134, 144
 growth 27, 29, 144, 202, 275
 male 5, 10, 30-1, 34-6, 65, 76, 134
 manufacturing 5, 8, 78
 service 5, 8, 78, 103-4, 128, 184
employment policy
 neo liberal 2, 11, 24-5, 32-3, 59-60, 166, 185-92, 254
 social democratic 2, 11-12, 40, 100-1, 166, 185, 192-200, 254
equality 74, 267-8
equilibrium 7, 23-4, 26, 51-3, 58, 186, 191-3
Europe
 job creation 12, 128, 157-8, 163-6
 monetary union 1, 25, 29, 40
 unemployment 1-2, 4, 23-5, 184
exclusion *see* social exclusion

F
family 9-10, 73, 109
feminist political economy 7, 69-75, 77-9, 81-2, 145, 209
fiscal policy 27, 32-3, 37, 193
flexibility 8-10, 14, 16, 18, 24, 26-9, 40, 59, 71, 75-81, 100, 123, 125, 131, 135, 138, 152, 157, 164-6, 184-5, 188-9, 192, 196-7, 200, 207, 220-1, 223-4, 226-7, 255-6, 258-9, 261, 263-4, 276-7
flexitime 108, 124-6, 134, 207, 220
Folbre, N. 70, 72, 79-80, 83
Fordism 73, 75, 87, 89, 196
France 1-2, 4, 15, 20, 83, 119, 121-8, 147, 163, 220-2, 224-6, 228, 245, 259, 278
full employment 2-4, 7, 23-4, 26-7, 32-3, 40, 69, 71-5, 80, 127-9, 144, 148, 254, 259

G
gender
 division of labour 7, 15, 70-3, 75, 78-9, 81, 83, 144-51, 205, 209-10, 215, 260, 275, 277-9
 relations 3, 6-9, 12-13, 16, 69-71, 110, 146, 148-9, 154, 209, 278
Germany 1-2, 83, 119, 121-4, 126, 163, 166, 196-7, 199, 201, 207, 221-3, 228, 251, 259
global

economy/market 32-3, 39, 161-2, 198-9, 201, 251
globalisation 4, 8, 34, 57, 161-2, 168, 183, 199-201, 251-2, 256, 271
Glyn, A. 17-18, 261
golden age 29-30, 32, 73, 195, 206-7
Greater London Council (GLC) 245-6, 249
green theory 7, 35, 85-96

H
household 7, 11, 14, 30, 60-6, 70, 72, 78-9, 81, 91, 110, 144-51, 206
human capital 28, 65, 188-9
hysteresis 25, 191

I
identity *see* youth identity
idleness 3, 5-7, 13-14, 71, 95, 99-102, 105, 107, 109, 114, 261, 271-2, 277
income
differentials 159-60, 212
distribution 158-9, 162, 167, 212
incomes policy 32-3, 193, 266
inequality 2-3, 10-11, 28-30, 35, 37, 74, 78, 82, 129, 136, 152-4, 157-63, 165-6, 168, 184, 190, 200-1, 210, 261
inflation 23-7, 30, 32-3, 36, 51, 58, 148
insecurity 3-6, 8-11, 17-18, 93, 136, 141, 164-5, 183, 207, 214, 270, 280-1
investment 25, 27, 32, 34, 192-3, 250
Italy 76, 121-2, 197, 221, 245, 250-1, 282

J
job creation 12, 15, 16, 27-31, 34, 36-7, 40, 93, 129, 157-8, 163-4, 169, 207-8, 228, 262-3, 265, 268
job search 24, 37, 187, 189
job security 3-4, 58-9, 241, 255, 270
job sharing 12, 15, 31, 38-39, 59, 206, 220
Jospin, L. 2, 20, 106, 226, 277-8

K
Kalecki, M. 259
Keynes, J. 26-8, 92, 192-3
Keynesian
theory 7, 26-8, 32-4, 72, 189, 192-3, 197
policies 12, 27, 33, 35-7, 73, 186, 193-4, 196, 254

L
labour market flexibility *see* flexibility
labour market participation/activity rates 14, 30, 34, 36, 65, 74-5, 77, 102, 119, 132-3, 138, 144-5, 147-8, 150, 208, 220, 224
Layard, R. 25, 40, 52, 55-6, 67

leisure 61, 72, 78, 85, 102, 109, 206, 270
Local Exchange Trading Schemes (LETS) 17, 114, 127, 238, 248-9, 283

M
Maastricht criteria 12, 25, 29, 40, 120, 201
Marxism 78, 88-89, 101, 106-7, 189, 202,
masculinity 70, 73, 78, 80, 82, 149, 260
minimum wage *see* wages
mismatch, labour market 25, 34-5, 41, 56-7, 74, 187-8, 194, 196
monetarism 23, 31, 3, 197
monetary policy 25, 27, 32-3, 193

N
Non-Accelerating Inflation Rate of Unemployment (NAIRU) 24-5, 27, 29, 35, 37, 51, 55, 72, 74, 186, 189, 192
needs 17, 35, 70, 88, 249, 270-1
negative income tax 15
neo-classical theory 6-7, 23-6, 40, 51-66, 72, 74-5, 77
neo-liberal policy and ideology 2, 11, 23-6, 33, 40, 105, 185-92, 207, 235, 251
Netherlands 1, 4, 83, 119, 121, 123-4, 128, 134, 147, 164, 221, 222-4, 228, 259, 282
New Labour 3, 9, 18, 40, 106, 113, 154, 201
New Right 101, 105, 113, 207-8

O
occupational structure 28, 34, 78, 103, 121, 145, 184
OECD 5-6, 25, 29, 32, 52, 56, 76, 122, 162, 185, 200
Offe, C. 260, 270, 272, 283
oil shocks 33, 195
older workers 30, 119-29, 132, 135, 137
orthodox models *see* neo classical theory
overtime 5, 15, 16-17, 108, 220, 223
Owen, R. 239-40, 249

P
paid work 5-6, 8, 12, 14, 31, 35, 69, 71, 73, 81, 145-6, 148, 152, 160, 209, 270
part time work 5, 9, 16-17, 31, 36, 66, 71, 75-8, 82, 109, 121-5, 128, 131, 134-7, 146, 152, 207, 221-2, 224, 227-8, 282
pensions 120, 124-5, 128, 136, 206-7, 250, 278
Phillips curve 24-5, 40, 186
Polanyi, K. 258, 264
poverty 13, 30, 131, 162-3, 165-6, 168, 255
productivism 86-7, 89
productivity 28-9, 34, 39, 53, 57, 73, 87, 91, 160, 167, 184-7, 197, 212-3, 240, 26: 3, 275
privatisation 10, 18, 76, 246

public sector employment 17-18, 38, 202, 208, 261, 273
public services 38, 131-2, 138, 237, 245-6, 262, 266, 268, 276-7

R
race 7, 70, 74, 162, 165-6
recession 9, 30, 191
redistribution of work 2-3, 12-13, 15-16, 19, 38-9, 69, 71, 78, 80, 82, 95, 114, 153, 202, 205, 210, 253-8, 270-1, 274, 276-81
reproduction *see* social reproduction
reserve army of labour 30, 100, 106, 202
retirement 15-16, 31, 59, 119-28, 206-7, 259-60
risk 8-9, 136
Robinson, J. 28, 202
Rogers, J. 254-5, 268, 278, 282

S
sabbatical 15, 224, 263
Say's law 192
Schumpeter, J. 194-5
self employment 6, 31, 108, 121, 133-8
service sector 5-8, 34, 83, 103-4, 128, 150, 184
skilled workers 57-8, 160-1, 189, 193
skills 9, 74, 102, 105, 138, 161, 185, 188-92, 194-200, 255-6
small business 6, 262
social cohesion 89, 205, 216
social democratic policy 11-12, 40, 93, 100-1, 105-6
social economy *see* third sector
social exclusion 2, 15, 18, 95, 99, 131, 216
social reproduction 6, 13-14, 16, 71, 79, 81-2, 150, 210-1, 213, 216
solidarity 3, 8, 17, 26, 87, 213, 258, 260-2, 273-6
Solow, R. 27, 40, 197, 199
stagflation 23, 33, 40, 183
state *see* welfare state
    intervention 27, 32-3, 35, 37, 55, 120, 123, 133-4, 238, 267-8, 273, 277-9
Streeck, W. 196, 199, 254-5, 278
supply-side policy 24-5, 194-5, 201, 254
Sweden 57, 76, 90, 122-3, 127, 134, 148, 199, 201, 208, 221-2, 226-8, 266, 273, 282

T
tax policy 15, 37-8, 56, 79, 189, 206-8, 214-15, 248, 250, 261-2, 264, 266, 279
technological change 9, 34, 57, 92-3, 135, 157, 160, 194-5, 256
time (*see* working time)
third sector 2, 13, 17-18, 38, 94, 114, 127, 131, 140-1, 217, 237-52, 255-7, 261-2, 264-5, 267-9, 272-3, 275-9
third way 3, 201-2

trade unions 2, 5, 9, 20, 24, 26, 32, 34, 39, 56, 87, 104, 119, 121, 184, 208, 219, 221-8, 240, 242-3, 250, 259-60, 282
training 8-11, 56, 59, 78, 102, 104, 106, 109, 121-2, 125, 127, 131, 184-6, 188-92, 196-202, 207, 244, 247, 265, 273
transition *see* youth transition

U
underclass 105
underemployment 28, 77, 100, 133
unemployment *see* Europe, United Kingdom and United States
    disguised/hidden 37, 202
    female 4, 30, 132
    involuntary 24, 28, 72, 193-4, 198
    long term 25, 30, 34, 36, 59, 163, 216, 247
    male 4, 30-1, 74, 132, 148
    mass 2, 4, 12, 15, 23, 30-1, 157, 166, 205, 264
    voluntary 24, 40, 74, 186-8, 216
United Kingdom
    Conservative governments (1979-97) 27, 29, 33, 35, 106, 112, 152, 195
    economic growth 4, 6, 33-5, 59, 207
    employment policy 4, 6, 33-5, 59, 207
    inequality 11, 29-30, 163
    job creation 29, 31, 34, 36-7
    unemployment 4, 5, 29-33, 36-7, 132
United States
    economic growth 29, 32, 157
    employment policy 4-5, 10-11, 28, 76, 157, 161, 165-6, 196, 199-202, 207
    inequality 11, 29, 40, 157-63, 165-6, 200
    job creation 2, 23, 28, 40, 157-8, 163-4
    unemployment 29, 103, 157-8, 165, 184
unpaid work 3, 5-8, 12, 14, 16, 18, 71-3, 77-80, 85, 91, 110, 126-7, 143-51, 207, 209-11, 224, 260
unskilled workers 5, 8, 10, 57, 103, 164, 167, 184, 189

V
voluntary sector 141, 235, 237, 245-6, 268-9
voluntary work 8, 17, 122, 127, 141, 209, 273
Van Parijs, P. 14, 264, 267, 276

W
wages
    efficiency 24, 53
    growth 159-61, 187
    inequality 78, 158-9
    low 8-10, 28, 37, 103-4, 160-1, 261, 264
    minimum 9, 29, 158, 161, 184, 187-8

reservation 187-8
rigidity 25-7, 40, 164-5, 187, 189, 193
welfare
dependency 14, 105, 131, 134, 207
state 14, 79, 83, 106, 128, 132, 205-7, 250, 266-7
welfare to work 18, 113, 134, 202, 216, 247-8, 255
work
ethic 88, 207, 211, 215-6, 271-2
hours 5, 15-16, 30-1, 39, 65-6, 71, 76-7, 81-2, 92, 95, 122, 129, 134-5, 153, 159-60, 198, 207, 212-3, 220-8, 258-60, 272
ideologies of 69, 71-4, 80, 86, 95, 107-8, 112-3, 205, 209, 211, 236, 246, 273, 277
intensification 5-6, 77, 183
rich/poor 4, 11, 30, 37, 41, 129, 205, 260
sharing *see* job sharing
unpaid *see* unpaid work
voluntary work *see* voluntary
work-and-spend 7, 85, 88, 106, 189, 191, 200, 206-7, 216-7
workfare 18, 100, 106, 189, 191, 200, 206-7, 216-7
working time 2, 5, 9, 12-13, 15-17, 20, 31, 35, 38-9, 69, 76, 78, 82, 85, 95, 108, 126, 205, 208, 211-14, 219-28, 250, 257-60, 262-3, 265-6, 270-1, 273-8

Y
youth
culture 100, 102, 105, 107-8, 111-2
identity 108, 110-1
ideologies of 99-102, 104-5, 271
transition 100-1, 104, 106-7, 109-10
unemployment 4, 18, 100, 102-3, 105, 109, 116, 191, 207